CATHOLIC MORAL THEOLOGY IN THE UNITED STATES

SELECTED TITLES
from the
MORAL TRADITIONS SERIES
James F. Keenan, SJ, series editor

The Fellowship of Life: Virtue Ethics and Orthodox Christianity
JOSEPH WOODILL

Feminist Ethics and Natural Law: The End of the Anathemas
CRISTINA L. H. TRAINA

The Global Face of Public Faith: Politics, Human Rights, and Christian Ethics
DAVID HOLLENBACH SJ

The Ground Beneath the Cross: The Theology of Ignacio Ellacuría
KEVIN F. BURKE, SJ

Heroes, Saints, and Ordinary Morality
ANDREW M. FLESCHER

Introduction to Jewish and Catholic Bioethics: A Comparative Analysis
AARON MACKLER

Jewish and Catholic Bioethics: An Ecumenical Dialogue
EDMUND D. PELLEGRINO, & ALAN I. FADEN, EDITORS

John Cuthbert Ford, SJ: Moral Theologian at the End of the Manualist Era
ERIC MARCELO O. GENILO, SJ

Josef Fuchs on Natural Law
MARK GRAHAM

Loyal Dissent: Memoir of a Catholic Theologian
CHARLES E. CURRAN

Medicine and the Ethics of Care
DIANA FRITZ CATES, & PAUL LAURITZEN, EDITORS

The Moral Theology of Pope John Paul II
CHARLES E. CURRAN

The Origins of Moral Theology in the United States:
Three Different Approaches
CHARLES E. CURRAN

Prophetic and Public: The Social Witness of U.S. Catholicism
KRISTEN E. HEYER

Theological Bioethics: Participation, Justice, and Change
LISA SOWLE CAHILL

United States Welfare Policy: A Catholic Response
THOMAS J. MASSARO, SJ

CATHOLIC MORAL THEOLOGY IN THE UNITED STATES

A History

Charles E. Curran

GEORGETOWN UNIVERSITY PRESS

144772063

Georgetown University Press/Washington, D.C.
Georgetown University Press, Washington, D.C. www.press.georgetown.edu

Library of Congress-in-Publication Data
Curran, Charles E.
Catholic moral theology in the United States: a history / Charles E. Curran.
p. cm. — (Moral traditions series)
Includes bibliographical references and index.
ISBN–13: 978–1–58901–195–3 (hardcover: alk. paper)
ISBN–13: 978–1–58901–196–0 (pbk. : alk. paper)
1. Christian ethics—Catholic authors—History.
2. Christian ethics—United States—History. I. Title.
BJ1249.C78 2008
241' .04273—dc22
2007025020

♾ This book is printed on acid-free paper meeting the requirements of the American National
Standard for Permanence in Paper for Printed Library Materials.

15 14 13 12 11 10 09 08   9 8 7 6 5 4 3 2

First printing
Printed in the United States of America

To the moral theologians who have gone before
especially

Tom Dailey

Joe Fuchs

Bernard Häring

Dick McCormick

May they rest in peace

CONTENTS

PREFACE

This book tells the story of Catholic moral theology in the United States. Those interested in the discipline of moral theology will find here the first monograph telling the story that began in the middle of the nineteenth century in this country. The title clearly indicates what the book attempts to do, but three aspects of the title need further explanation.

First, what is moral theology? Moral theology is the name the Roman Catholic tradition gives to the theological discipline that deals with Christian life and action. Protestants often call the same discipline by the name of Christian ethics. In one sense all theology is one, but to facilitate the study of the various aspects of theology, separate disciplines have come into existence. The various theological disciplines today include systematic theology (in the past often called dogmatic theology), which deals with Christian faith, moral theology, spiritual theology, pastoral theology, liturgical theology, historical theology, and biblical theology. Divisions are necessary for the study of theology, but they always remain somewhat artificial. The boundaries of moral theology are quite porous because Christian life and action are clearly connected with faith as well as with spiritual, pastoral, historical, liturgical, and biblical theologies. Thus, at times, it is difficult to discern what belongs to moral theology and what does not. This book follows the practical criterion of determining the field of moral theology on the basis of how people who call themselves moral theologians have dealt with these issues.

Within moral theology different divisions exist to facilitate the study of the subject matter of the discipline itself. This volume follows the often-used divisions of fundamental moral theology, sexual, bioethical, and social moral theology. Fundamental moral theology considers those aspects of the discipline such as the person as moral agent and subject, virtues, principles, conscience, and human actions in general that come into play in all the different areas and issues of human moral activity. The division among sexual, bioethical, and social moral theology derives from the areas and subjects considered. These divisions are certainly helpful, but there is the danger that some aspects of personal morality tend to be overlooked by this tripartite division.

Second, what is meant by *Catholic* moral theology? This book considers those theologians who write from the Catholic moral tradition. The ecumenical character of Catholic moral theology in the United States in the last half century, however, tends to blur somewhat the boundaries of Catholic moral theology. Catholic moral theology, especially after Vatican II, has learned much from ecumenical dialogue especially with Protestant thought. The subsequent pages occasionally recognize the influence and importance of the ecumenical dialogue, but the focus is on Catholic moral theology and not on the broader discipline of Christian ethics understood as involving all those who write from the broader Christian tradition. In the present ecumenical climate, Catholic moral theologians will sometimes write from the general Christian perspective and address a broad Christian audience rather than from a specifically Catholic perspective and for a specifically Catholic audience. Parameters of Catholic moral theology were much more clear and sharp in the pre-ecumenical era before Vatican II.

Third, the United States part of the title also raises some boundary issues. The Catholic Church is universal and the universal Church strongly influences what occurs in any individual country. In the world of theology in general and moral theology in particular, Europe was the primary home of Catholic theology well into the post–Vatican II era. Books by European authors frequently had English translations and exerted a great influence in the United States. In addition, English-speaking theologians, especially from England, Ireland, Canada, and Australia, have been in dialogue with moral theologians in the United States. This book recognizes the existence of these contributions, but because of space and the need for strict limits, the focus remains on moral theologians from the United States.

I have written in some detail about aspects of the history of Catholic moral theology in the United States, especially with regard to the nineteenth century, and with regard to Catholic social ethics in the twentieth century. In this book I will depend on these earlier writings. I have always been interested in the history of Catholic moral theology, and in the back of my mind I had the intention at some time to write a complete history of Catholic moral theology in the United States. My intention has come to fruition in the present volume.

Catholic theology lately is very conscious of social location and the effect that has on one's theology. My social location has certainly influenced how I have approached this history. I received doctorates in moral theology in Rome in 1961 and began teaching moral theology even before the start of Vatican II. As a result I have personal familiarity with much that has occurred in Catholic moral theology in the United States, including the pre–Vatican II period.

I write this history as a participant observer and do not claim to be neutral. The challenge is to strive to be objective in reporting and assessing what has occurred in moral theology but at the same time to explain my own approaches and positions. This role of a participant-observer is not an easy one. In this context I use the third person to refer to my past writings and actions and the first person to refer to the judgments and positions I take as the author of this history. The reader will have to determine for oneself how well I have dealt with the tensions involved in such a role.

As a participant in the story of Catholic moral theology in the United States, I have been privileged to be part of an ongoing community of theologians committed both to the scholarly discipline of moral theology and to the Church. I have learned from all the moral theologians mentioned in this text, and I have personally known all the leading figures in Catholic moral theology since the 1950s. To be a part of this ongoing tradition of ideas and community of people has been a marvelous experience for me, and I am truly grateful.

Finally, I want to recognize significant debts and publicly express my gratitude. Southern Methodist University has provided me a congenial and challenging academic environment and many good colleagues. I am privileged to hold the Elizabeth Scurlock University Chair of Human Values, generously endowed by Jack S. and Laura Lee Blanton in honor of her mother. Laura Lee Blanton passed away a few years ago, but her memory lives on at SMU thanks to the many benefactions of the Blanton family. The Birdwell Library and its accomplished and friendly librarians continue to facilitate my research. Richard Brown, the director of the Georgetown University Press, and James F. Keenan, the editor of the Moral Traditions series, together with the very efficient staff of the press, have been most helpful and easy to work with. Richard Brown, Richard Gula, Kenneth Himes, and James Keenan read the manuscript and made very helpful comments. My most immediate cooperator is my associate, Carol Swartz, who in addition to preparing this manuscript for publication, assists me in many ways with her efficient, cheerful, and friendly help.

THE NINETEENTH CENTURY

Moral theology is a systematic, thematic, and reflexive study of Christian moral life and actions. From the very beginning, the community of the disciples of Jesus concerned itself with how Christians should respond to God's gift in Christ Jesus through the Holy Spirit. Even in New Testament times, Christians referred to their religion as "the way." Morality is the actual living out of the Christian life; moral theology is a second-order discourse that stands back and reflects in a systematic way on Christian life and actions.

Moral theology involves different degrees of systematization. From the earliest times, it has been associated with the sacrament of penance.[1] In sixth-century Ireland, a new form of penance emerged, which then spread to the continent and to the whole Catholic world. Penance now involved the confession of sins to a priest who imposed a penance and through the mercy and forgiveness of God absolved the sinner and reconciled the sinner to the community of the Church and to God. The older form of penance was called "public penance" and generally could be received only once in a lifetime. Now penance could be received frequently. To assist the priest, *libri paenitentiales* came into existence to point out the appropriate penance that should be assigned for particular sins.

A more academic and systematic approach to moral theology began in the twelfth and thirteenth centuries. Three significant factors influenced this more systematic approach—the founding of universities, dialogue with Aristotelian thought, and the founding of religious orders dedicated to scholarship. The teachings of Thomas Aquinas (d. 1274) well illustrate a systematic approach to moral theology. In the theology of Aquinas, no separate discipline called "moral theology" existed. Aquinas dealt with the human response to God's gift and the moral life in the second part of the *Summa theologiae*. The term *moral theology* appeared for the first time in the writings of Alan of Lille (d. 1202).[2] Later academics, especially in the sixteenth-century Thomistic renewal, developed moral theology through commentaries on the second part of the *Summa*. At the same time, as

1

the more academic and systematic approach to moral theology occurred on the pastoral level, books also called *Summae* gave guidance for confessors in the sacrament of penance. The cruder form of these practical *Summae* simply followed an alphabetical approach to all issues, but the *Summa* of Antoninus of Florence (d. 1459) was more systematic, providing a good picture of the life of fifteenth-century Florence. Among other topics, long discussions were included of the obligations of all the professions and states in life of the Christian people.

Moral theology has always experienced the tension between a more practical and pastoral approach, associated especially with the sacrament of penance, and a more theoretical and academic approach, associated with the university world. This tension continues to exist in contemporary Catholic moral theology.

MANUALS OF MORAL THEOLOGY

This chapter focuses on the origins of moral theology in the United States in the nineteenth century. At that time, moral theology was identified with what were called "manuals of moral theology." What was the nature of these manuals, and how did they come into existence?

The manuals of moral theology owe their origin to the Council of Trent, the sixteenth-century council that tried to reform the Catholic Church after the Protestant Reformation.[3] In its fourteenth session, in 1551, Trent dealt with the sacrament of penance. Its focus was twofold. Although the Fourth Lateran Council in 1215 required all Catholics to confess their mortal sins once a year, the fifteenth century saw a crisis with regard to the use of auricular confession. Trent reiterated the obligation to confess mortal sins once a year. In addition to addressing the practical problem, Trent also responded to the teachings of the Reformation with regard to penance. Private confession in his own life was esteemed by Luther, but he emphasized the forgiveness of God, which comes from the word of God as preached by ministers of that word. The other reformers did not give much importance to penance.

The Council of Trent in its teaching recognized two characteristics of Catholic moral theology—mediation and the human response to God's gift. The divine is mediated through the human; God's forgiveness comes to us in and through the visible Church in the person of the priest. The human response to God's gift called for contrition, the confession of one's sins, and personal works of satisfaction.

Trent understood the sacrament of penance primarily in juridical terms, with the priest acting as a judge to determine whether absolution is to be given or denied. The penitent is required by divine law to confess all mortal sins according to number and species so that the confessor can pronounce the sentence of remission or retention of sin. The confessor also determines an appropriate penance. Trent overemphasized the juridical nature of penance, but its approach profoundly influenced the development of moral theology.

A second important Tridentine influence on the future of moral theology came from the council's insistence on the founding of seminaries to ensure that future priests were trained to carry out their role and mission in general and specifically in the sacrament of penance. These two emphases in Trent gave rise to what became known as the "manuals of moral theology" that continued in existence in the Catholic world until Vatican Council II in the 1960s.

The new genre of moral theology, the *Institutiones morales* (generally referred to in English as the "manuals"), came into existence through the Society of Jesus (Jesuits). The Society of Jesus was founded in 1540 with the special mission of carrying out the reform of the Church in light of the Council of Trent. In 1603 the Jesuit John Azor published his *Institutiones morales* based on the two-year course he taught to Jesuit seminarians in accordance with the *Ratio studiorum* of the Jesuits to prepare future priests to hear confessions. In light of the Tridentine understanding of penance, the sacrament was often called "confession" rather than "penance." The first-year course covered human acts, conscience, sins, and the Decalogue, excluding the seventh commandment. The second year treated the seventh commandment, sacraments, censures, and the different duties of particular individuals.

The *Institutiones morales,* or manuals, came into existence to train seminarians for the hearing of confessions in their future ministry. In a sense, they were a creative adaptation to the needs of the time, but unfortunately the manuals later became identified with the whole of moral theology. Trent's view of penance was too juridical and did not emphasize enough other aspects of the sacrament of penance, such as praise and thanks to God for the gift of forgiveness. The manuals separated moral theology from all other theological aspects, including the dogmatic, the spiritual, and the sacramental. The use of scripture was frequently reduced to providing proof texts for particular conclusions based on natural law. With their practical orientation, the manuals of moral theology paid little attention to the theoretical aspects. Furthermore, they said nothing about grace and the virtues. The purpose of the manuals was to point out which acts were sinful and the degree to which each was sinful.

To understand nineteenth-century moral theology, one must be acquainted with the major developments that occurred in the seventeenth and eighteenth centuries. In these centuries a sharp discussion between the two extremes of laxism and rigorism arose. The Holy Office (the predecessor of the Congregation for the Doctrine of the Faith), under Pope Alexander VII, in 1665–66, condemned forty-five laxist propositions, and under Pope Innocent XI, in 1679, condemned sixty-five laxist propositions. In 1690 the Holy Office, under Pope Alexander VIII, condemned thirty-two rigorist positions often associated with Jansenism, a French-based approach to the Christian moral life. These actions constituted the first major involvement of the papacy in specific moral actions and had the beneficial effect of condemning the extremes. But these condemnations did not bring peace and tranquility to moral theology. The eighteenth century witnessed a continuing struggle between rigorous and benign approaches. The primary issue was the uncertainty that arose when the existence of a law or obligation was doubtful. Historians describe this debate as the struggle over probabilism. Adherents of the more rigorous position maintained that one had to follow the law unless the argument for freedom was more probable. (The word "probable" comes from the Latin and really means "provable," not the contemporary "likely.") Moderate probabilism maintained that one did not have to obey the law if the opinion for freedom was truly probable.

The details of this bitter struggle lie beyond the focus of this book, but in the eighteenth century Alphonsus Liguori's moderate probabilism struck the middle way between rigorism and laxism. Alphonsus's moral theology followed the general approach, style, and format of the manuals. He began teaching Redemptorist students in 1744 and chose the manual of the Jesuit Hermann Busenbaum for a textbook. The first edition of his moral theology in 1748 consisted of his annotations on the text of Busenbaum. Such an approach was very common among the manualists. In later years Alphonsus toyed with the idea of moving away entirely from Busenbaum, though he never did. However, he added more and more of his own material and in later editions no longer mentioned Busenbaum on the title page. Alphonsus ultimately published nine editions of his moral theology. Leonard Gaudé in 1905 published a critical edition of Alphonsus's moral theology.[4]

Alphonsus's middle way and his outstanding contribution to moral theology in the eighteenth century came not only from his theory of moderate probabilism but also from his pastoral prudence and his understanding of conscience and the sacrament of penance. Although Alphonsus followed the manuals in seeing law as the primary ethical model and was concerned primarily with determining what actions were sinful and the degree to which each was sinful, he showed a sensitive pastoral prudence in regard to the solution of particular cases and issues. His commonsense approach led him to consider all the different circumstances of a case. Alphonsus himself pointed out that he began as a rigorist whose approach was based on Genet, the textbook he used as a student, but he changed his approach as a result of his own pastoral experience, which led him to embrace a benign understanding.[5]

Alphonsus followed the legal method of the manuals but with a somewhat nuanced understanding of that approach. Law constitutes the remote and material norm of human actions, but conscience is the proximate and formal norm of human actions. The formal norm ultimately gives final meaning to the act. Conscience should follow the dictates of the law, but the goodness of human action becomes known to us through its approbation by conscience. Such an approach opposes the rigorism that sees the objective law alone as determining all morality.[6] Thus, for example, Alphonsus recognizes that a person could be invincibly ignorant of the more remote conclusions of the natural law. Alphonsus invokes Aquinas in defending his position on conscience; in fact, he actually goes beyond Aquinas. Aquinas maintained that an individual following an invincibly erroneous conscience does not commit sin (the error is not the individual's fault), but the act itself is not good. Alphonsus, with his understanding of conscience as the formal norm of action, maintains, in fact, that a person acting with an invincibly erroneous conscience performs a good and meritorious act.[7]

With regard to the sacrament of penance, Alphonsus, in keeping with the manualistic approach, sees the confessor primarily as judge. But Alphonsus is also true to the motto of the Redemptorist order that he founded—"overflowing is the mercy of God" (copiosa apud eum redemptio). Yes, the confessor is primarily a judge, but in the very beginning of his discussion of penance, Alphonsus also insists on the role of the confessor as father and doctor.[8] Marciano Vidal goes so far as to maintain that Alphonsus brought about a Copernican revolution with regard to the sacrament of penance.[9] In practice, Alphonsus sees the spiritual welfare of the penitent as the primary consideration in dealing with such practical dilemmas as delay of absolution or granting of absolution to a person who continues to commit the same sin.[10]

Alphonsus exemplified the best of the manualists. He was not primarily an academic but a devoted minister of the Gospel working for the evangelization of people—in particular the rural poor. His practical prudence, realistic anthropology, and belief in the superabundant mercy of God made him a true guide for casuists and confessors. Nonetheless, his many strengths supported the genre of the manuals of moral theology, which tended to become identified with the totality of moral theology. Moral theology in this perspective followed a legal model and emphasized the determination of sin and the degree of sinfulness. The manuals did not see moral theology as touching all aspects of the Christian life, including the basic call of all Christians to holiness, the role of grace, and the virtues in the Christian life. Furthermore, the practical nature of the moral theology of the manuals cut moral theology off from dogmatic theology, scripture, and sacramental theology. In fairness to Alphonsus, he was a person of his time responding to the needs of his time.

NINETEENTH-CENTURY CATHOLIC MORAL THEOLOGY IN EUROPE

To understand the origins of moral theology in the United States in the nineteenth century, one must know what was occurring in Europe, the center of Catholic life at that time. Four characteristics of nineteenth-century European moral theology stand out—the dominance of the manualist tradition, the general acceptance of the Alphonsian approach, a growing ultramontanism stressing the primacy and central role of the papacy in the Church, and the isolation of moral theology from the political, economic, and intellectual influences of the nineteenth century. The manual remained the primary way of understanding moral theology. The intellectual home of moral theology was the seminary, where future priests were trained to carry out their ministry with a heavy emphasis on their role as judges in the sacrament of penance.

The Tübingen School in Germany expressed dissatisfaction with the narrow, minimalistic, and legalistic approach of the manuals. It advocated that moral theology should deal with the fullness of the Christian life and not just with the minimal aspect of what is sinful. Moral theology needs to be intimately connected with scripture, dogmatic theology, and sacramental theology. But this new approach, associated especially with John Michael Sailer (d. 1832) and John Baptist Hirscher (d. 1865), had no influence outside Germany and only limited influence in Germany.[11] The manuals of moral theology, with their narrow scope, continued to be the approach to moral theology in the Catholic world.

Influence of Alphonsus and of Ultramontanism

The nineteenth century saw the growing acceptance of Alphonsus Liguori's approach to moral theology. At the beginning of the nineteenth century many manualists, especially in France, opposed the Liguorian approach as being too benign. Raphael Gallagher calls the period of 1800–1850 a period of struggle for the acceptance of Alphonsus's approach.[12] Thanks especially to Thomas Gousset in France and Peter Scavini in Italy, moral theology eventually became Liguorian.

Jean Guerber speaks of an apparently unique phenomenon in the history of theology: The teaching of one author quickly became the teaching of the Church.[13]

John Peter Gury, a French Jesuit, published in 1850 the most influential manual of moral theology in the nineteenth century—a book that went through forty-three editions between 1850 and 1890. Many later Jesuit moral theologians in many countries used Gury's text, which they then updated and accommodated to the situation of their own countries. We will consider the manual of Aloysius Sabetti, whose textbook of moral theology in the United States is based on the Gury manual. The Jesuits had always been heavily interested in moral theology, but in the latter part of the eighteenth century they were on the defensive because of many enemies in the Church. Ultimately, they were suppressed in 1773 and restored only in 1814. The Gury manual, the first Jesuit manual published after the restoration of the Jesuits, became the primary textbook for moral theology among the Jesuits and the whole Catholic world. Gury was a strong supporter of the Liguorian approach. Before publishing his compendium in 1850, he made accessible to his students in 1845 a lithograph bearing the title *Praelectiones theologiae moralis ex probatis auctoribus, praesertim ex S. Liguorio concinnata*.[14]

However, another factor heavily influenced the acceptance of Alphonsus's approach in moral theology—approbation from Church authority. In 1803 the Congregation of Rites, with the approval of Pope Pius VII, declared that nothing in Alphonsus's voluminous writings was deserving of censure. The Sacred Penitentiary responded in 1831 that the confessor could safely follow all the opinions of St. Alphonsus. In 1839 Alphonsus was canonized.[15] These three factors—the intrinsic merits of his writings, the acceptance by other moral theologians, and official Church recognition—thus contributed to making Alphonsus Liguori's approach the accepted understanding of moral theology in the Catholic Church in the nineteenth century.

Nineteenth-century Catholic Europe saw the growth and predominance of ultramontanism, literally meaning "beyond the mountains." This was a movement in European countries beyond the Alps, such as France, Germany, and England, that emphasized the centrality and authority of the papacy in the Church, often seeing the papacy as the best defense against the political and intellectual liberalism of the day. Ultramontanism triumphed over other movements that had been strong in the eighteenth century. In France, Gallicanism had a long history of downplaying the central role of the papacy while supporting a greater role for the French Church. It was still quite strong at the beginning of the nineteenth century. In the eighteenth century, Febronianism in Germany and Josephinism in Austria tried to subordinate the Church to national interests. In the nineteenth century, however, ultramontanism ultimately succeeded in strengthening the papacy at the expense of the local churches. Many ultramontanists saw the papacy as a staunch defender against political liberalism and the Enlightenment. The Syllabus of Errors, issued by Pope Pius IX in 1864, defended papal prerogatives and condemned aspects of political liberalism.[16]

As a result of the triumph of ultramontanism, the Catholic Church became more centralized, more authoritarian, and more defensive in the nineteenth and twentieth centuries right up to Vatican II. Ultramontanism played a great role in the First Vatican Council in 1870, which emphasized the primacy of the papacy and defined papal infallibility. The term "papal ordinary magisterium," referring to the pope's teachings in a noninfallible way, also came into common usage in the nineteenth century.[17] As a result of this greater emphasis on papal authority and centrality, the papacy, often using the congregations of the Roman Curia, such as the Holy Office, which dealt with faith and morals, and the Sacred Penitentiary, which dealt with internal forum matters of confession, played a significant role in moral theology. For example, casuistic issues about abortion and the definitions of direct and indirect abortions were solved for the whole Church by the rulings and decisions of curial congregations.[18] Thus the nineteenth century saw the growing role of papal moral teaching even involving the solution of particular cases and problems. This emphasis continued and increased in the twentieth century.

A connection exists between the primary role of Alphonsus in moral theology and the growing emphasis on the role of papal authority in the Church in the latter part of the nineteenth century. Alphonsus had always been a strong supporter of the papacy, an ardent promoter of Marian devotion, and a staunch opponent of the intellectual and political developments associated with the Enlightenment and liberalism. He gradually became identified with the cause of ultramontanism throughout most of Europe in the second part of the nineteenth century. Alphonsus's identification with ultramontanism at the time undoubtedly influenced the papal decision to name him a doctor of the Church in 1871.[19]

Alphonsus's identification with the cause of ultamontanism and the strong approbation of Church authority distorted his own approach to moral theology in the second part of the nineteenth century. Ph. Lécrivain describes this distortion in terms of the twofold dangers of rigorism and Liguorianism. Many of Alphonsus's own Redemptorists were responsible for this development. They engaged in a sterile debate with Antonio Ballerini and some Jesuits over the true meaning of Alphonsus's teaching on probabilism, which they termed "equiprobabilism." They insisted on a Liguorian school of moral theology, neglected Alphonsus's emphasis on God's mercy and the role of prudence in the application of the law, and used him to defend the status quo and oppose any new developments in the Church.[20]

Gallagher refers to the "fossilization" of Liguori's moral theology. The seeker of the pastorally viable middle way based on intrinsically convincing reasons became the establishment theologian whose authority was used to prevent change or development.[21] Marciano Vidal points to an ideological reading of Alphonsus in the late nineteenth century and the first part of the twentieth. Aphonsus, who wrote a moral theology with doubts and hesitations and who never developed his own system apart from Busenbaum, was used as a guarantee of doctrinal certitude. The individual who had struggled against rigorism in his day was now used to combat the moral laxism of the times.[22] All moral theologians in the late nineteenth century and the first half of the twentieth century claimed to be following Alphonsus Liguori, but many, including members of his own religious order, were not following the true spirit of Alphonsus.

Isolation of Manuals

The manuals of moral theology were very pragmatic books used to train confessors to be judges in the sacrament of penance. This narrow role tended to insulate these manuals from dialogue and contact with the broader world of their times. Significant events were occurring in the economic, political, cultural, and intellectual worlds of the nineteenth century, but the manuals of moral theology give no indication of these activities.

The very practical nature and narrow focus of the manuals constitute the principal reason for their intellectual isolation. The extended discussion over probabilism also contributed to this situation. A position is probable and can be safely followed in practice if there are intrinsic reasons to support it or if a number of authorities or previous authors held such a position to be probable. The method of the manuals was to cite the number of past authors who held such a position in order to prove that it was probable. The citations and footnotes in these books referred only to other moral theologians from the present and the past. Louis Vereecke has pointed out in his study of eighteenth-century moral theology that the manuals were little affected by the more theoretical and philosophical debates of the time.[23] The same judgment is true for the manuals of the nineteenth century.

The manuals of moral theology also failed to reflect contemporary discussions in dogmatic theology. Moral theology deals with Christian life and actions, whereas dogmatic theology deals with beliefs. The manuals of moral theology never considered the important role of grace in the moral life. Dogmatic theology itself went through some very significant developments in the nineteenth century in interaction with the intellectual and political aspects of the Enlightenment.

Many in the Catholic Church and in the papacy, however, feared these new developments in the intellectual and political spheres. The writings of theologians trying to work out some accommodation and dialogue with the Enlightenment were condemned. As the nineteenth century progressed, a renewal of Thomism in the form of neo-scholasticism came to the fore as a means of combating new approaches. The Jesuits teaching in Rome, especially Joseph Kleutgen and Matthew Liberatore, spearheaded this Thomistic revival. In 1879 Pope Leo XIII issued the encyclical *Aeterni patris,* which called for the restoration of Catholic philosophy according to the mind and method of Thomas Aquinas.[24] This imposition of neo-scholasticism had some positive results. However, the primary result was a very defensive posture opposed to any dialogue with contemporary thought.

Without doubt Catholic philosophy and theology in general became neoscholastic. Some historians have concluded that the manuals of moral theology now went through a significant change and became neo-Thomistic or neoscholastic.[25] But this is not the case. Despite the imposition of neo-scholasticism, the manuals of moral theology did not fundamentally change their basic structure and approach. Thus reference to the manuals of moral theology as neoscholastic or neo-Thomistic is inaccurate. Later in this chapter I will discuss at some length the criticism of Thomas Bouquillon, professor of moral theology at the Catholic University of America, who also has said that the manuals were not Thomistic.

The question naturally arises: Why did the manuals of moral theology not change with the introduction of neo-scholasticism? First, the very nature and focus of the manuals would have to change if they were to become fully neoscholastic. Thomas Aquinas's understanding of moral theology (even though he did not use the term and did not see moral theology as separate from the rest of theology) had an entirely different focus and method in dealing with the study of Christian moral life. Aquinas did not use a casuistic approach.

Second, the nineteenth-century papacy not only called for Thomistic philosophy and theology but also strongly endorsed Alphonsus's moral theology. The authors of all the manuals at this time claimed to be following in the footsteps of Alphonsus.

Third, Alphonsus himself testified to the important role of Thomas Aquinas in moral theology. In the preface to his moral theology, which basically was unchanged from the second edition, Alphonsus claims to use the work of Aquinas assiduously, the only theologian he mentions by name in this context.[26] In his discussion of conscience, Alphonsus refers to Aquinas as "the most distinguished [*princeps*] of theologians."[27]

As a result of these factors it was easy to conclude that Aquinas and Alphonsus used the same approach to moral theology. Church authority joined the two together, with Alphonsus himself claiming to be following Aquinas. With their pastoral purpose of training confessors as judges, the manuals were so entrenched in practice that nothing was going to change their basic approach. The focus and method of the manuals were not the focus and method of Aquinas. But the manuals fully endorsed the spirit of neo-scholasticism, emphasizing the defensiveness of the Church and the failure to dialogue with the modern world.

NINETEENTH-CENTURY AMERICA

In the nineteenth century the scene in the United States was quite similar to the European scene. Although the early Catholic Church, centered in Maryland, showed some tendencies toward a national Church influenced by a republican spirit and the Enlightenment, by the early part of the nineteenth century it was moving in the same direction as the European Church. The most striking characteristic of the Church in the United States at this time was the growth through immigration from European countries and the need to care for the immigrants' spiritual and even temporal and cultural lives. Jay Dolan describes four focuses of this nineteenth-century Catholic Church: authority, sin, ritual, and miracles.[28]

The emphasis on sin and ritual gave great importance to the sacrament of penance. The aspects of Roman Catholicism that distinguished it from American Protestantism were the Eucharist and the sacrament of penance—confession. Especially on the frontier, priests were not able to provide weekly Eucharist for Catholics. On the few occasions of priestly visits, they spent most of their time hearing the confessions of Catholics. The experience of the confessional was perhaps the most intimate religious experience for frontier Catholics. Stephen Badin, an early missionary in Kentucky, spent most of his days in these pastoral visits hearing confessions, and because of the large number of people even had to issue tickets to them.[29]

Prayer books at the time emphasized sin and the need for confession. Devotional practices stressed the sins people commit and the need for reparation and forgiveness. The parish mission was an important spiritual event each year in the parish and gave prominence to the reality of sin, the fear of hell, and the need for confession of sins. Yes, the emphasis was on sin and the fear of hell, but the last and most important word was the mercy and forgiveness of God.[30]

A major concern for bishops was to have an adequate number of priests.[31] In the beginning, priests were in short supply; most were immigrants from Europe. Bishops recognized the need to have more native priests, but providing and staffing seminaries was a problem. French priests from the Society of St. Sulpice

11

(Sulpicians) founded the first seminary in the United States in 1791—St. Mary's Seminary in Baltimore. Mt. St. Mary's Seminary in Maryland came into existence in 1809. Some attempts were made in individual dioceses to start small seminaries in the house of the bishop, which usually had very few students and only one professor responsible for all the courses in addition to his other pastoral work. As the century progressed, the bishops recognized the need for bigger and better-staffed seminaries. Finally, in 1884 at the Third Council of Baltimore, the bishops proposed a model curriculum for the seminary consisting of two years of philosophy and four years of theology.

From an intellectual viewpoint, the Sulpicians, who ran a number of seminaries in addition to St. Mary's in Baltimore, did not give their members training beyond the ordinary seminary courses until the late 1870s. The Vincentian Fathers, founded by St. Vincent de Paul, also staffed seminaries in this country, but until the 1880s they forbade their members to earn academic degrees because of their fear of the vanity of learning.[32]

The emphasis in the seminary was on moral theology. Because of the needs of ministry, bishops often shortened the seminary training of their priests, provided they had courses in moral theology. In 1813 John Carroll, the first bishop of Baltimore, told the Jesuit superior to ordain priests early even if they had not studied all the courses in theology, provided they knew the obvious and general principles of moral theology.[33] Samuel Eccleston, a later archbishop of Baltimore, told the seminary president that he could not ordain a seminarian until he had a good course in moral theology, but dogmatic theology could be postponed.[34] Father Ferdinand Coosemans, the provincial of the Missouri Province of the Society of Jesus, testified to the same approach among Jesuits.[35]

The Third Plenary Council of Baltimore in 1884 set new standards for the training of diocesan seminarians. The committee report placed an equal emphasis on moral theology and dogmatic theology, requiring six hours of each in the first three years of theology and three hours in the fourth year.[36] As a result, diocesan seminarians in the United States had more instruction in moral theology than their counterparts in Europe, who always had more hours in dogmatic theology than in moral theology. This approach shows the importance attached to moral theology in the United States.

The Sulpicians and Vincentians, who were early founders of seminaries in this country, each brought with them a French theological background that was somewhat Gallican in its dogmatic theology and ecclesiology but somewhat rigorous in its moral theology. Louis R. Deloul (1787–1858), the Sulpician superior in the United States, illustrates such an approach. From the Gallican perspective, he urged a transformationist synthesis between Catholicism and American culture.[37]

But in moral theology he found Alphonsus to be "too sweet."[38] However, as in France, here too the more benign Alphonsian approach soon predominated, as seen in the influential approach of Jean Baptiste Bouvier, which spread from his native France to this country.[39]

FRANCIS P. KENRICK

The early seminaries used moral manuals written in Europe. The text of the manuals was in Latin so that they could be used in all countries of the world. The first manual of moral theology written in this country came from the pen of Francis Patrick Kenrick—a three-volume textbook published in 1841–43 for the seminarians at St. Charles Seminary in Philadelphia, which Kenrick had started.[40] Kenrick, a native Irishman, had studied in Rome and volunteered for the American mission in Kentucky. He first taught all of the theology courses at St. Joseph's Seminary there and quickly gained a reputation as a theologian. History remembers him as the foremost theological scholar in the Catholic Church in the United States in his time. In 1829 he was named secretary of the First Council of Baltimore. He became coadjutor bishop of Philadelphia with full jurisdiction when he was not yet ten years ordained.[41]

Despite his long and rigorous administrative functions as a bishop (he became the archbishop of Baltimore in 1851), Kenrick managed to publish in all areas of theology. His apologetic writings defended, in a somewhat irenic way, the primacy of the Apostolic See, transubstantiation, and the Catholic approach to baptism and confirmation. Gerald Fogarty devotes one chapter in his *American Catholic Biblical Scholarship* to Kenrick's work of translating the books of the Bible into English. Unfortunately, he was never able to publish all his translations in one Bible.[42] From 1834 to 1840 he published four volumes of dogmatic theology for his seminarians in Philadelphia. Kenrick did not originally intend to write a moral theology manual for his students, but even before finishing the dogmatic theology he recognized the need for a manual of moral theology for American students.[43] Kenrick was a very intelligent man with great discipline, but he did not pretend to be an expert in all areas.

Kenrick's moral theology retained the focus and the ethical method of the manuals. The purpose of his book was to prepare seminarians for hearing confessions. He followed the legal model of the manuals by emphasizing conscience as the proximate norm of morality and law as the remote norm. In his preface he mentioned only two sources for his work: St. Thomas, of the older school, and Alphonsus, of more recent times.[44] He later elaborated on both of these sources in greater detail. Thomas Aquinas stands out above all the other scholars of his time. Because of his clarity and genius, Aquinas has rightly been called the "angel of the schools." His writings accurately and auspiciously proposed the holiest and purest teaching. For this reason Kenrick kept Aquinas accessible as he was writing his textbook. Alphonsus had proposed an eminent approach to moral theology based on his deep knowledge and his many years of pastoral experience. Kenrick used Alphonsus and willingly followed his authority in writing his book, often even using Alphonsus's own words.[45]

Not everyone who claimed to follow Alphonsus in the nineteenth century was true to his nuanced pastoral and prudential approach. In fact, so-called followers often distorted Alphonsus's own approach. Raphael Gallagher, himself a contemporary Redemptorist moral theologian teaching in Rome, points out that Kenrick, unlike even many later Redemptorists, had a truly sophisticated understanding of Alphonsus's approach.[46] Like Alphonsus, Kenrick brought to his moral theology his own pastoral experience in ministry.

In addition to his understanding of Aquinas and Alphonsus, Kenrick brought to his work a theoretical and practical understanding of the American scene. In keeping with the understanding of his time, he recognized that the moral norms derived from scripture (note again the heavy emphasis on a legal model where morality is seen in terms of norms) do not and cannot change, but they must be applied to the changed conditions of time and place. For his students Kenrick attempts to make this application to the conditions of the United States.[47]

Based on his understanding of the American scene, Kenrick disagreed, for instance, with the famous position of Alphonsus that the visit of betrothed couples to each other's house would inevitably lead to sin. Kenrick even became chauvinistic on this point. Alphonsus took the harsher position based on what he regarded as the depraved morals of Italians, but Americans, Kendrick believed, could be more trusted in these matters.[48]

Concerning the subject of sexuality, Peter Gardella maintains that "the positive bond that Kenrick forged between love, sex, and general behavior in marriage was something entirely new in Catholic moral theology."[49] Kenrick appears to be the first Catholic moralist to see love as one of the rational purposes of marital intercourse. Gardella also praises the sermon on love that Kenrick placed at the beginning of the section on marriage. Gardella maintains that Kenrick's teaching on the role of love and marriage came from the American cultural influence. The American bishop said more than Liguori or any other Catholic moralist about the role of love and pleasure in marriage.[50] Perhaps Gardella at times confuses the ends or purposes of sexual intercourse and the ends or purposes of marriage, but this problem does not totally invalidate his thesis that American culture influenced Kenrick's understanding of the role of love and pleasure in sex and marriage.

Kenrick addressed the subject of slavery in the preface to his moral theology, and his teaching on slavery was definitely influenced negatively by the American scene. European manuals no longer discussed slavery, but he considered it because it was an important question in the United States.[51] He defined slavery as a state of perpetual subjection by which one gives one's labor to another in return for maintenance. Contemporary listeners hear this as an imaginary notion of slavery. Kenrick maintained that slaves are persons but that in accord with Catholic teaching, slavery is not opposed to natural law. Theologians proposed four legal titles to justify slavery: capture and war, sale, punishment for a crime, and nativity. Kenrick admitted that the ancestors of the present slaves were brought to this country unjustly, but he still justified such slavery in the present day by appeal to prescription. The defect of title was validated by the lapse of a very long time. Here he also indicated that concern for the common good could justify limiting the freedom of contemporary slaves.[52] Joseph Brokhage, in a doctoral dissertation in 1955, correctly maintains that the slavery Kenrick defended as not being against the natural law was not the slavery practiced in the United States.[53] John Noonan points out how Kenrick, in denying any condemnation of slavery in the Letter to Philemon, concluded that the Gospel "does not indulge vain theories of philanthropy to the prejudice of the social order."[54] Kenrick's position on slavery indicated that he was greatly influenced by the American scene and subordinated the rights of slaves to the existing social order. In fairness to Kenrick, very few Catholics supported the immediate abolition of slavery before the Civil War.

Kenrick's application of moral theology to the American scene comes to the fore especially in his discussion of justice and rights. The consideration of the seventh commandment on justice was the longest of the sections in the manuals. Kenrick followed the older manuals in devoting two hundred pages to the subjects of ownership and contracts. The very nature of the matters treated required a somewhat in-depth knowledge of the particular legalities governing the various types of ownership and contracts. In his treatment of justice Kenrick frequently cited the well-known works of Sir William Blackstone, Kent's *Commentaries*, and Purdon's *Digest*, as well as the laws of individual states, especially those of Pennsylvania, Delaware, and New Jersey, obviously because of their geographical relationship to Philadelphia.[55] His knowledge of American law appears throughout his moral theology. Kenrick pointed out, for example, that priests who officiate at marriages of minors who have not consulted with their parents are subject to civil penalties. He then discussed those penalties in the laws of Pennsylvania, New

Jersey, and Delaware.[56] Obviously, he spent much time studying the laws of different states.

In light of the pluralistic religious practices in the United States, Kenrick made a creative contribution to the manual tradition by frequently citing non-Catholic authors. He pointed out in his preface that he would frequently mention non-Catholic authors, especially Anglicans, in the footnotes since it is helpful to know that they often agree with Catholics and share much common ground. His approach here too is irenic.[57] The second and third footnotes in the first volume refer to Jeremy Taylor, the Anglican bishop.[58]

On the other hand, Kenrick showed some acceptance of ultramontanism, with its emphasis on the prerogatives of the papacy. His preface includes a recognition that moral theology deals with many contingent matters that have not been determined by a decree of the Church, so he could easily have erred on some points. He asked to be instructed and corrected by those more wise than he on these matters. He ended by promising in all things obedience to the Roman See, which we acknowledge as the teacher of all Christians, the divinely constituted judge and guardian of faith and morals.[59]

Kenrick's moral theology volumes were used in the seminaries at Louisville, St. Louis, New York, Cincinnati, Charleston, Baltimore, Emmitsburg, and Philadelphia. The Fifth Provincial Council of Baltimore agreed that the archbishop of Baltimore should recommend Kenrick's work to all American seminaries, but this never happened. Kenrick himself explained this as the result of a fear of offending the majesty of Rome by introducing the work of an American theologian.[60] A revised second edition of the moral theology was published in Malines, Belgium, in 1861, but there were no subsequent editions. As the nineteenth century progressed, Kenrick's moral theology influenced the American Church less and less.

Given Kenrick's status as the outstanding theologian in the United States and his important role as a bishop in Philadelphia and later in the Primatial See of Baltimore, one would expect that his moral theology would go through many editions and have an enduring influence on U.S. Catholicism. Why did his moral theology not have an extended life through future editions?

Different answers have been given to this question. John Tracy Ellis maintains that the primacy of the Gury manual in the United States came from the fact that he wrote from Rome,[61] but as John P. Boyle points out, Gury taught in Rome for only one year and wrote his moral theology in France.[62] Joseph White suggests that Kenrick's teaching on slavery made the book inappropriate after the Civil War.[63] But a subsequent editor could have corrected this erroneous teaching on slavery. Others claim that Kenrick's difficult Latin prose made it hard for American seminarians to read and understand his textbooks.[64] I think there was a more practical reason. The manuals that went through many editions were written by priests in a religious order. Subsequent editors were fellow religious from the same order who felt a commitment to continue the work of their predecessors. Kenrick was a diocesan priest; apparently no one felt compelled to come out with future editions of his book.

ALOYSIUS SABETTI

Aloysius Sabetti (1839–98), a Neapolitan Jesuit, studied in Rome and France and came to the United States after ordination in 1868 to become a missionary in New Mexico. But plans changed when Woodstock College, the Jesuit seminary in Maryland, needed a professor. In 1871 Sabetti began teaching dogmatic theology but moved to moral theology in 1873 to replace a Jesuit who had died. He continued teaching moral theology until his death in 1898. Sabetti had no training to teach theology beyond the course required of all Jesuits for ordination. He was not a scholar or an intellectual, but he had the characteristics necessary for a good author of a manual of moral theology. He was a practical man of common sense, sympathetic, committed to the pastoral scope of moral theology, unpretentious, and a loyal son of the Church.[65]

In 1884 Sabetti brought out the first edition of his one-volume *Compendium theologiae moralis,* which went through thirteen editions in his lifetime. His successors at Woodstock, Timothy Barrett and Daniel Creeden, continued to produce updates of the manual, especially incorporating the material from the new code of canon law that came into effect in 1918. A thirty-fourth edition appeared in 1939.[66] The title page of the *Compendium* describes the work as first written by John Peter Gury, updated by Anthony Ballerini, and now shortened and accommodated for seminarians of this region by Aloysius Sabetti. The excellent quality of the Gury manual edited by Ballerini influenced Sabetti's desire to adapt the book for the American scene rather than write his own volume. Sabetti's redaction aimed to make the manual shorter, clearer, and more concise in light of recent Roman documents and adapted to local conditions in the United States.[67]

Analyzing the Sabetti manual will at the same time indicate the approach of the manuals in general. Sabetti's *Compendium* has the role of all the manuals of training seminarians for their role as confessors in the sacrament of penance. His book is a brief and practical manual aimed at seminarians preparing for priesthood in the United States. These students did not need dense dissertations, controversies, doubts, or new and strange approaches but brief and solid solutions. Sabetti pointed out that priests already ordained would find in the manual a short treatment in which solutions that had perhaps been forgotten would at a moment's notice be perceived.[68]

In this context, the *Compendium* focuses on what is sinful and the degree of sinfulness. The discussion of faith clearly illustrates such a narrow focus. One would expect faith to be a basis for the entire moral life of the Christian, but this is not the approach of the manuals. Sabetti warns us at the beginning that he will not cover the aspects of faith that belong in dogmatic theology. He touches on only three topics: the necessity of faith, the object of faith, and the sins opposed to faith. By the very nature of faith, an explicit act of faith by adults is necessary to obtain justification. Furthermore, it is necessary by law to make an act of faith sometime during one's life, but when precisely is it required to make an internal act of faith? Pope Innocent XI condemned the proposition that it is sufficient to make an act of faith only once in a lifetime. Theologians commonly maintain that a Christian should make an act of faith often. The meaning of "often" is debatable, but one can safely conclude that it does not require greater frequency than once a year.[69]

In discussing the material object of faith, the focus again is minimal. Here Sabetti makes a distinction he frequently uses, between a necessity of means, which is required by the very nature of the reality, and the necessity of precept, which is required by an authoritative command or precept. A "necessity of means" demands that a person believe in the existence of God and that God is the remunerator. A "necessity of precept or command" holds the faithful to an explicit belief in all that is contained in the creed and the efficacy of the major sacraments. Authors disagree about whether it is required by a necessity of means to explicitly believe in the Trinity and the Incarnation. But the opinion denying such an obligation is certainly probable.[70]

The third section deals with the two sins of infidelity and heresy.[71] In reality, the discussion of the virtue of faith deals not with the virtue of faith but with the acts of faith from the perspective of what is sinful and what are the minimal faith requirements—the basic perspectives of the manual tradition. Important to note also is that Sabetti places the emphasis not on what is morally true but on what is morally safe in practice.

Sabetti's legal model sees morality primarily in terms of obedience to law. This legal model permeates his *Compendium*. His book begins with three short treatments of human acts, conscience, and law. This approach follows, without ever making it explicit, the moral approach that law is the remote norm of morality and conscience is the proximate norm of morality. Conscience must conform itself to law. In accord with this approach, Sabetti defines sin as the free transgression of a law obliging in conscience.[72] Sabetti then uses the Ten Commandments as the primary scheme for understanding the Christian moral life.[73] A section on the laws of the Church follows.[74] The *Compendium* devotes three hundred pages to the sacraments. For each sacrament, he discusses the matter and form of the sacrament, the minister of the sacrament, and the subject or recipient of the sacrament. In all these considerations, the primary concern is what is necessary for the validity of the sacrament (if a sacrament is invalid, there is no sacrament) and what is necessary for liceity or lawfulness. If an action is only unlawful, the sacrament remains valid. For example, according to Catholic law, the eucharistic bread must be unleavened. To use leavened bread is unlawful, but the sacrament is still valid.[75]

The legal model can easily become negatively legalistic in the sense of an extrinsic morality. Thomistic morality is intrinsic—something is commanded because it is good. However, the manuals often give the reverse impression that something is good because it is commanded. The previously mentioned distinction between a necessity of means and a necessity or obligation of precept logically gives the impression that the command or precept makes something right or wrong. In speaking about prayer, Sabetti goes so far as to say that prayer is certainly necessary for all adults by a necessity of precept based on scripture. In addition, many theologians hold that it is necessary by a necessity of means.[76] In this case, therefore, the precept is the more important category.

The approach of Sabetti and the manuals is individualistic. The focus is on the sins of the individual penitent. The *Compendium* gives a comparatively long discussion of justice—more than 150 pages—which begins by describing the four types of justice: legal, distributive, vindictive, and commutative. Legal justice treats the individual's obligations to society. Distributive justice deals with how society distributes its goods and burdens among its members. Vindictive justice discusses the punishments meted out to protect society. Commutative justice involves giving to another individual what is due her.[77] But Sabetti then considers only commutative justice with regard to the two realities of ownership and contracts. The focus on the confession of an individual's sins suggests that the concerns of society are not mentioned in these manuals. In light of the focus on individual sins, it is easy to think of the person as an isolated individual and not in terms of the individual's relationships with God, neighbor, world, and others.

Sabetti's approach is very practical and pragmatic. As mentioned in his preface, he is interested in giving brief and safe solutions and not in extended treatises.[78] His interest is in practice, not theory. Sabetti's treatment of the more theoretical aspects of moral theology is very truncated. The first section on human acts is only twenty pages long. His description of natural law, which he uses often in his arguments, is only one page.[79] As his manual demonstrates, his primary concern is not for moral truth as such but for solutions that can be safely followed and practiced.

Sabetti employs a casuistic approach. He is interested in giving practical solutions. He generally begins with a definition and distinctions to clarify what he is talking about. Next he proposes the principle or norms that are applicable in this matter. Finally he applies the principles to particular cases. His discussion of divination with regard to the first commandment demonstrates this approach. Divination is the attempt to learn the occult through the work of the devil. Sabetti proposes two principles or norms. Explicit divination, which is done through the expressed invocation of the devil, always involves mortal sin. Tacit divination, which invokes the devil by means that are in no way proportionate to obtain the desired effect, even if the person protests that he is in no way dealing with the devil, is per se a mortal sin. Sometimes, however, tacit divination can be excused because of guilessness, ignorance, or the fact that one really does not put faith in what transpires. Sabetti then applies these principles to six particular cases. Is it a grave sin to go to a fortune-teller? Generally it is not a grave sin because the person does not really put faith in the fortune-teller and does it more out of curiosity or as a joke. What about the use of a divining rod to detect water or precious metals? If one intends no role for the devil in the process, most recent authors see no problem with the practice.[80]

Sabetti also employs casuistry in contexts other than his moral theology book. Once a week he proposed and solved a case of conscience for the Jesuit community at Woodstock to help them in their sacramental practice.[81] In the first issue of the *American Ecclesiastical Review* in 1889, the editor, Father Herman J. Heuser, happily informed his readers that Father Aloysius Sabetti, "the highest authority on moral theology in this country," had agreed in the future to answer moral cases in this journal.[82] Pastoral publications such as the *American Ecclesiastical Review* invariably had someone discuss cases of conscience to help priests in their confessional work. Moral theology thus appears not only in the textbooks for seminarians but also in articles that appear in different types of journals. Sabetti was planning to publish a book of cases of conscience using the materials about which he had written and talked, but his health failed before he could finish this work.[83]

For Sabetti the highest authority in practice is the teaching of the popes, even when done only through the decrees and statements of the congregations of the Roman Curia, such as the Holy Office and the Penitentiary. He developed his thought here in two articles published in the *American Ecclesiastical Review*. Speaking of the teaching office of the pope, he says it is not the congregation itself that acts "but the Holy Father, himself, who in the exercise of his supreme power, makes use of the same congregation as a means to promulgate it. The binding power of the decree is thus the greatest; to disobey it would be a sin."[84] Note the superlatives—"supreme" and "greatest." But surely even Sabetti would recognize that infallible papal teaching has a greater teaching authority.

Sabetti himself was personally involved in some practical decisions of the Roman congregations about abortion. In the latter part of the nineteenth century, in keeping with the increased role of the papacy as a moral teacher, questions about particular issues were often submitted to the curial congregations for a response. Sabetti himself, in his manual and in a longer article in the *American Ecclesiastical Review,* dealt with the issues of abortion, craniotomy, and ectopic pregnancy.[85] In his *Compendium,* he mentions that previous responses from the congregations were somewhat doubtful and unsure, but now there is certainty in Catholic approaches as a result of the May 31, 1884, response from the Holy Office declaring that the acceptance of craniotomy cannot be safely taught.[86] In an 1869 reply to a query about the lawfulness of craniotomy, the Penitentiary responded to a petitioner that he should consult the approved authors. But some of these authors defended craniotomy to save the mother's life. Two further responses were still somewhat vague and uncertain. But in May 1884 the Holy Office responded to the archbishop of Lyons that it cannot safely be taught that craniotomy to save the life of the mother is permitted.[87] In light of this response, Sabetti claims "that an opinion which cannot be safely taught will never be held as probable by Catholic theologians." He further explains that Rome "could not have spoken more clearly."[88] Again his tendency is to give the strongest authority to any type of curial response.

Rome continued to receive questions dealing with abortion and especially with the distinction between direct and indirect abortion and whether the fetus could be killed as a materially unjust aggressor. Sabetti argued that an ectopic pregnancy (a pregnancy outside the uterus) could be removed because it was an unjust aggressor.[89] In 1902, after Sabetti's death, the Holy Office responded that it is not acceptable to remove a nonviable ectopic fetus from the mother in order to save her life.[90] Subsequent editions, published by Sabetti's successors, fully accepted this teaching. In light of his understanding of the teaching role of the papacy and the Roman congregations, Sabetti would have done the same thing himself. By the time of Sabetti's death, the curial congregations were frequently involved in authoritatively deciding concrete moral dilemmas. Sabetti, with his ultramontanist sympathies, was a strong supporter of such actions by the Roman congregations.

With more than thirty editions published, Sabett's manual was the most influential and long-lasting of the nineteenth-century moral manuals written in the United States.[91] In addition to its use by Jesuits, ten of thirty-two seminaries training diocesan priests in the mid-1930s still used Sabetti's textbook.[92] I have given extensive coverage to Sabetti's manual because his work is illustrative of the genre of manuals of moral theology that stayed in existence in the United States and elsewhere practically until the beginning of Vatican Council II. Later manuals basically share the same general approach and will not be discussed in detail.

Anthony Konings, a Dutch Redemptorist who taught moral theology and canon law in Holland before coming to teach in the United States, published the first edition of his moral manual in 1874. Joseph Putzer, his successor as teacher of moral theology in the Redemptorist seminary in Maryland, revised and updated the manual, but there were no further editions in the twentieth century.[93]

Adolphe Tanquerey (1854–1932), a French Sulpician who taught for a time at St. Mary's Seminary in Baltimore, published two volumes of his moral theology in 1902 and a third volume a few years later, after he returned to France. Tanquerey had earlier published a two-volume synopsis of dogmatic theology and was perhaps best known for his later writings in spirituality. His original moral theology manual did not pay much attention to the American scene. However, revisions by F. Cimetier made accommodations to the U.S. scene, and Sulpician-run seminaries in this country continued to use the Tanquery manual until Vatican II.[94]

THOMAS J. BOUQUILLON

The moral manual flourished in the institutional home of the seminary, but near the end of the nineteenth century a new institution appeared on the scene—the Catholic University of America. As the nineteenth century progressed, there was some talk about the need for the Catholic Church to have a Catholic university in this country to supply graduate degrees for students, especially in theology. Opposition, however, existed in many circles, even among some of the bishops themselves. The Third Plenary Council of Baltimore in 1884, spurred on by the work of Bishop John Lancaster Spalding of Peoria, Illinois, which included securing a gift of $300,000 made by Mary Gwendolyn Caldwell, voted to start a Catholic university. The Catholic University of America (CUA) officially opened its doors on November 13, 1889, with ten faculty members and forty-six students, but soon other schools opened and laypeople came in as well. The first rector, John J. Keane, had acquired his faculty from Europe, including the Belgian Thomas J. Bouquillon (1840–1903), professor of moral theology. Bouquillon, a priest of the diocese of Bruges, received a doctorate from the Gregorian University in Rome in 1867 and taught moral theology at the seminary in Bruges before going to the newly founded Catholic University of Lille.[95]

Bouquillon was a scholar. He had a love for books and assembled a personal library of more than ten thousand volumes in his lifetime. He was interested in history and even started writing a history of theology, and read widely in the social sciences. He helped form and contributed to the *Catholic University Bulletin*, which aimed to bring scholarly ideas to the intellectual public. More than half the articles he contributed to that journal in his lifetime were not in the field of moral theology.[96]

Catholic historians in the United States have remembered Bouquillon not for his work in moral theology but for his identification with the liberal wing of the Catholic Church at the end of the nineteenth century. This group espoused the defense of the Americanization of immigrants, the promotion of the Catholic University, cooperation with the state in the work of education, Catholic participation in the Knights of Labor, and opposition to the condemnation of Henry George's single-tax theory and the excommunication of George's priest supporter, Father Edward McGlynn of New York. The bishops linked with the liberal approach included John Ireland of St. Paul, Denis O'Connell, and others. Archbishop Michael Corrigan of New York and Bernard McQuaid of Rochester, along with some Jesuits, were heavily identified with the conservative camp.[97]

In 1891 Bouquillon published a pamphlet defending the position of Archbishop Ireland proposing that Catholic schools should start with mass and catechism in the early morning, afterward becoming public schools paid for by the local communities.[98] The debate was intense and somewhat bitter. Responses back and forth included a strong attack on Bouquillon in *Civiltà Cattolica*, the semiofficial Vatican journal published by the Jesuits. Bouquillon's approach to the role of the state in education was scholarly, irenic, and explicitly based on the approach of Thomas Aquinas and the scholastics as well as on that of Pope Leo XIII in his encyclicals. Such was Bouquillon's role in this dispute that the *New Catholic Encyclopedia* includes all the theoretical, practical, and historical aspects of this debate under the one entry "Bouquillon Controversy."[99]

Bouquillon was also intimately involved in the effort to overturn the excommunication of Father McGlynn by Archbishop Corrigan and was solidly identified with the liberal wing at the Catholic University, especially in the publication of the *Catholic University Bulletin*. Bouquillon strongly advocated the role of the social sciences; and two students greatly influenced by him, John A. Ryan and William J. Kerby, played a very significant role in American intellectual, cultural, and social life in the twentieth century.[100]

In 1899 Bouquillon published a devastating critique of the manuals of moral theology in the *Catholic University Bulletin*.[101] Unlike Thomas Aquinas and the great scholastics, the manuals separated the practical aspects of moral theology from the theoretical, the theological, and the scientific aspects. The dogmatic, the liturgical, and the ascetical aspects were all missing. He castigates the manuals in light of the *Summa* of Aquinas. The manuals say little or nothing about the important first reality in moral theology, the ultimate end of human beings; treat human acts in a jejune way; ignore the supernatural aspects of the moral life; and say nothing about virtues and vices. Addressing law in a very simplified way, the manuals do not touch on its theological aspects and put the primary emphasis on canon law. The treatment of conscience is almost totally devoted to the question of probabilism and how one solves the problem of acting in theoretical doubt. Truth is no longer the primary concern. Instead, the focus is on the safety of following a practical position on an issue that usually involves collecting the opinions of theologians from the past three centuries to demonstrate that a position is probable. Casuistry has become a lifeless way of teaching solutions to problems. No longer is it a living reality that directs human life in all its aspects. In special moral theology that treats specific and particular actions, the manuals, unlike Aquinas's model, offer little or nothing about the theological virtues and only superficially mention the moral virtues.

Part of the problem comes from the fact that the secularization movements in the political realm had driven theology out of the university and into the seminary and the sacristy. However, the major problem comes from the failure to follow the spirit and approach of Thomas Aquinas. Bouquillon was a convinced neoscholastic, totally accepting the leadership of Pope Leo XIII, who called for the primary place of Aquinas in Catholic philosophy and the use of this approach in dealing with the questions of the contemporary world. In 1887, before he came to the United States, Bouquillon published two editions containing Pope Leo's official writings, and the following year wrote six articles dealing with various aspects of Leo's approach.[102] No doubt Bouquillon was a convinced neoscholastic despite the fact that in American Church history he is identified as a strong supporter of the liberal wing of the Church in opposition to the conservatives, many of whom strongly identified with neo-scholasticism.

Disappointed with the manuals of moral theology, Bouquillon wrote a one-volume fundamental moral theology in 1873. In 1890 he drastically augmented the earlier edition, almost doubling its size. In 1903, the year after he died, the third edition, which was very similar to the second edition, was published.[103] He never published a special moral theology dealing with the specific areas of Christian living.[104]

A significant and unique feature of the second and third editions, illustrating Bouquillon's more scholarly approach, was a discussion of the history of moral theology that ran to almost one hundred pages.[105] From the twelfth century on he distinguishes three different epochs. The first epoch includes the golden period from the twelfth to the early fourteenth century, which was spurred on by the foundation of universities and religious orders committed to scholarship. The *Summa* of Thomas Aquinas stands at the apex of this period. The second period, from 1660 to 1830, is a period of change and especially a progressive fall into ruin. The *Summa* is no longer the textbook, and moral theology is developed totally apart from dogmatic theology with the growth of the manuals. A third stage of renewal begins with the restoration of the theology and philosophy of Thomas Aquinas, led by the powerful actions of the nineteenth-century popes.

One is somewhat surprised to find Alphonsus Liguori in the period of great decline, especially in light of the strong support Alphonsus and his approach received from the popes. Bouquillon praises Alphonsus for his extraordinary Christian perception and his wise choice of opinions, as a man who found a middle way between the laxism and the rigorism that had existed in his time. But Alphonsus, despite his many admirable pastoral involvements, clearly was not a scholar and did not develop the scientific aspects of moral theology.[106] In short, Alphonsus was an outstanding casuist but not a scientific moral theologian. In the preface to his fundamental moral theology, Bouquillon is positive about Alphonsus without mentioning the negative aspects. The preface mentions Bouquillon's debt to three principal masters and teachers: Aquinas, Suarez, and Alphonsus Liguori for his practical application of principles.[107]

Bouquillon understands moral theology as the science of the means and laws by which the human being is helped and directed toward his or her supernatural end. His fundamental moral theology consists of five major treatises or divisions: the ultimate end of human beings; the means to that end, including the religious and civil societies to which the individual belongs, the rules directing human beings to their end, developed in terms of law and conscience; the free, moral, and salutary characteristics of the acts by which we attain the end; and a very short final section on attaining or losing the final end. By far the longest discussion, of almost four hundred pages, or 60 percent of the book, considers law and conscience.[108]

Bouquillon acknowledges reason and revelation as the primary sources for moral theology, but reason receives the overwhelming attention. Reason recognizes the fundamental moral principles and deduces practical conclusions from these principles. His discussion of natural law develops his understanding of the role of reason. He insists on the Thomistic aspects that the manuals, for the most part, fail to develop in any detail. The natural law is necessary, universal, perpetual, and indispensable.[109] Human nature consists of three God-given inclinations: the inclinations we share with all substances (to conserve ourselves in existence), the inclinations we share with animals (to procreate and educate offspring), and the inclinations proper to human beings (to know God and to live together in human society).[110] In discussing natural law, Bouquillon insists more than Aquinas on the role of the will and the coercive aspects of law.[111] These aspects, which differ somewhat from the Thomistic approach, seem to come from the influence of Suarez.[112]

Revelation is the other general source of moral theology. Bouquillon's six-page discussion of scripture gives only two pages to the New Testament and spends most of the time on the Old Testament, insisting that one cannot appeal to the Old Testament to disagree with some existing teachings of the Church. Sacred scripture does not influence the basic outline of his moral theology or the development of its principal parts. The book's primary use of scripture is as a prooftext.[113]

In this section on revelation, Bouquillon discusses the authoritative magisterium of the Church. The pope can either teach infallibility or efficaciously teach a doctrine, but not infallibly. The pope can also delegate his authority to the Roman congregations. A true, internal, and religious assent must be given by Catholics to these teachings of the congregations. However, one must be cautious in deriving conclusions from the decrees of congregations, especially the Penitentiary, which deals with prudential applications of principles and safe ways of acting.[114] His third edition does not repeat his earlier criticism of theologians' and bishops' having recourse too quickly and too readily to the congregation to solve complex issues. The criticism centers on those individuals making the request and not on the congregations as such. When the congregations respond that one is not to be disturbed in taking such a particular position, the manualists often do no more work or research to arrive at the truth.[115]

Doubtless Bouquillon has strongly supported the role of the papal teaching office in condemning the errors of the modern world. However, in a footnote in his discussion of conscience, he seems to recognize that in conscience one might be called to act against a decree of the Penitentiary.[116]

In his other writings Bouquillon showed a strong interest in and emphasis on the importance of other sciences, such as economics, law, anthropology, and sociology. One is surprised, therefore, to see little or no mention of the sciences in his fundamental moral theology. In a brief discussion of moral science in the introduction, he recognizes a role for the sciences in moral theology that deals with the specific human acts done in all spheres of life. Moral science is the superior science on which the other sciences depend, but moral theology receives data from these other sciences.[117] One is left with the impression that the other sciences do not contribute to the moral norms governing life, but these norms are applied to particular actions in light of the other sciences.

In an 1899 article Bouquillon insisted that moral theology could be renewed by the following steps: use of the philosophy of Thomas Aquinas, a more intimate union with the theoretical truths of revelation, critical study and research into the fundamental ideas and principles of the moral life, and consistent application of these principles to all aspects of contemporary life.[118] Does his 1903 edition carry out these reforms?

Without doubt the 1903 edition emphasizes the important role of Aquinas (and also Suarez) and closely follows Aquinas by beginning his consideration of moral theology with the ultimate end of human beings. His discussion of law and conscience is much more rigorous, scientific, lengthy, and in-depth than in Sabetti. But, in the end, I do not think that his book brings about a total reform in light of Thomistic understandings. Two reasons stand out. First, Bouquillon still accepts the purpose of the manuals of moral theology of training confessors for the sacrament of penance. With this somewhat limited perspective, he never deals with the totality of the moral life in the same way that Aquinas did. Second, as a result of this focus, he adopts the legal model of moral theology rather than the teleological model of Aquinas, which was based on understanding the nature of one's ultimate end and the means by which it is attained. Aquinas gives the primary means toward the ultimate end not to law but to virtue. Although Bouquillon begins with a treatise on the ultimate end and has a short final treatise on attaining or losing that end, 60 percent of his book is devoted to his understanding of law and conscience. Law is the remote norm of morality, whereas conscience is the proximate norm of morality. The legal model definitely predominates in Bouquillon's model. Thus Bouquillon's moral theology fails to be a full development of the Thomistic approach.

After Bouquillon's death there were no more editions of his fundamental moral theology, and that is readily understandable. He had written only a one-volume fundamental moral theology and had not covered special moral theology, as all the manualists had done. Furthermore, he had no successor at Catholic University interested in carrying on his tradition. Even more significantly, his book had little appeal as a textbook. In the climate of moral theology, with its pragmatic emphasis on training confessors for the sacrament of penance, his book was too theoretical; it even included a hundred-page treatise on the history of moral theology. Teachers in seminaries wanted the pragmatic approach of the manuals, which concentrated on pointing out what was sinful and the degrees of sinfulness, with a special emphasis on what actions were safe in practice.

JOHN BAPTIST HOGAN

Thomas Bouquillon was not the only critic of the manuals. John Baptist Hogan (1829–1901), an Irish-born, French-educated Sulpician priest, also criticized the manuals of moral theology. His manner of presentation was very restrained, but his content was quite radical. Hogan, who devoted his whole life to seminary education, served twice as president of St. John's Seminary in Boston and taught moral theology as well as other theological disciplines.[119]

Hogan was not a publishing scholar, but he was an intellectual in dialogue with much of contemporary thought and friendly with many French Catholic intellectuals who advocated new approaches to theology. His 1898 book *Clerical Studies,* based on articles that had appeared earlier in the *American Ecclesiastical Review,* offered his understanding of the seminary curriculum. Hogan was interested in history and open to dialogue with all the historical developments in theology, philosophy, and science that occurred in the nineteenth century—a position different from the proponents of neo-scholasticism. Hogan also accepted historical consciousness, with its emphasis on development. History has brought about great changes in the convictions of human beings and in their intellectual methods.[120] Hogan's acceptance of historical criticism in scripture and historical development in dogmatic theology well illustrates his historical consciousness.[121] In *Clerical Studies,* the irenic, tactful, and nonconfrontational tone of his writing tends to camouflage his more radical approaches. Alfred Loisy complained that Roman authorities condemned in him what they approved in Hogan.[122] Christopher Kauffman describes him as a moderate Americanist and a moderate modernist.[123]

Both his historical consciousness and his tactful approach come through in his discussion of moral theology, which is the longest treatise in the book.[124] The first part of the discussion highly praises the present development of moral theology and its fundamental importance in the seminary curriculum. Yes, moral theology deals with the minimal level of duty, but that is necessary in light of its purpose to train confessors for the sacrament of penance. For the same reason, law and not virtue must be primary in moral theology. Casuistry as well plays a very significant role. Moral theology rightly gives primacy to human reason because almost all Christian moral duties are natural duties.[125]

But moral theology, like any science, has some imperfections and limitations.[126] Hogan then proposes a radically different understanding of the method of casuistry without ever explicitly disagreeing with the existing approach or with any theologian in particular. Hogan sees rules as standing midway between principles and concrete cases. Rules come from a variety of different sources, but history reminds us that rules change over time. The formation of rules depends on a dialogue with the principles above them and with the concrete cases below them. Practice is as much a part of theory as theory is of practice.[127] Casuistry is much more an intuition of the cultured mind than a matter of applying or deducing from principles.[128] Such an approach differs from both the manual and neoscholastic approaches, with their emphasis on the eternal, the immutable, and the unchanging natural law and a deductive reasoning process.

Hogan recognizes the important role played by Church authority and the popes, including the decisions of the curial congregations. The supreme regulative action belongs to popes, but theologians will test every regulation, using reason to weigh all the aspects.[129] In another context in which he strongly defends papal infallibility, Hogan recognizes that there have been errors in noninfallible papal teaching.[130]

In addition to his emphasis on historical consciousness, Hogan downplays and even challenges in his usual irenic way the distinction between mortal and venial sin. Human good and human evil are very complex and involve great variety; this complexity makes it difficult to distinguish mortal sin and venial sin accurately. The consequences of mortal sin and venial sin are dramatic, but at times the lightest of mortal sins and the worst of venial sins seem very close. He strongly opposes using the fear of mortal sin to secure prompt obedience to the merely positive laws of the Church, but he never points out that this approach was universally accepted and consistently used in Catholic instruction. Even if it were possible to have a clear distinction between mortal and venial sin, this distinction would refer only to the objective aspect of sin. The real meaning of an act comes primarily from the subjective side—the mental and moral state of the person who is doing the deed. Thus moral science cannot know this most important aspect: whether or not a mortal sin has been committed.[131]

Such an approach logically challenges and undercuts the whole purpose and focus of the manuals. Today it also challenges the canonical requirement of the individual confession of sins according to number and species, and therefore opens the door to other forms of sacramental penance. But, again, the irenic Hogan does not develop at all the logical consequences of his positions.

John Talbot Smith (1855–1923), a priest of Ogdensburg, New York, who wrote in a more popular historical and literary vein, published a scathing criticism of American seminaries in 1896.[132] The seminaries today look upon moral theology as the primary discipline, but Smith reduced it to the fifth most important discipline. The existing manuals claimed an almost mathematical type of certitude and are not written at all for the American scene.[133] Despite his severe criticism, Smith did not challenge the purpose and function of the manuals.

At the end of the nineteenth century, the manuals remained the textbooks used in all the seminaries in the United States, but some significant voices raised criticisms about the existing manuals. Would this criticism bring about a new and different approach to moral theology? The following chapters will explain how the manualistic approach continued in the twentieth century until Vatican Council II (1962–65).

NOTES

1. There is no definitive history of moral theology. Louis Vereecke is the recognized authority in the field, but he has not published books as such or a general history. He has published four volumes of printed notes for his students at the Academia Alfonsiana in Rome. Titled *Storia della teologia morale moderna*, these volumes have been widely diffused and cited and are for public sale. They cover the period from 1300 to 1789—*Storia della teologia morale dal XIV° al XVI° secolo: Da Guglielmo di Ockham a Martin Lutero (1300–1520); Storia della teologia morale in spagna nel XVI° secolo e origine delle "Institutiones Morales" (1520–1600); Storia della teologia morale nel XVII° secolo: La crisi della teologia morale (1600–1700); Storia della teologia morale nel XVIII° secolo: Concina e S. Alfonso de' Liguori, l'Aufklarung (1700–1789).* Summaries of his research on the history of moral theology have appeared; see Vereecke, "History of Moral Theology," 1119–22; Vereecke, "Storia della teologia morale," 1314–38. A very helpful collection of his essays has been published under the title *De Guillaume d'Ockham à Saint Alphonse de Liguori.* The best available one-volume history of moral theology is Angelini and Valsecchi, *Disegno storico della teologia morale.* For a significant historical work that claims to be neither complete nor systematic, see Mahoney, *Making of Moral Theology.* Although I have written summary histories of moral theology (e.g., *Encyclopedia of Religion, Encyclopedia of Bioethics, Westminster Dictionary of Christian Ethics*) and have had an interest in some historical issues, I do not claim expertise in this area. In what follows I depend heavily on Vereecke and other secondary sources.
2. Vereecke, "History of Moral Theology," *New Catholic Encyclopedia* 9:1120.
3. Vereecke, "Concile de Trent."
4. Vidal, *La morale di Sant' Alfonso,* 69–114.
5. Ligorio, *Dissertatio scholastico-moralis,* 45.
6. Capone, "Per la norma morale," 220–22.
7. Vereecke, "Conscience selon Saint Alphonse de Liguori."
8. Ligorio, *Theologia moralis,* 3:459.
9. Vidal, *La morale di Sant' Alfonso,* 270–72.
10. Gallagher, "Fate of the Moral Manual since St. Alphonsus," 213–16.
11. Angelini and Valsecchi, *Disegno storico,* 128–30.
12. Gallagher, "Fate of the Moral Manual since St. Alphonsus," 216–26.
13. Guerber, *Le ralliement du clergé français,* 4–5, and throughout.
14. Ph. Lécrivain, "Saint Alphonse aux risques"; Campana, "Gury, Jean Pierre."
15. Vidal, *La morale di Sant' Alfonso,* 207–16.
16. For the best overview of the Catholic Church in the nineteenth century, which I am following here, see Aubert et al., *Church in the Age of Liberalism.*
17. Boyle, *Church Teaching Authority,* 10–42.

18. Connery, *Abortion*, 225–95.

19. Weiss, "Alphonso de Liguori"; Lécrivain, "Saint Alphonse aux risques," 387–93; Gallagher, "Fate of the Moral Manual since St. Alphonsus," 233–35.

20. Lécrivain, "Saint Alphonse aux risques."

21. Gallagher, "Fate of the Moral Manual since St. Alphonsus," 237.

22. Vidal, *La morale di Sant' Alfonso*, 201–2.

23. Vereecke, *Ockham à Liguori*, 49–50.

24. The best study in English of intellectual developments of the Catholic Church in the nineteenth century is McCool, *Catholic Theology in the Nineteenth Century.*

25. E.g., Gallagher, *Time Past, Time Future*, 48–122.

26. Ligorio, *Theologia moralis*, 1:lvi.

27. Ibid., 1:26.

28. Dolan, *American Catholic Experience*, 221–40.

29. Crews, *American Holy Land*, 50–51.

30. Dolan, *American Catholic Experience*, 226–30.

31. For the history of diocesan seminaries in the United States, see White, *Diocesan Seminary.*

32. Ibid., 131–33.

33. Ibid., 124.

34. Ibid., 139.

35. Ellis, "Formation of the American Priest," 8.

36. White, *Diocesan Seminary*, 139.

37. Kauffman, *Tradition and Transformation*, 110–11, 312.

38. Quoted in White, *Diocesan Seminary*, 139.

39. Ibid., 140.

40. Kenrick, *Theologia moralis*, 3 vols.

41. For the life of Kenrick before he became archbishop of Baltimore, see Nolan, *Most Reverend Francis Patrick Kenrick.*

42. Fogarty, *American Catholic Biblical Scholarship*, 14–34.

43. Kenrick, *Theologia moralis*, 1:iii.

44. Ibid., 1:iv.

45. Ibid., 1:2–3.

46. Gallagher, "Fate of the Moral Manual since St. Alphonsus," 220–22.

47. Kenrick, *Theologia moralis*, 1:iii.

48. Gallagher, "Fate of the Moral Manual since St. Alphonsus," 221.

49. Gardella, *Innocent Ecstasy*, 23.

50. Ibid., 9–24.

51. Kenrick, *Theologia moralis*, 1: iv.

52. Ibid., 255–58.

53. Brokhage, *Kenrick's Opinion on Slavery*, 242–43.

54. Noonan, *Church That Can and Cannot Change*, 109.

55. Kenrick, *Theologia moralis*, 2:2–212.

56. Ibid., 1:100.

57. Ibid., 1:iv.

58. Ibid., 1:2–3.

59. Ibid., 1:v. Commentators disagree on whether or not Kenrick is a neoscholastic. White (*Diocesan Seminary,* 139) maintains that, in scripture and doctrine, Kenrick ignored the scholastic authors. Fogarty (*American Catholic Biblical Scholarship,* 34) claims that Kenrick's theology was not based on the scholastics and that he would have opposed the imposition of Thomism by Pope Leo XIII. But McGreevy (*Catholicism and American Freedom,* 53) characterizes Kenrick as a neo-Thomist and an ultramontanist.

60. Nolan, *Most Reverend Francis Patrick Kenrick,* 244.

61. Ellis, "Formation of the American Priest," 32.

62. Boyle, "American Experience in Moral Theology," 8.

63. White, *Diocesan Seminary,* 140.

64. Nolan, *Most Reverend Francis Patrick Kenrick,* 244; Konings, *Theologiae moralis,* 7.

65. For more detailed information on Sabetti, see Curran, *Origins of Moral Theology,* 83–93.

66. Sabetti, *Compendium theologiae moralis,* 34th ed.

67. Sabetti, *Compendium theologiae moralis,* 7th ed., v–viii. Subsequent references will be to this edition, but the section numbers as well as the page numbers will be given to help those who might use a different edition.

68. Ibid., vii.

69. Ibid., 107–8nn152–53. In church documents, n. refers to the paragraph number.

70. Ibid., 112–14nn155–57.

71. Ibid., 114–15nn158–61.

72. Ibid., 85n124.

73. Ibid., 140–232nn200–325.

74. Ibid., 233–51nn326–44.

75. Ibid., 459n679.

76. Ibid., 143n202.

77. Ibid., 253–54n346.

78. Ibid., vii.

79. Ibid., 75nn107–8.

80. Ibid., 146–49nn207–9. The term *casuistry* is used here in the broad sense employed by the manuals to refer to the application of principles to particular cases. For the understanding of casuistry as opposed to a principle-based approach, see Jonsen and Toulmin, *Abuse of Casuistry.*

81. Dooley, *Woodstock and Its Makers,* 86–89.

82. Heuser, "Note," 70. This journal for a time changed its name to *Ecclesiastical Review* but then went back to the original title. Subsequent citations are to the *American Ecclesiastical Review.*

83. "Father Aloysius Sabetti," 228.

84. Sabetti, "Commentary on the Decree 'Quemadmodum,'" 166.

85. Sabetti, "Animadversiones" and "Catholic Church and Obstetrical Science."

86. Sabetti, *Compendium theologiae moralis,* 274n273.

87. Connery, *Abortion*, 225–92.

88. Sabetti, "Catholic Church and Obstetrical Science," 130–31.

89. Sabetti, "Animadversiones."

90. Bouscaren, *Ethics of Ectopic Operations*, 22; Connery, *Abortion*, 201–3.

91. Connell, "Theological School in America," 224; McKeever, "Seventy-Five Years"; Boyle, "American Experience," 26.

92. Heck, *Curriculum of the Major Seminary*, 46–47.

93. Sampers, "Konings, Anthony."

94. Laubacher, "Tanquery, Adophe Alfred"; McKeever, "Seventy-Five Years," 21; Kauffman, *Tradition and Transformation*, 183–84; Heck, *Curriculum of the Major Seminary*, 46–47.

95. For the history of the Catholic University of America, see Nuesse, *Catholic University of America*.

96. For a more in-depth study of Bouquillon's life and moral theology, see Curran, *Origins of Catholic Moral Theology*, 171–254.

97. For the classical but somewhat dated study, see Cross, *Emergence of Liberal Catholicism*.

98. Bouquillon, *Education*.

99. Ryan, "Bouquillon Controversy." See also Reilly, *School Controversy, 1891–93*.

100. Nuesse, "Thomas Joseph Bouquillon."

101. Bouquillon, "Moral Theology."

102. Bouquillon, *Leonis Papae XIII*. The following six articles by Thomas Bouquillon appeared in *Le Messager des Fidèles de Maredsous* 5 (1888): "Dix années de pontificat," 4–9; "Léon XIII et la Bavière," 74–87; "Condemnation des doctrines Rosminiennes," 199–207; "Le libéralisme d'après l'Encyclique *Libertas*," 361–70; "La liberté chrétienne d'après l'Encyclique *Libertas*," 399–404; "Les droits de l'Eglise," 533–46.

103. Bouquillon, *Institutiones theologiae moralis fundamentalis; Theologia moralis fundamentalis*, 2d ed.; and *Theologia moralis fundamentalis*, 3d ed.

104. In 1880 Bouquillon published one volume dealing with the virtue of religion: *Institutiones theologiae moralis specialis*. In this 461-page tome, the first treatment on prayer covers more than one hundred pages and, unlike Sabetti, develops a full discussion of all aspects of prayer, and not just the minimum obligation.

105. Bouquillon, *Theologia moralis fundamentalis*, 2d ed., 49–140; 3d ed., 71–167. Subsequent references are to the third edition.

106. Ibid. (3d ed.), 140n7.

107. Ibid., viii.

108. Ibid., 216.

109. Ibid., 237–38.

110. Ibid., 225, 235–36.

111. Ibid., 218–29.

112. Bouquillon, "Moral Theology," 252–53.

113. Bouquillon, *Theologia moralis fundamentalis*, 29–35.

114. Ibid., 53–70.

115. Bouquillon, "Moral Theology," 267.

116. Bouquillon, *Theologia moralis fundamentalis*, 525n1.

117. Ibid., 7.

118. Bouquillon, "Moral Theology," 267–68.

119. The best available source for Hogan is Kauffman, *Tradition and Transformation*, 168–77.

120. Hogan, *Clerical Studies*, 370.

121. Ibid., 152–66, 176–86.

122. Kauffman, *Tradition and Transformation*, 275.

123. Ibid., 176–79.

124. Hogan, *Clerical Studies*, 196–262.

125. Ibid., 197–242.

126. Ibid., 235ff.

127. Ibid., 221–22.

128. Ibid., 247–49.

129. Ibid., 214–19.

130. Hogan, "Christian Faith and Modern Science," 386–88.

131. Hogan, *Clerical Studies*, 256–61.

132. Smith, *Our Seminaries*.

133. Ibid., 266–72.

THE TWENTIETH CENTURY BEFORE VATICAN II

This chapter will consider the development of Catholic moral theology from the beginning of the twentieth century until the Second Vatican Council (1962–65). During this period, the manuals continued to be the Catholic approach to moral theology. This chapter will also discuss sexual and medical ethics.

MORAL THEOLOGY IDENTIFIED WITH THE MANUALS

Reasons connected with the very nature of moral theology help to explain the continuing primary role of the manuals despite some rather sharp criticism at the end of the nineteenth century. The seminary remained the home institution for the discipline of moral theology. The first sixty years of the twentieth century emphasized the importance of confession in Catholic life. People were encouraged to receive the sacrament on a regular basis, and many did. The growing emphasis on more frequent communion also encouraged more frequent celebration of the sacrament of penance. Priests and seminarians continued to see their role as confessors as a most significant aspect of their ministry. In this context, the manuals of moral theology continued to thrive and be identified as *the* approach to moral theology.

Condemnations of Americanism and Modernism

Another significant development affecting the Church also discouraged newer approaches to moral theology. The papal condemnations of Americanism in 1899 and of modernism in 1907 made Catholics all over the world, including the United States, fearful of new and different approaches to theology in all its forms.

Americanism, like the later modernism, received its description from the papal condemnation. Americanism was a broad movement that urged the Catholic Church to adapt to American culture and experience in many different areas. The liberal wing of the American hierarchy (Archbishop John Ireland, Bishops Denis O'Connell and John Keane, and Cardinal James Gibbons of Baltimore to a great extent) urged the Americanization of immigrants and a greater accommodation of the Church to American culture. These same prelates also supported the separation of church and state as it existed here in the United States as being good for the Church. The theological controversy on Americanism primarily took place in Europe as a result of the French translation and introduction, by Felix Klein, of the biography of Isaac Hecker, the founder of the Paulist Fathers. Hecker was convinced that many Americans would convert to Catholicism if the Church accommodated itself more to American culture, with particular emphasis on the active virtues rather than the passive virtues of humility and obedience.[1]

Pope Leo XIII, in his 1899 apostolic letter *Testem benevolentiae,* condemned Americanism as accommodating the faith to American culture in order to gain converts and for its emphasis on the active virtues over the passive virtues and the natural virtues over the supernatural. The conservative bishops in the United States, led by Michael Corrigan of New York City and Bernard McQuaid of Rochester, were quite pleased with the condemnation. The liberal bishops, however, said that although they agreed with everything in the encyclical, the encyclical did not portray what actually was occurring in the United States. Earlier, in his 1895 encyclical *Longinqua oceani,* Leo had praised aspects of the American Catholic Church but had maintained that the American separation of church and state was not the desired approach and should not be the norm.[2] The condemnation of Americanism obviously created a climate in which American Catholics became very cautious about proposing any change or development in Catholic faith, life, and practice.

The worldwide condemnation of modernism in 1907 solidified the status quo in American Catholic theology and life and encouraged suspicion of anyone who proposed innovation.[3] Again the pope described and defined modernism in his condemnation. The general thrust of the modernist approach was to call for an evolution and development in faith that would recognize the historical aspect of all human knowledge. The danger, of course, was an uncritical acceptance of contemporary thought. The pope condemned Alfred Loisy for maintaining that Christianity went through historical developments and evolutions in the very beginning that were not envisioned by Jesus. He also condemned the writings of the Irish Jesuit George Tyrell for emphasizing the experiential basis of revelation and the metaphorical character of religious language. At that time modernism came in many forms, ranging from the moderate to the more radical, and it played out primarily in Europe.

However, some people in the United States were involved in one way or another with some modernist approaches. In his book on the modernist impulse in America, Scott Appleby mentions John Zahm, the Holy Cross priest who wrote on theological evolution; the Paulist William L. Sullivan; and the Josephite John R. Slattery. The latter two ultimately left the Church. The strongest institutional presence of a moderate modernist approach was at Dunwoodie Seminary in New York and in its journal the *New York Review*, which began publishing in 1905. After the condemnation of modernism, even moderate followers ceased to exist in the United States. Archbishop John Farley of New York removed James Francis Driscoll as rector of the Dunwoodie Seminary in 1908, and the *New York Review* ceased publication in the same year.

The liberal professors at Catholic University and the editors of the *Catholic World,* published by the Paulist fathers, and the *Catholic University Bulletin,* which had accepted some articles of a moderate modernist approach, completely reversed their earlier position, with vigorous denunciation. The *American Catholic Quarterly Review* and the *American Ecclesiastical Review* avoided scrupulously any further treatment of critical studies in archeology, history, biblical science, and theology. The board of trustees at Catholic University established a committee to find modernist books in the library. The university, under orders from Rome, did not renew the contract of Father Henry Poels, a Dutch scripture scholar who accepted modern critical biblical scholarship and refused to take the oath against modernism. Appleby describes an ecclesiastical climate in which "certain persons, in public controversy against modernism, in brochures, newspapers, and other periodicals, go to the length of detecting the evil [of modernism] everywhere or any rate of imputing it to those who are very far from being infected with it."[4]

The condemnation of modernism created an intellectual climate in the Church that was fearful of theological creativity and innovation and insisted on neo-scholasticism as the Catholic philosophy and theology. There was to be no dialogue with modern thought. After the condemnation of modernism, all Catholic professors and priests had to take an oath against modernism. Vigilance committees were set up in every diocese to make sure that modernism never again surfaced. Historical consciousness and critical thinking were allowed no room in the Church. The condemnation of Americanism and modernism had a very negative effect on Catholic intellectual life in general and on the development of theology in this country. In this atmosphere of caution and suspicion, the manuals of theology and philosophy flourished.

Theological studies at CUA languished.[5] The university conferred nine doctorates in theology from 1895 to 1909 but no more until 1917. From 1917 to 1935, CUA conferred only thirty-four doctoral degrees in theology.[6] One of the primary reasons for the lack of strong theological scholarship at CUA was the fact that most students were sent to Rome for a doctorate. Before 1931, students in Rome often received a doctorate for having finished the ordinary four-year theology seminary course. During this time frame CUA did have some professors who made significant contributions in other fields, but theology did not prosper.[7] According to Joseph White, by the mid-1930s the theology school at CUA had a handful of students and only a skeleton faculty.[8]

Seminaries continued to use the Latin manuals of moral theology, most of which originated in Europe; some were never adapted to the conditions of the United States by later editors. When I began teaching moral theology at St. Bernard's Seminary in Rochester, New York, in 1961, we used the thirty-third edition of the Latin manual of Jerome Noldin, which had originally been published in Innsbruck and had been brought up to date by his successors in Innsbruck. According to a 1962 study, more than one-half of the seminaries responding to a questionnaire reported that they used the Noldin textbook in moral theology.[9] Interestingly, no American editor had ever adapted this textbook to the conditions of the United States.

During the period 1900–1960, Charles Callan and John McHugh, two Dominican priests, wrote the only American manual of moral theology (1929).[10] Written in English rather than Latin, it was not used in seminaries. Callan and McHugh were not specialists in moral theology. They taught together at the Maryknoll Seminary in Maryknoll, New York, were coeditors of *Homiletic and Pastoral Review,* and published sixteen books together covering a range of topics. Their primary interest and scholarship were probably in scripture.[11] In the preface to their two-volume work, they recognize that moral theology is broader than just training confessors. They also call for a more scientific approach to moral theology, and, as Dominicans and followers of Aquinas, they give a greater role to the virtues.[12] But, in reality, they follow the scope and approach of previous manuals. For example, their manual divides all of special moral theology into three parts—the duties of all classes of men, the duties of particular classes of men, and the duties of men in the use of the sacraments.

The first official codification of Church law came in 1917, after more than ten years of preparation. *The Code of Canon Law* had a significant influence on the manuals of moral theology, and all manuals had to be updated in light of the new code. The new code especially affected the treatment of the administration of the sacraments, which often constituted one of the three volumes in manuals of moral theology. The greater emphasis now given to canon law encouraged the very close relationship between moral theology and canon law, strengthened the role of the law model as *the* approach to moral theology, and concentrated the focus of moral theology on what was forbidden and sinful.

First Steps toward a More Academic Approach

Although the Latin manuals originating in nineteenth-century Europe remained the textbooks in U.S. seminaries until Vatican II, some institutional support arose for a more scholarly approach to moral theology within the context of the manuals themselves. In the late 1930s and early 1940s, societies and journals in Catholic theology began to take a more scholarly approach to all aspects of Catholic theology. In 1939 the Dominican Fathers started publishing the *Thomist,* a scholarly review of philosophy and theology.[13] Also in 1939, the newly formed Catholic Biblical Association began publishing the *Catholic Biblical Quarterly.* The Canon Law Society of America began in 1939, and in 1940 the canon law faculty of CUA began publishing the *Jurist.* The Catholic Theological Society of America began in 1946.

In 1940 the American Jesuits started *Theological Studies*—the journal that has had the greatest influence on moral theology. Until the present day, *Theological Studies* has published on a regular basis what from early on were called "Notes on Moral Theology." These "Notes," which bring in literature from other scientific fields (e.g., medicine, sociology) and cite articles and books in most of the European languages, address priests in their role as confessors. The "Notes" usually appear every year, sometimes more often, and are critical reflections on what was written that year about moral theology.

John C. Ford, SJ, the professor of moral theology at the Jesuit theologate in Weston, Massachusetts, started writing the "Notes" in 1941 and was later joined in these annual and semiannual "Notes" by Gerald Kelly, SJ, from the Jesuit theologate in St. Mary's, Kansas. Both Jesuits had received doctorates in moral theology from the Gregorian University in Rome in the late 1930s, both specialized in the area of moral theology, and both wrote the "Notes" in *Theological Studies* until 1954.[14] Their many writings, but especially the "Notes," made them leading figures in moral theology in the United States and to some extent in Europe.

In 1958 Ford and Kelly published *Contemporary Moral Theology,* volume 1, *Questions in Fundamental Moral Theology,* which was to be part of an ongoing series expanding and updating their earlier "Notes" in *Theological Studies.*[15] In the late 1950s Ford and Kelly became aware of some criticism of the manuals of moral theology coming from Europe. They were open to some of these criticisms but believed that moral theology must continue to have as its primary purpose the training of confessors to know what is sinful and what is not. Professors of moral theology and confessors, however, needed to bring more than this to their understanding of the discipline and of the confessional. Realistically, moral theology itself needed to remain separate from dogma and from ascetical theology. Until new textbooks came along, the manuals would have to continue to be the textbooks for moral theology.[16]

In this light, Ford and Kelly continued to see moral theology operating within a legal model. In keeping with the manuals, the objective norm of morality is law in all its different forms. Obligations and law remain the key categories.[17] The "Notes," like their other scholarly writings, use the casuistic method of applying principles to particular cases. Jesuit moral theologians from the seventeenth century onward had used this casuistic method, and Ford and Kelly both carried on and updated this tradition. As casuists, they are clear, concise, and quick to point out how pertinent principles are applied to particular cases.

In 1951 Gerald Kelly himself wrote a popular little book, *The Good Confessor,* which emphasizes the intimate relationship between moral theology and confession and the importance of the casuistic approach. According to the *Roman Ritual,* the qualities of a good confessor are goodness, knowledge, prudence, and respect for secrecy. A confessor must have knowledge of moral theology and canon law to be able to solve the ordinary cases presented in the confessional and "to doubt prudently about the more difficult cases."[18] The confessor has the fourfold office of father, teacher, physician, and judge, but 50 percent of the book deals with the role of the confessor as judge.

In their book on fundamental moral theology, Ford and Kelly strongly defend the principles and conclusions of Catholic moral theology and give considerable attention to Pius XII's condemnation of situation ethics in the 1950s. This new morality, or situation ethics, stressed freedom, creativity, and initiative in an unorthodox way that denied the objective norms of morality.[19] A number of chapters deal with freedom and subjective imputability under stress in light of some contemporary psychological and legal understandings. The authors strongly uphold free will but recognize that we should judge more leniently than in the past subjective culpability in individual cases of human misconduct and frailty.[20]

John Ford himself wrote extensively on alcoholism and was the first moral theologian to do so.[21] The Ford and Kelly book, which devotes one chapter to alcoholism, recognizes it as a pathological reality with some moral aspects. Society and all concerned within it should work to overcome alcoholism and support the role of Alcoholics Anonymous. The alcoholic's culpability is generally diminished to a considerable extent and frequently beyond the point of mortal sin.[22]

Ford and Kelly's 1958 book shows the primary role in moral theology now played by papal teaching. Ultramontanism in the nineteenth century extolled the centrality and authoritative aspect of the papal role in the Church. The twentieth century saw a continuing and growing role for papal teaching in moral theology. The condemnation of Americanism and modernism emphasized the papal role. Encyclicals on sexual issues (*Casti connubii* in 1930) and social issues (*Quadragesimo anno* in 1931) again highlighted the primary papal role in moral teaching.[23] As the twentieth century progressed, the Roman congregations continued even more often to give solutions to particular issues and problems. Papal moral teaching reached its apex in the pontificate of Pius XII (1939–58). Pius XII spoke out often on moral issues, especially in the areas of sexuality and medical ethics. Gerald Kelly, in his *Medico-Moral Problems,* refers to the teaching of Pope Pius XII on twenty-two specific issues.[24] John P. Kenny's *Principles of Medical Ethics* lists in the index forty issues on which the pope has spoken.[25] Ford and Kelly show the importance of papal teaching by devoting the first three chapters of their book on fundamental moral theology to this topic. The first page of their book distinguishes the human science of ethics, with reason as its supreme norm, from moral theology, with authority as its sovereign guide.[26]

Papal moral teaching comes in different forms, with encyclicals being the most authoritative way of proposing papal teaching, but also in addresses and speeches—a form frequently used by Pius XII. Ford and Kelly developed their understanding of the authority of papal teaching based on the pope's own 1950 encyclical *Humani generis,* in which Pius XII understood the hierarchical magisterium as the proximate and universal norm of truth for theologians. Pius XII applied to the ordinary, noninfallible papal magisterium the words of Jesus from Luke 10:16: "He who heareth you, heareth me." As a result, the document maintains that whenever the pope goes out of his way to speak on a disputed point, it is no longer a matter for free debate among theologians.[27] Ford and Kelly recognize that *Humani generis* primarily discusses papal encyclicals, but they give the same authority to other papal teachings, such as the addresses of Pope Pius XII on medical issues. In fairness, Ford and Kelly are not literalists or fundamentalists—papal documents require some interpretation. If it is clear that the pope intends to settle a controversial issue decisively in these addresses or talks, then theologians can no longer disagree.[28]

Ford and Kelly's first volume of *Contemporary Moral Theology* is not a systematic work and does not discuss natural law at any great length. Their second volume, on marriage questions, published in 1963, well illustrates their heavy dependence on natural law theory. Catholic sexual ethics in general and the specific hierarchical teaching condemning artificial contraception are based on the fact "that from time immemorial the church held and applied the natural-law principle that forms the basis for the teaching of Pius XI and Pius XII, namely, that the inherent procreative design of the conjugal act must always be respected: hence, it is never licit to perform the act and try to frustrate that purpose or mutilate that design."[29] Furthermore, "the concept of the 'natural marriage act' as a criterion of sexual morality, so fundamental to Catholic theological thought, seems to make little if any impression on Protestants."[30]

Ford and Kelly brought a more scholarly approach to moral theology, but they still accepted the basic approach of the manuals, defended the Catholic natural law approach and the teachings based on it, and maintained that theologians cannot disagree with a papal teaching on a moral issue.

Also beginning in 1940, Francis J. Connell, a Redemptorist priest, advanced the academic aspect of moral theology, especially through his work at CUA, which was the one place in this country that offered doctoral degrees in theology, but it had fallen on hard times in the 1930s. Connell came to CUA in 1940 after having written a doctoral dissertation in Rome in 1923 with the noted neoscholastic Father Garrigou-Lagrange, OP, and having taught dogmatic theology for more than twenty years at the Redemptorist theologate. Connell had regularly written articles on current theology for the *American Ecclesiastical Review* and was hired to teach dogmatic theology at CUA. Because of a vacancy, he shifted to moral theology.[31] During World War II, dioceses and religious orders could not send priests to Rome or elsewhere in Europe to earn doctoral degrees. CUA was now the only place available to train future seminary professors. From 1941 to 1950 Connell directed about twenty doctoral theses in moral theology. These dissertations often dealt with casuist issues (e.g., organ transplantation, lying, boxing), but all of them were published and thereby added to the scholarly character of moral theology in general and to the academic reputation of CUA. Connell made CUA a center for the study of moral theology. After the war doctoral students continued to come to work with him.[32] When Connell retired in 1958, John Ford came to CUA to take his place.

Connell was a casuist who applied the principles of moral theology to contemporary issues in his answers to moral cases in the *American Ecclesiastical Review* from 1944 to 1957, in the *Catholic Nurse* from 1953 to 1967, and in the *Liguorian* from 1954 to 1967.[33] He condemned the dropping of the atomic bomb on Hiroshima and maintained that "the destruction or maiming of hundreds of thousands of innocent persons has inflicted a permanent blot of shame on the United States."[34] He also condemned the immorality of professional prize fighting in the United States.[35]

Francis Connell was a manualist, as illustrated in a book based on lectures to laity that was really a popularization of the existing manuals. For example, he follows the traditional importance of the role of law. The eternal law is the plan of God for the world. The natural law is the participation of the eternal law in the rational creature. The proximate norm of human morality is human nature considered in its totality.[36] In keeping with the manualist approach, Connell accepts three sources or factors for determining the morality of human acts: the object, the end, and the circumstances.[37] He recognizes, however, some of the problems contemporary revisionist moral theologians have raised in their unwillingness to identify the human moral object with the physical structure or aspect of the act. Connell insists that the moral object of the act has to include the first moral circumstance; for example, the moral object is murder and not killing. He applies such an approach to lying but not to any of the sexual issues that later became controversial.[38] Thus Connell staunchly defended the existing Catholic sexual teaching.

Connell's tenure at Catholic University coincided with the papacy of Pius XII, which, according to a contemporary admirer of Connell, produced "an unprecedented and intensive series of allocutions, exhortations, and messages whose scope is genuinely vast and, at times, quite detailed." Connell sometimes concluded a discussion simply by citing the authoritative teaching of Pius XII. For Connell, the authoritative magisterium of the pope determines the intellectual assent of the Catholic faithful.[39]

Connell was a convinced neoscholastic, a casuist, a theological conservative, a defender of the manuals, and a strong advocate of the central role of papal teaching in moral theology. But he was also a scholar who in his work with doctoral students provided a more academic environment for Catholic moral theology.

SEXUALITY

The manuals of moral theology generally presented the same basic approach to all issues, including sexuality. Sexual teaching was based on natural law. The eternal law is the plan or ordering of God for the world, and the natural law is the participation of the eternal law in the rational creature. Human reason reflecting on human nature (which God has made) can determine how God wants human beings to act.

In keeping with their practical purposes, the manuals propose the reasoning behind the teaching on sexuality succinctly but without great elaboration. In the words of the manual of Jerome Noldin—used by more than half of the diocesan seminaries in the United States in the middle of the twentieth century—sins of impurity (*luxuria*) involve the abuse of the generative faculty against the order established by God. Sexual pleasure, which is acceptable only within marriage and according to the laws of marriage, induces one to act against this order. The malice of impurity consists in abusing the generative faculty against its God-given purpose. The intrinsic purpose of the generative faculty and the proper ordering of sexual acts call for the sexual act to be done by two people joined in a permanent commitment of marriage to secure the procreation and education of offspring, and with the act done in such a way that procreation can occur.[40]

The manuals then discuss three different types of sins of impurity: externally consummated sins of impurity, external acts that do not involve full sexual actuation, and internal acts. The external consummated sins fall into the two categories: sins according to nature, in which the act can lead to procreation, and sins against nature, in which the act does not lead to procreation. Sins according to nature include fornication, adultery, incest, sacrilege, and rape. Sins against nature include masturbation, sodomy (including homosexuality), bestiality, and birth control.[41]

Nonconsummated external sins of sexuality involve direct sexual arousal without total consummation. Acts such as looks, touches, embraces, kisses, and reading, which are not in themselves sinful, are grave sins of impurity if they are calculated to arouse sexual pleasure. The manuals all develop an elaborate casuistry to discuss these various acts in light of the danger of causing sexual arousal. Of interest is the fact that such a casuistry replaces prudential judgments with specific descriptions applicable in all circumstances. To look at the private parts of a person of the opposite sex is gravely sinful unless unexpectedly, briefly, or at a distance. Such an observation, by its very nature, excites corruptible nature. To look at the semiprivate, or less arousing, parts of a person of the opposite sex is not, per se, a mortal sin because such looks do not notably arouse the observer. However, to continue looking for a long time is a mortal sin. It is venially sinful to look at the nude body and private parts of another person of the same sex because ordinarily this does not involve sexual arousal, but looking intentionally and for a long time becomes seriously sinful, especially if there is affection for the other person. By their very nature, such looks involve the approximate danger of sexual arousal. To look at one's own nude body and its private parts is no sin if it is done for reasons of necessity, utility, and without any bad intention. To look at one's self out of curiosity or with no reason does not exceed a venial sin because such looks do not cause sexual arousal. But even here such looks could involve mortal sin if they are done in a morose way in order to bring about sexual arousal.[42] Internal sins of impurity include impure thoughts, morose delectation, and impure desires that are purposely considered in order to bring about sexual arousal or involve a free consent to sexual arousal.[43]

The manualist treatment of sexuality thus illustrates the natural law and ca- suistic approach characteristic of this genre. But one aspect of the approach to sexuality is unique. In sins against sexuality there is no parvity of matter.[44] What does this mean? According to the manuals, a sin is mortal if three conditions are met: grave matter, advertence of the intellect, and consent of the will. No parvity of matter means that the matter of sins of impurity, even internal sins, is always grave. The sixth commandment is the only commandment that does not involve parvity of matter. Stealing a small amount of money, for example, is a light matter and only a venial sin. Because the manuals deal with the matter itself, they tend to assume the advertence of the intellect and the consent of the will and sometimes explicitly say that sins of impurity are always grave or mortal sins. In everyday Catholic parlance, all sins of impurity, even internal sins of consenting to slight sexual arousal, are always mortal sins. Gerald Kelly, in his very popular college textbook, *Modern Youth and Chastity* (1941), spells out the external and internal actions that involve mortal sins.[45] Such an approach gives great importance to sexuality and exaggerates its role and importance in the Christian life.

Why is there no parvity of matter in sexuality and why are all sins of impurity, even internal sins, always mortal? According to Noldin, the sin is always grave because it goes against a most significant ordering established by God, the author of nature. Even brief, direct sexual pleasure is a mortal sin because it goes against this ordering of God about the purpose of human sexuality.[46] Callan and McHugh explain that even brief, directly willed sexual arousal is gravely wrong because it can easily lead to full sexual arousal. "A small spark of fire is not trivial in the vi- cinity of a powder magazine, a minute flaw in a machine is not unimportant if it may bring on disaster, a first step is not safe if it is made on a slippery downward declivity."[47]

ARTIFICIAL CONTRACEPTION

The Catholic position on the immorality of artificial contraception for spouses was the most significant moral issue discussed by Catholics in the twentieth cen- tury. In practice, birth control touched on the lives of all married Catholics. Its theoretical considerations involved especially natural law and the authoritative teaching of the Church. During the twentieth century practically all non-Catholic churches changed their teaching on birth control, but official hierarchical teaching did not change. Various historical, cultural, and social circumstances affected the debate about birth control in the twentieth century. Urban life raised the question of birth control more acutely than did rural life. After 1929 the Depression affected the size of families. After World War II larger families were more acceptable, but this trend did not last. Demographics began to reveal the dangers of overpopulation in many parts of the world after 1950. These social, cultural, and economic factors affected families on a broad scale. But there were also social, economic, and medical factors that affected individual families. The Catholic teaching on artificial contraception for spouses unfolded in this context.[48]

Catholic teaching had consistently condemned "onanism" (the older and often used European term for what Americans call artificial contraception or birth control), but the question became much more pressing in the twentieth century. According to John T. Noonan, the first full discussion of birth control or family limitation in the United States came from the pen of John A. Ryan, of CUA, in the 1916 issue of the *American Ecclesiastical Review,* the pastoral review for priests then published at CUA.[49] Ryan, who is best known for his many contributions to social ethics, believed that many Catholic spouses were practicing artificial contraception in this country and did not think it was a mortal sin. Such couples, Ryan felt, should not be left in good faith. With proper instruction, married Catholics in America would desist from what they were doing. His article condemned artificial contraception as the "immoral perversion of a faculty." To exercise a faculty in such a way as to prevent it from attaining its natural end is contrary to nature. The end of the generative faculty is procreation, and artificial contraception goes against the God-given purpose and finality of the sexual act. But in addition to this argument Ryan also developed an argument against contraception based on consequences, recognizing the need to bring in long-term consequences.[50]

But such an approach was neither his first published word on this subject nor his last. In a 1906 article Ryan had argued against those who employed a teleology of the ultimate end as the basis for all moral activity. He claimed that, on the basis of consequences alone, one could not prove the Catholic teaching that all acts of impurity (alluding also to birth control) were always wrong. One had to consider rational human nature in order to show that impure actions are always wrong.[51]

In 1928 and 1929 in the *American Ecclesiastical Review,* however, Ryan pointed out the weakness of the perverted faculty argument against birth control.[52] Many Catholic theologians today reject the perverted faculty argument in the case of lying. Arguments against contraception based on the misuse of the faculty, a perversion of function, a frustration of the sexual act, and a defeat of its primary end are not convincing. Ryan accepts that artificial contraception is opposed to the good of rational nature, but he proposes an argument based on both direct and indirect consequences, rather than the perverted faculty argument, to prove the point. In fact, he claims that the consequentialist approach is the best argument for defending all Catholic sexual teaching. His argument, based on consequences rather than the nature of the faculty or the act, goes against the generally accepted notion of contraception as intrinsically evil. (A following section on social justice will consider in greater depth Ryan's understanding of the role of consequences.)

In his 1930 encyclical *Casti connubii*, Pope Pius XI strongly condemned artificial contraception as going against the nature and purpose of the sexual faculty and its act. "Since, therefore, the conjugal act is destined primarily by nature for the begetting of children, those who in exercising it deliberately frustrate its natural power and purpose sin against nature and commit a deed which is shameful and intrinsically vicious. . . . Our mouth proclaims anew: any use whatsoever of matrimony exercised in such a way that the act is deliberately frustrated in its natural power to generate life is an offense against the law of God and of nature, and those who indulge in such are branded with the guilt of a grave sin."[53] The strong and authoritative condemnation of artificial contraception and the reasons for it as found in this encyclical thus became the official teaching of the hierarchical Church that was accepted by all theologians until the 1960s.

Even before *Casti connubii* in 1930, many Catholic theologians had accepted the fact that a married couple could use the infertile period in the woman's cycle to avoid conception. The use of the infertile period does not involve the invasion and infringement of the physical integrity of the marital act. Before the work of Knaus and Ogino in 1929 and 1930, however, many scientists were not certain when the infertile time occurred in the woman's cycle; some even suggested midway between her periods.[54] In keeping with the growing role of papal teaching authority, discussions of rhythm after 1930 took the form of commentaries and interpretations of papal teaching. *Casti connubii* acknowledged that married couples who perform the marital act in the proper natural way, even though timing or natural defects prohibit procreation from occurring, do nothing wrong.[55] Subsequent debates ensued about the dangers involved in the use of the rhythm method and what constitutes a legitimate or serious reason for practicing it.[56] Orville Griese, for example, in a doctoral dissertation directed by Francis Connell, held the conservative position that the use of the rhythm method was, per se, illicit but under some circumstances might be justified.[57]

In his 1951 address to midwives, Pius XII dealt in some depth with the use of the rhythm method or the infertile period. The pope insisted that married couples have a duty to procreate, but serious reasons or indications of a medical, eugenic, economic, or social nature can excuse them from the positive obligation to procreate for a long time and even for the entire duration of the marriage.[58] Theologians continued to develop casuistry to discuss the reasons justifying the use of the rhythm method and whether or not the positive obligation to procreate is a grave obligation that involves mortal sin. Theologians such as Lawrence Riley and John A. Goodwine, writing in 1957, insisted that, in theory, procreation is a grave obligation binding under pain of mortal sin, but because of ongoing theological debate and no clear teaching of the magisterium, they would not insist on this strict understanding in their role as confessors.[59]

In the late 1950s the new anovulant pills raised a number of significant moral issues. Once again the theological discussion centered on an address of Pope Pius XII, who in 1958 applied the principle that direct sterilization is always wrong but that indirect sterilization can be permitted for a proportionate reason. The anovulant pill, which was just coming into use, prevents ovulation and is customarily used with the intention to prevent conception, but it can also be used for other purposes. Contraception interferes with the sexual act; sterilization interferes with the sexual faculty. Direct sterilization is an act that by the nature of the act or the intention of the agent aims at sterilization as a means or as an end. To take the pill to prevent conception is a direct and temporary sterilization. But there can be other reasons for preventing ovulation, since the sexual faculty has both a generative aspect and also an aspect related to the well-being and health of the individual person. The pope mentioned that it is acceptable to take the pill to remedy a malady of the uterus or of the sexual organism even though the indirect effect of sterilization occurs.[60]

All Catholic theologians at that time agreed with the pope that direct sterilization or using the pill to prevent procreation is morally wrong but that therapeutic use of the pill to overcome a problem or malady of the generative faculties can be acceptable even if sterilization is an indirect effect. Many theologians claimed that a woman has a right to a regular cycle and that an irregular cycle is a malady or pathology. One could then use the pill to regulate the menstrual cycle, even though it also indirectly brought about sterilization. Some moral theologians also justified using the pill as "rebound therapy" to help infertile women become fertile by preventing ovulation for a period after which, evidence had shown, they were better able to procreate. According to some experts, breastfeeding prevents ovulation and is nature's way of spacing children. On this basis, some theologians maintained that ovulation during breastfeeding is an anomaly or "pathological condition" and that one can use the pill to prevent it.[61]

Ford and Kelly, in their book on marriage written early in the 1960s, before the Second Vatican Council, present their understanding of the Catholic teaching on birth control. Their analysis gives primacy to the teaching of the papal magisterium, especially Popes Pius XI and Pius XII. Following their usual approach, they discuss what other theologians have said about the authority and the status of the Catholic condemnation of artificial contraception by the hierarchical magisterium. Four distinguished theologians claim that the teaching found in *Casti connubii* is an *ex cathedra* infallible teaching of the pope. A few others claim that the teaching is infallible by reason of the teaching of the ordinary and universal magisterium of the Church—that is, all the bishops together with the pope always and everywhere have condemned artificial contraception as something to be definitively held by all the faithful. Other theologians do not go so far as to claim infallibility for the teaching. Ford and Kelly conclude that the condemnation of birth control is irrevocable and can safely be said to be at least definable and is very likely already taught infallibly. For this reason, there can be no change in this teaching.[62]

Why is artificial contraception wrong? Again, the Jesuit theologians begin with the reasoning proposed in papal documents. They basically accept the perverted faculty argument. God has written a certain, definite plan into the nature of the generative and sexual powers, and human beings are not free to interfere with or change that plan. Artificial contraception goes against the God-intended purpose that the sexual faculty exists for the purpose of procreation, and human beings cannot interfere with that divine plan. But Ford and Kelly go on to develop another aspect of the perverted faculty argument that was not found explicitly in papal documents but had recently been proposed by other theologians. The marital act is also a personal act of love. Contraception is wrong because it violates the marriage act as procreative, but it also violates the marriage act as an act of loving, total self-giving of a couple to each other.[63]

Why do most Protestants not accept the Catholic approach? The two Jesuit moral theologians propose three reasons for the Protestant failure to consistently condemn artificial contraception.[64] First, Protestants have developed a new understanding of sexuality that is deprived of all reference to procreation. The sexual act is seen only in terms of the loving relationship of the couple. Second, Protestants have lately accepted situation ethics, which denies absolutely binding moral norms and places the ultimate moral decision solely in the conscience of the individual reacting to the situation. Ford and Kelly discuss situation ethics in two chapters in their first volume.[65] The description given here, however, tends to be a caricature of what some of the situationists had been saying.

The third and "even more important and fundamental reason" for the Protestant position in accepting birth control comes from their rejection of a religious teaching authority.[66] Ford and Kelly point out the need for a religious authority for an adequate knowledge of the natural law. Within five years of the publication of Ford and Kelly's 1963 book, Catholic moral theologians themselves would raise serious objections to the understanding of natural law and of the papal magisterium proposed by Ford and Kelly. In the early 1960s, however, their work was very much in the mainstream of Catholic theological self-understanding in the United States.

MEDICAL ETHICS

By the 1950s medical ethics was a thriving branch of Catholic moral theology in the United States. In fact, more work was done in medical ethics in the United States than in any other country. Once again institutional factors helped to explain the emphasis on medical ethics in this country. Catholic nursing schools and medical schools had courses in medical ethics for their students, and professors published textbooks for these students. The Catholic Hospital Association came into existence in 1915 because of the large number of Catholic hospitals that continued to grow, and the association published a brief code of ethics in 1921 that dealt primarily with questions of pregnancy and reproduction. A more comprehensive "Ethical and Religious Directives for Catholic Hospitals" was published in 1949 and modified in later editions. The Catholic Hospital Association (now called the Catholic Health Association) began publishing *Hospital Progress* (now called *Health Progress*) in 1920. The National Federation of Catholic Physicians' Guild and its journal the *Linacre Quarterly* began in 1932.[67] These institutional aspects of Catholicism in the United States strongly supported the discipline of Catholic medical ethics.

Catholic moral theology has always been concerned about the obligations of the various professions. St. Antoninus of Florence (d. 1459), in the third tome of his four-volume *Summa,* discussed the duties and obligations of physicians.[68] The nineteenth century saw the publication of books often with the title *Pastoral Medicine.* The German physician Carl Capellmann, in his *Medicina Pastoralis* (Pastoral Medicine), provided the knowledge of medicine that the priest needed to carry on his ministry and the knowledge of moral principles that the physician needed to carry out the moral obligations of the profession.

In the United States in the twentieth century, books in medical ethics evolved from this earlier literature to meet the needs of Catholic colleges and hospitals. In 1897 Charles Coppens, a Jesuit priest teaching at the Creighton Medical School in Omaha, published the first—and very well-received—book about what would later be called medical ethics: *Moral Principles and Medical Practice: The Basis of Medical Jurisprudence.* In 1922 Patrick Finney, a Vincentian priest, published his *Moral Problems in Hospital Practice: A Practical Handbook,* primarily for nuns in charge of Catholic hospitals but secondarily for nurses, physicians, and seminarians. This book dealt almost exclusively with reproductive issues. A second edition was published in 1956. Other books were published in this general area before 1940, but they were not as significant as those of Coppens and Finney. In the 1940s the term "medical ethics" came to be commonly used to describe the systematic study of the moral issues connected with medical care. But in the nineteenth century and early twentieth, "medical ethics" referred to a field of discussion among physicians themselves dealing primarily with matters of etiquette. Therefore Catholic writers in the early twentieth century did not use the term "medical ethics."[69]

In the 1940s and 1950s the most popular textbook in medical ethics was written by Charles J. McFadden, an Augustinian priest and professor of philosophy at Villanova University, whose *Medical Ethics for Nurses* was first published in 1946. The book went through numerous printings and six editions, the last one in 1967. It first served as a textbook for the author's classes to nurses at Villanova University, but from the second edition on, the author cast the book also for medical students and doctors.[70] John P. Kenny, a Dominican priest and professor, in 1952 published *Principles of Medical Ethics* based on his lectures to nursing and premed students. Kenny revised his text in 1962. Two other significant textbooks for doctors and students in Catholic medical schools, but also addressing the needs of non-Catholic doctors to understand what is required in Catholic hospitals, were written by Edwin Healy, a Jesuit priest who taught at the Gregorian University in Rome from 1952 to 1957, and Thomas J. O'Donnell, a Jesuit priest teaching at Georgetown University Medical School.[71]

Gerald Kelly, SJ, was the most influential Catholic medical ethicist in the United States in the 1950s. Kelly had published articles on medical ethics in *Theological Studies* and other journals in addition to his "Notes on Moral Theology" in that journal. He had been involved with the 1949 "Ethical and Religious Directives for Catholic Hospitals" and in 1958 published *Medico-Moral Problems* as an extended commentary on these directives.

Characteristics of Medical Ethics

Catholic medical ethics in the 1950s followed the general approach of the manuals of moral theology, with their emphasis on a legal model. Three important characteristics of Catholic medical ethics in the 1950s were the natural law method, a greater reliance on papal teaching, and a casuistic approach that applied principles of medical ethics to problematic cases and issues.

In light of all that is now known about Catholic moral theology in general, one would expect Catholic medical ethics to rely on natural law. According to

McFadden in his first chapter, "Practically all of the moral conclusions in this work, save those that are expressly related to the sacraments, are simply expressions of Natural Law."[72] Natural law is "the participation in the eternal law (Divine Wisdom guiding all creatures to their proper ends) by a rational creature inclining the rational creature toward the end and actions proper to its nature." The natural law is universal, immutable, and absolute.[73]

All the medical ethics books in the 1950s recognized the importance and even primary place of the teaching of the hierarchical magisterium, especially that of the recent popes. Jesus Christ has given to the Church a teaching authority extending to the whole of revelation, including the natural moral law. In interpreting natural law, the Church explains the demands of human nature itself, and therefore these demands are true and binding on all people, not just Catholics.[74]

The late 1940s and 1950s saw a tremendous growth in the moral teachings issued by Pope Pius XII. Kelly admits that official Church declarations on medical issues were comparatively infrequent before Pius XII, who responded to many requests from medical societies to address different medical issues.[75] In the preface to his revised edition, John P. Kenny points out that Pius XII delivered seventy-five allocutions on medical issues, touching practically every conceivable topic. This second edition "contains numerous quotations from the allocutions of Pius XII who will go down in history as the 'Pope of Medical Ethics.'"[76] Thus, by the end of the 1950s, the primary source for Catholic medical ethics was the teaching of the papal magisterium.

Magisterial papal teaching was accepted by all Catholics as the final word. Gerald Kelly, in articles published in 1939 and 1947, accepted as truly probable the artificial insemination of the wife with the husband's semen, provided the semen was not obtained by actuation of the sexual faculty (e.g., masturbation) but by extracting semen directly from the epididymis or massaging the seminal vesicles.[77] But after papal allocutions in September 1949 and October 1951, this position, according to Kelly, was no longer acceptable.[78]

What is the relationship between the natural law based on human reason as applied to all human beings and the teaching authority of the Church? As a philosopher, McFadden stresses above all the rational aspect of his approach. In his first chapter he insists that ethics is a branch of philosophy, a science that discerns its truth from the accurate use of unaided human reason and is based on neither the revealed word of God nor the traditional teaching of Christ's infallible Church. However, "the infallible teaching of Christ's Church is of indirect value to the study of Ethics. Such teachings serve as an excellent guide and constant 'checkup' on the accuracy of our reasoning processes."[79] Here McFadden wrongly refers to the Church teaching on ethical matters as infallible, whereas all theologians, even at that time, agreed that at the very minimum most of the Church's teaching on ethical matters was not infallible.

Kelly proposes the same basic approach in his book on medical ethics that he and Ford later developed in their book on marriage. In fact, Kelly explains in detail the relationship between human reason and the authority of Church teaching in his discussion of contraception. Ford and Kelly honestly recognized the problem that McFadden never faced. If natural law is based on human reason and knowable by all, why do most Protestants and practically all philosophers and ordinary non-Catholic people disagree with Catholic teaching on contraception? Kelly begins his answer by appealing to Pope Pius XII's 1950 encyclical *Humani generis* to explain the ability of human beings to know the natural law. To apply human truths about God and the relationship between God and human beings requires some self-surrender and self-abnegation. Here the human intellect is hampered by impulses of the senses and by evil passions stemming from original sin. For this reason divine revelation is morally necessary for human beings in their present condition to know with ease, with certitude, and without any admixture of error those religious and moral truths that are not beyond the reach of their natural reason.[80] But nowhere does Kelly explain how precisely the papal magisterium learns and knows these moral truths that belong to the natural law. After Vatican II, many Catholic theologians would no longer accept the understandings of natural law, papal teaching authority, and the relation between them as proposed by Kelly.

A third characteristic of Catholic medical ethics in the late 1950s was its casuistic nature. The casuistry consisted in applying the principles derived from natural law to the practical cases and issues that arose in medical and nursing practice. A good pedagogue, McFadden ends each chapter with a section of problems for discussion, and most focus on casuistry.[81] Healy explicitly deals with 171 cases, which he lists directly after his table of contents.[82] Kelly's book consists of commentaries on the "Ethical and Religious Directives," which themselves often employed casuistry. He discusses the ethical directives dealing with specific procedures; each group of directives is divided into "Principles" and "Particular Applications."[83]

Principles and their application constitute the primary approach found in Catholic medical ethics. These principles are derived from natural law and share the natural law characteristics of universality, unchangeableness, and absoluteness. According to Kelly, there can be no substantial change in the principles of medical ethics. This is also true of some of the practical applications, such as direct abortion, direct attack on fetal life, euthanasia, contraceptive sterilization, immoral sterility tests, and so forth. In these issues, the application of the general principle is so immediate and logical that a change in the particular teaching is inconceivable. There can be changes in those particular applications that involve a question of sufficient reason, such as the justification of lobotomy to treat serious mental illness and intractable pain.[84] But in Catholic medical ethics at the end of the 1960s, the basic principles and most of their applications were certain and unchangeable.

Principles

The textbooks of medical ethics followed the casuist approach of moving from principles to their application to particular questions. The most significant principles proposed by all Catholic medical ethicists include the right to life, the stewardship humans have over their bodies and persons, the principle of totality, the purpose and ends of the sexual organs, the principle of double effect, and principles of cooperation and scandal.[85]

The most fundamental principle and the foundational principle is the right to life. However, these textbooks do not emphasize the right to life as much as later twentieth-century Catholic theological approaches do in light of their opposition to the newly proposed justifications for abortion and euthanasia. Human beings are made by God, the author of all life, and life is a natural right that belongs to all human beings. The right is irrevocable and is violated by acts such as murder. The right to life in a positive fashion empowers the person to achieve the end of protecting, promoting, and preserving human life, but death reminds us that humans do not have full control over their lives. The right to life is not absolute, as exemplified in the acceptance of some forms of killing, for example, in the case of unjust aggression and just war. The state and political authorities must respect the right to life, which is a God-given and natural right and does not come from secular or political authority.[86]

The human being has stewardship, or the right of use with regard to life and body, but not full dominion. God is the author of life and has full dominion over life; the human creature is a steward or administrator who must care for life in light of what God has intended. God's intentions are found in the human nature that God has given us in creation. The principle of stewardship serves as a basis for the care one should exercise over one's life and body.[87]

The principle of totality, formulated first by Pope Pius XII but with a long history in Catholic tradition, maintains that a part may be sacrificed for the good of the whole. This principle serves as the justification for surgeries or amputations of the body for the good of the whole. The purpose of a part of the human body (e.g., an arm, a leg) is to serve the entire body, and thus the part can be sacrificed for the good of the whole. Catholic moralists were quick to point out that the principle of totality cannot be used to justify totalitarian states' sacrificing the individual for the good of the state precisely because the individual has a proper finality of one's own and is not totally subordinated to the state. Catholic medical ethics at this time followed Pius XII's 1958 teaching that the particular organ is subordinated to the good of the bodily organism, but the bodily organism is subordinated to the good of the spiritual finality of the person. On a somewhat mundane level, this understanding justifies some cosmetic surgery.[88]

The finality and purpose of sexual organs exist not only for the good of the individual but also for the good of the species. With regard to marriage and sexuality, the Church teaches that the primary purpose of marriage and of the sexual organs is the procreation (and education) of offspring. Consequently, the sexual organs are not totally subordinated to the good of the individual bodily organism or the person and cannot be sacrificed for the good of the body or the person. The principle of totality cannot apply to the sexual organs in their species or procreational aspect. Thus one cannot sterilize a person in order to prevent procreation, no matter how much good might ensue for the individual person. Such direct sterilizations are always wrong. But the sexual organs have a twofold aspect: the species or procreational aspect and the individual aspect. Thus one could remove a cancerous testicle or uterus that is a threat to the good of the bodily organism. The threat comes not from the species aspect of the sexual organ but from its individual aspect. The sterilization in this case is indirect. However, the species finality of the sexual organs means that the principle of totality cannot be used to sacrifice the species aspect of the sexual organs for the good of the person.[89]

The principle of double effect deals with conflict situations in which an act has two or more effects, one or more of which is good and one or more of which is bad. All authors agree on four conditions to justify an act under the principle of double effect, although all do not follow the same order in proposing the four conditions. The conditions that justify an act with a possible evil effect are

(1) The act itself must be good or at least indifferent.
(2) The individual must intend the good effect and not the evil effect.
(3) The good effect must follow equally immediately as the bad effect. The good effect cannot be produced by means of the evil effect.
   A good end cannot justify an evil means.
(4) There must be a proportionate reason for doing the act that has a bad effect.

If these four conditions are fulfilled, the evil is produced indirectly and can be justified by the proportionate reason required in the fourth condition. If any of the first three conditions are not met, the evil is done directly and is morally wrong. To do evil directly is morally wrong; thus direct killing, direct abortion, direct sterilization, and direct cooperation are always wrong.

The most significant condition is the third—the good effect must follow equally immediately as the bad effect and cannot be caused by means of the bad effect. This condition refers to the physical causality of the act itself. To intend directly or to do evil directly either as an end or as a means is always wrong. If the good effect would occur, even if the bad effect does not occur, the good effect is not achieved by means of the bad effect.[90] This principle will be explained in greater detail in its application to abortion.

The books of medical ethics also discuss the principles of cooperation and the understanding of scandal regarding the work of doctors and nurses. Cooperation is participation in the wrong or sinful act of another. Formal cooperation, which intends the evil act, is always wrong. Immediate material cooperation, sometimes called "formal cooperation," is defined as actual participation in the performance of the wrong act itself and is likewise always wrong. Mediate material cooperation, which presupposes that there is no intention to do evil and involves doing an act which is good or indifferent, may be permitted if sufficient reason exists. A doctor, for example, can never do an immoral operation since this involves at least immediate material cooperation. A nurse's cooperation in such an operation usually involves only mediate material cooperation and might be justified, especially if it is not proximate cooperation by a number of different reasons, including the good such a person can do in the hospital in which one is employed.

Scandal is a sinful or seemingly sinful word, action, or omission that tends to incite or tempt another to sin. Direct scandal, in which the sin of the other is intended, is always wrong. Indirect scandal, in which the sin of the other is not intended but only permitted, may be allowed under two conditions: if the act giving scandal itself is not morally wrong and if sufficient reason exists for doing such an act.[91]

Application of Principles

The principle of totality, in light of the principle of stewardship, justifies surgery or procedures affecting parts of the body (except for the sexual organs) when this is done for the good of the whole body.[92]

The principles of stewardship and the double effect govern issues involving life and death. The direct killing of an innocent person is always wrong. Catholic medical ethics condemns suicide and euthanasia. The good end of alleviating suffering does not justify the bad means of directly killing the person.[93]

What is the obligation to conserve one's own life? Here Catholic ethics in the 1950s appealed to the important distinction between positive and negative natural law commands. One can never go against a negative command of the natural law such as the direct killing of the innocent or lying. But positive commands of natural law are not always so obliging because the good required by positive natural law can be in conflict with some other goods. For example, one can never tell a lie, but one does not always have to tell the truth. In certain cases, an individual has no right to the truth. Similarly, one can never directly take one's own life, but one does not have to do everything possible to prolong human life.[94] Centuries before the emergence of Catholic medical ethics in the United States, the Catholic tradition recognized that one had to use ordinary means to preserve life, but there was no obligation to use extraordinary means.[95] Gerald Kelly proposed an understanding of the difference between ordinary and extraordinary means that found general acceptance among Catholic medical ethicists. Ordinary means are all medicines, treatments, and operations that offer reasonable hope of benefit and that can be obtained and used without excessive expense, pain, or inconvenience. A classic case based on earlier writings maintained that a person with a serious lung problem did not have to leave family and home and move to a better climate in order to live somewhat longer. Even in the 1950s, the Catholic approach strongly challenged the predominant medical practice that required the doctor to do everything possible to preserve life.[96]

Catholic medical ethicists in the 1950s applied the same principle against direct killing to the question of abortion. Direct abortion is always wrong; indirect abortion can be permitted for a proportionate reason. The abortion issue involves two basic questions: When does truly individual human life or the human person begin to exist, and how do you solve conflict situations? At this time, most other religions and the general public condemned abortion but recognized some justification for what were called "therapeutic abortions."

In keeping with the rather practical approach, some of these books simply presuppose that the fetus is a human person from the moment of conception and do not develop arguments for this position.[97] However, Kelly and Healy recognize the older common opinion, including that of Thomas Aquinas, that the soul is not immediately infused at the moment of conception. Even in the 1950s a substantial number of Catholic moral theologians still held this speculative position. Speculatively, this question is still open for Catholics, but in practice one must follow the safer course of action. If a hunter is not sure whether the object he sees is a deer or a human being, he must follow the safer course and not shoot. In a similar manner, the speculative doubt about when ensoulment takes place concedes in practice to the need to follow the safer course that ensoulment takes place at conception. Here again the teaching of Pius XII provides the certain answer for Catholics.[98]

The major debate in the broader society at that time was the distinction between criminal abortions and therapeutic abortions that might be necessary to save the life and health of the mother. Catholic ethics also recognized the existence of conflict situations and solved them by using the principle of double effect, which condemned the direct killing of the fetus in order to save the life of the mother.

The "Ethical and Religious Directives for Catholic Hospitals" in the 1950s (n. 15) states that "direct abortion is never permitted, even when the ultimate purpose is to save the life of the mother. . . . Every procedure whose sole immediate effect is the termination of pregnancy before viability is a direct abortion."[99] In light of the principle of double effect, partially incorporated in this directive, direct abortion is understood as an act that either by the intention of the agent or by the nature of the act aims at abortion either as a means or as an end. Such an understanding of forbidden, direct abortion came about as a result of decisions by the Holy Office in the late nineteenth century. Some respected Catholic theologians held that the fetus threatening the life of the mother could be aborted as a materially unjust aggressor. The second argument proposed by some Catholic ethicists for aborting the fetus maintained that craniotomy in this case was not a direct and forbidden killing. A third argument justifying abortion in case of a threat to the mother's life was based on a conflict of rights in which the right of the mother was judged more important. But the Holy Office at the end of the nineteenth century condemned all these positions. Later, the Holy Office also condemned the position of August Lehmkuhl, who admitted that craniotomy to save the mother's life was wrong but that simply removing the fetus from the womb was not a direct abortion and could be done to save the life of the mother even if the fetus were then to die indirectly. T. Lincoln Bouscaren, in his 1928 dissertation at the Gregorian University and in the subsequent book based on it, maintained that as a result of the decisions of the Holy Office, positions allowing the killing of the fetus to save the life of the mother were forever closed to Catholics.[100]

The two primary examples of an acceptable, indirect abortion are the removal of a pregnant cancerous uterus and a diseased fallopian tube containing an ectopic pregnancy. If the pregnant uterus is cancerous, the abortion is indirect because the act does not directly target and kill the fetus but directly targets the cancerous uterus. Here the physical causality of the act is the determining factor.[101] Bouscaren, in his study of ectopic pregnancies, recognized that Catholics cannot directly target the ectopic pregnancy and remove it from the fallopian tube because that would be a forbidden, direct abortion. But the fetus infects the tube, which ultimately will rupture. The already infected but still intact tube is pathological and can be removed even though it contains a fetus. The action is indirect because it does not directly target or touch the fetus but directly targets and touches the pathological tube. Thus, in the Catholic understanding, licit, indirect abortions were few, and one could never justify the abortion of the fetus in order to save the mother's life.[102]

The purpose and finality of the sexual faculty governs the eleven directives of the Catholic hospital code dealing with procedures involving reproductive organs and functions. The unnatural use of the sex faculty (e.g., masturbation) is never permitted, not even for a laudable purpose such as providing sperm for sterility testing. Artificial contraception is always morally wrong. Based on the personal nature of the marital act, artificial insemination, even with the husband's sperm, is wrong because it is not in accord with the divine plan for human procreation. The sexual organs have a species finality, but they also have a finality for the good of the individual person. The species finality, however, cannot be subordinated to the good of the individual. In light of these twofold finalities, direct sterilization, as an act that by the intention of the agent or the nature of the act aims at preventing conception, is morally wrong. Indirect sterilization, however, such as removing a cancerous uterus, is permitted.[103]

In the 1950s other religions, philosophers, and the general public were not terribly interested in medical ethics. There were no controversies in this area because good medicine and good morality accepted the same criterion—the welfare of the patient. Catholics called this the "principle of totality." Most non-Catholics disagreed with the Catholic approach to the reproductive organs because Catholics claimed that the principle of totality did not apply: Finality for the good of the species cannot be subordinated to the good of the individual. A large portion of Catholic medical ethics dealt with the reproductive organs.

In Europe, as the twentieth century progressed, some Catholic moral theologians called for newer approaches to moral theology, but, as this chapter has shown, Catholic moral theology in the United States continued to use the manuals as the textbook for the discipline and followed existing approaches in sexual and medical ethics. As a result, theologians in this country were not prepared for the new perspectives ushered in by the Second Vatican Council (1962–65).

NOTES

1. For the classical study of Americanism, see McAvoy, *Americanist Heresy in Roman Catholicism;* see also Reher, "Pope Leo XIII and Americanism"; and *U.S. Catholic Historian* 11 (summer 1993), entire issue.

2. Leo XIII, *Longinqua oceani*, 363–70.

3. For modernism and its effects on U.S. Catholicism, see Appleby, *Church and Age Unite.* For a summary and evaluation of the many papers on modernism given at the American Academy of Religion, see McKeown, "After the Fall." The issue of *U.S. Catholic Historian* 20 (summer 2002) is devoted to modernism.

4. Appleby, *Church and Age Unite,* 230.

5. White, "Theological Studies."

6. Catholic University of America, School of Religious Studies, *Century of Religious Studies,* 23–25.

7. Carey, "Introduction."

8. White, "Theological Studies," 464.

9. Boere, "Survey of the Content," 73. See also White, *Diocesan Seminary,* 380–81.

10. McHugh and Callan, *Moral Theology* (1929). Edward P. Farrell later revised and enlarged these two volumes; the last edition appeared in 1960. For two vernacular manuals written by English Jesuits that were never officially used as textbooks in American seminaries, see Slater, *Manual of Moral Theology,* and Davis, *Moral and Pastoral Theology.*

11. Fogarty, *American Catholic Biblical Scholarship,* 191–221. For biographical information, see Coffey, "Callan, Charles Jerome"; Coffey, "McHugh, John Ambrose"; Langlois, "Callan, Charles Jerome"; Langlois, "McHugh, John Ambrose."

12. McHugh and Callan, *Moral Theology,* 2: iv–v.

13. Wister, "Theology in America," 1382.

14. Ford and Kelly, *Questions in Fundamental Moral Theology,* v.

15. Ibid.

16. Ibid., 42–103.

17. Ibid., 42–103, 141–73.

18. Kelly, *Good Confessor,* 18.

19. Ford and Kelly, *Questions in Fundamental Moral Theology,* 104–40.

20. Ibid., 147–276.

21. Ford, *Man Takes a Drink.*

22. Ford and Kelly, *Questions in Fundamental Moral Theology,* 277–312.

23. Pius XI, *Casti connubii,* 391–414; Pius XI, *Quadragesimo anno,* 415–43.

24. Kelly, *Medico-Moral Problems,* 363.

25. Kenny, *Principles of Medical Ethics,* 272.

26. Ford and Kelly, *Questions in Fundamental Moral Theology,* 1.

27. Pius XII, *Humani generis,* 178n20. In church documents, n. refers to the paragraph number.

28. Ford and Kelly, *Questions in Fundamental Moral Theology,* 19–41.

29. Ford and Kelly, *Marriage Questions,* 277.

30. Ibid., 14.

31. Moran, "Connell, Francis (1888–1967)."

32. Catholic University of America, School of Religious Studies, *Century of Religious Studies,* 36–33.

33. Smith, "Selected Methodological Questions," 32–54.

34. Connell, *Morals in Politics,* 47–48.

35. Connell, "Prizefighting and Boxing."

36. Connell, *Outlines of Moral Theology,* 28–31.

37. Ibid., 20–22.

38. Smith, "Selected Methodological Questions," 249–56.

39. Ibid., 76–78.

40. Noldin, *Summa theologiae moralis,* 15–17.

41. Ibid., 21–43.

42. Ibid., 43–55.

43. Ibid., 55–58.

44. Ibid., 16–20.

45. Kelly, *Modern Youth and Chastity,* 82–84.

46. Noldin, *Summa theologiae moralis,* 16–18.

47. McHugh and Callan, *Moral Theology* (1960), 521.

48. For an excellent historical study, see Tentler, *Catholics and Contraception.*

49. Noonan, *Contraception,* 422.

50. Ryan, "Family Limitation."

51. Ryan, "Method of Teleology in Ethics."

52. Ryan, "Immorality of Contraception," and "Comment by Dr. Ryan."

53. Pius XI, *Casti connubii,* 399–400nn54–56.

54. Tentler, *Catholics and Contraception,* 104–6.

55. Pius XI, *Casti connubii,* 400n58.

56. Tentler, *Catholics and Contraception,* 106–83.

57. Griese, *Morality of Periodic Continence,* 18.

58. Pius XII, "Italian Catholic Union," 12–15nn29–37.

59. Riley, "Moral Aspects"; Goodwine, "Problem of Periodic Continence."

60. Pius XII, "Morality and Eugenics."

61. For a full discussion of these issues, see Ford and Kelly, *Marriage Questions,* 38–77.

62. Ibid., 256–78.

63. Ibid., 279–90.

64. Ibid., 305–14.

65. Ford and Kelly, *Questions in Fundamental Moral Theology,* 104–40.

66. Ford and Kelly, *Marriage Questions,* 312.

67. Kelly, *The Emergence of Roman Catholic Medical Ethics,* 140–42. Kelly's book is the best available history of Catholic medical ethics in North America, and I have followed him in my short discussion of nineteenth- and early twentieth-century Catholic medical ethics in the United States. For my perspective on the history, development, and current state of Catholic medical ethics and bioethics, see Curran, "Roman Catholicism," 2321–31.

68. St. Antoninus, *Summa theologica, pars tertia,* Titulus VII, col. 277–92.

69. Kelly, *Roman Catholic Medical Ethics,* 81–94.

70. Subsequent references to McFadden's *Medical Ethics* are to the fourth edition (1956). After Vatican II, McFadden published a volume for the general reader, *The Dignity of Life,* that maintained the basic positions developed in his earlier text.

71. Healy, *Medical Ethics;* O'Donnell, *Morals in Medicine.* After Vatican II, O'Donnell published a revision of this text under the title *Medicine and Christian Morality.*

72. McFadden, *Medical Ethics,* 6.

73. Ibid., 18.

74. Kelly, *Medico-Moral Problems,* 31.

75. Ibid., 33.

76. Kenny, *Principles of Medical Ethics,* 2d ed., vii–viii.

77. Kelly, "Morality of Artificial Insemination" and "Current Theology."

78. Kelly, *Medico-Moral Problems,* 243.

79. McFadden, *Medical Ethics,* 2.

80. Kelly, *Medico-Moral Problems,* 152.

81. E.g., McFadden, *Medical Ethics,* 73–74, 102–4.

82. Healy, *Medical Ethics,* xvii–xxii.

83. Kelly, *Medico-Moral Problems,* 19.

84. Ibid., 20.

85. Given that all Catholic ethicists discussed these principles in basically the same way, subsequent references cite single authors as illustrative of the common approach.

86. Healy, *Medical Ethics,* 10.

87. McFadden, *Medical Ethics,* 265–329.

88. Kenny, *Principles of Medical Ethics,* 2d ed., 151–58.

89. McFadden, *Medical Ethics,* 330–72.

90. Kelly, *Medico-Moral Problems,* 12–16.

91. Kenny, *Principles of Medical Ethics,* 2d ed., 24–28.

92. Kelly, *Medico-Moral Problems,* 246.

93. Healy, *Medical Ethics,* 11, 266–71.

94. McFadden, *Medical Ethics,* 265–66.

95. Cronin, *Moral Law in Regard,* 47–87.

96. Kelly, *Medico-Moral Problems,* 128–41.

97. E.g., McFadden, *Medical Ethics,* 140–41; Kenny, *Principles of Medical Ethics,* 2d ed., 197–201.

98. Kelly, *Medico-Moral Problems,* 66–67; Healy, *Medical Ethics,* 192–94.

99. Kelly, *Medico-Moral Problems,* 69.

100. Bouscaren, *Ethics of Ectopic Operations,* 3–16.

101. McFadden, *Medical Ethics,* 193–94.

102. Bouscaren, *Ethics of Ectopic Operations,* 147–71.

103. Healy, "Ethical and Religious Directives," 397–98nn29–39.

TWENTIETH-CENTURY SOCIAL
ETHICS BEFORE VATICAN II

The manuals of moral theology, Catholic sexual ethics, and medical ethics all follow the same basic approach. The manualists themselves discussed sexuality under the sixth commandment, or the virtue of chastity. Separate textbooks existed in medical ethics but the manuals themselves treated issues of medical ethics briefly, most often in their discussion of the fifth commandment. The orientation to the sacrament of penance, with its emphasis on what was sinful, characterized these approaches. The primary concern involved what actions are wrong or sinful in light of Catholic teaching. All three approaches (the manuals, sexual ethics, and medical ethics) followed the legal model, with law being the objective norm of morality. All three used the casuistic approach, moving from principles to the discussion of particular cases. All three approaches strongly defended the existence of absolute norms that are always and everywhere obliging. As a result, they accentuated the characteristics of natural law as being universal, absolute, and unchangeable.

Catholic social ethics takes a different approach. The primary orientation of Catholic social ethics is not the confessional. Social ethics, by definition, deals with what is good for society, not what is good or bad for the individual. The manuals did not generally consider what is good for society. In the context of the seventh commandment, or the virtue of justice, the manuals pointed out individual acts that were wrong, but they did not develop what was good for society. The different orientation of social ethics gives it a unique methodological approach.

Social ethics does not primarily use a casuistic approach. The primary concern is to develop what is a good and just society. In keeping with the understanding of the period, Catholic social ethics based itself on the neoscholastic understanding of natural law, but it employed natural law in ways different from the approach of the manuals. Social ethics generally understood natural law as a teleological approach that was more in keeping with the original purpose of Thomas Aquinas than the legal model used in the manuals. Likewise, social ethics did not stress the characteristics of natural law as absolute and unchangeable as much as the manuals did because it was more conscious of the changes that had occurred in society over time. The secondary or tertiary principles of natural law are not as certain and absolute as the primary principles. Thus significant methodological differences exist between Catholic personal ethics and Catholic social ethics. In addressing Catholic social ethics before Vatican II, this chapter identifies and develops these differences.

JOHN A. RYAN

The dominant figure in Catholic social ethics in the first half of the twentieth century was John A. Ryan (1869–1945). Institutional connections gave him considerable exposure and influence. Ryan, a priest of the archdiocese of St. Paul, Minnesota, received his doctorate at CUA. His dissertation on the living wage was published by a secular publisher in 1906.[1] He came back to CUA as a professor of moral theology in 1915 after having taught at the seminary in St. Paul. From 1920 to 1945 he served as director of the Social Action Department of the National Catholic Welfare Conference, the national organization of the U.S. bishops. Thus, he held the most prestigious theoretical and practical posts dealing with Catholic social ethics and practice.

Ryan was a pragmatic reformer with regard to U.S. economic and political life. In his quest for social justice he worked with many secular groups as well as with Catholic and other religious groups throughout his life. Ryan was popularly identified with the movement for progressive reform in the United States. In fact, Francis Broderick titled his biography of Ryan *The Right Reverend New Dealer*. In reality, Ryan did not influence Roosevelt that much and in fact often criticized Roosevelt for not going far enough with his social policies. For Ryan, there was no incompatibility whatsoever in being an orthodox Roman Catholic and a progressive social reformer. That is, he acknowledged no basic incompatibility between his Catholic understanding and the progressive American ethos.[2]

Ryan's Method

The natural law method supplied the ultimate basis for Ryan as both a Catholic theologian and a progressive social reformer.[3] Ryan accepted the neoscholastic distinction between the supernatural order and the natural order. The ultimate end of human life consists in eternal happiness with God, which is the supernatural order that comes about because of God's gift of grace to us. The ultimate or supernatural end can never be attained in this life and can never be attained without God's grace. But God, through the eternal and natural law, has appointed an end to the law of human nature. This natural and proximate end of human beings is the basis for judgments about what is good and bad for humans. The ultimate criterion for Ryan, the believer, is the eternal law or plan of God for the world, and the proximate criterion is the natural law as discovered by human reason as a consequence of reflection on human nature. Philosophers and some politicians and legislators might not acknowledge the eternal law, but they are rational people who could reflect on their own rational nature.[4]

Harlan Beckley, a Protestant ethicist from Washington and Lee University, astutely characterizes Ryan's approach to social reform as "an ethicist to politicians" with the strategy of achieving social justice through moral arguments for legislative action. Ryan sought to achieve social justice primarily through the rational action of the state. He did not place his hope for reform in powerful social movements such as labor, socialism, or even the Church.[5]

The manuals of moral theology, as we have seen, employed a legal model and saw natural law in light of such a model. Ryan was a student of Thomas Bouquillon at CUA and strongly defended the understanding of natural law as a teleological model or approach. Teleology comes from the Greek work *telos*, meaning "end" or "goal." Something is good if it moves toward the end and bad if it prevents one from arriving at the end. Most teleologists today are what I call "extrinsic teleologists" who determine morality by the consequences that follow an action. Aquinas and his followers in the United States, Bouquillon and Ryan, are what I call "intrinsic teleologists." Human beings have an intrinsic nature or principle of operation given by God, and they must act in accordance with the end and nature they have been given. Human happiness, or fulfillment, comes about through arriving at the end or goal of their nature.[6]

The true basis of ethical judgments is the end or norm of conduct. The fundamental ethical determinative can be understood as the end to which acts should be directed or the standard to which they should conform. An act that is directed to the proper end will necessarily agree with the norm.[7]

Ryan's anthropology or understanding of human beings also illustrates this teleological approach. The end to which the person tends is the development and perfection of her personality—the fulfillment of her rational nature. From his published doctoral dissertation through his last writings, Ryan insisted that this end, or obligation of self-perfection or development—which has its ultimate source in God and its proximate source in human nature—constitutes the true basis and justification for human rights. Natural rights constitute the moral means by which the human being is enabled to reach the obligatory end of self-development.[8] Ryan's social ethics is thus not based on a legal model but on an intrinsic teleology grounded in human nature.

But Ryan added something to and modified somewhat the understanding of natural law found in the generally accepted neoscholastic view of the time. Ryan was trained as an economist and frequently appealed to economics in his work on ethics. Ryan's ethics, in contrast to the manualist approach to natural law, placed more importance on experience, induction, and prudential aspects. In his consideration of land ownership at the beginning of *Distributive Justice,* he insists that "past experience is our chief means of determining whether an institution is likely to be socially beneficial, and therefore morally right, in the future."[9]

As both an economist and a Catholic ethicist, Ryan recognized the Catholic insistence on a harmony between good economics and good ethics that is characteristic of the Catholic emphasis on divine ordering in all aspects of human life. He defended the economic feasibility of his moral proposal for a living wage. The living wage would bring about an enormous improvement in individual and social conditions. The enlarged consuming capacity of workers would overcome the perpetual economic danger of overproduction.[10] He especially insisted on John A. Hobson's underconsumption theory during the Depression. If workers have a just and living wage, they will be able to increase consumption. Thus the possibility of a depression will be eliminated.[11]

During the Depression Ryan insisted that the fundamental task for activist Catholics was to bring about the identification of morality and expediency in our industrial world.[12] In his 1913 debate on socialism with Morris Hillquit, Ryan formulated the principle of expediency. "In the matter of social institutions, moral values and genuine expediency are in the long run identical."[13] Some significant qualifications should be noted here. He is speaking of "social institutions," "genuine expediency," and "in the long run." But still this is not the language one finds in neo-scholasticism.

How does this emphasis on feasibility, experience, and expediency fit into Ryan's natural law theory? Ryan was not primarily an ethicist interested in theory for its own sake. Near the end of his life, he published a small book called *The Norm of Morality,* but even here he does not explicitly develop his emphasis on expediency, feasibility, and experience. Ryan, the Catholic natural law thinker, is obviously not a consequentialist who makes consequences his only moral consideration.

Some indications in his various writings allow one to see how experience, expediency, and consequences fit into his natural law theory. In keeping with Thomas Aquinas himself, Ryan distinguishes the primary and secondary principles of natural law. The most fundamental of the primary principles is that good is to be done and evil is to be avoided. All human beings intuit this principle. From this most general principle other primary principles follow, such as: adore God, do not steal, do not murder, honor parents, protect health, do not commit adultery. In addition, there are secondary principles of the natural law that contribute to public and private moral good but are not absolutely necessary and depend on circumstances, conditions, and consequences.[14]

A good illustration of a secondary principle of the natural law is the right to land ownership, or private property. Natural rights are grounded in the dignity of the human being and supply the means necessary for the individual to achieve the end of self-perfection and development. There are three classes of natural rights. The first class has as its object what is intrinsically good—that is, good for its own sake as an end in itself, namely, the right to life itself. The second class of rights has as its object those things that are per se morally necessary for the individual person to achieve her end—such as the right to marry, to personal freedom, to own consumptive goods such as food and clothing. The third class of rights includes those realities that are means to human welfare but are not directly necessary for any individual person. Such realities are necessary as social institutions and thus are only indirectly necessary for the individual. The right to private property is a right of the third class.[15]

Ryan bases his defense of private property on empirical and consequentialist grounds and not on the intrinsic nature of the human person. If and when a better system is discovered, he argues, the state has a moral obligation to put it into practice.[16] I suggest that for Ryan the right to private property is thus a secondary principle of the natural law that is not as certain as the first principles, is only indirectly necessary for the individual person, and might even change in other contexts.[17] Thus Ryan's understanding of Thomistic natural law differs from the manualistic approach in using a teleological rather than a legal model and in recognizing that the secondary principles of natural law are not absolutely certain and can change.

Ryan's understanding of natural law influenced his approach to some questions in sexual ethics. He was a firm opponent of artificial contraception in the 1920s, but he rejected the argument that artificial contraception is intrinsically evil and instead proposed a consequentialist argument to condemn it. Earlier, and before any papal condemnation, Ryan had maintained that direct sterilization is not intrinsically evil, and he even justified compulsive legal sterilization in eugenic programs to achieve the end of protecting society.[18]

Ryan well illustrates the growing role of papal teaching in Catholic moral theology as the twentieth century progressed, but with a peculiar twist. Ryan had already shown an interest in economic issues as a student in the college seminary at St. Paul, but he only read Leo XIII's *Rerum novarum* in his junior year in college, in 1894, three years after the encyclical was issued.[19] His most systematic work, *Distributive Justice*, written in 1916, mentions Leo XIII's *Rerum novarum* only three times.[20] By the 1930s, however, papal encyclicals constituted the primary source for Ryan's ethical analysis of socioeconomic issues.[21] In the 1940s Ryan thought the best description of himself was neither liberal nor progressive but "papalist."[22]

What explains this later emphasis on papal teaching? Ryan's positions were progressive and liberal, and he often was challenged by conservatives within the Catholic Church. In the 1930s, in his attempt to overcome the problems of the Depression and his criticism of Roosevelt, Ryan wrapped himself in the papal mantle. His conservative Catholic opponents were not merely disagreeing with John Ryan; they were disagreeing with the pope.

Ryan's Positions

The cornerstone of Ryan's social ethics is the insistence on the rights of all human beings to a decent livelihood. All persons are of equal dignity and have an equal intrinsic importance. The goods of creation exist to serve the basic needs of all human beings. Consequently, every human being has a right to a minimally decent livelihood and human existence. This conviction serves as the basis for his arguments for a living wage for all workers and even a family living wage.[23] Ryan recognizes other canons of distribution in addition to needs: equality, efforts and sacrifices, productivity, and scarcity. In light of these other canons, an individual might receive a greater wage than a fellow worker, but all have a right to a minimally decent human existence.[24]

The Catholic University professor gave a very significant role to the state in economic reform and often was criticized by fellow Catholics for such a proposition.[25] He accepts the basic Catholic natural law position that human beings are social by nature and that the state is a natural society based on God's creation to provide for the common good and allow individuals thus to achieve their self-development, which could not occur if they remained isolated from each other. He rejects a totalitarian notion of the state, maintaining that the state must respect the rights of individuals, families, and voluntary associations, but he strongly opposes the individualistic theory of the state that was common in the United States at that time. The individualistic theory, based on an erroneous concept of the freedom of the individual, restricts government functions to a minimum because government involvement means interference in the freedom of the individual. The state plays the primary role of promoting human welfare or social justice, which includes the basic right of all to a decent livelihood.[26] Unlike almost all Catholics at the time, Ryan distinguished various levels of socialism, although he strongly opposed its approach to religion, philosophy, and morality.[27] In the 1930s he found only two objectionable planks in the mitigated approach of the U.S. Socialist Party, and even these, he believed, could be interpreted in accordance with Catholic teaching.[28]

His program for social reform, which can accurately be called "economic democracy," went through stages: reform by legislation; a new status for workers sharing in management, profits, and ownership; and the occupational group system proposed by Pope Pius XI. His interest in bringing about reform as quickly as possible fueled his insistence on legislation and the role of the state. From the beginning, he advocated a living wage and other benefits and protections for workers. He wanted legislation to overcome the abuses in land ownership, to control and break up monopolies, and to bring about progressive taxation.[29]

In the political order Ryan staunchly defended and supported democracy, especially civil rights and liberties. He was a member of the national committee of the American Civil Liberties Union and titled a chapter of his autobiography "In Defense of Civil Rights and Liberties."[30] Such freedom and rights were often supported by individualists who absolutized the freedom of individuals. Catholic thought in the nineteenth century, as illustrated by the teachings of Pope Leo XIII, condemned the modern liberties. Ryan defended the unrestricted freedom of expression; tolerating the evil involved in such freedom, he believed, avoided the greater evil of provoking continual strife by trying to contain the error.[31] American liberals were happy to have the strong support of this significant Catholic figure and in general did not worry about how he justified his conclusions.

Ryan's tolerant approach to religious freedom caused a political and public storm during the 1928 presidential election involving the Roman Catholic candidate, Alfred E. Smith. On this issue Ryan proposed the generally accepted Catholic approach that the ideal order calls for a union of church and state. However, this union applies only to a completely Catholic state, and probably not even Spain qualifies as such a state today. In a religiously pluralistic society such as ours, religious freedom can be tolerated as the lesser of two evils. Nonetheless, Ryan maintained that even in this country non-Catholic sects might decline to such a point that the union of church and state could become feasible and expedient.[32] Commentators pointed out, in the context of the 1928 election, that even John A. Ryan, the Catholic liberal, could not wholeheartedly support the separation of church and state and American freedoms.[33] Ironically, John A. Ryan—the progressive Catholic social reformer—is best known in American history for his inability to support fully the American understanding of freedom.

OTHER DEVELOPMENTS

Ryan was the most academic, the most published, and the best-known Catholic social ethicist in the first half of the twentieth century. There were other, less scholarly voices, some of which proposed approaches quite different from Ryan's. The *Central Blatt and Social Justice Review*, a publication for German-American Catholics, basically following the approach of the German Heinrich Pesch, SJ, feared that Ryan gave too great a role to the state and saw too great a harmony between Catholicism and the progressive American ethos. Writers in this journal had a romantic longing for the Middle Ages and a fear of liberalism, and used the natural law approach to justify a more corporative understanding of society based on the medieval guild system.[34]

Paul Hanly Furfey (1896–1992), a priest and sociologist at CUA in the 1930s, wrote popular works, most notably *Fire on the Earth*, which explained the social ethics of the Catholic Worker Movement founded by Dorothy Day. Furfey advocated a supernatural sociology (in opposition to a natural law approach), a literal and radical interpretation of the New Testament teachings, and strategies of separation, nonparticipation, and bearing witness in relation to the U.S. culture and ethos, emphasizing above all the issues of peace, poverty, and racial discrimination.[35] Virgil Michel (1890–1938) was a Benedictine monk of St. John's Abbey in Collegeville, Minnesota, with broad theological and philosophical interests. Michel wrote more popular books and articles that insisted on the need to bring together social change and reform with a change of heart and active participation in the liturgical movement.[36] Joseph Husslein (1873–1952), an associate editor of *America* magazine and the founder of the School of Social Service at St. Louis University, wrote many popular articles and books on social justice; throughout his thirty years of writing he illustrates the trajectory toward finding the primary source of Catholic social justice in papal teachings.[37]

Peace was a significant issue for Ryan, and he was interested in extending his social reform to the international scene. In 1927 he founded the Catholic Association for International Peace. This group worked for peace in the world but from a just war perspective, and in the late 1930s it strongly supported American involvement in World War II and opposed American neutrality and isolationism in the face of Nazi aggression. Furfey and especially the Catholic Worker Movement were stalwart pacifists even during World War II.[38] In 1944 John C. Ford wrote a very significant article in *Theological Studies* condemning the saturation bombing of German cities by the Allies. Such attacks violated the just war principle of discrimination by directly targeting and attacking innocent civilians.[39] Francis

Connell agreed with Ford and later also condemned the dropping of the atomic bomb on Hiroshima.[40]

The 1950s brought new faces and new issues to the fore in Catholic social ethics. John F. Cronin (1908–94), a Sulpician priest who taught in seminaries and served as the assistant director of the Social Action Department for the U.S. bishops from 1948 to 1967, continued the work of John A. Ryan in a more popular way. His *Social Principles and Economic Life* (1959), based on an earlier work and later revised to include the encyclicals of John XXIII, served as a textbook in many Catholic colleges and universities. In this book Cronin follows the natural law approach, adopts a reforming rather than a radical approach to the social order, and insists on institutional and structural change, while downplaying the need to change one's heart. Cronin begins each chapter with extended citations from appropriate papal (and occasionally episcopal) documents. Thus Catholic social ethics involves a commentary on and an application of papal documents. But in 1971, after Vatican II, Cronin wrote a fascinating article criticizing his own naïve hermeneutic of papal documents for failing to recognize their historical and cultural conditioning. He also pointed out the limited and fundamentalist ecclesiology that had influenced him.[41]

Cronin also touched on two other issues in the 1940s and 1950s—communism and racism—but not in a thorough or scholarly way. In 1945 he presented a long report on communism to the U.S. bishops. He also wrote two popular pamphlets published by the bishops and, anonymously, three widely distributed pamphlets for the U.S. Chamber of Commerce. He feared the infiltration of communism into American culture and political life and complained that many liberals failed to appreciate this danger. He worked closely with the FBI and with Richard Nixon, for whom he was a primary speechwriter in the 1950s. Cronin truly was a cold war warrior. The subject of U.S. Catholicism's relationship to communism abroad and in this country is complex, but moral theologians contributed practically nothing to the discussion.

In the late 1950s Cronin urged the U.S. bishops finally to write a pastoral letter on racism and proposed some drafts. Many were already criticizing the Catholic Church for not speaking out on this issue. Finally, in the fall of 1958, the bishops released their document.[42] Unfortunately, moral theologians seldom mentioned racial discrimination, let alone studied it deeply. To his great credit, Paul Hanly Furfey and the Catholic Worker radicals recognized and addressed the huge problem of racism in the United States.[43] John Ryan had urged Father Francis Gilligan to write his doctoral dissertation on race in the late 1920s and attempted unsuccessfully to get a commercial publisher to accept the book.[44] Ryan himself addressed racism in a 1943 lecture at Howard University in which he called for education, working together with people of goodwill to overcome the problem, and nonviolence and patience. But he never called for legislation and government intervention as he had in dealing with industrial and labor problems.[45] It is appropriate to mention here that Catholic moral theologians in the first half of the twentieth century merely accepted, without any great comment or study, the traditional role of women as mothers and homemakers with the primary duty of caring for the family.[46]

JOHN COURTNEY MURRAY

John Courtney Murray, SJ (1904–67), was the best-known and most academic Catholic social ethicist in the United States in the pre–Vatican II period and throughout the 1960s. Murray received his doctorate in Rome in the 1930s, taught at the Jesuit theologate at Woodstock, Maryland, primarily in the area of dogmatic or systematic theology, and was the editor of *Theological Studies* from 1941 until his death in 1967. But Murray is best known for his work in the area of social ethics.[47]

The Catholic-American relationship was problematic from the beginning of Catholicism in this country and became even more so with Catholic immigration and the growth of Catholicism in what had been a traditionally Protestant country. Anti-Catholicism took many different forms in the nineteenth and early twentieth centuries. Even John A. Ryan could not fully accept religious freedom. John Courtney Murray argued that one could be both Catholic and American, but his primary allegiance was obviously to Catholicism. Romans (the popes and the Vatican and the traditional Catholic position) were suspicious of American pluralism and freedom, feared that Catholics would become too Protestant in the United States, and insisted that the ideal order in America should be a union of church and state. Many Americans were suspicious of Catholics as not being able to accept fully the American political and cultural ethos. Murray proved to the Romans that religious liberty was completely in accord with Catholic tradition and theology. To other Americans he maintained that the U.S. Catholic could readily accept American democracy and freedom and that only natural law theory as maintained by Roman Catholics could give an adequate philosophical foundation to American political ethos and culture.[48]

Murray's writings on church and state in the 1950s brought him into conflict with the Vatican, and he was silenced by the Vatican through his Jesuit superiors in 1955. He did not write again on religious freedom until the Second Vatican

Council.[49] He was, in his own words, "disinvited" from the first session of the Second Vatican Council but came to the second session as the *peritus* (expert) of Cardinal Francis Spellman of New York and ultimately became the primary influence on the conciliar document on religious liberty, *Dignitatis humanae.*[50] In the 1950s, after his silencing, he primarily addressed issues of the Catholic relationship to American political ethos and culture.

Murray's Approach to Natural Law and Papal Teachings

Contemporary scholars point out significant development in Murray's methodology and approach over the years.[51] For our purposes, we are primarily interested in the period 1948–64, when Murray dealt extensively with the two sides of religious freedom and American political ethos and relied heavily on natural law. In an earlier period Murray had recognized the need for Christianity to permeate and transform society and thus appealed to many explicitly theological concerns. During and after Vatican II he again turned to what Leon Hooper has called a more theological approach. At the same time, under the influence of Bernard Lonergan, Murray accepted the need to move from a classicist approach to a historically conscious methodological approach.[52] The later changes in Murray are most significant for Catholic theologians today in their consideration of the way in which the Christian believer and the Church try to transform the world.

As mentioned earlier, natural law has a theological as well as a philosophical aspect. From a theological perspective that is based on creation, Catholic theology justifies human reason, reflecting on human reason as a source of moral wisdom and knowledge. Murray himself never dealt explicitly with this issue but obviously he agreed with it. In keeping with the neoscholastic concept of his time, Murray distinguished the natural order from the supernatural order, or grace—the temporal order from the spiritual. But he did not want a complete separation between the two orders. In the 1940s Murray made this distinction to justify the position that Catholics could and should cooperate with all others for the common good and social peace of human society. On the basis of natural law we can find agreement with those of other faiths and of no faith in working for the common good of the temporal order. This agreement does not involve us in an unacceptable cooperation on the level of the supernatural or of faith.[53] This basic distinction between the spiritual and the temporal, the supernatural and the natural, paved the way for Murray to recognize a rightful separation of church and state. At the same time, on the basis of this distinction, Murray showed how Catholics could, in the natural order, fully accept the American political ethos. The temporal order is governed by reason and natural law.

In *We Hold These Truths,* his book of essays published in 1960, Murray defends the philosophical aspect of natural law—the meaning of human nature and reason—as proposed by Thomism. Murray maintains in the penultimate chapter that for many people the doctrine of natural law is dead. But in the final chapter he maintains that the doctrine lives.[54] Natural law gives us not a blueprint for all of society but rather a skeletal law to which flesh and blood must be added by competent, rational, political activity. According to Murray, four premises of natural law are the elaboration by the reflective intelligence of a set of data that are ultimately empirical. First, natural law presupposes a realist epistemology that asserts the real to be the measure of knowledge and also maintains the possibility that intelligence can reach the real—the nature of things. Second, natural law implies a metaphysics of nature. Nature is a teleological concept, and the "form" of a thing is its final cause—the goal of its becoming. There is a natural inclination in human beings to achieve the fullness of one's own being. Third, natural law supposes a natural theology that acknowledges a God with eternal reason—the author of all nature—who wills that the order of nature be fulfilled in all its purposes. Fourth, natural law presupposes a morality that is based on the discovery through human reason of God's ordering and the human will that freely conforms to it.[55]

Murray develops in a somewhat analogous way the understanding of the different levels, or principles, of the natural law as proposed by Aquinas and later accepted by Ryan. First, intelligence grasps the ethical a priori, the first principle of moral consciousness, not by argument but merely by being conscious of itself. Good is to be done and evil is to be avoided. Second, after some basic experience of human existence, intelligence can grasp the meaning of good and evil in basic human relationships and situations. Third, as human experience unfolds, simple reason can arrive at the derivative natural law principles generally associated with the Ten Commandments. A fourth level, or achievement, which is beyond the capacity of most human beings, involves the requirements of rational human nature in complex human relationships and amid institutional developments in the progress of civilization. Here we deal with what were traditionally known as the more remote principles of natural law, which require the greatest knowledge, experience, reflection, and dispassion. These principles are not the province of all but rather of the wise. Murray willingly acknowledges that he is an elitist. On this fourth level, the role of the wise people and of the university comes into play to develop and promote a common consensus.[56]

Murray argues for the superiority of natural law over three other approaches found in American society. He disagrees with the law of nature proposed in the Enlightenment and by John Locke because of its rationalism, individualism, and nominalism. Without naming names, he then condemns two approaches found within Protestant Christianity in the United States. He condemns the Social Gospel school for a voluntarist approach that makes morality subjective and, again, is too individualistic and thus unable to deal with complex social problems. He also disagrees with Christian realism in the United States, which puts such stress on complexity and ambiguity, because of the presence of sin in the world, that making a right or wrong moral judgment is impossible.[57]

Murray also dealt, in a very creative way and differently from any of his contemporaries, with the role of papal teaching in Catholic moral theology. In light of the heavy emphasis on papal teaching at the time, Murray had to deal with the strong teaching of Pope Leo XIII in the nineteenth century that condemned religious liberty and the separation of church and state. As discussed below, Murray creatively used a historical hermeneutic to justify changing Leo XIII's nineteenth-century teaching in the changed conditions of the twentieth century.

Religious Liberty

Murray began studying the issue of religious liberty in the mid-1940s. Over the years he developed a position favoring religious liberty and was strongly opposed by three conservative American Catholic theologians: Joseph Clifford Fenton and Francis Connell of Catholic University, and George Shea of the seminary of the archdiocese of Newark. Thomas Love, a Protestant, has traced the historical development of Murray's thought over the years.[58] Our goal here will be to give a more synthetic understanding of the approach he finally developed.

Murray's definition of religious liberty involves a twofold immunity: no one can be forced to act against one's conscience in religious matters and no one can be coerced from acting in accord with conscience.[59] For Murray, religious liberty is not primarily a theological or ethical question but a juridical or constitutional concept that has foundations in theology, ethics, political philosophy, and jurisprudence.[60] Murray's understanding of religious liberty depends on the role and function of the limited constitutional state.

Four principles or distinctions help to ground his understanding of limited constitutional government. First, the distinction between the sacred and the secular orders of human life recognizes that every person has a transcendental and supernatural end that is beyond the power and competency of the state. The state deals with the temporal order of human existence. Second, the distinction between society and the state means that corporate and personal freedom exist in public, societal life, whereas the state has the limited role in society of using coercive power. The third distinction is between the common good—which involves all the goods of public life—and public order—which refers to the good that can and should be obtained by the coercive power of the state. Public order is thus much more limited than the common good, involving a threefold content of justice, public peace, and public morality. Public order serves as the criterion to justify coercive intervention by the state. The fourth principle is a substantively political truth and the primary rule of political procedure: the freedom of human beings is to be respected as much as possible and curtailed only when and insofar as necessary. In all of this, Murray sees great continuity between medieval constitutionalism and the present limited constitutional state.[61] The state thus has no competency in religious matters and must respect the religious freedom of its members.

How does and should the Church relate to such a state? Murray builds his understanding of the relationship between the Church and the constitutional state on the basis of the fourteenth-century Dominican John of Paris's understanding that the spiritual power is exclusively spiritual and has no direct power in temporal matters. In today's context, the Church comes into contact or relationship with the state only indirectly or mediately through the conscience of the person who is both a Christian and a citizen. The Christian believer freely accepts the magisterial authority of the Church and then freely participates in the institutions whereby the processes of temporal life are directed to their proper end.[62] In this way the Church carries out its mission to work for a better temporal society.

Murray, with his understanding of historicity, insists that there is no ideal church and state relationship but that there are transtemporal principles of Catholic understanding that need to be present in all situations—the freedom of the Church, the harmony between the Church and the state, with recognition of the primacy of the spiritual over the temporal, and an ordered cooperation between church and state. Murray sees these three transtemporal principles in limited constitutional government. The Church is free to exercise its own religious functions. The Church, through the consciences of its Christian people, who are also citizens, is able to work for the improvement of human society. Such an understanding recognizes the proper roles of church and state and avoids both the one-sided secularism that has no public role for the Church in society and the one-sided religion approach that gives the Church some direct power over the temporal realm.[63]

At the same time that Murray was developing his defense of religious liberty in the 1950s, he devoted six articles in *Theological Studies* to the authoritative teaching of Pope Leo XIII, who at the end of the nineteenth century strongly condemned religious freedom and upheld the union of church and state as the ideal. Murray applied his historical hermeneutic to Leo's official teaching and insisted on distinguishing the doctrinal, the historical, and the polemical aspects of Leo's position.[64]

Leo was primarily interested in the broader question of the role of faith and the spiritual in affecting the temporal order and society. His enemy was continental liberalism, or totalitarian democracy, which defended the absolute autonomy of individual human reason and conscience with no relationship whatsoever to God and God's law. In the political order, continental liberalism called for a thoroughgoing monism—one society, one law, one secular faith. The spiritual and the Church were reduced to the private realm and could have no role or influence on public society itself.[65] A second factor was the existence of the illiterate masses throughout the Catholic world, whose faith had to be protected.[66]

In this context Leo defended the confessional state with his theory of the ethical- or society-state, in which there is no distinction between society and the state. The total care of the common good was given to the princes who ruled and guided the illiterate masses. Only with a growing emphasis on personal responsibility and political awareness did the notion of a limited constitutional government arise, with a juridical understanding of the state as opposed to the ethical understanding of the state Leo proposed. In this context Leo had to accept the confessional state and the union of church and state as the ideal, although religious liberty could be tolerated to avoid a greater evil or to attain a greater good.[67]

The doctrinal aspect of Leo's teaching consisted of the transtemporal principles developed earlier. First, Leo insisted on the freedom of the Church (*libertas Ecclesiae*)—its freedom to pursue its own supernatural role but also to enter by proper spiritual action into the temporal sphere. Second, Leo worked out the harmony of church and state in light of his understanding of the person as a *res sacra in temporalibus*—a spiritual reality in the temporal sphere. Church and state meet in the conscience of the individual person who is both Christian and citizen. The Church enters and influences the temporal sphere through the conscience of the Christian citizen who tries to transform the temporal order in light of the grace and teaching coming from the Church. Third, this understanding also grounds the proper cooperation between church and state.[68] These transtemporal principles, in the context of a limited constitutional government with a juridical understanding of the state, now call for religious freedom.[69]

The Church and the American Political Consensus

Murray also proved to other Americans that Catholics wholeheartedly support the American political ethos; in fact, Catholics, thanks to the natural law, are the only ones today in the United States who can properly defend and explain the American consensus. The United States recognizes religious pluralism in the context of civic unity that rests on the public consensus of the truths laid out in the

Declaration of Independence. We hold these truths as self-evident that all are created equal and endowed by their Creator with certain inalienable rights. Among these are life, liberty, and the pursuit of happiness. American constitutionalism as found in this understanding is in continuity with medieval constitutionalism. These natural and inalienable rights are proximately grounded in human nature and ultimately have their source in God. The First Amendment, dealing with religious liberty, involves not articles of faith but articles of peace by which different types of believers and nonbelievers can live together in peace and harmony.[70]

The doctrine of natural law has no Catholic presuppositions about it, but, unfortunately, American universities and intellectuals no longer accept it. The principles of the American consensus belong to the remote principles of natural law, which is the task not of the people as a whole but of the wise. Murray maintained, somewhat audaciously, that not only can Catholics accept the American consensus but, on the basis of natural law, Catholics are the only ones with the ability to rebuild and to rearticulate the consensus.[71]

On a number of practical issues Murray believed that American policy was theoretically erroneous and practically harmful because it was not based on natural law. He strongly opposed Communist Russia but saw the problem not primarily in terms of military force but in terms of doctrine. Soviet theory dictates a policy of maximal security and minimal risk. Our policy, in return, should involve a minimum of security and a maximum of risk.[72] Murray insisted on the need for the natural law principles of just war, which avoid the sentimental pacifism of the Social Gospel and the cynical realism of the Niebuhrian school. Here Murray appeals to the conditions required to justify going to war—a just cause that, in accord with the teaching of Pius XII, is now limited to a defensive war, last resort, proportionality of good over evil, and hope of success. He also recalls the limits in the exercise of war called for by both proportionality and especially the principle of discrimination calling for noncombatant immunity. But he thought these principles could justify even some use of atomic weapons.[73] With regard to public aid to religious schools, the government should accept the principle of accommodation. Since schools fulfill the public service of education, they should receive some governmental financial support.[74]

Murray has been criticized, especially by contemporaries looking back at his work.[75] Like Ryan, Murray distinguishes and even separates too much the spiritual and the temporal, the supernatural and the natural. The theological realities of grace and sin also directly affect the world in which we live, but Murray paid little or no attention to them. The Christian role in the world should be seen as more intimately connected with theological realities as a constitutive dimension of the Gospel itself. He places too much emphasis on reason and harmony and fails to recognize adequately the roles of conflict, power, sin, and the need for individual change or conversion of heart. His understanding of history has also been challenged. Is American constitutionalism really in that much continuity with medieval constitutionalism? Would Leo XIII be willing to accept Murray's view of how historical conditioning limited his denial of religious freedom? Murray's concept of historical development in explaining official Church teaching on religious liberty fails to recognize that at times the official teaching was wrong. Is it true that natural law is the only way to defend and support the American consensus? Murray rightly recognizes the need for religious pluralism in the United States, but he seems to call all Americans to a metaphysical unity based on natural law theory.

In the last few years of his life Murray made two significant changes in his thought. Under the influence of Bernard Lonergan, he accepted historical consciousness, which in one sense built on his own earlier recognition of historicity. Historical consciousness recognizes that there is no truth out there but that truth is gained by historically conditioned individuals in and through a process of social interaction with others. Such an understanding would call for some change in his earlier approach to natural law. Murray also called for a more theological approach and a theological understanding of religious liberty not just as an immunity but also as an empowerment for religious people to participate in public society in light of their religious convictions.[76]

Catholic social ethics in the United States before Vatican II had much greater diversity than did other areas of moral theology. Catholic social ethicists took different positions in their dialogue with the political, cultural, and economic ethos in this country. John Courtney Murray was the most academic and creative figure in U.S. Catholic moral theology in the pre–Vatican II period, and his legacy is still being discussed today. Murray's thinking foreshadowed two significant developments in post–Vatican II moral theology: a historical, critical hermeneutic of papal teaching, and the revision of natural law in light of historical consciousness.

NOTES

1. Ryan, *Living Wage.*

2. For Ryan's autobiography, see Ryan, *Social Doctrine in Action.*

3. For a perceptive study of Ryan's social ethics in an ecumenical context, see Beckley, *Passion for Justice.* See also Kennedy et al., *Religion and Public Life.* For my analysis and criticism, see Curran, *American Catholic Social Ethics,* 26–91.

4. Ryan, *Norm of Morality,* 7–18.

5. Beckley, *Passion for Justice,* 181–86.

6. Ryan, "Method of Teleology."

7. Ryan and Boland, *Catholic Principles of Politics*, 7–11.

8. Ryan, *Living Wage*, 43–66. Substantially the same treatment is found in Ryan and Boland, *Catholic Principles of Politics*, 13–28.

9. Ryan, *Distributive Justice*, 7.

10. Ryan, *Living Wage*, 312–31.

11. Ryan, *Better Economic Order*, 1–30, and *Seven Troubled Years*, 38.

12. Ryan, *Seven Troubled Years*, 59.

13. Hillquit and Ryan, *Socialism*, 58.

14. Ryan and Boland, *Catholic Principles of Politics*, 4–5; Ryan, *Norm of Morality*, 25–26.

15. Ryan, *Distributive Justice*, 56–59, and *Norm of Morality*, 56–63.

16. Ryan, "Private Ownership and Socialism."

17. For a similar approach, see Beckley, "Theology and Prudence." Beckley sees economics as shaping the content of human rights in determining the best means to achieve human welfare.

18. Broderick, "Encyclicals and Social Action," 3. Broderick cites Ryan, *Moral Aspects of Sterilization.*

19. Broderick, *Right Reverend New Dealer*, 19.

20. Ryan, *Distributive Justice*, 64–66, 306–9, 377.

21. Ryan, *Seven Troubled Years.*

22. Broderick, "But Constitutions Can Be Changed."

23. Ryan, *Living Wage*, 43–122.

24. Ryan, *Distributive Justice*, 243–53.

25. Curran, *American Catholic Social Ethics*, 29–30.

26. Ryan and Boland, *Catholic Principles of Politics*, 108–39.

27. Hillquit and Ryan, *Socialism*, 103–22, 143–54.

28. Ryan, *Seven Troubled Years*, 87–91.

29. Curran, *American Catholic Social Ethics*, 51–60.

30. Ryan, *Social Doctrine in Action*, 159–76.

31. Ryan, *Declining Liberty*, 38–42.

32. Ryan and Millar, *State and Church*, 32–39. Ryan basically repeats the same position in Ryan and Boland, *Catholic Principles of Politics*, 313–21.

33. Broderick, *Right Reverend New Dealer*, 170–85.

34. For the definitive history of this movement, see Gleason, *Conservative Reformers*. For my analysis and criticism of this approach, see Curran, *American Catholic Social Ethics*, 92–129.

35. Furfey, *Fire on the Earth*. For an appreciative but critical contemporary analysis of Furfey, see McCarraher, "Church Irrelevant." For my evaluation, see Curran, *American Catholic Social Ethics*, 133–71.

36. Michel, *Christian Social Reconstruction* and *Social Question*. See also Himes, "Eucharist and Justice"; Franklin and Spaeth, *Virgil Michel.*

37. Husslein, *Christian Social Manifesto*. For different perspectives and evaluations of Husslein, see Werner, *Prophet of the Christian Social Manifesto*; McDonough, *Men Astutely Trained*, 50–64.

38. Whitmore, "Reception of Catholic Approaches to Peace and War," 496.

39. Ford, "Morality of Obliteration Bombing."

40. Connell, *Morals in Politics and Professions*, 47–48.

41. Cronin, "Forty Years Later."

42. Donovan, "Crusader in the Cold War," 117–46.

43. Furfey, *Fire on the Earth*, 12–13, 51–52, 84, 92, 111, 118; Furfey, *Respectable Murderers*, 29–49.

44. Broderick, *Right Reverend New Dealer*, 117, 262.

45. Ryan, "Place of the Negro in American Society."

46. E.g., Ryan, *Declining Liberty*, 101–14. For a critique of Ryan's positions, see Swidler, "Catholics and the E.R.A."

47. For the best available biography of Murray, see Pelotte, *John Courtney Murray*.

48. Curran, *American Catholic Social Ethics*, 175–78.

49. Pelotte, *John Courtney Murray*, 27–73.

50. For Murray's work on the Declaration on Religious Freedom at Vatican II, see Regan, *Conflict and Consensus*.

51. For a helpful overview of different contemporary understandings of development in Murray's approach and methodology, see Whitmore, "Growing End."

52. Hooper, "General Introduction," 27–39.

53. Murray, "Intercreedal Co-operation," 274; Murray, "Letter to the Editor."

54. Murray, *We Hold These Truths*, 275–336.

55. Ibid., 327–28.

56. Ibid., 109–23.

57. Ibid., 275–330. For a criticism of Murray's understanding of natural law as being intuitionist, see Porter, "In the Wake of a Doctrine."

58. Love, *John Courtney Murray*. See also Pelotte, *John Courtney Murray*, 3–73.

59. Murray, *Problem of Religious Freedom*, 25. This book was originally published in 1964 as *Woodstock Papers 7*.

60. Ibid., 20–22.

61. Ibid., 28–31.

62. Murray, "Contemporary Orientation."

63. Murray, "Problem of State Religion."

64. The first five articles published by John Courtney Murray in *Theological Studies* are "Church and Totalitarian Democracy"; "Leo XIII on Church and State"; "Leo XIII: Separation of Church and State"; "Leo XIII: Two Concepts of Government"; and "Leo XIII: Two Concepts of Government II." The sixth article, which existed in galley proofs but was not allowed to be published because of Vatican intervention, was titled "Leo XIII and Pius XII: Government and the Order of Religion." This article was subsequently published in Murray, *Religious Liberty*, 49–125.

65. Murray, "Church and Totalitarian Democracy," 525ff.

66. Murray, "Vers une intelligence," 127–28.

67. Murray, *Problem of Religious Freedom*, 53–58.

68. Murray, "Leo XIII: Separation of Church and State," 206–9.

69. Murray, "Vers une intelligence," 118.

70. Murray, *We Hold These Truths*, 27–43.

71. Ibid., 117–21, 275–336.

72. Ibid., 221–47.

73. Ibid., 249–73.

74. Murray, "Dr. Morrison and the First Amendment" and *We Hold These Truths*, 143–54.

75. For my evaluation of Murray, see Curran, *American Catholic Social Ethics*, 323–32.

76. Hooper, "Theological Sources of John Courtney Murray's Ethics," 118–25; Hollenbach, "Freedom and Truth," 144–48; Whitmore, "Growing End."

THE SETTING OF MORAL THEOLOGY
AFTER VATICAN II

Moral theology in the United States in the period before the 1960s was quite mono-lithic. The approach to moral theology in the manuals was based on natural law in both its theological and philosophical aspects. The seminary, as the primary place for moral theology, gave the discipline a pastoral orientation focused primarily on the sacrament of penance. Later in this period, thanks to the founding of scholarly societies and more scientific journals, this approach became more academic. The number of moral theologians was limited to priests who were professors, and the contributing and writing scholars in this field were few. Social ethicists John A. Ryan and John Courtney Murray contributed more creative approaches. The discussion of the first six decades of the twentieth century, therefore, concentrated on the comparatively few primary authors writing in the field of moral theology.

The post–Vatican II period brought startling changes. Moral theologians began to question both the theological and philosophical aspects of natural law. Catholic moral theology was no longer tied to one methodology. A pluralism of different methodological approaches now existed in this discipline. The number of moral theologians grew exponentially. The moral theologians in the first six decades of the century were only of the clergy, but now the clergy forms a small minority of those in the United States who are engaged in the discipline of moral theology. The discipline itself has become much more academic and complex than it was earlier. In the late 1970s it became evident that no one person could ever again deal with all aspects of moral theology. As a result, no one person—or even two or three persons—could dominate the discipline. To explain in general the dramatic changes that occurred in moral theology in the United States after 1960, this chapter considers the three publics that influenced moral theology: the Church, the academy, and the broader society.

THE CHURCH

The three most significant aspects of the Church affecting moral theology were the Vatican Council II, Pope Paul VI's encyclical *Humanae vitae,* and the long papacy of Pope John Paul II (1979–2005).

Vatican II

Vatican II had an enormous impact on Catholic life and theology in general and on moral theology in particular. The two-pronged principle of renewal at Vatican II was *ressourcement* and *aggiornamento. Ressourcement* called for a return to the sources of scripture and tradition; *aggiornamento* called for the Church to bring itself up to date and to engage in dialogue with the modern world. In the nineteenth century the imposition of Thomism and neo-scholasticism came about precisely to prevent any dialogue with modern thought. After Vatican II the differences between the approaches of *ressourcement* and *aggiornamento* became apparent. The *ressourcement* school in general feared many post–Vatican II developments in the Catholic Church, whereas the *aggiornamento* school generally maintained that the spirit of Vatican II called for further reform and change in Catholic life and theology. But at Vatican II the two approaches and their adherents strongly disagreed with the existing neo-scholasticism.[1] After Vatican II new approaches in all areas of Catholic theology, including moral theology, came to the fore. Pope John Paul II recognized that the Church does not canonize one particular philosophy in preference to others.[2] This pluralism of approaches contrasts strongly with the monolithic approach of the manuals that prevailed in the first six decades of the twentieth century.

Vatican II also enlarged the scope of moral theology. Yes, seminarians still needed preparation for their work as confessors in the sacrament of penance, but Vatican II, in the fifth chapter of the Constitution on the Church, insisted on the call of all Christians to holiness.[3] Moral theology thus should deal with the call to perfection and all the dispositions and attitudes that accompany that call. The discipline of moral theology could no longer insist only on the lower level of the Christian moral life, which dealt with sin and the different degrees of sin.

In general, Vatican II called for a more theological approach to moral theology. Vatican II's Decree on Priestly Formation maintained that all theological disciplines should be renewed by livelier contact with the mystery of Christ and the history of salvation. Moral theology in particular should be more thoroughly nourished by scriptural teaching; it should express the nobility of the Christian vocation of the faithful to bring forth fruit in charity for the life of the world.[4]

Gaudium et spes, the Pastoral Constitution on the Church in the Modern World, lamented the split between faith and daily life and believed that it deserved to be counted among the more serious errors of our age.[5] In its first part, the Pastoral Constitution considers the human person, human community, and human action. In all these areas it mentions not only the role of creation but also the reality of sin and the redeeming role of Jesus Christ. Life in this world is not merely the sphere of natural law, but the whole of Christian faith affects what occurs in our daily life and actions.[6]

Unfortunately, the documents of Vatican II also missed an opportunity to stress the theological aspects of moral theology. The Constitution on the Liturgy reminds seminary professors: "Moreover, other professors, while striving to expound the mystery of Christ and the history of salvation from the angle proper to each of their own subjects, must nevertheless do so in a way which will clearly bring out the connection between their subjects and the liturgy, as also the unity which underlies all priestly training. This consideration is especially important for professors of dogmatic, spiritual, and pastoral theology and Holy Scripture."[7] The document, unfortunately, does not explicitly recognize the connection between liturgy and moral theology, even though the document on the training of priests said that all theology, including moral theology, should be renewed in light of contact with the mystery of Christ and the history of salvation.

In its Decree on Ecumenism Vatican II called for all theology, including moral theology, to be ecumenical. Catholics share with other Christians an appreciation of the dignity of human beings, the pursuit of peace, the application of Gospel principles to social life, the need to relieve the afflictions of our times—illiteracy, poverty, homelessness, and the unequal distribution of wealth. All human beings are called to cooperate in working for a more just world; those who believe in God have a stronger summons than others, but the strongest demands are placed on Christians, for they have been sealed with the name of Christ.[8] In the realm of action in this world, all Christians should work together. On the more theoretical level, the document calls for ecumenical dialogue. Professors should present theology from an ecumenical point of view.[9] Thus Vatican II called for significant changes in moral theology.

HUMANAE VITAE

Pope Paul VI's encyclical *Humanae vitae,* written in 1968, reaffirmed the teaching of the hierarchical magisterium that condemned artificial contraception for spouses. In light of changes at Vatican II, many Catholic theologians had argued for a change in the teaching on artificial contraception. Pope John XXIII had established a small commission to study the question, and Pope Paul VI enlarged the commission. Unfortunately, in light of the commission's study, Pope Paul VI maintained that Vatican II should not discuss this issue. In April 1967 reports were leaked to the press showing that the vast majority of commission members were in favor of changing the teaching.[10] It is not surprising that the condemnation of artificial contraception in *Humanae vitae* met with much opposition even within the Church. The day after the encyclical was released, Charles E. Curran acted as the spokesperson for eighty-seven theologians (the number ultimately swelled to more than six hundred) who signed a statement affirming that in theory and practice one could be a loyal Catholic and still disagree with the teaching of the encyclical condemning artificial contraception.[11] Pope Paul VI himself referred to the "lively debate" set off by the encyclical.[12] Andrew M. Greeley maintained that the encyclical influenced the large number of Catholics who dropped out of the Catholic Church in the United States in the decade 1963–1973.[13]

The teaching of Pope Paul VI in *Humanae vitae* is founded on natural law. The teaching authority of the Church is competent to interpret even the natural moral law.[14] The natural law basis is "the inseparable connection, willed by God and unable to be broken by man on his own initiative, between the two meanings of the conjugal act: the unitive meaning and the procreative meaning" (n. 12). As a result, "every action which, either in anticipation of the conjugal act or in its accomplishment, or in the development of the natural consequences, proposes whether as an end or as a means, to render procreation impossible" is morally wrong (n. 14). But the encyclical makes clear that the primary reason for the papal ban on artificial contraception is the authoritative teaching of the Church. The pope states that the conclusions of the commission could not be definitive or dispense him from his own examination. The proposals justifying artificial contraception "departed from the moral teaching on marriage proposed with constant firmness by the teaching authority of the Church" (n. 6). *Humanae vitae* thus made the understanding of natural law and the role of the teaching authority of the Church in moral matters most significant and important issues for Catholic moral theology.

Pope John Paul II

John Paul II was bishop of Rome for more than twenty-six years (1978–2005) and had a profound influence on the Church in all areas, including moral theology. As the authoritative hierarchical teacher in the Church, he wrote fourteen encyclical letters and issued many other authoritative statements.[15] Before becoming pope, Karol Wojtyla had been trained in and taught ethics. Two of his encyclicals—*Veritatis splendor* (1993) and *Evangelium vitae* (1995)—deal with moral theology. *Veritatis splendor* develops in depth the foundational issues of moral theology in light of the crisis of truth that exists not only in the world but also in the Church. Truth is the ultimate foundation for moral living and moral theology. In this letter the pope condemns many of the developments in the so-called revisionist Catholic moral theology that disagree with older Catholic positions. *Evangelium vitae* contrasts the culture of life and the culture of death in our contemporary world and strongly defends the condemnation of contraception but especially of direct abortion and euthanasia. It also argues against capital punishment.

John Paul II's three social encyclicals deal with different topics. *Laborem exercens* (1981) commemorates the ninetieth anniversary of Pope Leo XIII's first social encyclical, *Rerum novarum*, and elaborates his theological understanding of the meaning of human work, with special emphasis on the person who does the work. *Sollicitudo rei socialis* (1987) explains the authentic meaning of human development, deploring the economic underdevelopment in the third and fourth worlds as well as the economic superdevelopment in the industrial world. The two blocks of East and West contribute to the problems of the developing world. *Centesimus annus* (1991) elaborates the social teaching of the Church in light of Leo XIII's original encyclical on workers and especially in light of the collapse of communism in Eastern Europe in 1999.

In his many travels throughout the world, John Paul II strongly advocated the need for democratic governments and pointed out the plight of the poor, calling on Christians and others to make a preferential option for the poor. John Paul II spoke out against many of the wars and the violence that occurred including the two U.S. wars against Iraq. He often opposed war and violence so deeply that he had to profess publicly that he was not a pacifist. He still followed the just war principles and criteria, but he interpreted them stringently. War, at best, can stop or prevent an evil, but it can never bring about true peace.[16]

In *Veritatis splendor* John Paul II strongly supports the accepted Catholic understanding of natural law, with its defense of intrinsically evil actions and negative absolute norms. The supreme rule of life is the divine law itself, the eternal, objective, and universal law by which God, in his wisdom and love, directs and governs the world. The participation of the eternal law in the rational creature is called "natural law." Seen in this light, there can be conflict neither between law and human freedom nor between nature and freedom. John Paul II strongly upholds the immutability of natural law, objective norms of morality, and perennial, structural elements of human nature. The truths of natural law remain valid in their substance despite all historical change and growth.[17]

John Paul II, in his own understanding of ethics before he became pope, proposed a personalistic approach, which also comes through in his papal teachings.[18] In his discussion of work he recognizes the objective aspect of labor—that which is done—but maintains that the primary aspect of labor is the subjective aspect— the person who does the work. Such a personalism thus grounds the priority of labor over capital and supplies the basis for the rights of workers.[19] John Paul II's personalism, unlike that proposed by some Catholic theologians, does not call for change in any existing Catholic moral teachings based on natural law. John Paul II explicitly sees his developing personalistic reasons against artificial contraception as trying "to elaborate more completely the biblical and personalistic aspects of the doctrine contained in *Humanae vitae.*"[20] The language of the human body should express the total reciprocal self-giving of husband and wife to each other in the marital act. Contraception, however, involves a contradictory language of spouses not giving themselves totally and reciprocally to one another.[21]

John Paul II later described his very first encyclical, *Redemptor hominis,* as addressing the subject of "the truth about man."[22] The Church continues in time and space the mission of Jesus the Redeemer, by fully revealing the meaning of, and teaching the truth about, the human being. "By Christ's institution the Church is its [truth's] guardian and teacher, having been endowed with a unique assistance of the Holy Spirit in order to guard and teach it [truth] in its most exact integrity."[23] "The Church in her life and teaching is thus revealed as 'the pillar and bulwark of truth' (Tim 3:15), including the truth regarding moral action."[24] The rich young man in Matthew 19:16 asks the question about morality: What must I do to have eternal life? The answer to the question has been entrusted by Jesus Christ in a particular way to the pastors of the Church.[25]

More than any other pope, and more than all the earlier popes combined, John Paul II apologized for the sins and mistakes of the members of the Church.[26] But he could not say that the Church itself was wrong or made mistakes. The Church acknowledges and confesses the weaknesses and sins of its members, but it also gratefully acknowledges the power of the Lord, who fills it with the gift of holiness.[27] Precisely because of this divine element in the Church, John Paul II could not say that the Church itself did wrong or was sinful. But if the Church is the pilgrim people of God, then the Church will never be perfect and will always fall short. In a true sense, the Church itself is sinful. However, John Paul II had a very triumphalistic view of the Church and saw the divine aspect of the Church as preventing the Church itself from being sinful.

While insisting that the Church and the hierarchical magisterium teach the truth about humanity, John Paul II never addressed the basic question about how the hierarchical magisterium learns the truth. Undoubtedly the magisterium has to learn the truth before it teaches it. Moral teachings have developed and even changed over the years. The Catholic Church's acceptance of slavery for more than eighteen hundred years is not one of the better chapters in its history. Change has occurred in many specific areas of Catholic moral teaching, including the understanding of marriage, the rights of the defendant to remain silent, the taking of interest on loans, the acceptance of democracy, and religious liberty. Even in core matters of faith, the hierarchical Church in the fourth and fifth centuries learned the understanding of the basic mysteries of Christianity: three persons in one God in the Trinity, and two natures, human and divine, in Jesus.[28] The hierarchical Church, especially in specific moral matters, has to learn the truth before it can teach it. The hierarchical magisterium learns this truth only through a discernment process with the help of the Holy Spirit in dialogue with the whole Church.

In *Veritatis splendor* John Paul II dealt with the issue of dissent from authoritative and noninfallible Church teaching. He wrote *Veritatis splendor* because of the discrepancy between the traditional teaching of the Church on moral matters and certain theological positions in moral theology that were being proposed even in Catholic seminaries. The Church is "*facing what is certainly a genuine crisis,* which is no longer a matter of limited and occasional dissent, but of an overall and systematic calling into question of traditional moral doctrine."[29]

Veritatis splendor explicitly addresses the role of moral theologians and dissent. Moral theologians are to set forth the Church's teaching and give, in the exercise of their ministry, an example of loyal assent, both internal and external, to the magisterium's teaching in the areas of dogma and morality. Moral theologians must work in cooperation and communion with the hierarchical magisterium. *Veritatis splendor* recognizes some possible limitations of the human arguments employed by the magisterium and calls for moral theologians to develop a deeper understanding of the reasons underlying the magisterial teaching and to clarify more fully the biblical foundations, the ethical significance, and the anthropological concerns of these teachings.[30] *Veritatis splendor* strongly condemns dissent, which it defines in a narrow and very pejorative sense, as "in the form of carefully orchestrated protests and polemics carried on in the media."[31]

In footnote 177, *Veritatis splendor* refers to *Donum veritatis,* the Congregation for the Doctrine of the Faith's 1990 Instruction on the Ecclesial Vocation of the Theologian, in particular numbers 32–39, devoted to the problem of dissent.[32] According to *Donum veritatis,* loyal submission to noninfallible teaching must be the rule. The instruction provides three points for the theologian who cannot give internal assent after serious study. First, the theologian has the duty to make his problem known to the magisterial authorities. Second, the theologian can suffer in silence and prayer with the understanding that truth will ultimately prevail. Third, dissent, understood as public opposition that causes severe harm, can never be justified.[33] The papacy of John Paul II did not explicitly accept any legitimacy of dissent from noninfallible teachings. One could argue that this papacy did not condemn a form of public dissent from the papal teaching that was not in the form of public opposition, polemical, and harmful to the Church. To my knowledge, all those Catholic theologians who dissented would maintain that their dissent did not fit the very negative description found in these documents.

In many other ways the papacy in the last quarter of the twentieth century shored up the teaching authority of the magisterium and insisted on the need for theologians to teach what the magisterium teaches. The 1990 Apostolic Constitution, *Ex corde ecclesiae,* required a mandate (*mandatum*) for all Catholic college teachers of theology, a requirement that had been promulgated earlier, in the 1983 Code of Canon Law. Catholic leaders of higher education in the United States strongly fought this requirement as a violation of academic freedom and helped convince the American bishops in 1996 to propose norms for Catholic higher education in this country by a vote of 224 to 6, which did not include the need for a mandate. However, the Vatican insisted. In 1999, by a vote of 223 to 31, the U.S. bishops reversed themselves and required the mandate for teachers of theological disciplines in Catholic colleges and universities in the United States.[34] Perhaps because of all the problems the U.S. bishops have had over the pedophilia scandals and their cover-up, there has been no public dispute over the conferral or withdrawal of a mandate.

In June 1998 John Paul II inserted into the Code of Canon Law some changes that first appeared in the Profession of Faith issued by the Congregation for the Doctrine of the Faith in 1989. The 1983 Code of Canon Law referred to two categories of magisterial teaching: the infallible teaching of a divinely revealed truth, which must be believed by divine and Catholic faith, and noninfallible teaching, to which the faithful owe the religious *obsequium* of intellect and will. The new category inserted between these two is the definitive (i.e., infallible) teaching by the magisterium of a doctrine concerned with faith and morals that is not directly revealed but is necessarily connected with revelation.[35] In an unofficial document, Cardinal Ratzinger, then the prefect of the Congregation for the Doctrine of the Faith, mentioned the following teachings as belonging to this second category: the ordination of women, the invalidity of Anglican orders, and the moral teachings on euthanasia, prostitution, and fornication.[36]

In practice, the Congregation for the Doctrine of the Faith in the last part of the twentieth century, especially in the papacy of John Paul II, took action against a number of Catholic theologians. One of the principal areas of Vatican concern was moral theology and the dissent of Catholic moral theologians, especially in the area of sexuality. Various forms of investigation and disciplinary action have been taken against many moral theologians. Cardinal Ratzinger singled out the United States as being the primary place of moral dissent because the moral teaching of the Church is significantly opposed to the practice and ideas prevalent in the United States. "Consequently many moralists believe they are forced to choose between dissent from the society or dissent from the magisterium. Many choose this latter dissent."[37]

On the U.S. scene, the Vatican criticized the books of Anthony Kosnik and John McNeill and took disciplinary action against them and also removed the imprimatur from Philip Keane's book.[38] Often some type of compromise was worked out, and the full process of investigation by the Congregation for the Doctrine of the Faith was not followed. In the case of Charles Curran, the Congregation for the Doctrine of the Faith followed its process and, with the approval of the pope, concluded that Curran was neither suitable nor eligible to teach Catholic theology. The Congregation disagreed with Curran's nuanced dissent on artificial contraception, sterilization, masturbation, homosexuality, premarital sex, abortion, and euthanasia. On the basis of that condemnation, CUA fired Curran. Furthermore, no other Catholic university would hire him.[39] This was the strongest disciplinary action ever taken against a U.S. Catholic moral theologian.

Many progressives in the Catholic Church view the papacy of John Paul II as providing a restorationist agenda and putting the brakes on reform in Catholic life and theology. John Paul II appointed bishops throughout the world who carried out this agenda. Clearly the Wojtyla papacy strongly upheld the papal teaching authority, by not acknowledging error or even change in past papal teaching. Furthermore, it never explicitly accepted the legitimacy of dissent from noninfallible teaching.[40]

THE ACADEMY

The academic aspect of moral theology in the United States changed dramatically after Vatican II. As the latter half of the twentieth century progressed, the home of moral theology moved primarily to the university and the college; the discipline itself became much more academic and complex, and the number and diversity of Catholic moral theologians increased dramatically.

Changes in Catholic Higher Education and Theology

The United States is unique in the Catholic world in its number of Catholic colleges. A few small Catholic colleges have closed in the last few years, but today there exist more than 220. The self-understanding of Catholic colleges and the role of theology in these institutions felt the beginning winds of change in the 1950s, but in conjunction with Vatican II, very significant changes occurred in the 1960s.

Before the 1960s Catholic higher education was outside the mainstream of American higher education in general and even somewhat opposed to the notion of research. The Catholic institutions handed down the traditional wisdom of the past. The leading figures in administration and faculty were the priests and sisters and brothers of the religious communities who staffed most of these institutions. Even in the late 1950s laypeople still often felt like second-class citizens on Catholic college campuses. Change came from a number of directions. In the late 1940s Catholic colleges expanded, with the return of war veterans and an upwardly mobile Catholic population. These colleges continued to grow in the 1950s and 1960s. More laypeople, even some who were trained in non-Catholic institutions, had to join the faculties of these growing institutions. Many people began to call for Catholic colleges to focus on their professionalism and academics and to fully adopt accreditation standards similar to those of non-Catholic institutions of higher education.[41]

In a famous article in 1955, John Tracy Ellis of CUA complained about the lack of Catholic intellectual contributions to the cultural life of the United States. Despite the large number of Catholic colleges, he wrote, Catholics made little or no impression on American intellectual life. Ellis's article called for critical reflection upon Catholic higher education.[42] The most dramatic sign of this change was the demand for academic freedom in Catholic higher education that suddenly came to the fore only in the late 1960s with the Land O'Lakes Statement, which was signed by twenty-six prominent Catholic educators under the leadership of Father Theodore Hesburgh of Notre Dame. Before that time, the leaders of Catholic higher education often gloried in their differences from non-Catholic higher education and strongly opposed the research aspect and academic freedom of non-Catholic colleges and universities. In general, Catholic colleges did not strongly accept the standards of American higher education until the 1970s.[43]

The role of theology in Catholic higher education also went through a similar change.[44] Before 1960 every Catholic college required its students to take a good number of courses in religion. These courses, however, were primarily catechetical and pastoral in orientation, and the teachers were professed religious or priests who often had no advanced degree or training in theology. The Jesuits and Dominicans made some attempts to pursue an academic approach to these religion courses. In the mid-1950s a small group of Catholic teachers of religion founded the Society of Catholic College Teachers of Sacred Doctrine, which in

1967 changed its name to the College Theology Society. This society came into existence in response to the need, recognized by many people on Catholic campuses, for theology to be taught from a much more academic perspective. Catholic educators generally recognized that these religion courses were not in keeping with the academic nature of what a college tries to be.[45]

A strong aspect of the professionalization of Catholic theology required that the teachers and professors themselves have advanced degrees in theology. This development was occurring just as Vatican II was unfolding. Both interest in theology and recognition of its importance were growing. Previously, doctoral degrees in theology were granted only at CUA and at a very creative and courageous program that awarded doctoral degrees to women, started at St. Mary's in Notre Dame, Indiana. Consequently, in the 1960s a number of Catholic universities established doctoral programs: Marquette, Fordham, Boston College, Notre Dame, and others also followed.[46] The professors at these doctorate-granting institutions formed a core of publishing academics who insisted on the need for research and publication in Catholic theology. In addition, the teachers of theology in Catholic colleges were expected to meet the standards of all other academics and therefore to publish articles in refereed journals and to publish books, especially with university presses.

Catholic theologians in the pre–Vatican II era would not recognize Catholic theology as it exists today. More Catholic theological articles and books are published in one year than were published in twenty years in the previous era. Theology professors before Vatican II were almost all priests. After Vatican II many religious women received doctoral degrees, and then laypeople of all stripes came into the profession. Today, Catholic lay theologians dominate the profession.

With this research and publication, the discipline of Catholic theology became much more academic, more profound, and more complex than it had been previously. Before, one person could master all of moral theology. Now that is impossible because of the complex nature of the discipline. Moral theologians today need to specialize in one particular area, such as bioethics, political ethics, the history of moral theology, or the use of scripture in moral theology.

Moral Theology after Vatican II

This striking change came about only gradually in the post–Vatican II period. Until around 1980, moral theology in the United States was still dominated by a few theologians. Many of the leading figures in Catholic moral theology in the pre–Vatican II American Church had died: Gerald Kelly in 1964 and Francis Connell in 1967. John Ford, after the Vatican Council, continued to write articles defending the Catholic teaching against contraception and opposing dissent on this and other issues.[47] Many professors of moral theology trained in the older manualistic approach were not happy with the Vatican II changes and the negative reaction to *Humanae vitae,* and they ceased to teach and publish. John R. Connery, SJ, who six times wrote the "Notes on Moral Theology" in the 1950s, continued to write after Vatican II, generally defending, in a gentlemanly way, the existing hierarchical teachings and method.[48]

One continuity between the pre– and post–Vatican II periods was the leadership role of European theologians. The U.S. Church, except for John Courtney Murray, made no real contributions to Vatican II. U.S. Catholicism was a brick-and-mortar church with little or no interest in scholarship and the intellectual aspects of theology. In systematic theology, figures such as Yves Congar, Karl Rahner, Edward Schillebeeckx, and Hans Küng had a great influence throughout the Catholic world. The translation of their books into English made them leading figures in this country.

The influence of European moral theologians in the United States in the immediate post–Vatican II period was likewise strong. The two most influential European moral theologians in this country were Bernard Häring and Josef Fuchs. Because of their work as professors in Rome—Fuchs at the Jesuit-run Gregorian University and Häring at the Alfonsian Academy—they had a great influence throughout the Catholic world.[49] Louis Janssens, of Louvain, did not write as extensively as Fuchs and Häring, but he had considerable influence in this country with his personalist moral theology. For Janssens, ontic evil is not the same as moral evil and can be justified by a proportionate reason.[50]

Fuchs's book on natural law was translated into English in 1965, and five subsequent books of his essays were published in English.[51] Fuchs also had a considerable influence on many American moral theologians who both made his work known to others and developed it themselves. Richard A. McCormick and Charles E. Curran met Fuchs when they were students in Rome and later became good friends with him. Timothy O'Connell wrote his doctoral dissertation on Fuchs and relied heavily on Fuchs in his 1978 textbook *Principles for a Catholic Morality.*[52] James Keenan was one of Fuchs's last doctoral students, and his published dissertation demonstrated the basis in Thomas Aquinas for Fuchs's characteristic distinction between goodness and rightness.[53] Keenan later directed the published dissertation of Mark Graham on Fuchs's understanding of natural law.[54]

Bernard Häring, the German Redemptorist teaching in Rome at the Alfonsian Academy, had the greatest influence on Catholic moral theology in the United States at this time. Häring's *Law of Christ,* originally published in German in 1954, was translated into more than fifteen languages, which made him the leading moral theologian in the Catholic world. This three-volume work appeared in English in the early 1960s. Häring had a very public and influential role in the work of Vatican II, significantly influencing what the council said about moral theology and also contributing substantially to the Pastoral Constitution on the Church in the Modern World.[55] At this time Häring, who spoke English very well, lectured widely in the United States and taught at different universities. He also taught many American students at the Alfonsian Academy in Rome. The German Redemptorist was a prodigious worker and published numerous books, of which the University of Notre Dame library has eighty-one. In the late 1970s and early 1980s Häring wrote *Free and Faithful in Christ*, an entirely new three-volume textbook of moral theology, written first in English and later translated into German and other languages.

In the United States, new faces replaced those of previous leaders in moral theology. The two most significant figures in the immediate post–Vatican II and post–*Humanae vitae* period were Richard A. McCormick, SJ, and Charles E. Curran. In continuity with the pre–Vatican II era, the institutional support of *Theological Studies* (McCormick) and CUA (Curran) gave added prominence to their work. McCormick had earned his doctoral degree writing on medial ethics at the Gregorian University in Rome in 1957. He began teaching at the Jesuit theologate then at West Baden, Indiana, and started writing the "Notes on Moral Theology" in 1965. At first he shared the writing of the "Notes" with others, but he soon became the acknowledged master of the literary genre of the "Notes." His very first writings were much in accord with the older approach of moral theology, but as he wrote the "Notes" from 1965 to 1984, he disagreed with the older methodologies and practices on significant issues and developed his influential ethics of proportionalism.[56]

The "Notes" was not just a bibliographical survey. McCormick read thoroughly the pertinent periodical literature in moral theology in many languages from the previous year and selected the most significant authors and articles. He then analyzed, criticized, and compared different approaches but always ended the discussion by developing his own position. McCormick possessed a clear and uncluttered mind that identified the central issues without getting bogged down in peripheral matters. In addition, his writing was succinct and respectful and often refreshingly humorous.

The primary method that McCormick employed in the "Notes" was that of casuistry. McCormick had learned the casuistic method in his training in the pre–Vatican II manuals of moral theology. He used the skills of the casuist to make the "Notes" a leading vehicle for the development of post–Vatican II revisionist moral theology. McCormick discussed primarily the controverted issues facing the post–Vatican II Catholic Church. He did not deal primarily with broader methodological and systematic approaches to the discipline. The person, the virtues, and the positive actions of the Christian called to live out the Gospel, as well as social and political ethics, did not receive that much attention, except for controversial issues such as war and capital punishment. Most of McCormick's other writings, including his books of essays, followed the basic method and format of the "Notes."

Richard McCormick's own vocational journey as a moral theologian illustrates the developing academic ethos of the discipline. From 1957 to 1974 he taught moral theology in a Jesuit theologate but then became the Rose F. Kennedy Professor of Christian Ethics at the Kennedy Institute of Ethics at Georgetown University. In 1986 he became the John A. O'Brien Professor of Christian Ethics at the University of Notre Dame. McCormick died on February 12, 2000.

Curran was Häring's student and earned the first doctoral degree granted by the Alfonsian Academy, in 1961, and was the most prominent young voice in the United States speaking for a Vatican II approach to moral theology. In 1963, while teaching at St. Bernard's Seminary in Rochester, Curran was invited to give the major paper on moral theology at the Roman Catholic/Protestant colloquium sponsored by Harvard University.[57] This colloquium brought together the major Protestant and Catholic scholars in all disciplines and was the first and probably the largest ecumenical dialogue ever held in the United States. Cardinal Augustin Bea, the head of the Vatican Secretariat for Christian Unity, gave three plenary addresses at this convocation.

In 1965, even before the end of the council, Curran gave a paper at the Theological Institute of the National Liturgical Conference calling for the renewal of moral theology in four areas. First, moral theology needs a more biblical approach, which takes seriously the implications of the radical demands of the Sermon on the Mount. Second, the liturgy is a great source and school for Christian morality. In and through the liturgy, Christians become conscious of who they are and what they are called to be in their lives. Third, the contemporary challenge is to spell out how Christians should live their vocation to holiness and perfection in all aspects of their daily life. Fourth, on the philosophical level, moral theology needs to recognize that human nature is more personal, more historical, and more relational than manualistic natural law theory allows.[58] In a 1968 study Curran presented the consequences of the shift from classicism to historical consciousness in moral theology.[59]

Having studied under both Fuchs and Häring in Rome, Curran went to CUA in 1965. In April 1967 the trustees of Catholic University voted not to renew Curran's contract because of his teaching on contraception and his call for changes in other Church teachings. The faculty and students of CUA staged a successful strike and the trustees reinstated and promoted him. In 1968 Curran was the principal author and spokesperson for a statement ultimately signed by more than six hundred Catholic academics in the sacred sciences who disagreed with the condemnation of artificial contraception in *Humanae vitae*. In the same year he edited *Absolutes in Moral Theology*, arguing for change in the approach to natural law and Church teaching on a number of specific issues. Curran continued to publish extensively, mostly in article form, calling for a new approach to natural law, disagreeing with some hierarchical Church teachings on such issues as sterilization, divorce, masturbation, homosexuality, and the beginning of human life, and justifying dissent from noninfallible moral teachings. As mentioned above, in 1986, after a seven-year investigation, the Congregation for the Doctrine of the Faith, with the approval of the pope, decreed that Curran was neither suitable nor eligible to teach Catholic theology. He has been teaching at Southern Methodist University since 1991.[60]

James M. Gustafson, universally recognized as the most influential Protestant ethicist during this period, testifies to the leading role of Häring, Fuchs, McCormick, and Curran in his 1978 *Protestant and Roman Catholic Ethics: Prospects for Rapprochement*. Gustafson cites these authors together with Karl Rahner much more than any other Catholic authors. In McCormick's collected *Notes on Moral Theology, 1965–1980*, the greatest number of citations refer to Curran, Häring, Fuchs, and Bruno Schüller, a German moral theologian. Other Catholic moral theologians receiving more than occasional mention in McCormick's "Notes" include Louis Janssens of Belgium, Daniel Maguire of Marquette University, and John Giles Milhaven. Milhaven, then teaching at the Jesuit theologate in Woodstock, Maryland, published a number of significant essays that were brought together in his *Toward a New Catholic Morality* (1970). Milhaven proposed an ethic based on a proper empirical evaluation of the consequences of our actions in light of love. He acknowledged the similarity of his approach to the situation ethics of Joseph F. Fletcher.

These moral theologians belonged to the progressive, or revisionist, wing of Catholic moral theology. Other moral theologians who were trained as philosophers strongly disagreed with the newer revisionist approaches and defended the existing hierarchical teachings. Germain Grisez, a lay philosopher who taught for many years at Mt. St. Mary's Seminary in Emmitsburg, Maryland, is the most significant figure in this group. Grisez published *Contraception and the Natural Law* in 1964, defending the condemnation of artificial contraception. Grisez, either alone or with others, has written prolifically on a number of specific issues, including abortion, euthanasia, and nuclear weapons. He developed a new and creative approach to natural law, now often called the "new natural law theory." In addition, he published a three-volume manual of moral theology.[61] John Finnis, an Australian legal philosopher trained and teaching now in England and at Notre Dame, also works on the new natural law theory.[62] Less original than Grisez but also prolific is William E. May of Catholic University and now of the John Paul II Institute on the Family in Washington, DC. May staunchly defends the existing Catholic teachings on many specific issues and argues against the revisionist school.[63]

The striking change in moral theology in the post–Vatican II Church became quite evident in 1980. Many new figures were writing in the discipline. The college and university, rather than the seminary, became the primary homes of moral theology. The new Catholic graduate schools trained new moral theologians. The discipline itself was becoming so complex that moral theologians had to specialize in particular areas.[64]

The "Notes on Moral Theology" in *Theological Studies* well illustrate the change in the discipline. McCormick ended his twenty-year stint of writing the "Notes" in 1984. By that time it was impossible to review all the periodical literature and monographs in moral theology published only in English in the past year. *Theological Studies* has continued to publish "Notes" every year, but the genre and format have changed dramatically. Now a different author discusses in depth a significant issue or area of moral theology. No attempt is made to relate this discussion to other areas or to the whole of moral theology. More than twenty moral theologians have contributed to "Notes" since 1985. "Notes" thus illustrate the complexity of the discipline of moral theology today, the need for specialization in a particular area, and the fact that no one or two people will ever again dominate the discipline. The new face of moral theology makes it even more difficult to write a history of contemporary moral theology because so much material and so many authors must be covered. At the very least, one must distinguish the early period, before about 1980, when a few figures dominated, from the later period, which welcomed many new voices.

SOCIETY AT LARGE

Moral theology serves and is in dialogue with the broader human society of which it is a part. The aspects of contemporary society are so many and varied that one cannot attempt to summarize them adequately. The issues that surfaced in the first part of the twentieth century continue to be important, but often in very different circumstances. Poverty and economic issues are now worldwide. The division between the developed and developing worlds continues to grow, but poverty also persists in urban and rural America. Heated debates continue about the best way to structure the economic system in our country and in the world to bring about justice and overcome the horrendous problems of poverty. What is the proper role of government in these issues? The poor and the marginalized themselves are now speaking up and demanding to be heard. Racial and ethnic problems have taken on new faces in our own country and in the world. Discrimination against African Americans has not been eliminated in the United States, and the growing problems of a burgeoning Hispanic population have raised serious problems about American democracy. Issues of housing, schooling, and medicine are very complex. The woman's issue has come to the fore in the last forty years. Issues of justice and peace are urgent in all parts of the world. Can war and violence ever be justified, and, if so, under what conditions? Globalization today affects practically every aspect of human existence, from climate to industrial production and trade. Technological breakthroughs in many areas such as bioethics, computers, and communication raise new issues.

The cultural and intellectual life of contemporary society strongly affects moral theology. Liberationist and feminist approaches have come to the fore. The turn to the subject, to language, to narrative, and to tradition have all affected moral theology. Postmodernism raises significant issues for the discipline. This very cursory and inadequate summary indicates some of the multitudinous issues and different intellectual approaches existing in our contemporary world and affecting moral theology.

Three publics—the Church, the academy, and society at large—shaped moral theology after Vatican II. Based primarily on the Church aspect, today one can distinguish three generations of moral theologians. The first generation was directly involved with the immediate aftermath of Vatican II and *Humanae vitae*. The second generation began writing somewhat later; having been trained in light of these two significant events, they wrote in this historical context. At the turn of the century, a third generation appeared—people not yet born in the era of Vatican II and *Humanae vitae*. Subsequent chapters will discuss the work of these three generations of Catholic moral theologians.

NOTES

1. Komonchak, "Church in Crisis."
2. John Paul II, *Fides et ratio*, 879n49.
3. Abbott, "Dogmatic Constitution on the Church," 65–72nn39–42.

4. Abbott, "Decree on Priestly Formation," 452n16.

5. Abbott, "Pastoral Constitution on the Church," 243n43.

6. Ibid., 210–38nn12–32.

7. Abbott, "Constitution on the Sacred Liturgy," 144–45n16.

8. Abbott, "Decree on Ecumenism," 354–55n12.

9. Ibid., 353–54nn9–10.

10. Kaiser, *Politics of Sex and Religion*.

11. Curran, et al., *Dissent In and For the Church*.

12. Pope Paul VI used the expression *la vivida discussión* in an address delivered to the Second General Conference of Latin American Bishops held at Medellín, Columbia, on August 24, 1968, and published in *Acta Apostolicae Sedis* 60 (1968): 639–49.

13. Greeley, McCready, and McCourt, *Catholic Schools in a Declining Church*, 103–54.

14. Paul VI, *Humanae vitae*, n4. Subsequent references are given parenthetically in the text by paragraph number (n.).

15. For a one-volume collection of Pope John Paul II's encyclicals, see Miller, *Encyclicals of Pope John Paul II*. Subsequent references, when appropriate, are to paragraph number (n.) of the document and page number in Miller.

16. Joblin, "Le Saint-Siege," 333–52.

17. John Paul II, *Veritatis splendor*, 607–20nn35–53.

18. Wojtyla, *Person and Community*.

19. John Paul II, *Laborem exercens*, 172–84nn14–21.

20. John Paul II, *Theology of the Body*, 421.

21. John Paul II, *Role of the Christian Family*, 51–52n32.

22. John Paul II, *Dominum et vivificantem*, 244n1.

23. John Paul II, *Redemptor hominis*, 62n12.

24. John Paul II, *Veritatis splendor*, 602n27.

25. Ibid., 657n114.

26. John Paul II, "Tertio millennio adveniente"; "Incarnationis mysterium," 450–51n11; "Jubilee Characteristic." See also Ford, "John Paul II Asks for Forgiveness"; Sullivan, "Papal Apology"; Kalbian, "Catholic Church's Public Confession."

27. John Paul II, *Ut unum sint*, 783n3.

28. Noonan, *Church That Can and Cannot Change*; Curran, *Change in Official Catholic Moral Teachings*.

29. John Paul II, *Veritatis splendor*, 586–87nn4–5. Emphasis in original.

30. Ibid., 653–55nn109–10.

31. Ibid., 656n113.

32. Ibid., 656n177.

33. Congregation for the Doctrine of the Faith, "Ecclesial Vocation," 123–24nn30–32.

34. U.S. Catholic Bishops, "*Ex Corde Ecclesiae*," 401–9.

35. John Paul II, "Ad tuendam fidem."

36. Ratzinger and Bertone, "Profession of Faith's Concluding Paragraph."

37. Messori, "Colloquio con il cardinale Josef Ratzinger," 77.

38. For the texts of the Congregation for the Doctrine of the Faith's observations on the books by Kosnik and McNeill, see Curran and McCormick, *Dialogue about Catholic Sexual Teaching*, 485–97.

39. For the correspondence between the Congregation and Curran, see Curran, *Faithful Dissent*.

40. Küng and Swidler, *Church in Anguish*.

41. Greeley, *From Backwater to Mainstream*.

42. Ellis, "American Catholics and Intellectual Life." See also O'Dea, *American Catholic Dilemma*.

43. For the changing Catholic attitude toward academic freedom, see Curran, *Catholic Higher Education*, 26–153.

44. For a helpful overview of the changing role of theology in Catholic higher education, see Carey, "College Theology in Historical Perspective."

45. Mize, *Joining the Revolution in Theology*; Rodgers, *History of the College Theology Society*; Sloyan, "Present at the Sidelines"; Mize, "On Writing a History."

46. Carey, "College Theology in Historical Perspective," 259–66.

47. Menius, "John Cuthbert Ford, S.J."

48. For Connery's significant historical monograph, see Connery, *Abortion*.

49. For Häring's story, see Häring, *My Witness for the Church*. For a helpful study in English of Fuchs's work, see Graham, *Josef Fuchs on Natural Law*.

50. Christie, *Adequately Considered*. For a festschrift in honor of Janssens, see Selling, *Personalist Morals*.

51. These were *Human Values and Christian Morality*; *Personal Responsibility and Christian Morality*; *Christian Ethics in a Secular Arena*; *Christian Morality*; and *Moral Demands and Personal Obligations*.

52. O'Connell's dissertation was titled "Changing Roman Catholic Moral Theology."

53. Keenan, *Goodness and Rightness*.

54. Graham, *Josef Fuchs on Natural Law*.

55. Häring, *My Witness for the Church*, 52–69; Dietrich, "*Gaudium et spes* and Häring's Personalism"; McDonough, "'New Terrain' and a 'Stumbling Stone'"; Hill, "Bernard Häring and the Second Vatican Council."

56. See Odozor, *Richard A. McCormick and the Renewal of Moral Theology*.

57. Curran, "Problem of Conscience."

58. Curran, "Relevance: Contemporary Moral Concerns."

59. Curran, "Absolute Norms in Moral Theology."

60. See Curran, *Loyal Dissent*.

61. George, *Natural Law and Moral Inquiry*. For a personal and intellectual biography of Grisez, see Shaw, "Making of a Moral Theologian."

62. For the most systematic development of this theory, see Finnis, *Natural Law and Natural Rights*.

63. The home page of William E. May is www.christendom-awake.org/pages/may/may.html.

64. Curran and McCormick co-edited the series *Readings in Moral Theology* (New York: Paulist Press, 1979–2004), to provide an in-depth discussion of significant issues in moral theology culled from already published articles and representing all sides in the debate.

THE AFTERMATH OF
HUMANAE VITAE

Vatican II called for a more scriptural and theological approach to moral theology, and this direction had a significant impact on Catholic moral theology throughout the world. But the most immediate impact on moral theology came from Pope Paul VI's 1968 encyclical *Humanae vitae,* condemning artificial contraception, which brought about what the pope himself called "a lively discussion" in the Church.[1] This lively discussion, as it took place in the United States, gave rise to what has been called "revisionist moral theology." Revisionist moral theology dissented from the encyclical's condemnation of artificial contraception and thus began a long discussion about sexuality and moral norms. Revisionist theologians focused on the two primary characteristics in pre–Vatican II moral theology: natural law and the hierarchical teaching office and role in the Church. The majority of publishing moral theologians accepted the general approach of revisionism and realized that the criticism of natural law as found in *Humanae vitae* logically led to questions about other hierarchical moral teachings, especially in sexual and medical ethics. Some moral theologians defended the encyclical and supported the pre–Vatican II understanding of natural law and Church teaching authority. Germain Grisez and his school supported the teaching of the hierarchical magisterium and Catholic sexual teaching in general but developed a creative new natural law theory to support these positions.[2]

REVISIONIST MORAL THEOLOGY

Revisionists found some weaknesses and problems in the natural law method used in the manuals and in *Humanae vitae* as well. We are dealing here with what has been called the "philosophical aspect of natural law." But these revisionist theologians on the whole did not totally reject natural law theory and hence were often regarded as revisionists. Revisionists pointed out three problems in the natural law approach found in the encyclical and proposed alternative approaches. First, the older natural law theory embodied a classicist worldview; the revisionists called for a historically conscious worldview. Second, the older approach absolutized the physical aspect of the human act at the expense of the total human aspect. Third, the older method emphasized the nature and finality of the faculty, whereas the revisionists emphasized the person and the person's relationships as more signifi-cant than the faculty itself.[3]

The Shift from Classicism to Historical Consciousness

Bernard Lonergan claimed that the ultimate reason for the changes at Vatican II came from the shift from classicism to historical consciousness.[4] John Courtney Murray picked up this understanding of historical consciousness and incorporated it into his approach in the last years of his life. Revisionist moral theologians used historical consciousness to criticize the pre–Vatican II natural law approach and the approach found in *Humanae vitae.*

Classicism sees the world in terms of the immutable, the eternal, and the unchanging. Historical consciousness places greater significance on the particular, the contingent, and the historical. Historical consciousness recognizes that the human subject, who is knower and actor, is also embedded in a history and culture that affect the ways in which the individual thinks and acts. Historical consciousness is a middle way between classicism and sheer existentialism, which sees the particular human person today with no real connection to past and future and no binding relationships with others in the present. Historical consciousness recognizes the need for both continuity and discontinuity. Historical consciousness, by definition, is thus more open than classicism to some change and development.

The shift to historical consciousness affects the method of moral theology. The manualistic natural law employed a deductive methodology using the syllogism. The syllogism consists of the major premise, the minor premise, and the conclusion. For example, the major states that actions going against the God-given purpose of the faculty or power (e.g., the eye or the sexual faculty) are wrong. But plucking out your good eye and artificial contraception go against the God-given purpose of the faculty and are therefore morally wrong. The syllogism claims that the conclusion is just as certain as the premises, provided the logic is correct. Thus the goal of deductive and syllogistic thinking is certitude.

Historical consciousness calls for a more inductive approach that considers many different aspects of the act, including the experience of people of goodwill. The move to historical consciousness, with its more inductive approach, affects natural law in a number of ways. First, the manuals assume that a monolithic natural law theory exists that can be applied deductively to moral problems and issues as they arise. We thus have the theory that gives us the method of evaluating particular issues and problems as they appear. But in reality it seems that the understanding of the morality of particular acts (e.g., lying, stealing, adultery) came first in the consciousness of the Christian community, and that the theory of natural law then arose to explain systematically and coherently why these particular actions were wrong. The individual teachings were established long before the Thomistic natural law theory came into existence.

Second, the classicist approach to natural law, with its deductive method, insists that natural law is eternal, immutable, and unchanging, and that its conclusions are certain. A more historically conscious methodology can never claim as much certitude as the deductive approach. Such an understanding of the historically conscious approach, with its recognition of possible change and development, fits in well with the historical reality that Catholic teaching on specific moral issues—slavery, usury, the defendant's right to silence—and on the role of procreation in marriage have all changed in the course of history.

Physicalism

A second problem with the manualistic understanding of natural law, especially in sexual issues, is physicalism. Physicalism refers to the a priori identification of the human moral act with the physical or biological aspect of the act. For the most part, the Catholic tradition has not identified the physical with the moral. Killing is a physical act, but not every killing is a morally condemnable act of murder. Think, for example, of killing in self-defense. Mutilating the body is a physical reality, but one can mutilate or sacrifice a part of the body (e.g., an infected organ) in order to save the whole. Even abortion is a physical term referring to a physical act, and the Catholic tradition has never condemned all abortion, only direct abortion.

In sexual ethics there exists an a priori identification of the physical structure with the moral aspect of the act. The manuals and *Humanae vitae* recognize as morally normative the physical act of depositing the husband's semen in the vagina of the wife. You cannot interfere with the physical act to avoid procreation, as in the case of contraception; likewise, you cannot interfere with this physical act in order to have children, as in artificial insemination with the husband's seed. The physical act is sacrosanct and must always be present and respected.

One of the basic problems of physicalism comes from the Thomistic acceptance of Ulpian's understanding of natural law as that which nature teaches humans and all the animals. Thomas Aquinas distinguishes Ulpian's understanding of natural law from the *ius gentium*, which is deduced from human reason.[5] The resulting anthropology sees the human person as composed of two layers: a bottom layer of what is common to humans and all animals and a top layer of what is proper and unique to humans—human reason. But human reason cannot interfere in the animal, biological finalities. Why should the physical structure of the marital act always be morally obliging? Why cannot human reason interfere with the physical structure of the act for a proportionate good? In most other areas, the Catholic tradition does not totally identify the moral aspect of the act with its physical structure.

A More Personalist or Relational Approach

The manuals and *Humanae vitae* employ the perverted-faculty argument to condemn artificial contraception. The God-given purpose of the sexual faculty is procreation; therefore, every act of this faculty must be open to procreation. A more personalist or relational anthropology does not absolutize the finality of the faculty itself. The sexual faculty or power exists in light of the total person and the person's relationships. Thus, for the good of the person or the good of the marriage, one can and should interfere with the sexual faculty or power.

Richard McCormick frequently cited the criterion of morality proposed by Louis Janssens—that the human person be integrally and adequately considered. The human being is an embodied subject, a historical being living in relationship with other persons, social groups, and institutions, and called to love and worship God. Persons are utterly original but fundamentally equal.[6] Charles Curran has criticized the conclusion of *Humanae vitae* in light of a relationality-responsibility criterion that he later expanded upon in terms of the individual existing in multiple relationships with God, neighbor, world, and self.[7]

Revisionist theologians appeal to the changed understanding of lying. An older approach, based on the nature and purpose of the faculty of speech, defined a lie as a violation of the God-given purpose of speech. Speech exists to put on my tongue what is in my mind. In the early twentieth century, some moral theologians proposed a different understanding of the malice of lying in order to deal with some conflict situations. The faculty of speech cannot be absolutized but exists in service of the person and the person's relationship to others. The ultimate malice of lying consists in the violation of my neighbor's right to truth. If this neighbor has no right to truth, my speech is false but it is not morally a lie. Note here the distinction between the "physical act" of false speech and the moral act of lying.[8] Civilians who hid Jews in countries occupied by the Nazis in World War II morally told the Gestapo that Jews were not hidden in their homes. The Gestapo did not have the right to know the truth. As noted in the previous chapter, John A. Ryan in the 1920s had appealed to the newer approach to lying in order to reject the perverted-faculty argument as the basis for condemning artificial contraception for spouses.[9]

The two criticisms of the natural law theory as found in the manuals and in papal documents—the identification of the human moral act with the physical structure and aspect of the act and the criterion of the nature and purpose of the faculty rather than the good of the person and the person's relationships—help to explain the questioning by revisionist theologians of almost all the disputed specific issues that have arisen in moral theology in the past fifty years. This short section does not try to prove or support a dissenting position on these issues but only to explain why these are the issues that are being debated in Catholic moral theology. The problem of physicalism and the finality of the faculty explain why questions have been raised about sterilization, masturbation, artificial insemination, and homosexual acts between two committed persons with a homosexual orientation. The most important condition of the famous principle of the double effect is based on the physical causality of the act. The good effect cannot be achieved by means of the bad effect, which explains why many have questioned this condition. There has been a discussion about the beginning of truly individual human life because some do not want to identify truly individual human life with only the physical and biological union of the ovum and sperm. The manualist approach talked about the existence of the bond of marriage that comes into effect when two people make their commitment to each other. But does a bond truly exist when the relationship of love has ceased to exist? A few have questioned why euthanasia, as the physical act of bringing about death, is always wrong. But a word of caution is also in order. The physical, the biological, and the body are a part of the human and, in general, can never be totally dismissed. The generally accepted understanding of the death of the human person is based on the physical realities of the breakdown of the circulatory or respiratory systems or the lack of total brain function.

The debate over these issues has also raised the question about the existence of absolute moral norms and intrinsically evil acts. Revisionist moral theologians are not opposed to either. They maintain that torture, rape, and lying (understood as the violation of my neighbor's right to truth) are intrinsically wrong and constitute absolute norms that have no exception. But revisionists hold that actions that are described only in terms of the physical aspect or structure are neither necessarily always wrong nor intrinsically evil.

The traditional Catholic natural law approach maintained that the morality of an act is determined by its object, the end, and the circumstances. Some acts are intrinsically wrong by reason of the object. Revisionists can accept such an approach if the object is defined in terms of the moral reality of the object and not just the physical aspect of the object.[10]

Revisionist theories arose as an attempt to explain systematically and coherently the positions often taken by revisionist theologians, especially in the area of sexuality and the principle of double effect. Individual moral judgments and positions came into being first; the theory came later to explain the existing positions. At a very minimum, there will always be a two-way relationship between theory and individual moral judgments. Individuals and the Church community often make their individual moral judgments based on the broadest possible moral experience, including more theoretical aspects, but individual judgments influence and sometimes even call for a change in the theory.

PROPORTIONALISM

The proponents of revisionism involved many Catholic moral theologians from Europe: Peter Knauer, Josef Fuchs, Bruno Schüller, and Louis Janssens were the primary European voices. Richard McCormick and Charles Curran were the leading revisionists in the United States.[11] In his "Notes on Moral Theology" in *Theological Studies,* McCormick chronicled the debate and also developed and defended his own understanding of proportionalism. One can do premoral evil if there is a proportionate reason for so doing.[12]

The development and defense of proportionalism took place in two overlapping contexts: the dissatisfaction with the manualistic and hierarchical Church teaching on sexual issues and its natural law basis, and the contemporary debate among Christian ethicists and philosophical ethicists over teleology and deontology. Utilitarianism or consequentialism, one form of teleology, makes the net good of the consequences of the act the moral criterion. In other words, the end justifies the means. The deontological position in general maintains that some actions are always wrong, no matter what the consequences. McCormick recognizes his own position as avoiding the two extremes of absolute deontology, as found in the Catholic manualist tradition and in Germain Grisez, and absolute consequentialism, as identified with Joseph Fletcher and some utilitarians. His moderate teleology sees the role of consequences as necessary but not sufficient for determining the morality of actions.[13]

McCormick maintains that proportionate reason is the criterion used even in the manuals themselves and in the Catholic hierarchical teaching in most areas, except in the areas of sexuality and the principle of double effect. For example, the Catholic tradition justifies breaking promises or killing people if there is a proportionate reason for doing so. In reality the objection to the manualist teaching on sexual issues such as masturbation, contraception, sterilization, and homosexual relations does not in any way imply the danger of accepting absolute consequentialism or utilitarianism. Many theologians and philosophers accept such positions and strongly oppose utilitarianism. The specter of absolute consequentialism arises especially in issues of justice and the direct killing of noncombatants in war. One case that illustrates the justice issue is the framing of an innocent person in order to avoid very great evils. A southern sheriff framed and handed over to the white mob an innocent person in order to prevent the mob from killing, raping, and pillaging in the African American section of the city, even though he knew that the mob would kill the innocent person. McCormick will not accept the framing of an innocent person, or the direct killing of noncombatants to end a war quickly and save more lives in the long run.

McCormick's final understanding of proportionate reason indicates how he differs from the absolute consequentialists. The very fact that he speaks of premoral values shows that he recognizes that these values have some moral meaning apart from consequences. He does not want to base morality on aggregating all the consequences of the action. There has to be a proportionate reason for choosing a premoral evil in order to achieve this particular end or value.

Another way to avoid consequentialism is to bring in the concept of associated goods. McCormick holds that there are basic human goods grounded in our natural inclinations and tendencies. His theory of the association of basic goods implies some indirect way to make them commensurate. The sheriff should not hand over the innocent prisoner to the mob to avoid the horrendous consequences to the black community in the town. The good of life, the end of the sheriff's action, would be undercut in the long run by serious injury to the associated good of human freedom. The mob should recognize its moral obligation not to participate in such violence.[14]

In addition to associated goods, McCormick insists that a proportionate reason is present when the means are in a necessary causal relationship to the end.[15] There is no necessary connection between killing innocent people and ending a war, thereby avoiding greater evil. But there is a necessary connection between aborting a fetus to save the life of the mother. McCormick refers to such prohibitions as virtually without exception, but James Walter points out that the requirement of a necessary connection between the premoral evil committed and the good consequences means that these prohibitions are intrinsically evil.[16]

In the process of defending his theory of proportionalism, McCormick responds to three criticisms of his approach: Once one knows that there is a proportionate reason to justify the act, one cannot choose a wrong option; the basic goods are themselves incommensurate; and one cannot establish a hierarchy or order among the basic goods.[17]

By the latter part of the twentieth century the defense of proportionalism was no longer a major topic in moral theology. James Keenan claims that proportionalism was a temporary attempt to deal with particular issues because it shared the basic focus of avoiding evil rather than the pursuit of the good. Basically, it followed the logical approach of the manuals without their concept of intrinsic evil.[18] Aline Kalbian makes basically the same point by showing that newer approaches, such as feminism, virtue ethics, and casuistry, have taken over the concerns of proportionalism.[19]

NEW NATURAL LAW THEORY

Proponents of the natural law approach of the manuals strongly object to revisionism and its dissent from official Catholic teachings. But the most creative and innovative defense of the negative moral absolutes proposed by the hierarchical magisterium comes from the theory often called the "new natural law theory" or the "basic human goods theory" proposed by Germain Grisez, frequently writing with Joseph Boyle and others.[20] Later, John Finnis, an Australian teaching legal jurisprudence at Oxford and now also teaching at Notre Dame, proposed and defended the same basic approach.[21]

Grisez strongly disagrees with the manualistic approach to natural law. He accepts the basic insight of David Hume that one cannot go from an "is" to an "ought." This approach is the naturalistic fallacy. Nature itself has no normative character. The argument against contraception as violating the God-given purpose of the sexual faculty—the perverted-faculty argument—is not valid. Many times we go against the purpose of a faculty, as in holding our noses to avoid a repugnant smell.[22] Thus, Grisez, in a certain way, joins the proportionalists in objecting to the physicalism of the manualistic approach. But Grisez strongly opposes revisionism and proportionalism. It is impossible to make a judgment about the greater good because diverse basic values or goods cannot be compared. Moral situations are complex and without fixed borders, and so we can never know all that is involved in a situation and its consequences. Basic human goods (e.g., justice and truth) are incommensurate. There is no common denominator for judging what is the greater good.[23]

Grisez and others have recognized that their approach is not Thomistic and that their theory is neither teleological nor deontological. Aquinas begins with the teleology of the ultimate end and recognizes inclinations in nature that have moral content. For Grisez, Aquinas's first principle of practical reason—good is to be done and pursued and evil is to be avoided—is not itself a moral precept.[24] For Grisez, the first principle of morality is this: "In voluntarily acting for human goods and avoiding what is opposed to them, one ought to choose and otherwise will those and only those possibilities whose willing is compatible with the will toward integral human fulfillment."[25]

Modes of responsibility are intermediate principles that are somewhat formal in nature and involve not moral actions but ways of choosing and acting that spell out the first general principle. The first mode of responsibility, for example, maintains that one should not be deterred by inertia from acting for intelligible goods. The most significant of the modes of responsibility for the defense of the absolute moral norms taught by the hierarchical magisterium is the eighth and final mode: one should not be so moved by desire for one instance of an intelligible good that one chooses to destroy, damage, or impede some other instance of an intelligible good to obtain it. In other words, one cannot go against a basic human good in trying to achieve some other human good.[26]

What are these basic human goods? Grisez maintains that there are eight self-evident basic human goods. They are not deduced from any first principle or derived from our understanding of human nature. We know them just by knowing the meaning of their terms. Four are existential goods—integration; practical reasonableness or authenticity; friendship and justice; and religion or holiness. Three are substantive goods—life and bodily well-being; knowledge of truth and appreciation of beauty; and skill for performance and play. The eighth good is the complex good of marriage and family. The permanent union of man and woman, which normally unfolds in parenthood and family life, is both substantive and reflexive. This is a substantive good insofar as it fulfills the natural capacity of men and women to complement one another, have children, and bring them up; but it is also a reflexive good insofar as it includes the free choices of a couple marrying and committing themselves to fulfill all the responsibilities of marriage.[27] Contraception is the choice to prevent the passing on of human life. But this is a choice to impede a basic human good (life) in a particular instance. Such a choice against an instance of the basic human good of life violates the eighth mode of responsibility. William E. May has also written extensively to explain and defend the Grisez approach in areas of general moral theology, sexual ethics, and bioethics.[28]

With many I disagree about the theoretical and practical aspects of this theory. On the basis of a relational ethical model, one easily recognizes that many basic human goods, such as justice and truth, might come into conflict.[29] In fact, from a different perspective, Pope Pius XII, in his defense of using only ordinary means to preserve life, recognized that life and health are subordinated to spiritual ends.[30] Grisez in reply points out the incommensurability of basic goods, but it seems that the Catholic tradition has recognized the existence of these conflicts and has tried to deal with them. On the practical issue of contraception, contraception itself does not have a very close connection with the basic good of human life. In fact, there is no human life present when contraception occurs. Would someone who did not hold that contraception and masturbation are intrinsically grave evils ever come to the conclusion that these acts go against the basic good of life itself?

DISSENT

Theological dissent from noninfallible teaching became a burning issue in response to Pope Paul VI's 1968 encyclical *Humanae vitae,* which condemned artificial contraception for Catholic spouses. The whole Catholic world knew that in the previous years a special papal commission had been studying the issue and that a majority of the commission's members were in favor of change. The encyclical created greater furor than any other Church document, since it directly affected so many people. Great publicity surrounded its issuance and the reactions to it.[31]

The questioning of some absolute norms taught in the Catholic Church coincided with this related issue of the binding force of the teaching of the papal magisterium on moral issues. Revisionist theologians challenged some of these norms, while the new natural law theorists and proponents of the neoscholastic natural law approach staunchly defended them. A significant factor in the discussion about dissent from the teaching of *Humanae vitae* on artificial contraception for spouses was the practice of many married Catholics—and today the vast majority of Catholic married people—who do not condemn artificial contraception. Chapter 7 discusses the Catholic teaching that one must follow one's conscience, but conscience can be wrong. This section supports that understanding of the role of conscience by emphasizing the importance of the reception of hierarchical teaching in the Church and the *sensus fidelium*—the sense and practice of the faithful—as a true source of wisdom for the Church community. In light of these factors, revisionist theologians point out that the hierarchical teaching on a number of issues in the past has changed precisely because of the practice of the Christian people who did not go along with the former teaching.

Many theologians contributed to the debate supporting the legitimacy of dissent from the teaching on contraception and the possibility of dissent from authoritative noninfallible Church teaching. This section synthesizes the primary reasons proposed in this debate and concentrates heavily on the work of two moral theologians: Charles E. Curran and Richard A. McCormick, singled out by Germain Grisez, a strong opponent of such dissent, as the primary representatives of what he calls "radical dissent."[32]

The Constitution on the Church of Vatican II addressed the issue of the hierarchical magisterium, or teaching office, of the Church. To infallible teachings, a Catholic owes the assent of faith. The religious submission (*obsequium*) of will and intellect is owed to authoritative noninfallible papal teaching.[33] Proponents of theological dissent from the papal teaching on artificial contraception and the possibility of dissent from other noninfallible Church teachings proposed three generic types of reasons: from history, from ecclesiology, and from moral theology.

Historical Reasons

The first historical reason concerns the proper meaning and understanding of Vatican II's teaching on the religious *obsequium* of intellect and will, which is owed to authoritative noninfallible teaching. This terminology came into existence only in the nineteenth century, when the First Vatican Council proclaimed the infallibility of the pope. One had to distinguish from this infallible teaching the category of noninfallible teaching. Objections were raised against papal infallibility at the time of the council on the basis of the historical teachings of Pope Liberius (352–66), Pope Vigilius (540–55), and Pope Honorius (625–38). These three were cited as teaching erroneous doctrines in the course of the debate over papal infallibility.[34] A threefold answer responded to the objection that these erroneous statements argued against papal infallibility. First, some of these events and statements might not be historically certain. Second, they do not pertain to the subject of infallibility, which involves only *ex cathedra* statements. Third, they do not pertain to the object of infallibility, which is a doctrine about faith and morals.[35] Such discussions at Vatican I recognized the need to realize the existence of a category of teaching—noninfallible teaching—that might be wrong or erroneous.

An early and important study by Joseph Komonchak analyzed the teaching of the accepted manuals of dogmatic theology, the textbooks used in the seminaries throughout the world. These authors were often called in Latin the *auctores probati*, the approved authors. The manualists maintained that one owes an internal religious assent to authoritative noninfallible teaching that differs from the assent of faith owed to infallible teaching. Divine faith is absolutely certain and firm, whereas internal religious assent is not absolutely or metaphysically certain. Most authors speak of a morally certain teaching that excludes the likelihood of error but not the possibility of error.[36]

According to many of these approved authors, internal religious assent is conditional. Different authors propose the condition differently: An equal or superior Church authority should decree otherwise; the Church changes its teaching or the contrary becomes evident; a grave suspicion arises that the presumption is not verified; an issue may become positively and clearly wrong; unless there is something that could prudently persuade one to suspend assent. But there is a presumption in favor of the teaching, so that assent cannot be suspended rashly, casually, or out of pride. Generally, these authors thought it highly unlikely that error would ever be taught by the authoritative magisterium. Some of the manualists explain more fully than others the possibility of error and its correction. Ludwig Lercher maintains that ordinarily the Holy Spirit preserves the Church from error through the assistance given to the pope. But it is possible that the Holy Spirit might actually overcome error through the detection of that error by subjects who, therefore, would not give their internal assent. Thus the manuals, which were the official textbooks of theology in Catholic seminaries throughout the world, recognized that some noninfallible teaching might be erroneous and that Catholics could, at times, suspend their internal assent from such teaching.[37]

This understanding seems to be behind some events that occurred at Vatican II. The first schema on the Church proposed to the council fathers was rejected. This schema cited Pope Pius XII's 1950 encyclical *Humani generis*, which maintained that when the Roman pontiff goes out of his way to speak on a heretofore controverted subject, the subject can no longer be regarded as a matter for free debate among theologians. Subsequent schemas and the finally approved Constitution on the Church no longer included that statement, which was found in the first schema.[38]

During the conciliar debate, three bishops proposed an emendation (modus 159) about an educated person who for serious reasons cannot give internal assent to a noninfallible teaching. The Doctrinal Commission responded that approved theological explanations should be consulted.[39] The obvious reference is to the authors of the manuals. In the conciliar debate on religious liberty, one proposed emendation would have changed the statement that, in the formation of their consciences, "the Christian faithful ought carefully attend to the sacred and certain doctrine of the church." The proposed substitution would have read, "ought to form their consciences according to" rather than "ought carefully attend to." The commission in charge of the text responded that the proposed emendation was too restrictive. The obligation was sufficiently expressed in the text as it stands.[40]

The actual meaning and translation of the Latin word *obsequium,* which is frequently translated as "assent," has been much discussed. Francis Sullivan, for example, finds "submission" an adequate translation.[41] Bishop Christopher Butler of England prefers "due respect."[42] John Boyle points out the confusion resulting from the fact that *obsequium* originally was limited to describing the response to definitive Church teaching of revelation but has now been extended to matters that are not definitive and not based on revelation—the category of noninfallible teaching.[43] Ladislas Örsy recognizes the various usages of *obsequium,* which basically signifies communion or being one with the Church. *Obesequium fidei* is being one with the believing Church, whereas *obsequium religiousum* is being one with the searching Church. The duty to offer *obsequium* calls for respect or submission or any other similar and related attitude.[44]

What, then, is the meaning of the religious *obsequium* of intellect and will? Among the many theologians recognizing the possible legitimacy of dissent from noninfallible teaching, general agreement exists that such a religious *obsequium* calls for a docile and honest attempt to assimilate and accept the proposed teaching, but such an attempt can result in the inability to give such an assent, in other words, dissent.[45]

The second historical reason supporting dissent from authoritative noninfallible Church teaching comes from the change that has occurred in specific moral teachings in history. John Noonan has analyzed the changes that have occurred in Catholic moral teaching on slavery, usury, religious liberty, and divorce. For more than nineteen hundred years the Catholic Church did not condemn slavery.[46] In addition, change has taken place in respect to the right of the defendant to remain silent, the ends of marriage, and human rights.[47] Some want to refer to development rather than change, but in all these cases the specific norm changed. With regard to usury, Noonan points out that within thirty years three papal bulls, *Cum onus, In eam,* and *Debilitatis avaritia,* were deprived of force to influence anyone's behavior. "Acts of papal authority, isolated from theological support and contrary to the conviction of Christians familiar with the practices condemned, could not prevail, however accurately they reflected the assumptions and traditions of an earlier age." Theologians were to have the last word because those who cared consulted them, because they taught the next generation, and because acts of papal authority are inert unless supported by theologians.[48]

Avery Dulles pointed out that Vatican II quietly reversed the positions of the Roman magisterium on a number of important issues—the critical approach to the Bible, the acceptance of the ecumenical movement, the acceptance of religious freedom, and the acceptance of an evolutionary view of history. "By its actual practice of revision, the Council implicitly taught the legitimacy and even the value of dissent. In effect the Council said that the ordinary magisterium of the Roman Pontiff had fallen into error and had unjustly harmed the careers of loyal and able scholars."[49]

Ecclesiological Reasons

From the perspective of the theology of the Church (ecclesiology), a number of reasons support the possibility of such dissent. The first theological argument is linguistic. The very word "noninfallible" means that the teaching is fallible. If the teaching is fallible, it can be wrong.

The most fundamental ecclesiological reason for the possibility of dissent from noninfallible teaching is the recognition that the teaching function of the Church is broader than the hierarchical teaching function. The primary teacher in the Church is the Holy Spirit. Through baptism all Christians share in the threefold office of Jesus as priest, king, and teacher. Catholic theology has recognized the importance of the *sensus fidelium*.[50] Cardinal John Henry Newman's *On Consulting the Faithful in Matters of Doctrine* is a good example of recognizing the teaching role of all the faithful. The Constitution on the Church of Vatican II speaks of the *sensus fidei*. The whole of God's people share in the prophetic role of Christ. The universal body of the faithful who have received the anointing of the Spirit cannot be mistaken in belief. Vatican II recognizes the supernatural sense of faith in all the people of God. The Spirit distributes charismatic gifts among the faithful of every rank.[51] The Spirit bestows various gifts both hierarchical and charismatic.

Canonists and theologians today recognize the significant role of reception by the whole Church of hierarchical teaching.[52] The neoscholastic notion of the Church as a hierarchical pyramid ignored the role of reception. An ecclesiology of communion now recognizes the important role of reception of Church teaching by the whole Church. Such communion ecclesiology sees a two-way street between the hierarchical teaching office and all the people of God.[53]

In addition to a role of the *sensus fidelium* and the entire people of God, theologians also have a teaching role in the Church. In the medieval period, the triad that provided leadership and direction for the life of society was the *sacerdotium,* the *studium,* and the *imperium.* With the development of universities, beginning in

115

the twelfth century, theologians played an important teaching role in the Church. University schools of theology regularly presented judgments on the orthodoxy of various theological opinions. Theologians participated in even larger numbers than bishops in the Council of Constance (1414–18) and the Council of Basel (1431). By the time of the Council of Trent (1545–63), theologians were clearly only involved in a consultative manner, but they still had a significant influence.[54] The experience of Vatican II illustrates the significant role played there by theologians, even though they had no voting powers in the council itself. In speaking about Vatican II, most commentators give much more importance to the role played by theologians than the role played by individual bishops. In a 1980 article from which he later distanced himself, Avery Dulles discussed the two magisteria in the Church: the hierarchical magisterium and the theological magisterium.[55]

The word "magisterium" itself, until the nineteenth century, referred to the activity of an authority in a particular area, such as military endeavors or teaching. Before the nineteenth century, the term "magisterium" did not refer to what we call the magisterium today—the authoritative teaching role of pope and bishops—although this reality itself certainly existed. One of the reasons for the concentration of the magisterium in the teaching office of pope and bishops was the fact that the university faculties of theology no longer existed after the French Revolution.[56]

In a groundbreaking and perceptive article, Daniel Maguire in 1968, even before *Humanae vitae,* insisted that the word "magisterium" has a plural. There are many magisteria in the Church: papal and episcopal magisteria, the authentic magisterium of the laity, and the magisterium of theologians. Each of these provides a creative service and contributes to the search for the understanding of faith in the life of the community of Jesus.[57] As the years after Vatican II and *Humanae vitae* passed, Catholic theologians in the United States came to an awareness that the hierarchical magisterium does not involve the total teaching activity of the Church.

The changes that have occurred in specific Catholic moral teachings well illustrate the teaching role of the *sensus fidelium* and of theologians. The Declaration of Religious Freedom of Vatican II also recognizes the limits of the teaching role of the hierarchical magisterium. The declaration begins by noting the desires in society for the free exercise of religion. The document takes careful note of these desires and declares them to be greatly in accord with truth and justice.[58] Thus the declaration recognizes that the truth of religious liberty existed before the council adopted this new teaching.

These overlapping teaching roles are necessary for the life of the Church, but inevitably some tensions will always be present. Too often the tension has been expressed as a contest between authority and conscience. But that scenario is too simple. Actually, three terms are involved: truth, the magisterial teaching authority, and conscience. Both the hierarchical magisterium and the individual conscience are seeking the truth. Both can be wrong and have made mistakes in the area of noninfallible teaching.[59]

A third theological argument justifying the possibility of such dissent comes from the shifting understanding at Vatican II of the nature of the Church and the corresponding shift in the understanding of what it means to be an authoritative teacher in the Church. In the pyramidal model of the Church in the pre–Vatican II period, all authority and truth came from the top down. In such an understanding, the teaching role of the hierarchical magisterium was often seen as an exercise of the power of jurisdiction. As a result, the global response of the faithful to this teaching was obedience. The magisterium had the truth and imparted it to the faithful.[60]

In an illiterate society, the teacher is the person who provides answers and solutions for those who are ignorant. Anyone who teaches today in a college or university knows that the ideal teacher is also the one who inspires students to think for themselves. A great problem arises when the concept of teacher becomes closely identified with the concept of jurisdiction or ruling. The concept of "authoritative teaching" tends to tie the teaching and ruling functions in the Church too closely together. The proper response to ruling is obedience, but this should not be the proper response to teaching. One does not obey the teacher. For this reason *obsequium*, the response to noninfallible teaching, should not be called obedience.

Any teacher realizes that she has to learn the truth before she can teach it. This applies also to the hierarchical magisterium. Vatican II pointed out that the hierarchical magisterium is subject to the word of God and must conform itself to the word of God. The hierarchical magisterium, like the conscience of the individual believer, strives to know the truth. The history of the Church illustrates this important reality. In the fourth and fifth centuries, the early Church struggled for an understanding of the basic beliefs of the Catholic faith: the three persons in one God with two natures, human and divine, in the one person of Jesus. But these concepts of person and nature are not found in the New Testament but rather come from Greek philosophy. Only after a long discernment process could the hierarchical Church teach that there are three persons in one God and two natures in Jesus. The hierarchical magisterium learned this truth from others before it could teach it.

The need to learn the truth before teaching it is even more essential in moral matters. Specific moral teachings arise in a particular historical context.

In addition, the Catholic tradition has insisted that much of the moral teaching in the Catholic Church is based on the natural law or human reason. Over the centuries, the hierarchical magisterium changed some of its specific moral teachings. The hierarchical magisterium, with the help of the Holy Spirit, learned much of this teaching from the experience of Christian people. Since specific Catholic moral teachings are often based on human sources of moral wisdom and knowledge, the hierarchical magisterium has to use these sources of reason and experience to learn moral truth.

Reasons from Moral Theology

In addition to historical and ecclesiological justifications for the possibility of dissent, moral theology itself indicates why some specific norms cannot be absolutely certain. As a general rule, the greater the specificity and complexity, the less certitude one can have about a specific norm. In the Thomistic tradition, the secondary principles of the natural law generally oblige but can and do admit of exceptions precisely because of the complexity of the human situation. For example, the hierarchical magisterium has taught that direct killing and direct abortion are always wrong. But the distinction between direct and indirect cannot claim absolute certitude. This distinction is based on one philosophical approach and has been questioned by many others. Conflict situations, by their very nature, are very complex, and it is hard to imagine that one proposed solution can claim absolute certitude.

In addition, Catholic moral theology, to its credit, has insisted on an intrinsic morality—something is commanded because it is good. The will of the legislator or teacher does not make something good. Rather the teacher or legislator has to conform to the good as discovered through human reason. Law for Aquinas is not an act of the will of the legislator but rather an ordering of reason for the common good made by the one who has charge of the community. Such an approach also grounds the possibility of civil disobedience. For Aquinas, the justification of civil disobedience is simple, maybe too simple: An unjust law is no law and is not obliging in conscience.[61] In moral matters, the will of the teacher does not make something right or wrong, but the teacher must conform to right reason.

Other Aspects of Dissent

What about the assistance of the Holy Spirit given to the hierarchical magisterium? The Catholic Church is characterized by its acceptance of mediation—the divine is mediated in and through the human. The gift of the Holy Spirit does not substitute for the normal way of human knowing but rather assists and helps the two human processes of gathering evidence and assessing evidence.[62] The assistance of the Holy Spirit gives a special and distinct importance to the hierarchical teaching office. The hierarchical teaching office is not just another voice in the Church, not just another Catholic theologian or reflective believer. The assistance of the Holy Spirit grounds the special nature of the hierarchical magisterium and is the basis for the presumption in favor of its teaching, but that presumption always cedes to the truth.

The presumption in favor of the hierarchical teaching explains a primary grounding for the use of the word "dissent" when there is disagreement from such teaching. The hierarchical teaching is in place and presumed true unless and until reason and experience convince one to reject this presumption. More than any other American moral theologian, Charles Curran has been identified in theory and in practice with dissent from noninfallible Church teaching. But some people in basic agreement with Curran's positions disagree with his use of the term *dissent*. Kevin Kelly, and later Linda Hogan and Lisa Cahill, have objected to using the term *dissent* because it is negative and associated with opposition and confrontation. Also, the term *dissent* does not recognize all that is positive in this concern for truth, love of the Church, respect for tradition, and commitment to shared responsibility in the Church.[63] Curran recognizes that there are some pejorative aspects connected with dissent, although in our society dissent does not necessarily have only a pejorative connotation. Dissent, which is in the ecclesial order, is analogous to civil disobedience in the civil order and does not involve rebellion and revolution. But the word *dissent* clearly recognizes the presumption in favor of the teaching of the hierarchical magisterium.

Some have maintained that in light of the presumption in favor of authoritative hierarchical teaching, dissent should be a rare phenomenon. But dissent has now become somewhat widespread in moral matters in the Church. Yes, dissent does extend to a number of significant areas, but the same basic factors are involved in all these issues: a questionable understanding of natural law, an unwillingness to accept contemporary experience of the Christian faithful, a failure to dialogue with theologians, and a claim of too great a certitude. The presumption itself is weakened when the hierarchical magisterium fails to carry out the required human activities of amassing the evidence and assessing it.[64]

Proponents of the possibility of dissent from noninfallible Church teachings frequently point out the danger of creeping infallibility on the part of the hierarchical Church. Noninfallible teachings, by their very nature, are fallible. The hierarchical Church should not claim absolute certitude for these teachings. The West German bishops in a 1967 letter gave the following description of noninfallible teaching: "In order to maintain the true and ultimate substance of faith [noninfallible teaching] must, even at the risk of error in points of detail, give expression to doctrinal directives which have a certain degree of binding force and yet, since they are not *de fide* definitions, involve a certain element of the provisional even to the point of being capable of including error."[65] In this context Margaret Farley has recently called for the need for the grace of self-doubt in light of attempts by the hierarchical magisterium to claim too great a certitude for some of its teachings.[66]

In their dissent from *Humanae vitae,* the dissenting Catholic University theologians and others so clearly made the point about the possibility of dissent from noninfallible Church teachings that the U.S. bishops themselves publicly recognized the legitimacy of such dissent under certain conditions. "The expression of theological dissent from the magisterium is in order only if the reasons are serious and well-founded, if the manner of the dissent does not question or impugn the teaching authority of the church, and is such as not to give scandal."[67]

Some Catholic theologians put strict limits on dissent. William E. May recognizes that theologians can propose hypotheses, but they can never suggest that their views are to be preferred to the authoritative teaching of the magisterium. Theologians cannot assume the role of bishops.[68] Michael Novak insists that the Church needs dissenters but that theologians can only propose; the pope and the bishops dispose.[69] The positions developed above in favor of dissent refute these objections.

Public Dissent

Some individuals, including bishops, recognize the legitimacy of private dissent but oppose public dissent. Daniel Pilarczyk refers to those who oppose the Church's teaching openly.[70] William Levada accepts private dissent but not public dissent that places the theological judgment at parity with the magisterium's judgments.[71] Roger Mahony sees dissent existing between the two extremes of private dissent and organized dissent. Church teaching authority must responsibly intervene when theologians propose their personal theory as pastoral practice.[72] In my judgment, this assertion explains why it is important for theologians to call their position "dissent" and thereby recognizes that they are not authoritative teachers in the Church.

Without doubt, the opposition to public, organized dissent referred especially to the dissent from *Humanae vitae,* led by Charles Curran in 1968. More than six hundred Catholic scholars signed a statement maintaining that in theory and practice one could disagree with the encyclical's condemnation of artificial contraception and still be a loyal Roman Catholic. Historians have referred to "three Curran affairs."[73] The first Curran affair occurred at Catholic University in 1967. After a university-wide strike of faculty and students, the board of trustees, who were mostly bishops, at the national Catholic university rescinded their previous decision to fire Curran. The underlying, but never explicitly mentioned, reasons were Curran's liberal positions on a number of issues, especially his disagreement with official Church teaching on contraception.

The second Curran affair was the dissent from *Humanae vitae* in 1968 and its aftermath. The board of trustees of Catholic University called for an academic hearing to determine whether the dissenting professors had violated their various commitments as Catholic theologians teaching at Catholic University by their dissent from the encyclical and by the manner and mode of their dissent. The faculty inquiry board concluded that the professors had acted responsibly and the trustees of Catholic University took no action against them.

The third Curran affair occurred in the 1980s. In 1986, after a seven-year investigation, the Congregation for the Doctrine of the Faith, with the approval of the pope, declared that one who dissents from the magisterium as Curran had is neither suitable nor eligible to teach Catholic theology. The Congregation objected to Curran's generic defense of the possibility of dissent from authoritative noninfallible Church teaching and from his nuanced dissent on such issues as contraception, masturbation, premarital sexuality, divorce, homosexual acts, and abortion. Correspondence between the Congregation and Curran never stated precisely what the Congregation's position was on dissent despite his repeated requests that they do so. Curran continued to defend his dissent on the basis of its conformity with what the U.S. bishops said in 1968: that serious reasons exist to support dissent, that no impugning of the teaching authority of the Church had been made, and that there was no scandal.[74] The Curran affair caused a great stir in the U.S. Church.[75]

The procedures of the Congregation for the Doctrine of the Faith deal only with one's writings and thus the issue of public and/or organized dissent did not explicitly come up in the Vatican's investigation of Curran. But the 1990 "Instruction on the Ecclesial Vocation of the Theologian" from the Congregation for the Doctrine of the Faith condemns dissent understood as public opposition to the magisterium of the Church that causes the Church severe harm.[76] *Veritatis splendor,* the 1993 encyclical of Pope John Paul II, condemns dissent "in the form of carefully orchestrated protests and polemics carried on in the media."[77]

The CUA professors who dissented from *Humanae vitae* defended such public dissent at their academic hearing in 1968–69.[78] Academic practice in the United States at the time fully recognized such public statements signed by professors.

Church documents, including the Decree on the Media of Social Communications of Vatican II, insisted on the right of human beings to information about matters concerning individuals and the community. Theologians have a responsibility to communicate with many people: the pope and bishops, fellow theologians, individuals particularly affected by a specific issue, other members of the academic community, priests and pastoral ministers, and the public. The media invariably contact Catholic theologians to comment on events in the Church. The CUA professors feared that many Catholics would think they had to leave the Church if they did not agree with the condemnation of artificial contraception in *Humanae vitae*. This public dissent from *Humanae vitae* fulfilled the three conditions laid down by the U.S. bishops in their 1968 letter. Such public dissent was for the good of and not in opposition to the Church.

The public dissent of an individual theologian can take many forms: writing in a theological journal, publication in a popular journal, or being quoted in the public media. Organized public dissent involves groups of theologians making public statements. The important public role given to faculties of theology in the medieval period provides strong historical precedent for the public and even the organized role of theologians today.

OPPOSITION TO DISSENT

The strongest opposition to the somewhat widespread dissent of many U.S. Catholic moral theologians and ecclesiologists came from Germain Grisez. In his estimation, the present situation is truly a crisis; this widespread dissent is a cancer growing in the Church's organs and interfering with her vital functions.[79]

To overcome this crisis, Grisez proposed his own understanding of how in practice the roles of theologians and the hierarchical magisterium should function in the Church. Grisez is quite critical of the way Pope Paul VI used theologians and laypeople in the so-called birth control commission. When there is an issue of debate, the pope and other bishops should listen carefully to the theological opinions coming from all sides, then dismiss the theologians and engage in their own teaching efforts in light of the authority given them by the Holy Spirit. The pope should actively engage in this dialogue with all the bishops before making a final judgment.[80] Revisionists reject such a proposal as based on a very juridical model that can never replace the ongoing dialogue that is always required between bishops and theologians.[81]

But Grisez has proposed another position. The Constitution on the Church of Vatican II recognizes the ordinary universal magisterium. Bishops can proclaim

Christ's doctrine infallibly even when dispersed throughout the world, "provided that while maintaining the bond of unity among themselves and with Peter's successor, and while teaching authentically on a matter of faith or morals, they concur in a single viewpoint as that to be held definitively (*tamquam definitive tenendam*)."[82] Grisez maintains that the teaching condemning artificial contraception has been taught infallibly by the ordinary magisterium.[83] The vast majority of U.S. theologians have strongly disagreed with Grisez's contention.[84] Two major questions arise from this discussion: Can a natural law teaching, such as the condemnation of artificial contraception, be an object of infallible teaching? And how does one verify when the conditions necessary for an infallible teaching by the ordinary universal magisterium have been fulfilled?

With regard to the object of infallibility, Catholic scholars after (and even before) Vatican II recognized that the primary object of infallibility is what has been revealed for our salvation, whether explicitly or implicitly, whether written or handed down. The secondary object of infallibility is that which is necessary to safeguard adequately and faithfully expound the deposit of faith or that which has been revealed. Grisez maintains that if the norm against contraception is not contained in revelation, it is at least connected with it as a truth required to guard and faithfully expound the deposit of faith and thereby belongs to the secondary object of infallibility. This teaching has been constantly proposed by the bishops together with the pope as something to be held definitively by the faithful.

The vast majority of Catholic moral theologians and ecclesiologists maintain that teachings based on the natural law do not and cannot belong to the secondary object of infallibility. The determinations of the natural law with regard to specific and complex moral issues are neither formally nor virtually revealed, nor are they so necessarily connected with revealed truth that the magisterium could not defend revelation if it could not teach infallibly in these areas.[85] Here, it seems, Grisez has an unnecessarily and unacceptably broad interpretation of what is necessarily, or strictly and intimately, connected with revealed truth. Among the many theologians holding the majority position is William Levada, now the prefect of the Congregation for the Doctrine of the Faith This position was taken in his 1970 doctoral dissertation at the Gregorian University, written under the direction of Francis Sullivan.[86]

The other question concerns that which is required to verify that something has been taught infallibly by the ordinary universal magisterium. The most significant issue in this discussion concerns the condition that all the bishops must have taught that this matter is to be held definitively by all the faithful. Grisez gives a very broad understanding of the need for teaching something to be held definitively by all the faithful. This means that the point in question is not proposed as merely probable but as certain, not as something optional but as something that bishops are obliged to teach and Catholics are obliged to accept.[87] Francis Sullivan, who taught for many years at the Gregorian University in Rome, and others insist that to be held definitively does not mean just to teach something as a serious moral obligation but to maintain that this position is to be held definitely and with an irrevocable assent by the faithful.[88] To prove the consensus of all the bishops that an assertion is to be held definitely and irrevocably—and not just as a serious obligation—is difficult if not impossible.[89]

All would admit that the majority of publishing Catholic moral theologians recognize the legitimacy of dissent from some noninfallible Church teachings. The divisions, however, within the U.S. Catholic theological community have been institutionalized to a great extent. The major association of theologians, the Catholic Theological Society of America, includes among its members the primary advocates of dissent in the United States, and the society itself is very open to hearing these views. On the other hand, in 1977 more conservative Catholic scholars broke off from the Catholic Theological Society of America and founded the Fellowship of Catholic Scholars. This group, which includes both theologians and nontheologians, commits itself to accepting the teaching of the hierarchical magisterium.[90] The second-largest society involving Catholic theologians is the College Theology Society, whose membership somewhat overlaps with that of the Catholic Theological Society of America. This society, too, is basically very open to dissenting positions in the Church.[91] The major scholarly journals in theology, such as *Theological Studies,* published by the Society of Jesus in the United States, and *Horizons,* the journal of the College Theology Society, open their pages to dissenting theologians. But journals such as *Homiletic and Pastoral Review, Faith and Reason, Linacre Quarterly,* and *National Catholic Bioethics Quarterly* do not publish dissenting positions.

OTHER NATURAL LAW APPROACHES

In addition to the revisionist approach and proportionalism, on the one hand, and the new natural law approach, on the other hand, other authors have continued to accept and defend the generally accepted Thomistic natural law approach that was the primary basis for Catholic understanding in the pre–Vatican II Church. The Notre Dame philosopher Ralph McInerny and the Dominican moral theologian Romanus Cessario well illustrate this use of what they call the "classical Thomistic approach" in supporting the existing teachings of the hierarchical magisterium on contraception and other sexual issues.[92] Thus they disagree in theory with both revisionists and proportionalists and with the new natural law theory of Grisez. In opposition to the revisionists, Cessario refutes the charge of physicalism and the contention that the classical Thomistic natural law needs to be modified in light of personalism and historical consciousness. At the same time, he opposes the new natural law theory for its failure to accept an ontology and metaphysics of human nature. Whereas the revisionists in general reacted negatively to the 1993 encyclical of Pope John Paul II, *Veritatis splendor,* Cessario sees this document as the papal vindication of the classical Thomistic theory. He strongly supports *Humanae vitae* and the teachings of the hierarchical magisterium on issues of sexuality.[93]

At the end of the twentieth century and the beginning of the twenty-first, Jean Porter of the University of Notre Dame proposed a quite different understanding of natural law. Porter pays great attention to the medieval tradition of natural law and the teaching of Thomas Aquinas. Her 1999 *Natural and Divine Law: Reclaiming the Tradition for Christian Ethics* develops the thesis that the scholastic concept of the natural law is distinctively theological. The scholastic concept of natural law reinforces and specifies the theological interpretations of nature that it incorporates. The scholastics ground their understanding of natural law in a particular reading of scripture. Consequently, their understanding is distinctively Christian, not so much in its particular elements as in the overall shape given to those elements as synthesized through a particular reading of scripture. The distinctiveness comes through in the particular aspects of human nature given priority and in the interpretation of moral reasoning and law. The scholastics accept natural law as being rational but at the same time interpret it in terms of a distinctively Christian theology. These medieval theologians and canonists see no incongruity in affirming natural law as the common possession of humanity, in some sense, but still assert its theological distinctiveness.[94]

Porter developed this thesis in her 2005 volume *Nature and Reason: A Thomistic Theory of Natural Law.* Modern and contemporary approaches to natural law both in Protestantism and in Roman Catholicism changed the scholastic understanding by seeing natural law as based on human reason alone and as compelling for all people of goodwill. Porter rejects understanding natural law as based on the order of nature (as in the generally accepted neoscholastic and manualistic approach) and as based on the human mind (the Grisez approach). But Porter is a realist, not a relativist. She appeals to Alasdair MacIntyre's notion of rationality as "tradition guided inquiry." Situating natural law within a tradition calls for recognizing the theological and metaphysical component of that tradition.[95] But Porter insists that her understanding of natural law recognizes some universality and is open to criticism from other rational and theological perspectives.

Russell Hittinger, now at the University of Tulsa, makes the same point that the modernist understanding of natural law based on human reason alone, freed from any theological influence, falsifies the best of the scholastic understanding of natural law. Hittinger recognizes that Catholic approaches in the modern and contemporary period have adopted this understanding of natural law as based on human reason without any theological influence. *Ad extra,* even Church documents understand the natural law in this sense in order to convince the gentiles of the truth of its teaching. *Ad intra,* many Catholics discuss Aquinas's teaching on natural law apart from its important context and relationship to the theological realities found in his understanding of happiness, virtues, and the old and the new law.[96] Questions about this approach will continue as its authors further develop their thesis and its ramifications.

Although Porter and Hittinger agree that natural law is not based on human reason totally separate from any theological influences, they strongly disagree on what natural law calls for in specific cases. Porter does not understand natural law as an attempt to derive a comprehensive set of moral precepts from first principles that are regarded as compelling to all rational creatures. Human nature underdetermines the social conventions and practices stemming from it. Porter understands natural law as a fundamental capacity for moral judgment, not primarily as a set of specific precepts derived from first principles. Natural law more broadly conceived includes specific moral norms, although there is considerable room for both legitimate variation and sinful distortion at the level of particular norms.[97] On specific questions Porter disagrees with the hierarchical teaching on the legitimacy of suicide and of physician-assisted suicide for individuals near death. She also maintains that the early-stage fetus is not a person.[98] On the other hand, Hittinger strongly supports the existing hierarchical Church teachings on all moral issues. Whereas Hittinger strongly supported John Paul II's 1993 encyclical *Veritatis splendor,* referring to the traditionally accepted intrinsically evil moral actions, Porter strongly disagreed with the basis for intrinsically evil moral actions as set forth in the encyclical.[99]

The debate over the theory and applications of natural law in the Catholic tradition continues. As noted above, Curran adopts a revisionist position and dissents from the specific teachings of the hierarchical magisterium on such issues as contraception, sterilization, homosexuality, divorce, and aspects of the principle of double effect. Undoubtedly, the theoretical and practical discussions will continue and perhaps even take on new forms, as illustrated in the thesis of Porter and Hittinger, suggesting that the natural law is based on a theological tradition.

Historians agree that *Humanae vitae* was a very significant event in the life of the Catholic Church in the second part of the twentieth century. Vatican II had a deep and broad influence on Catholic life and theology, but *Humanae vitae* touched on specific issues involving moral theology and thus had a great impact on moral theology. The ensuing discussions in the aftermath of the encyclical focused on three different areas: the morality of contraception and other issues, the natural law theory that was used as the basis for the papal condemnation, and the issue of dissent, in both theory and in practice, from such noninfallible teaching. These three areas have continued to be discussed in Catholic moral theology. The words and actions of the papal and hierarchical magisterium under the papacy of John Paul II focused strongly on these issues. The reactions to the 1993 encyclical *Veritatis splendor* well illustrate the ongoing discussion.[100]

NOTES

1. Pope Paul VI used the expression *la vívida discusión* in a speech delivered to the Second General Conference of Latin American Bishops, held at Medellín, Colombia, on August 24, 1968. See *Acta Apostolicae Sedis* 60 (1968): 639–49.
2. See Shannon, *Lively Debate.* For an in-depth overview of the discussion, see Selling, "Reaction to *Humanae vitae.*"
3. The two moral theologians most identified with revisionism and dissent are Charles E. Curran and Richard A. McCormick. For McCormick's specific developments of particular points, check the index under the appropriate heading (contraception, dissent, historical consciousness, natural law, personalism, physicalism) in McCormick, *Notes on Moral Theology, 1965–1980,* and *Notes on Moral Theology, 1981–1984.* For Curran, see especially Curran et al., *Dissent In and For the Church;* Curran, *Loyal Dissent.*
4. Lonergan, "Transition from a Classicist World-View to Historical Mindedness."
5. Aquinas, *Summa theologiae, Ia IIae,* q. 90, a. 1, ob. 3; q. 96, a. 5, ob. 3; q. 97, a. 2; *IIa IIae,* q. 57, a. 3.
6. McCormick, *Health and Medicine,* 16–18; McCormick, *Critical Calling,* 49–52.
7. Curran, "Natural Law and Contemporary Moral Theology," 172–74. For his latest development of relationality, see Curran, *Catholic Moral Tradition Today,* 60–109.
8. Dorszynski, *Catholic Teaching.* This was originally a doctoral dissertation at Catholic University directed by Francis Connell.
9. Ryan, "Immorality of Contraception."
10. For a fuller development of the moral object of the act, see Porter, "Moral Act in *Veritatis splendor.*"
11. For a systematic study of proportionalism, see Hoose, *Proportionalism;* Hallett, *Greater Good.* For a negative evaluation of proportionalism, see Kaczor, *Proportionalism and the Natural Law Tradition.* For the critical debate occasioned by John Paul II's encyclical *Veritatis splendor,* see Allsopp and O'Keefe, *Veritatis splendor: American Responses;* Wilkins, *Understanding Veritatis splendor.*

12. For an overview of McCormick's position, see Odozor, *McCormick and the Renewal of Moral Theology*, 91–118. For critical but basically favorable analyses of McCormick's position, see Langan, "Direct and Indirect"; Walter, "Foundation and Formulation of Norms."

13. McCormick, "Commentary on the Commentaries," 245.

14. McCormick, *Notes on Moral Theology, 1965–1980*, 720–21.

15. McCormick, "Commentary on the Commentaries," 210; McCormick, *Notes on Moral Theology, 1980–1984*, 63–64.

16. Walter, "Foundation and the Formulation of Norms," 143.

17. Salzman, *What Are They Saying*, 36–44. In this book Salzman gives a good overview of the discussion between revisionism and the new natural law theory.

18. Keenan, "Moral Agent," 39.

19. Kalbian, "Where Have All the Proportionalists Gone?"

20. Germain Grisez, a prolific scholar, has written a three-volume systematic moral theology: *The Way of the Lord Jesus*, vol. 1, *Christian Moral Principles*, vol. 2, *Living a Christian Life*, and vol. 3, *Difficult Moral Questions*. For a very readable, succinct, and accurate summary of his basic theory, see Grisez and Shaw, *Fulfillment in Christ*. For a personal and intellectual overview of Grisez's life and work, see Shaw "Making of a Moral Theologian."

21. Among Finnis's most significant works are *Natural Law and Natural Rights*; *Fundamentals of Ethics*; and *Moral Absolutes, Tradition, Revision, and Truth*.

22. Grisez and Shaw, *Fulfillment in Christ*, 44–48.

23. Ibid., 56–71.

24. Grisez, Boyle, and Finnis, "Practical Principles," provides a good summary of the development of this theory.

25. Grisez and Shaw, *Fulfillment in Christ*, 80.

26. Ibid., 305–14.

27. Ibid., 54–56.

28. For May's many publications, see his home page at www.christendom-awake./org/pages/may/may.html.

29. Curran, *Catholic Moral Tradition Today*, 158–60.

30. Pius XII, "Prolongation of Life," 207.

31. For the history of the contemporary debate over contraception, see Kaiser, *Politics of Sex and Religion*.

32. Grisez and Shaw, *Fulfillment in Christ*, 421. For the position of Curran and McCormick, see note 3, and the following two coedited books: Curran and McCormick, *Magisterium and Morality*, and Curran and McCormick, *Dissent in the Church*.

33. Abbott, "Dogmatic Constitution on the Church," 47–49n25.

34. Bihlmeyer and Tüchle, *Church History*, 250–56, 292–99.

35. Salaverri, *Sacrae theologiae summa*, 710n650.

36. Komonchak, "Ordinary Papal Magisterium," 105–8.

37. Ibid., 108–14.

38. Ibid., 102–3.

39. Ibid., 104.

40. Sullivan, *Magisterium,* 169.

41. Ibid., 158–68.

42. Butler, "Authority and the Christian Conscience," 186.

43. Boyle, *Church Teaching Authority,* 63–78.

44. Örsy, *Church Learning and Teaching,* 85–89.

45. Gaillardetz, *Teaching with Authority,* 268.

46. Noonan, *Church That Can and Cannot Change;* Noonan, "Development in Moral Doctrine."

47. Curran, *Change in Official Catholic Moral Teachings.*

48. Noonan, "Amendment of Papal Teaching," 75.

49. Dulles, "Doctrinal Authority," 264–65.

50. For a bibliography of the abundant literature on this subject in the post–Vatican II Church, see Finucane, *Sensus Fidelium,* 655–89.

51. Abbott, "Dogmatic Constitution on the Church," 29–30n12. See also Rush, "*Sensus Fidei.*"

52. The entire issue *Jurist* 57 (1997) is devoted to reception and communion among churches. See also Pottmeyer, "Reception and Submission"; Coriden, "Canonical Doctrine of Reception."

53. Gaillardetz, *Teaching with Authority,* 227–54.

54. Boyle, *Church Teaching Authority,* 174.

55. Dulles, "Two Magisteria." For his later detachment from this approach, see Dulles, "Criteria of Catholic Theology."

56. Congar, "Brief History," 318–22.

57. Maguire, "Moral Absolutes and the Magisterium."

58. Declaration on Religious Liberty, n. 1, in Abbott, *Documents of Vatican II,* 675.

59. Congar, "Brief History," 328.

60. Gaillardetz, *Teaching with Authority,* 3–30.

61. Aquinas, *Ia IIae,* qq. 90–97; *IIa IIae,* q. 120.

62. McCormick, *Notes on Moral Theology, 1965–1980,* 262–66.

63. Kelly, "Serving the Truth," 479–80; Hogan, *Confronting the Truth,* 176–79; Cahill, "Sexual Ethics," 113–14.

64. McCormick, "Search for Truth," 425.

65. This letter is cited in Rahner, "Dispute Concerning the Teaching Office," 115.

66. Farley, "Ethics, Ecclesiology, and the Grace of Self-Doubt."

67. U.S. Catholic Bishops, "Pastoral Letter on Health and Health Care," 18.

68. May, "Catholic Moral Teachings," 100.

69. Novak, "Dissent in the Church," 124–26.

70. Pilarczyk, "Dissent in the Church," 157–59.

71. Levada, "Dissent and the Catholic Religion Teacher," 146–47.

72. Mahony, "Magisterium and Theological Dissent," 171–73.

73. Wister, "Curran Controversy"; Thomas, "'Final Disposition.'" For Curran's memoir, see Curran, *Loyal Dissent.*

74. For the correspondence between Curran and the Congregation, see Curran, *Faithful Dissent,* 113–287.

75. See Briggs, *Holy Siege.*

76. Congregation for the Doctrine of the Faith, "Instruction on the Ecclesial Vocation," 123–24nn30–33.

77. John Paul II, *Veritatis splendor,* 56n113.

78. Curran et al., *Dissent In and For the Church,* 133–53.

79. Grisez, "How to Deal with Theological Dissent," 456.

80. Ibid., 465–66.

81. Salzman, *What Are They Saying,* 118–24.

82. Abbott, "Dogmatic Constitution on the Church," 48n25. The last six words are the translations given by Grisez and Shaw, *Fulfillment in Christ,* 412.

83. Grisez and Shaw, *Fulfillment in Christ,* 412–16; Grisez, *Way of the Lord Jesus,* 1:839–49.

84. For an overview of the discussion about infallibility and natural law teachings, see Salzman, *What Are They Saying,* 124–39. For the protracted debate between Grisez and Francis Sullivan on this issue, see Grisez, "Infallibility and Specific Moral Norms"; Sullivan, "'Secondary Object' of Infallibility"; Grisez, "*Quaestio Disputata*"; Sullivan, "Reply to Germain Grisez."

85. Sullivan, *Magisterium,* 138–52.

86. Levada, "Infallible Church Magisterium."

87. Grisez and Shaw, *Fulfillment in Christ,* 413.

88. Sullivan, *Magisterium,* 147.

89. The discussion in the United States preceded the documents from the papal magisterium on the understanding of the infallible magisterium mentioned in chapter 4, but these have not affected the substance of the arguments. For a discussion and analysis of these recent hierarchical statements, see Gaillardetz, "Ordinary Universal Magisterium."

90. Hitchcock, "Fellowship of Catholic Scholars."

91. Rodgers, *History of the College Theology Society*; Mize, *Joining the Revolution in Theology.*

92. See McInerny, *Ethica Thomistica*; Cessario, *Introduction to Moral Theology.*

93. Cessario, *Introduction to Moral Theology,* 52–99.

94. Porter, *Natural and Divine Law,* 122–23.

95. Porter, *Nature as Reason,* 63–65.

96. Hittinger, *First Grace.* For an elaboration and development of the positions of Porter and Hittinger, see Mattison, "Changing Face of Natural Law."

97. Porter, *Nature as Reason,* 7–24.

98. Porter, *Moral Action and Christian Ethics.*

99. Hittinger, "Natural Law as 'Law'"; Hittinger, "Pope and the Theorists"; Porter, "Moral Act in *Veritatis splendor.*"

100. See Allsopp and O'Keefe, *Veritatis splendor: American Responses.*

THE AFTERMATH OF VATICAN II
AND OTHER DEVELOPMENTS

The previous chapter dealt with the far-reaching influence of *Humanae vitae* on Catholic moral theology in the United States. This chapter specifies in greater detail the effect of the Second Vatican Council (1962–65) and other developments in Catholic moral theology in general. Areas of fundamental moral theology, sexual, medical, and social ethics will be treated later. The vital ecclesial importance of *Humanae vitae* and the lively debate that ensued focused the attention of moral theology on what has been called "quandary ethics"—the morality of particular acts, such as contraception. Vatican II called for a broader approach to moral theology that included much more than just the consideration of the morality of particular actions. This chapter develops the broader and methodological aspects of moral theology called for by Vatican II.

THEOLOGICAL CONTINUITIES IN VATICAN II

Vatican II proposed some new and different approaches to Catholic theology, but Vatican II also stands in some continuity with the best of the Catholic theological tradition. The council supported and illustrated three significant aspects of the Catholic theological tradition: mediation, catholicity, with its "both-and" approach, and the understanding of the Catholic tradition as a living tradition.

Mediation refers to the fact that the divine is mediated in and through the human. Other names, such as the "incarnational principle," the "sacramental principle," or the "analogical imagination," refer to this same basic reality. Incarnation well illustrates how the divine comes to us in and through the humanity of Jesus. Catholic theology has consistently emphasized the analogy of being. No one has ever seen God, but from what we see on the basis of the goodness of creation and of the human, we can have some understanding of God. Thomas Aquinas proposed five ways by which human reason, going from the human to the divine, could prove the existence of God—a position that not all Catholics today accept. There can be and have been problems with the use of analogy, especially when one forgets that God is only partly like the human and always surpasses the human. The danger always exists of making God in our own image, but still the use of analogy is necessary to understand the God we have never seen.[1]

The theology of the Church found in Catholic tradition and in Vatican II is based on the reality of mediation. God comes to us in and through the visible human community of the Church with its human officeholders. The community of the Church mediates the love of God in Christ Jesus through the gift of the Holy Spirit. God comes to us in and through the Church, and we go to God in and through the Church.

The sacramental system shows the role of mediation. Sacraments are the signs of the reality of our saving encounter with God through the Church. The Eucharist is the heart and soul of the life of the Christian community, where the Christian community gathers around the table for the celebratory meal of the covenant. Thus the Eucharist takes over the human reality of the celebratory meal, which is such a central part of human existence even in these days of fast food. We all look forward to celebrations with family and friends on major holidays, feast days, birthdays, weddings, and even funerals. Other sacraments use the basic human realities of oil and water as signs communicating the saving power of God's love for us. The Catholic use of art, architecture, and music with regard to liturgy and the depiction and expression of the divine shows the importance of mediation.

The theological foundation of natural law theory is grounded in mediation. How do we know what God wants us to do? Do we go directly and immediately to God and ask her? No. The eternal law is the rational plan of God for the world and all creatures. The natural law is the participation of the eternal law in the rational creature. God created all things in accord with God's reason and plan. God now gives us our reason. Through reason, we can reflect on what God has made and discern what God wants us to do. Natural law mediates the eternal law, or the plan of God.[2] Thus natural law has a theological basis, but the criticism of natural law found in Vatican II and elsewhere insists that redemption and sin, and not just creation, must affect how Christians act and live their lives.

The Catholic tradition is also catholic, or universal and all-inclusive. The Catholic tradition embraces all reality and touches all. At times the danger has been that Catholic tradition wanted to control all reality and see it only in direct and immediate service to the good of the Church. Vatican II reversed the older teaching on the unity of church and state that saw the need for the state to be subordinate to and in service to the Church. Conscious of past dangers, the

Pastoral Constitution on the Church in the Modern World insisted on the rightful autonomy and independence of created realities and earthly affairs. Created realities in society enjoy their own laws and values, which must be gradually developed and put to use. But the independence and autonomy of earthly realities does not mean that the temporal order is not dependent on God the creator. When God is forgotten, creation itself becomes unintelligible.[3] Thus this approach is catholic and all-inclusive without, however, denying the legitimate autonomy of all that God created.

The Catholic Church lives out this catholicity and all-inclusiveness. The Church is open to and appeals to all people of whatever race, gender, language, or culture. The Catholic Church is a big church that includes not just saints but sinners also. In this aspect, therefore, the Catholic Church distinguishes itself from the sectarian approach, which emphasizes the Church as a small community of saints who separate themselves from the world and others.

Mediation and inclusivity ground what is perhaps the most characteristic aspect of the Catholic theological tradition—its insistence on "both-and" rather than "either-or" approaches. The "both-and" approaches of the Catholic tradition were recognized and reasserted again in Vatican II. The Catholic tradition insists on scripture and tradition, grace and works, faith and reason, the divine and the human, Jesus and the Church, and Mary and the saints. Some Protestants, such as Karl Barth, had strongly objected to the Catholic "and" and have insisted on scripture alone, grace alone, faith alone, the divine alone, Jesus alone. But the Catholic approach is inclusive.[4]

The acceptance of scripture and tradition opposes the scripture-only approach. This insistence grounds the fact that the Catholic tradition could never be fundamentalist with regard to scripture. (The Catholic problem has been a fundamentalism with regard to papal teaching.) Scripture and tradition mean that the Church must always understand, appropriate, live, and bear witness to scripture in light of the ongoing circumstances of time and place. The Catholic approach recognizes the presence of the Holy Spirit in the Church community and its leaders, helping the Church understand and interpret scripture in light of changing historical and cultural circumstances. The Catholic approach is never content with just citing scripture, because scripture must be seen in light of the ongoing tradition of the Church in changing times and circumstances. The early Christological and Trinitarian councils of the fourth and fifth centuries illustrate the role of tradition as interpreting and bearing witness to scripture in changing historical and cultural circumstances. These councils used the Greek understanding of person and nature to interpret the reality of Jesus and the reality of the Trinity.

Grace and works emphasize the need for both God's gift and the human response. The two must be present.[5] This might be the best place to recognize the danger in the Catholic approach of "both-and," of placing more importance on the second element (works) in the couplet than on the first (grace). At times the Catholic approach so stressed tradition that it did not give enough importance to scripture. Historically Catholics tended to put too much emphasis on works and often fell into the danger of pelagianism or semipelagianism, suggesting that we save ourselves by our own works and actions. Vatican II rightly insisted on the primacy of grace but also the need for the human response.

The Catholic tradition has emphasized the need for both faith and reason. A famous scholastic axiom maintained that faith and reason cannot contradict one another.[6] This does not mean that reason can prove the realities of faith, but the two spheres of faith and reason in principle cannot contradict each other. Catholic theology has often understood itself as faith seeking understanding and understanding seeking faith. The Catholic recognition of the role of reason inspired the founding of universities under Catholic auspices in the Middle Ages. The Catholic tradition has always given an important role to human reason, as exemplified, for example, in the natural law approach. Vatican II strongly supported this insistence on both faith and reason. "If methodological investigation within every branch of learning is carried out in a genuinely scientific manner and in accord with moral norms, it never truly conflicts with faith."[7] In its various documents Vatican II insists on the need for both faith sources of scripture and tradition and reason sources, including human experience and science, as sources of moral wisdom and knowledge.

Catholic theology traditionally has recognized how the divine and the human work together. An old axiom insists that grace does not destroy nature but builds on nature. Catholic theology has also accepted the well-known saying of St. Irenaeus that the glory of God is the human person come alive.[8] The Pastoral Constitution on the Church in the Modern World develops in great detail this emphasis on both the divine and the human. The document begins by asserting the dignity of the human being, who by creation is an image of God.[9] Christ, who is the perfect human being, fully reveals the meaning and supreme calling of the human. The Gospel message is in keeping with the secret desires of the human heart.[10]

The Catholic insistence on Jesus and the Church and Mary and the saints exemplifies the principle of mediation. Without doubt, Catholics have sometimes given more importance to the Church, Mary, and even to the saints than to Jesus. But the Constitution on the Church of Vatican II tried to provide a balanced understanding. The Church is the pilgrim people of God and is consequently a sinful Church, always in need of reform and never fully responding to the gift of the Spirit.[11] The Council also discussed Mary in the document on the Church and not in a special document to emphasize that Jesus alone is the savior and mediator between God and humans.[12]

The emphasis on mediation, catholicity, and "both-and" approaches means that the Catholic tradition is a living tradition and that its moral theology constantly strives to understand what human beings and human communities are called to be and to do in this world. Vatican II's insistence on a continuing and extensive dialogue with other Christians, other religions, sciences, human culture, and human experience demonstrates how a living tradition of moral theology should function.[13] The tradition must always be faithful to the word and work of Jesus, but this striving to be faithful means that the Catholic approach must also be open to the ongoing work of the Spirit in the Church and in the world as well as to all human sources of moral wisdom and knowledge that help us understand the purpose for human beings and human communities.

A MORE THEOLOGICAL APPROACH

As mentioned in chapter 4, Vatican II called for a more theological approach to moral theology than had been present before Vatican II, specifically maintaining that Jesus Christ, grace, faith, and scripture should influence all aspects of Christian being, life, and action. This section shows how U.S. Catholic moral theologians developed the theological aspects of the discipline as mentioned in Vatican II.

Natural law as generally understood in pre–Vatican II theology involved human reason directing us to our end in accord with our nature. As such, it does not explicitly use faith sources of knowledge, but even in that understanding there is still a theological basis for natural law. Natural law is the participation of the eternal law in the rational creature. The eternal law is the plan of God for all creation. Law, as has been shown, for Aquinas and the best of the Catholic tradition is an ordering of reason. God has created all things and has given us our human reason. Human reason reflecting on what the Creator has made can determine how God wants us to use what God has made. Natural law has a theological basis, but Jesus Christ, grace, faith, and scripture do not directly enter into or influence the way in which natural law works.[14] (The thesis of Jean Porter and Russell Hittinger disagrees with this neoscholastic concept of natural law and argues for direct involvement of faith in natural law.)

How precisely do faith, grace, Jesus Christ, and scripture affect and influence the Christian moral person and her actions? The answer to this question in the

Catholic tradition must recognize the role of mediation. Mediation means that grace, faith, and Jesus Christ come to us in and through the human. The post–Vatican II Catholic approach recognizes the role of scripture, Jesus Christ, grace, and faith in moral theology and also the need for human sources of moral wisdom and knowledge.

The emphasis on the theological aspect in post–Vatican II U.S. moral theology follows the trajectory mentioned in chapter 4. In the beginning, the strongest influence was still coming from European theologians whose works were being translated into English, especially Bernard Häring, whose many writings insisted on the theological aspect of moral theology. Comparatively few American theologians wrote in a post–Vatican II perspective, with McCormick and Curran being the most prominent figures. Many older Catholic moral theologians found it difficult to continue writing in the field after Vatican II and *Humanae vitae*. However, theologians writing in the United States in the period of the late 1960s and 1970s, in light of the significant pastoral importance of the issues raised by *Humanae vitae*, gave much attention to such issues. It took almost fifteen years for a somewhat younger group of Catholic moral theologians to begin to make their presence felt. But in the last two decades of the twentieth century, the number of contributing Catholic moral theologians increased exponentially, and the writings in the field grew in both number and depth in all areas, including quandary ethics.

The theological concept of conversion as a basic reality in the Christian moral life illustrates this trajectory. Bernard Häring, even before Vatican II, made conversion a basic aspect of his moral theology.[15] As Häring's student, Curran wrote a long essay in 1966 seeing conversion as the central moral message of Jesus.[16] Walter Conn in 1978 edited a volume of previously published essays on conversion and, in a 1986 book, situated conversion within a pattern of personal development. With a strong dependence on Bernard Lonergan, Conn showed how a critical understanding of conversion can be philosophically grounded in a theory of self-transcendence and empirically controlled by a psychology of development.[17] Also in 1986, Stephen Happel and James J. Walter developed conversion as the Christian foundation for ethics and doctrine.[18] In 1995 Mark O'Keefe wrote a small book that was actually the first single volume dealing explicitly with the relationship of moral theology and spiritual theology. He began by developing conversion as the heart of the Christian life. The unity of moral and spiritual striving is grounded in their common foundation in the experience of Christian conversion. In this work O'Keefe relies heavily on the earlier authors mentioned.[19] Thus, as time went on, more and deeper attention has been paid to conversion and its role in Christian life than ever before.

Scripture

Every moral theologian writing in the post–Vatican II era has recognized the role of scripture in moral theology.[20] In addition, many have explicitly addressed the significant methodological question of how scripture should be employed in moral theology.[21] In keeping with the principle of mediation and the existence of human sources of moral knowledge in addition to scripture and tradition, Catholic approaches generally fall between two extremes. The one extreme sees scripture as providing nearly every detail of moral theology; this is the belief of many fundamentalists who see scripture as revealed morality. The other extreme sees scripture as contributing very little to moral theology, which was basically the position of the pre–Vatican II manuals of moral theology. From the earliest discussions of the role of scripture since Vatican II, a basic continuity exists, but the later discussions develop the issue in depth. There is no need, therefore, to trace any great historical development during this period. The approach developed here will concentrate heavily on the work of William Spohn, who has written more on this issue than any other Catholic moral theologian.[22]

Some of the complexities and problems in the use of scripture in moral theology arise from the need to bring moral theologians into dialogue with the discipline of scriptural studies. Scriptural studies use many different approaches in interpreting the Bible: historical, form, source, redaction, and literary criticism. In addition, different forms of literary criticism are used in different scholarly approaches: structuralism, deconstruction, rhetorical, narrative, sociological, psychological, liberationist, and feminist criticism. Most moral theologians are not trained as biblical scholars and are not competent in these areas.

The general Catholic approach, based on mediation, recognizes the role of the human authors of scripture, with their own gifts and as well as their limitations. The historical and cultural circumstances of the original authors and redactors differ in many ways from the cultural and historical ethos of the present. The hermeneutical issue involves how one goes from the meaning of scripture in its own cultural, historical, and ecclesial contexts to the different historical, cultural, and ecclesial contexts of today. In addition, the moral theologian brings a specific ethical mindset to the question of the role of scripture in moral theology today. One's understanding of moral theology or Christian ethics enters into how one understands the role of scripture in moral theology. Thomas Ogletree, writing from a Protestant perspective, talks about the ethical preunderstandings the theologian brings to the interpretation of scripture and its role in moral theology.[23] David Kelsey develops the very important role of the imagination in bringing all of these aspects together.[24] Protestants have been grappling with the question of the role of scripture for a much longer time than Catholics, and Spohn recognizes their accomplishments and tries to build on the work of these scholars.[25]

The effect of these ethical presuppositions, or preunderstandings, is very evident in how both Protestant and Catholic authors have employed scripture. One who sees the moral life primarily in terms of law or duty (the deontological model), such as Richard Mouw, uses scripture primarily to develop a divine command ethics.[26] H. Richard Niebuhr sees the Bible in light of a responsibility model of ethics, a responsive love on our part toward God and neighbor.[27] Anthony Tambasco, a Catholic scholar at Georgetown University, has compared Juan Luis Segundo's use of the Bible with the approach of some first world moral theologians.[28] Elizabeth Schüssler Fiorenza, the well-known Catholic feminist, makes the ultimate criterion of her acceptance and use of scripture whether or not it supports the dignity and equal role of women and refuses to give any role to the patriarchal aspects found in scripture.[29]

The need to fuse the horizon of the scriptural ethos and the present ethos can easily lead to the problem of eisegesis: reading into scripture what we want to find there. Christians always want Jesus to be on their side, and history has shown that Jesus has been given many different and totally irreconcilable roles over the years. He has been portrayed as a warrior king, a victim of injustice, a violent revolutionary, an exponent of nonviolence, an obedient servant, a capitalist, and a socialist, among other things. All contemporary moral theologians must be conscious of the danger of seeing Jesus only through their own limited vision.

As important as scripture is as a source for moral theology, the use of scripture in moral theology has significant limitations. A unified or a systematic biblical or scriptural ethic is not a reality. The Bible consists of many different books written by different authors in vastly different circumstances over a long period of history. Different authors approach issues and concepts from different perspectives. Take, for example, the very basic Christian moral reality of love. The synoptic Gospels emphasize the twofold commandment of love of God and love of neighbor. Paul speaks of God's relationship to us as love but seldom if ever speaks of our relationship to God as love. For Paul, our relationship to God is one of faith. We must recognize a distinct difference between God's love for us and our love for God. God's love for us is the sheer, total, unmotivated willingness to give and to share, whereas our love for God is a response to what God has first given to us. Our love is definitely motivated by what God has first done for us. The synoptic Gospels emphasize that my neighbor is the person in need, but the Johannine writings emphasize that the neighbor is the sister or brother in the community. John was obviously dealing with a fractious and divided community and insisted on the need for love among the members of that community. The disciples of Jesus apparently understood that the love of friendship, the love of one in need, the love of the enemy, and the love of the sister or brother in the community are quite different realities.

Another problem in interpreting the Gospels and the New Testament is their eschatological expectation. Scriptural scholars often point out that the early Church expected the end of time to come very quickly. Such an approach obviously affects one's attitude toward the moral life. If the end time is coming soon, there is no need to worry about what you are going to eat or drink or wear. Likewise, there is no need for someone to remarry after the death of a spouse.

In addition, most Christians recognize that certain moral teachings found in scripture should not be followed today. The New Testament, for example, accepts slavery and tells slaves to obey their masters. Hopefully no Christian takes such a position today. Feminists have reminded us of the patriarchal aspects of the Bible and the subordination of women to men, which should not be followed today. Another obvious limitation of scripture with regard to moral theology is that many of the concrete issues we face today are new and were never envisioned in scriptural times. For example, stem cell research and all the many technological developments in the area of biomedicine could not have been imagined by the authors of the Bible.

How, then, should scripture be used in moral theology? As mentioned above, the moral theologian brings to this question some presuppositions of the different aspects of moral theology. William Spohn sees the scriptural picture of Jesus as affecting especially the identity of the Christian person and the virtues that characterize that person.[30] I am in fundamental agreement with Spohn, but one can spell out in great detail the presuppositions of moral theology and how scripture influences them. Moral theology includes at least the following aspects: the person as subject and agent, the fundamental orientation of the person, the virtues that modify the person, moral values, principles, norms, and practical decision making. Since the primary limitation on the use of scripture comes from the fact that scripture is historically and culturally conditioned, scripture will have a greater role to play in those areas where there is more communality than in other areas; aspects that are more general than specific will be more relevant.

In ethics, the reality of the person is more important and central than individual acts. The Pauline writings emphasize that we who have received the gift of the Holy Spirit must now walk in the Spirit and produce the fruits of the Spirit in our lives. Thus the character or identity of the person is most significant for moral theology. Scripture says quite a bit about the person, which continues to be applicable for all Christians. The Christian is the one who has received the Holy

Spirit, the one who has been baptized into the paschal mystery of Jesus, the one who has become a disciple of Jesus, the one who has been given a new heart. The Christian person as agent then tries to live out this reality and expresses herself in and through her acts. But the person is also the subject who, by her acts, continues to develop and make herself the type person she is. The next chapter discusses in detail the fundamental orientation or option of the person who is heavily influenced by what is found in scripture.

Scripture also tells us much about the different virtues that should characterize the life of the Christian person and develop the basic orientation of that person. The so-called theological virtues of faith, hope, and love are based heavily on scripture. Also included are the virtues of mercy, forgiveness, gratitude to God, and many others.[31]

Scripture also contributes a great deal to our understanding of the general moral values, such as truth, justice, and human dignity. But more specific values depend more heavily on human reason, human experience, and the human sciences than on scripture. Thus, for example, scripture says much less about the nature of distributive justice and what justice calls for with regard to a fair economic or political system.

Scripture can offer quite a bit to ground some general principles in the Christian moral life, such as the fact that the goods of creation exist to serve the needs of all. But human reason, experience, and human sciences such as economics are all necessary to develop the criteria for judging economic systems such as capitalism. There is much discussion today over the scriptural teaching on homosexuality and how it relates to the contemporary scene. No doubt scripture condemns homosexual acts to some extent, but many scholars point out that the scriptural authors had no understanding of sexual orientation. In effect, they condemned homosexual acts done by heterosexual persons. Thus for persons with a homosexual orientation, homosexual acts in the context of a relationship striving for permanency can be justified today.[32]

Scripture has a greater role to play in the more general aspects of moral theology and a lesser role to play in more specific aspects, where the historical and cultural circumstances are different from those of scriptural times. However, even in the very general areas, scripture alone will never be the only source for human decisions.

Christology

Catholic moral theologians have perceived Christology in two different ways: a Christology from above, starting with the divinity of Jesus, the second person of the Trinity, and a Christology from below, starting primarily from the mission and life of Jesus of Nazareth as portrayed in scripture. Christopher Steck, in his development and basic acceptance of the approach of the Swiss theologian Hans Urs von Balthasar, employs a Christology from above. Christ stands at the center of the drama of salvation, thus realigning all other images, aspects, and events of revelation. Christ the Son's relationship to the Father is obediential, and his earthly mission shows the meaning of Christian existence. We who are incorporated into Christ must now live out this new relationship. To make Christ visible is now the task of all who share in the one body of Christ.[33]

Matthew Lamb, writing from a liberationist perspective and developing a theology of social transformation, employs a Christology from below. Lamb develops the agapaic praxis of the historical Jesus in becoming one with the victims of injustice and oppression. The prophetic and apocalyptic narrative of scripture calls for a disjunctive imminent expectation of redemption by the victims of history. Christians are called to conversion, whereby the revelation of God's identification with victims begins to heal the irrationalities of the manifold biases that have hardened human hearts and darkened human reason.[34]

Spohn focuses on the story of Jesus as found in the synoptic Gospels. Jesus is the concrete universal of the Christian life, the paradigm that guides all Christian living. The Christian is not called to go and do as Jesus did.[35] Rather, the imagination of the Christian moves analogically from the story of Jesus in the Gospels to discern how to act faithfully in contemporary situations. The title of Spohn's book, *Go and Do Likewise,* underscores the need for the analogical imagination to move from the Gospel to the contemporary scene. The authors mentioned here have somewhat different approaches, but, in keeping with their belonging to the Catholic tradition, they accept mediation and recognize that one cannot go from the scriptural Jesus or the Christ to the present reality without mediation through the human. Steck, perhaps more so than von Balthasar himself, insists on the God-given desire for human freedom, which involves the desire to overcome sheer contingency and the desire to gain self-possession through interpersonal love. These longings find their end in, and only in, the human individual's participation in the Christ-form.[36] Lamb develops his solidarity with victims by using a Lonerganian approach and critical theory. Spohn employs the analogical imagination to move from the Jesus of the Gospels to present situations.

Moral Theology, Spirituality, and Liturgy

Only in 1995 did Mark O'Keefe of St. Meinrad Seminary produce the first slim book on the relationship between moral theology and spiritual theology. O'Keefe notes the absence of a large body of literature on the subject and points out that his own work is neither a comprehensive nor a systematic study but rather develops different aspects or facets of the relationship between the two disciplines. As the title, *Becoming Good, Becoming Holy,* indicates, he recognizes the need for the continued existence of both disciplines but argues that the relationship between them must be developed further.[37]

Ever since O'Keefe's small book was published there has been a wealth of material dealing with the relationship between spiritual and moral theology. The first impetus for this discussion is Vatican II's call for a more theological approach to moral theology, and especially the call to all Christians to holiness and perfection. The second impetus is the recognition that moral theology embraces more than quandary ethics, or the morality of particular acts. Contemporary moral theology recognizes that the person, the character, and the virtues are very important aspects of the moral life and of the discipline of moral theology.

Richard M. Gula, an excellent pedagogue from the Franciscan School of Theology at Berkeley who writes primarily for students and interested adult Catholics, has contributed more than any other author in the past decade to the literature regarding the relationship between moral and spiritual theology. His 1999 book, *The Good Life: Where Morality and Spirituality Converge,* developed the basic thesis found in the title. Spirituality is concerned with the wellsprings of our actions. Morality and spirituality cannot be separated into two different spheres. Spirituality affects and shapes the moral person, the person's character, and the virtues that modify the person. Virtue leads us to action by providing a sensitivity and an inclination to do what is right. Gula recognizes there will always be a place for the discussion of duty, principles, and the morality of particular actions, but the person as agent, the character, and the virtues are most significant for the everyday life of Christians. The book develops four basic biblical theses: the individual as image of God, the covenant, discipleship, and a community of friends. In keeping with his practical and pastoral perspective, at the end of each chapter Gula provides a variety of spiritual exercises that can be done individually or, even better, in a small group.

The Call to Holiness (2003), again addressed primarily to an adult Catholic audience, develops Gula's thesis that spirituality without morality is disembodied and morality without spirituality is rootless. We cannot separate our relationship to God (spirituality) from the way we live in the world (morality), for our relationship to God is mediated by the way we respond to all things. A spiritual practice is a deliberate soulful effort to develop one's awareness of and response to God. Spiritual practices are by no means the only factors that influence our character, but spiritual practices, such as prayer and participation in the Eucharist, carry a great potential for changing one's moral life.

James F. Keating has written and edited a number of volumes in the twenty-first century dealing with spirituality and morality.[38] As a former editor of the *Josephinum Journal of Theology*, he has also published articles on this subject in that journal. His aim is to elaborate on how Christian spirituality shapes character, the formation of the person, and moral deliberation, and to bring this important area out from under the shadow of other projects such as debates about moral methodology, moral norms, and Church authority, which have dominated moral theology since Vatican II. The relationship between moral theology and spirituality is not sufficient to sustain the entire content of moral theology, but it is a necessary field of inquiry that has lain fallow for too long. Keating recognizes the important pastoral and practical implications of this approach in order to show how Catholics can embrace the universal call to holiness proposed at Vatican II and grounded in their baptism, in their own parish setting.[39]

Closely connected to the relationship of spiritual theology to moral theology is the relationship between liturgy and moral theology. An in-depth study of this relationship has yet to be written in the United States. The article in the *New Dictionary of Sacramental Worship* is written by Enda McDonagh, an Irish theologian, who has insisted on the theological nature of moral theology perhaps more than any other contemporary English-speaking theologian.[40] The relationship between liturgy and moral theology, however, is obvious. The liturgical celebration forms the character and virtues of the Christian person and calls her to live out in daily life what has been celebrated in the liturgy. Here too the influence of liturgy is precisely in the areas of the formation of the person, character, and virtues, as well as in the recognition of the obligatory call to live out in daily life what has been celebrated.

Much emphasis has been given to the relationship between liturgy and social justice. A good number of edited volumes have appeared on this subject since 1980.[41] The sharing of love and bread and wine in the Eucharist calls for Christians to oppose the individualism so often present in our society and to share bread and wine with one another, especially with those in need, as Jesus first shared with us. Work has also been done on the relationship between liturgy and ecology. As in the case of social justice and liturgy, the faculty of the Chicago Theological Union has produced a volume of essays that address this issue.[42]

In the area of liturgy and social justice, a connection exists between the pre– and post–Vatican II approaches. Virgil Michel, a monk at St. John's Abbey in Collegeville, Minnesota, the founding editor of *Worship* magazine, and one of the founders of the liturgical movement in the United States, strongly insisted on the connection between worship and social justice.[43] His esteemed successor as editor of *Worship*, Godfrey Dieckmann, once told me that his greatest regret was the failure of *Worship* to continue to emphasize the close relationship between liturgy and social justice. The relationship between liturgy and moral theology needs more scholarly and in-depth attention. Catholic moral theologians who strongly disagree on specific issues and methodologies can find general agreement in this area.

The growing literature since 1995 on the relationship between faith and morality, especially seen in the relationship between spiritual and moral theology, has come primarily from scholars who teach in seminaries and theologates. Thus the writing comes from a more pastoral perspective rather than a purely academic perspective. There will always be some tension between the academy and the Church aspects of moral theology. Moral theology needs to serve both publics. The academic aspect of moral theology is very important, but sometimes the academy can lose sight of important pastoral dimensions, as illustrated in the significant dialogue between moral theology and spiritual theology.

The Debate about Unique Christian Moral Norms

Beginning in the late 1960s a discussion arose in Europe and the United States about what is distinctive or unique in Christian morality and in moral theology or Christian ethics.[44] In Germany, two schools of thought emerged: the autonomous ethic and the faith ethic. The autonomy school, associated primarily with Alfons Auer, Josef Fuchs, and Bruno Schüller, maintained that there is no unique, material content in Christian morality. The issue was often phrased only in terms of moral norms. Christian ethics brings to the discussion a new horizon of meaning and intentionality. Schüller, for example, maintains that scripture and the Gospel do not bring new content to morality but only *paranesis* (motivation) or intentionality. The Catholic approach before Vatican II had maintained that its teaching on particular moral norms—contraception, adultery, lying, torture, euthanasia, and capital punishment—was binding on all human beings and available to human reason. The faith ethic proposed by theologians such as Bernhard Stoeckle, Joseph Ratzinger, and Hans Urs von Balthasar insisted that certain aspects of Christian morality, including moral norms, are revealed and therefore unique to Christians. One is not really practicing Christian ethics if one appeals only to the moral order of natural law. Faith sheds a new light on all reality, including the way in which Christians should act.

In the United States, Norbert Rigali was the leading spokesperson for the faith ethic approach, maintaining a distinctive and unique Christian morality that is unavailable to the nonbeliever. Rigali has consistently insisted that Vatican II called for a moral theology to show how faith, grace, and Jesus Christ affect all that we do. Although he has not written a monograph on moral theology and spirituality, Rigali has been a significant voice in this area. Charity calls for some Christian secular obligations that are not based only on natural law but are found uniquely in revelation and in faith.[45] Rigali developed his position over the years in explicit dialogue with Richard McCormick and Charles Curran. Both McCormick and Curran held that there is no unique moral content with regard to the norms of Christian life in this world, what Rigali himself called "essential morality" and which is required of all human beings.[46] McCormick clearly follows Schüller in claiming that Christ added nothing new or unique to these claims that are considered obligatory for all people. At this level there is material identity between Christian moral demands and those proposed by reason. The Bible and faith give us an intentionality and a way of looking at the human as well as *paranesis* and motivation. Christian faith gives one a particular access to the human, but the ultimate reality consists of human norms, required of and accessible to all.[47]

Curran, who began the discussion on social ethics in the United States, also maintained that the moral norms proposed for all Christians living in this world are open to discussion by all human beings. For example, the teachings proposed in papal social encyclicals are also addressed to all people of good will. Curran, however, recognized the role of grace in affecting morality but held that grace can exist in all people of goodwill. In addition, he maintained that the scriptures contain more than motivation or intentionality.[48]

This discussion was intimately related to the sharp disagreement among Catholic theologians about the hierarchical magisterium and the possibility of dissent from noninfallible moral teachings. Auer and Ratzinger explicitly raised this connection. Auer and other supporters of the autonomy school basically disagreed with the papal teaching on contraception and appealed to human reason to refute it. Auer also maintained that statements by the magisterium would become less necessary the more autonomous morality offered reasonable arguments. Ratzinger in response went so far as to claim that the autonomy school has no place at all for the magisterium.[49]

This same connection between dissent and the magisterium also existed in the American debate. Rigali disagreed with the majority report of the birth control commission under Paul VI precisely because it and later dissenters did not take into account the role of charity or Christian love in the moral life. Christian morality is concerned with doing the will of the Father and following Christ. Contraception is incompatible with Christian perfection and involves a morally negative aspect. However, we are all striving for perfection, and no one is obligated to do the impossible. Thus Rigali recognizes that some Christians are not obligated by the ban on contraception. Moral theology must be the science of the life of Christ and truly be theology and not just philosophical ethics.[50] It should be noted here that thirty years later, in 2004, Rigali continued to insist, especially on the basis of historical consciousness, that Christian ethics must be a theological discipline based on the vocation of the follower of Jesus. He claims that the pre–Vatican II moral theology and revisionist approaches were not theology at all but merely philosophy. However, Rigali seems to move away from the radicalism of his own statement by praising the work of Bernard Häring and Richard Gula, who are often classified as revisionists.[51] Part of the problem might come from different understandings of who is a revisionist, but today all the Catholic moral theologians mentioned in this book insist that they are students of theology.

The discussion about a distinctive or unique Christian morality finally faded in the 1990s. In my judgment it was helpful in clarifying the role and limitations of the hierarchical magisterium and in recognizing that Christians can and should dialogue with all others about morality and work with all others for a more just human society. In our religiously diverse world, there is a place for Catholic teachings addressed to all people of good will that propose values, attitudes, and principles that all should follow. But the discussion itself looked only at the human act considered in the abstract and did not consider the relationship between the human act and the human actor. Existentially, the Christian person formed in the Christian life, but also informed by human reason and experience, performs the act. The next chapter develops an understanding of the moral person considered both holistically and relationally.

ECUMENICAL ASPECTS

Vatican II's decree on ecumenism opened the door of Roman Catholicism to dialogue. Mention has already been made of the historic 1963 Roman Catholic–Protestant Colloquium sponsored by Harvard University. After Vatican II the ecumenical dialogue was present in all Catholic theology, but moral theology, perhaps more than any other branch of theology, quickly became ecumenical and has grown in this ecumenical dimension over the years.

A primary reason for the rapid development of ecumenical dialogue and moral theology came from the openness of the leading Protestant Christian ethicists (Protestants usually refer to the discipline as "Christian ethics," whereas Catholics use the term "moral theology") to such dialogue and the fact that they were already familiar with the Catholic tradition. Paul Ramsey, in his 1961 book on war, depended heavily on the Catholic theory of the double effect and titled one chapter "The Just War and Contemporary Roman Catholic Thought."[52] James Gustafson, the other leading figure in Protestant Christian ethics, was very familiar with Aquinas as well as with European developments in moral theology before the council, as illustrated in the work of Gerard Gilleman, Bernard Häring, and Dietrich von Hildebrand.[53] Paul Lehmann, in his 1963 book, showed an awareness of pre–Vatican II developments in European Catholic moral theology.[54] These Protestant theologians thus welcomed a dialogue with Catholic moral theologians. Curran, Häring, McCormick, and Milhaven contributed essays to the 1968 volume *Norm and Context in Christian Ethics,* edited by Ramsey and his younger colleague, Gene Outka. McCormick opened "The Notes" on moral theology to ecumenical dialogue and later edited an important book with Ramsey on moral norms.[55] Curran published a monograph in 1973 on Ramsey's work, pointing out that although Ramsey often agreed with Catholic conclusions, his deontological methodology differed greatly from the Catholic approach.[56]

No Protestant scholar illustrates the thoroughly ecumenical aspect of Catholic moral theology better than James Gustafson. His significant *Protestant and Roman Catholic Ethics: Prospects for Rapprochement* (1978) has already been mentioned. At Yale, Chicago, and Emory universities, Gustafson directed the doctoral dissertations of more than twenty Catholic moral theologians, almost all of whom have published extensively and made significant contributions to moral theology. No Catholic moral theologian in the United States in the latter part of the twentieth century even came close to directing that number of dissertations by future Catholic scholars. Today one cannot study Catholic moral theology without dialogue with Protestant Christian ethicists. There has also been some dialogue with Jewish ethicists and lately a broader dialogue with other religious traditions.[57]

The academic society called the Society of Christian Ethics shows the ecumenical nature of moral theology today. What is now called the Society of Christian Ethics officially came into existence in 1959 as a small group of professors of social ethics in Protestant seminaries. Some Catholics first joined the society in 1964 and 1965. Charles E. Curran became the first Catholic president in 1971. Today, about one-third of the membership is Roman Catholic, and many Catholics have served as officers and presidents of the society.[58]

The ecumenical dimension has been present in Catholic moral theology since Vatican II. The vast majority of the first post–Vatican II generation of Catholic moral theologians primarily addressed the Catholic tradition and the Catholic community but often included an ecumenical perspective. The major exception to this tendency to speak primarily to the Catholic community is Daniel C. Maguire, who, throughout the twentieth century and into the present century, has written primarily for the broader Christian community and the broader landscape of Christian ethics as such. Maguire, who has spent most of his career at Marquette University, in 1981 became the second Catholic to serve as president of the Society of Christian Ethics. His prolific writings and lively writing style (few moral theologians would dare write in an introduction that books on ethics don't have to be dull!)[59] have made him a respected figure in Christian ethics.

His 1978 book *The Moral Choice* addresses the broad discipline of Christian ethics in general rather than the narrower discipline of Catholic moral theology. In chapter 4 I mentioned some of his earlier writings that were directed primarily to internal Catholic issues. But even in addressing a wider audience Maguire continues to rely on aspects of the Catholic tradition, as he illustrates by citing Thomas Aquinas much more than any other author. Maguire's major contribution in this book and throughout his writings has been his emphasis on the role of creative imagination, feeling, and affectivity. The book develops his "wheel model" of ethics, with the hub or center containing the reality-revealing questions that supply the facts or data of the moral situation. He then develops the nine spokes of moral evaluation. Creativity is the most important spoke for Maguire, but he is neither a relativist nor a reductionist. The other spokes are principles, reason, authority, affectivity, individual experience, group experience, comedy, and tragedy. Unfortunately, Maguire does not detail the possibility of conflicts between and among the different spokes.

Maguire is the most liberal of contemporary Catholic moral theologians. Many have challenged him, but all have learned from him. His 1974 *Death by Choice* argues for the legitimacy of euthanasia. His 1980 *A New American Justice: Ending the White Male Monopolies* makes an early and well-developed case for affirmative action. In a number of books he has emphasized what he calls the revolutionary aspect of the basic Judeo-Christian message. Within this classic tradition Maguire claims to find thermal energy that is retrievable and can create a new moral landscape, contributing to the saving of us, our children, and our environment.[60] Since the 1990s Maguire has served as president of the Religious Consultation on Population, Reproductive Health, and Ethics. This group supports family planning by means of contraception, with access to safe abortion as an option when necessary, and has published a number of books that support such an approach, including an edited volume of scholars from all world religions.[61]

The second and third generations of post–Vatican II moral theologians have continued in similar ways. Some write from a broader Christian perspective to a broader Christian and human audience. Some still continue to address specifically Catholic issues and Catholic audiences, but even here they bring an ecumenically oriented perspective to their work. Many address both audiences in their writings.

HISTORICAL STUDIES

In the post–Vatican II period, a growing number of studies on the history of moral theology have appeared. The Vatican II emphasis on historical consciousness probably made some contribution to the growing interest in history. But a more scholarly approach to the discipline was an important factor in encouraging historical studies.

In addition to many other historical and legal publications, John T. Noonan Jr., a legal scholar and retired judge, wrote long scholarly books on historical development and change with regard to usury, contraception, the indissolubility of marriage, and slavery, as well as on religious freedom. Noonan's 1957 book on usury showed that before the sixteenth century a series of popes, three general councils of the Church, and all bishops taught that everywhere and always, usury, the making of profit on a loan, is a sin. But by 1589 the new theological position, based on the experience of Christians and changing historical realities, replaced the official papal teaching. This newer approach of accepting usury, however, was formally acknowledged by the papacy only in the eighteenth century.[62] Noonan's history of contraception, published in 1965, was very timely. He served at that time as a special historical consultant to the papal birth control commission. Noonan concludes his exhaustive study by showing how the moral norm prohibiting contraception was based on protecting five important values: procreation, education, life, personality, and love. "About these values a wall had been built; the wall could be removed when it became a prison rather than a bulwark."[63]

On the indissolubility of marriage, Noonan showed how canonical practice developed so that in the Church today the only indissoluble marriage is the consummated marriage, properly entered into, between two baptized persons.[64] The vast majority of marriages in the world today are thus dissoluble, despite the continuing teaching of popes that from creation God intended the indissolubility of marriage. The Declaration on Religious Freedom of Vatican II involves a flat rejection of propositions once taught by the ordinary magisterium on religious freedom.[65] Vatican II's teaching that slavery is intrinsically evil was the first categorical condemnation by the Church of an institution with which it had lived and that it had permitted for more than nineteen centuries.[66] Noonan succinctly summarizes the conclusions of his extensive historical research as follows: "What was forbidden became lawful (the cases of usury and marriage); what was permissible became unlawful (the case of slavery); and what was required became forbidden (the persecution of heretics)."[67]

The edited volume *Change in Official Catholic Moral Teachings* (2003) contains essays on the issues discussed by Noonan as well as the historical changes that have occurred in other areas, such as democracy, human rights, the right of the accused to be silent, capital punishment, marriage and sexuality, family, the role of women, and also changes in anthropology and methodology in Catholic social teaching. These changes support the need for a historically conscious methodology in moral theology. Scholars like Noonan are also beginning to discuss exactly how development and change occur in Catholic moral teaching. Obviously, the *sensus fidelium* has played an important role in this consideration. Human experience is an important factor, but of course raw experience can be wrong and needs to be evaluated in light of a proper understanding of the human and of the Gospel. Change in particular moral teachings also points out the lack of certitude in concrete moral norms and supports the legitimacy, and even the necessity, of dissent from noninfallible moral teachings.

Other significant historical studies have also appeared. The work of Jean Porter on natural law in the medievalists and Aquinas has already been mentioned. As might be expected, quite a bit of historical work has been done on Aquinas.[68] John F. Dedek published four articles between 1977 and 1983, often working from manuscripts, that trace the teaching of Catholic theologians from Peter Lombard to Durand of St. Pourcain on moral absolutes. Dedek concluded that the contemporary Church teaching on intrinsically evil acts was not the teaching of Thomas Aquinas but an innovation by the anti-Thomist Durand of St. Pourcain.[69] In 1982 Charles E. Curran published an overview of Catholic social ethics in the twentieth century in the United States, and in 1997 a monograph on the origins of Catholic moral theology in the United States.[70] In the 1980s Theodore Mackin wrote three monographs on aspects of the history of marriage.[71] Julia Fleming, in a 2006 book, maintains that the commonly accepted appraisal of the seventeenth-century moralist Juan Caramuel as "The Prince of Laxists" is without foundation.[72] In the future, we will undoubtedly see more historical studies.

Walter J. Woods's *Walking with Faith: New Perspectives on the Sources and Shaping of Catholic Moral Life* differs diametrically from most of the historical writings that have appeared in the post–Vatican II period. Its primary aim is not moral theology itself but moral life in the faith community. He is not interested in issues of behavior or even in theological methodology, but still his work has important ramifications for moral theology. From the time of the Old Testament to Vatican II, Christian moral life has developed in light of the changing historical and cultural circumstances in which it has been embedded. The sources that have shaped the Christian moral life throughout Christian history primarily are faith, scripture, sacramental practice, intellectual currents both within and outside the Church, and relationship with the broader society in which the Church exists.

FEMINIST APPROACHES

Perhaps the most significant development in post–Vatican II moral theology has been the large number of women who have become moral theologians. Over time their numbers have grown, and the percentage of religious women has decreased. Almost all Catholic women who are moral theologians have adopted some type of feminist approach, but one does not have to be a woman to be a feminist or to employ a feminist methodology.

Catholic feminists follow the same basic methodology, which is based on a liberation model, beginning with the experience of oppression. The oppression in this case is patriarchy, the domination by men that has severely affected the role of women in all areas of life. Feminist methodology proposes two steps. The first is the hermeneutic of suspicion that unmasks the patriarchy that has colored all aspects of human existence. Patriarchy has also affected the Bible, and Catholic feminists cannot accept as the revealed word of God what denies the equal dignity and role of women. The structures of the Catholic Church today continue to be heavily patriarchal. Some feminists have left the Catholic Church because of its patriarchy, but there are a good number of Catholic feminists struggling to overcome patriarchy and reform the Church. In many ways Catholic feminists are on the cutting edge, working for renewal and change in the Church. The second step in the methodology is the hermeneutic of retrieval, or recovery, which then attempts to build a more just and equitable moral and social framework for all human beings as well as a conscientious regard for the environment.

Thus social location has a very significant place in feminist methodology. In some cases, those advocating the importance of the role of social location deny the possibility of any kind of universal considerations and adopt a radical postmodernist approach. But feminist moral theologians of the Catholic faith, in keeping with the Catholic tradition, generally recognize the need for an ethic that is inclusive and has some universal aspects about it, such as the recognition of fundamental human rights for all.

Margaret A. Farley wrote her doctoral dissertation on commitment under James Gustafson, began teaching full time at Yale University in 1972, and recently retired from an endowed professorial chair at Yale. As the senior woman moral theologian in the United States, she has participated in most of the internal debates facing the Catholic Church. She has disagreed with the hierarchical teaching on issues of contraception, sterilization, divorce, and homosexuality. But she has also written from this broader perspective of Christian ethics, as illustrated in her latest book on sexual ethics.[73] In the December 1975 special issue of *Theological*

Studies, Farley wrote one of the first articles on feminist ethics in a scholarly Catholic publication.[74]

Farley was one of twenty-four Catholic women religious who, with others, signed a statement printed as an advertisement in the *New York Times* on October 7, 1984, pointing out the legitimate diversity of opinions among Catholics on abortion and opposing legal restrictions on abortion. The cardinal in charge of the Vatican office on religion wrote to the superiors of the religious women involved and demanded a public retraction. Twenty-two of the religious women who signed, including Margaret Farley, found a way to settle the matter with the Vatican without making a public retraction.[75] Farley's address as president of the Catholic Theological Society of America in 2000 strongly objected to the policy of U.S. bishops who placed opposition to abortion at the center of the Church's political agenda and thus marginalized other important issues.[76] With regard to the claim of the hierarchical Church that it has the assistance of the Holy Spirit in its teaching of moral matters, Farley has called for all participants in the Church to pray for the grace of self-doubt and epistemic humility.[77]

Farley makes the human experience of oppression the starting point of her feminist ethics. In her anthropology, autonomy is very important, but it must be balanced by relationality to avoid one-sided individualism. She strongly opposes complementarity between the sexes and role differentiation because such complementarity never means equality. Farley proposes a universal ethic that seeks equality and justice for all people.[78] In keeping with the Catholic emphasis on "both-and," she tries to overcome polarized disputes by insisting on the two ethical realities of compassion and respect.[79]

Lisa Sowle Cahill, another doctoral student of James M. Gustafson, has taught at Boston College since 1976 and has been elected to the prestigious American Academy of Arts and Sciences. She has written on a wide variety of topics in moral theology, and her many books, edited volumes, and articles make her an important figure in this discipline. She has written significant articles and monographs on sexuality, medical ethics, and the family.[80] Her 1994 book *Pacifism and Just War* traces this debate in Christian theology and the contemporary discussion while developing her own option for a pacifist position.[81]

Cahill has written extensively on method in Catholic moral theology, and in this area she has been in dialogue with feminist ethicists. Cahill insists that feminist theology and ethics are thoroughly particular, historical, and concrete, but she also maintains that feminist ethics calls for an equal personal dignity, justice, and social power for women and men. She feels that some feminists under the influence of postmodernism and deconstructionism deny any possibility of the universal. At the same time, Cahill wants to move away from the manualistic natural law approach, with its emphasis on abstract essentialism, a priori reasoning, and deduction. Cahill chooses historical consciousness and the inductive ethical approach in the best of the Artistotelean-Thomistic tradition. Truth claims, especially through praxis and prudence, can be grounded in the culturally mediated and reliable stratum of common human experience.[82] Cahill has shown an admirable depth in dealing with a broad range of issues—methodology, the foundation of moral norms, sexuality, social ethics, and bioethics.

In 1985 Barbara Hilkert Andolsen of Monmouth University and Christine Gudorf of Florida International University, together with Mary Pellauer, edited one of the first readers in feminist ethics that focused on the broader Christian rather than just the Catholic perspective.[83] Andolsen has explicitly considered the notion of Christian agape, pointing out the danger from a feminist perspective of seeing love and the moral life totally in terms of self-sacrifice.[84] Likewise, she is critical of associating women with an ethic of care.[85] Andolsen has recognized the importance of some significant justice issues—racism in American feminism and a feminist critique of changes in clerical work.[86] One book centers on economic insecurity and the new job contract, with a closing chapter on the Eucharist, solidarity, and justice.[87] From her Christian-feminist perspective, Andolsen thus brings together a concern for justice across the board, especially for workers. She writes for both the Catholic community and the broader Christian and human community.

Christine Gudorf published her doctoral dissertation in 1980 on Catholic social teaching and liberation theology, which also included a final chapter on papal teaching on women.[88] In addition to proposing a sexual ethic for a broader Christian audience, she has also developed the liberation theme in a book on Christian complicity in victimization.[89] Gudorf, in conjunction with others, has also been involved in two books proposing the case method, or casuistic approach, as a good way of presenting both Christian ethics and world religious ethics in a cross-cultural perspective.[90] Thus Gudorf has a broad agenda, addressing methodological, sexual, and justice issues from the perspective of Christian ethics in general, but she also writes on specifically Catholic issues.

In the 1975 special issue of *Theological Studies* on women, Anne E. Patrick of Carleton College surveyed the significant literature on women and religion from 1965 to 1974.[91] Patrick's major work, *Liberating Conscience* (1996), discusses from a feminist and liberationist perspective important aspects of Catholic moral theology: community, authority, obedience, sexuality, language, and the common good. As the first feminist president of the Catholic Theological Society of America (1989–90), she emphasized the need to hear new voices in theology, especially the voices of minorities.

Sidney Cornelia Callahan, with an academic degree in psychology, has been a significant voice in Catholic thinking and theology for five decades. She has discussed issues of the day and spiritual concerns in her many writings, especially as a columnist for *Commonweal* magazine. Her most significant contribution to moral theology is her 1999 book *In Good Conscience,* which calls for a holistic understanding of conscience that recognizes the roles of grace, reason, and the affective and emotional aspects of the human being. Callahan maintains that gender identity makes no essential difference in moral decision making, but that women have different life experiences that may predispose them to moral decisions different from men's.[92] Callahan's most explicitly feminist writings insist on the need for feminists to adopt a prolife position on abortion and related issues.[93]

New Catholic feminist authors have appeared in the last two decades. Susan Ross of Loyola University of Chicago has emerged as a significant Catholic feminist voice. She has written primarily in the areas of liturgy and sacramentality but also has touched on ethics, sexuality, and justice.[94] Christine Firer Hinze has brought a feminist perspective to the analysis and criticism of aspects of Catholic social teaching.[95] Maura Ryan has used a feminist perspective to study assisted human reproduction and its related technologies.[96] In keeping with the best of the Catholic "both-and" approach, Cristina Traina has sought to find a compatibility between natural law and feminism, and Susanne DeCrane has discussed the common good in light of Aquinas and feminism.[97] Patricia Beattie Jung, as well as many authors already mentioned, has written on sexual ethics, which will be discussed below.[98]

The main voices of Catholic feminists first came into existence in the 1970s, but there can be no doubt that feminist ethics plays a major role in contemporary Catholic moral theology. These feminist ethicists have made an important contribution to all aspects of Catholic moral theology.

APPROACHES FROM OTHER SOCIAL LOCATIONS

The feminist perspective was the first distinctive new voice in Catholic moral theology in the second part of the twentieth century. By the end of the twentieth century, Hispanic and Latino/a theologies had become a significant part of the Catholic scene. Hispanic and Latino/a theology share with feminist theology a common foundation in liberation theology, beginning with the experience of the marginalized and oppressed. This theology, like feminist theology, also blurs the boundaries of moral theology and perhaps even questions the present division of theology into such areas as systematic, moral, liturgical, and historical. A liberation theology, by its very nature, addresses how people can and should live and act. The vast majority of Latino/a theologians identify themselves as systematic theologians.[99]

Virgilio Elizondo is the grandfather of Hispanic theology in the United States. He has been a longtime member of the board and editor of many volumes for the international journal *Concilium*, but his approach to theology is primarily pastoral. He was one of the founders and the president of the Mexican American Cultural Center in San Antonio, a Catholic institute for multicultural pastoral training. He served as rector of the Cathedral of San Fernando in San Antonio from 1983 to 1995. In addition to his many edited volumes and articles, he has written more than ten books and currently holds an endowed professorship in pastoral theology at the University of Notre Dame.[100]

Elizondo has developed a *mestizaje* theology. He recognizes a "double *mestizaje*"—the first being the *mestizo* of Spanish and indigenous people, and the second coming from the U.S. conquest of Mexican territory, where many Hispanics now live. *Mestizos* are neither Spanish nor indigenous, neither Mexican nor American. Growing up in San Antonio, Elizondo experienced what it meant to be a *mestizo* and consequently what it meant to be marginalized. In his theology he reflects on Jesus the Galilean as a *mestizo* who spoke from what was, from a Judean perspective, the marginalized and despised land of Galilee. Jesus comes with a message of inclusion and liberation, which will break down exclusion and the power of oppression.[101] Elizondo's 1988 book *The Future Is Mestizo,* which has gone through six editions, calls for a cosmic *mestizaje* in the world—a breaking down of all barriers of oppression and racism, with an inclusivity in the midst of the diversity of all races and cultures. Elizondo emphasizes the role of Our Lady of Guadalupe as a liberating icon for all *mestizos.* As rector of the Cathedral in San Antonio he has incorporated traditional aspects of popular piety such as the *posadas,* the taking up of the Christ child, and the Day of Death as liberating celebrations for Hispanic people.[102]

The growth of the Latino/a theology at the end of the twentieth century owes much to the institutional support subsequently given to such theology. In the late 1980s the Academy of Catholic Hispanic Theologians of the United States (ACHTUS) came into existence. The academy tries to provide a theological voice for the lived faith of U.S. Hispanics, who are rapidly becoming a very important part of the Catholic Church in the United States. In 1993 the academy began publishing a peer-reviewed theological quarterly journal, *Journal of Hispanic-Latino Theology.* The academy and the journal have stimulated the growth of Hispanic and Latino/a theology, which will only increase in the coming years. Since 1989 the academy has awarded the Virgilio Elizondo Award to an individual for distinguished achievement in theology in keeping with the themes of the academy. ACHTUS members, including Orlando Espin, Miguel Diaz, Alex Garcia-Rivera, Roberto Goizueta, Timothy Matovina, Alberto Lopez Pulido, Fernando F. Segovia, and Francisco Lozada have published significant books in this area.[103]

Ada Maria Isasi-Díaz has been the most significant voice in the Latina community to write from the perspective of moral theology. Isasi-Díaz, a Roman Catholic Cuban exile, received her Ph.D. from Union Seminary in New York, writing under the tutelage of Beverly Harrison, and now teaches at Drew University. She first coined the term "*mujerista* theology" to describe her Latina perspective as distinguished from the feminist theology coming from mainly white middle-class first-world women and the womanist theology of black women. As a liberation theology, *mujerista* theology arises from the experience of oppression and calls for a liberating praxis to overcome the exploitation, marginalization, and powerlessness of Latina women. An important part of her method is hearing the stories of Hispanas and Latinas. These women are to be the subjects of their own *mujerista projecto histórico*. The stuff of this *projecto* is *lo cotidiano*—the daily life of these women. This *mujerista projecto histórico* is a utopian project. Utopias serve as a condemnation of the present order and the proclamation of a new and better order. But Isasi-Díaz sees this as a struggle—*la lucha*. This liberation is the unfolding of the kin_dom of God. She does not use "kingdom" because of its sexist and class connotations. "Kin_dom" includes the notion of community and shared responsibility. Throughout her work she puts great emphasis on family and community. In her earlier writings she referred to this *lucha* as the struggle for survival.[104] She later referred to the struggle for the fullness of the human, "life-liberation."[105] Other authors from the Latina perspective include Jeanette Rodriguez, who has written on the struggle of Mexican-American women and their spirituality.[106] Maria Pilar Aquino has written about the struggle of women in the broader Latin American world outside the United States.[107]

Black Catholic theologians have only recently emerged in the Catholic Church. Whereas the vast majority of Hispanics in the United States are Catholic, the vast majority of blacks are not. This demographic helps to explain the late emergence of black Catholic theology and the relatively small number of black Catholic theologians today. Bryan Massingale, who writes as a moral theologian, has pointed out the failure of Catholic moral theologians in the United States to deal with the evil of racism in the post–Vatican II period.[108] In December 2000 *Theological Studies* invited a team of black Catholic theologians to reflect on the painful neglect of the evil of racism by Catholic theologians in general and by *Theological Studies*. This invitation was occasioned by the thirtieth anniversary of the publication of James Cone's *Black Theology of Liberation*.[109] Chapter 10 of this book discusses racism in detail.

Massingale is the only black Catholic moral theologian writing today, but other black Catholic scholars have been developing a black theology. Cyprian Davis's 1990 *History of Black Catholics in the United States* made people aware of the black Catholic presence and its historical development. A small number of black women theologians have made significant contributions to the developing black Catholic theology. These Catholic theologians have brought a black liberationist and womanist perspective to their theology. Jaime Phelps has edited two respected volumes and gives special attention to areas of systematic theology, including inculturation, Christology, ecclesiology, and grace.[110] More than anyone else, Diana Hayes has developed a Catholic womanist theology. She maintains that the black Catholic tradition is a proper source for doing liberation theology by developing a womanist theology that has a special place for Mary, the bold woman who challenged societal norms.[111] M. Shawn Copeland, who was the editor of the *Theological Studies* special issue on black theology in 2000, has written more than seventy articles emphasizing the role of method. Copeland recognizes four elements in black Catholic theology: critique, retrieval, construction, and social analysis.[112]

A NEW GENERATION

At the turn of the century some people started talking about a new generation of moral theologians who lived in and responded to new situations and new times.[113] These younger scholars were not even born at the time of Vatican II and *Humanae vitae*. Some feel the need to go beyond the conservative-liberal split that has characterized Catholic moral theology since *Humanae vitae*.

As the previous chapter pointed out, the issues sparked by the debate over *Humanae vitae*—norms in sexual ethics and dissent from hierarchical Church teaching—preoccupied most Catholic moral theologians for years. But, in fairness, both sides have recognized that moral theology must look into more than quandary ethics and dissent. Both sides recognize the need for a theological perspective and the importance of the moral person and her virtues. Germain Grisez's three-volume moral theology addresses much more than just the controverted issues. Grisez and Russell Shaw have written *Personal Vocation: God Calls Everyone by Name*. Benedict Ashley has written *Living the Truth in Love: A Biblical Introduction to Moral Theology.* On the liberal side, for example, Charles Curran, Richard Gula, and Timothy O'Connell have all emphasized the importance of discipleship and spirituality for moral theology.[114]

Julie Hanlon Rubio explicitly wants to get beyond the liberal-conservative debate over contraception.[115] Darlene Weaver has proposed an understanding of the Christian's basic response to God that avoids both the proportionality-based developments of fundamental option and the more constrictive approach of John Paul II.[116] All must recognize the need for a greater dialogue among Catholic moral theologians and the need for newer approaches, but the issues addressed in the liberal-conservative debate are not going to go away.

William Portier and others refer to many of these new voices as "evangelical Catholics."[117] Portier objects to calling some of these new approaches "conservative." According to Portier's thesis, the older generation of Catholics came out of a Catholic subculture. The new generation comes out of a pluralistic and postmodern culture and has willingly embraced their Catholicism and recognized the need to bear witness to it in their daily life and in their relationship to the world. With an emphasis on the theological dimension of moral theology, this approach claims to go beyond the older division between liberal and conservative. Nonetheless, some of the evangelical Catholics are opposed to the liberal approach. The editorial introduction to the symposium in *Communio,* titled "Evangelical Catholicism? A Symposium on the Prospects of Catholic Theology in America," expresses their goal as going beyond the left-right debate to achieve the true program of Vatican II—*ressourcement*—a creative return to the sources.[118] There is no mention of the other source of renewal at Vatican II—*aggiornamento*—bringing the Church up to date.

Some of these new voices are students of Stanley Hauerwas. Hauerwas, brought up as a Methodist but now an Episcopalian, taught at Notre Dame but has been at Duke University for more than two decades now. He has had many graduate students who are Catholic or who teach at Catholic colleges and universities. Hauerwas, a prodigious writer and creative thinker, was invited to give the famous Gifford Lectures in Scotland.[119] In 2004 he coedited with Samuel Wells, an English scholar, the *Blackwell Companion to Christian Ethics.* Fourteen of the thirty authors in this volume now teach in Catholic institutions in the United States and are either students of Hauerwas and/or frequently follow his approach. Thus Hauerwas has had a significant influence on Catholic moral theology in the United States.

Hauerwas, like most Christians, strongly opposes the individualistic liberalism that is prevalent in secular theory and practice in the United States. He criticizes Protestant Christian ethics and Catholic moral theology for their emphasis on quandary ethics. From his earliest writings he has recognized the importance of the character and virtues of the moral agent.[120] He opposes a universal ethic based on principles or concepts, such as justice, that are common to all people. Morality and ethics are limited to and specified by specific communities. The Christian community is the Church. Christian ethics is primarily a narrative approach that tells the Christian story to the Christian community. Christian ethics directly addresses the community of the Church and not the broader society. The Church has an interest in what happens in the world and in the broader society, but it fulfills its role by bearing witness to the story of Jesus in its own life and not by directly working with others to change society. Christians are called to be pacifists and must be true to their own story, thereby bearing witness to the world.[121]

At the 2006 meeting of the Catholic Theological Society of America, Christine Gudorf responded to a paper by Hauerwas. Gudorf, coming out of the Catholic tradition, with its emphasis on mediation and "both-and," criticized Hauerwas. The Catholic tradition sees faith as touching and influencing all reality and works with all people of goodwill for a better human society. The Catholic theological tradition has always recognized the importance of both faith and reason. Gudorf also criticizes Hauerwas for his triumphalistic understanding of church.[122]

In a 1985 plenary address to the Catholic Theological Society of America, James M. Gustafson, Hauerwas's own dissertation advisor, warned against the sectarian temptation in Hauerwas. The emphasis on Christian community, rooted in the Christian story and scriptural narrative, downplays and even sets aside Christian interaction with society, culture, and the world, as well as with human reason and human sciences.[123]

Hauerwas and his followers claim that they are not sectarian. Michael Baxter, a Hauerwas doctoral student who now teaches at Notre Dame, recognizes a role for reason and human nature in Catholic moral theology but says that grace radically transforms the human; it perfects the human by disturbing it. Baxter proposes what he calls a "dialectical" view of Aquinas.[124] From my perspective, he still fails to give enough importance to mediation and the Catholic "both-and."

Specifically, Catholic tradition disagrees with the Hauerwas approach in three significant areas: First, the Catholic tradition, precisely because it is catholic (with a small "c"), recognizes a universal morality applicable to all people. The social teaching of the popes addresses not only Catholics but all people of goodwill and gives important roles in morality to both faith and the human sources of moral wisdom and knowledge.[125] Yes, at times the Catholic Church has claimed too much universality and too much certitude for its universal moral teaching, (e.g., in its opposition to artificial contraception), but by definition the Catholic approach is truly catholic and open to the universal.

Second, the Catholic Church has traditionally seen itself as directly addressing the world and working together with all others for a more just human society. The 1971 International Synod of Bishops insisted that action on behalf of justice and the transformation of the world is a constitutive dimension of the preaching of the Gospel and of the mission of the Church.[126] The Church's mission is not simply to bear witness to the world but to work effectively with all others for a better human society.

Third, the Catholic understanding of the Church insists on a big and inclusive Church, open to and inviting all people of whatever race or geographical location. The big Church is also a church of saints and sinners, and not just of the perfect. This Church is always a sinful Church, constantly in need of reform. The Gospel obviously serves as a criterion for reform in the Church, but the Church that is big and catholic has also learned from the world, as, for example, in its appreciation today of human freedom in political life and the role of women in society. Hauerwas's ecclesiology tends to be too triumphalist and fails to recognize the pilgrim nature of the Church. Yes, the Church is animated by the Holy Spirit, but the Church is always in need of reform. Some of Hauerwas's Catholic followers have trouble with dissent from noninfallible hierarchical teaching and support existing papal teachings in sexual areas, often bringing in a strong theological dimension. For example, David M. McCarthy, who sees himself as an evangelical Catholic, strongly supports the teaching of *Humanae vitae*.[127]

The Hauerwas approach, however, rightly reminds Catholics of the perennial danger in the Catholic approach that the Church too readily conforms itself to the world. Think, for example, of the Church's failure to condemn absolutely slavery for nineteen centuries. The big Church living in the world and open to saints and sinners must always be vigilant and not lose its light and its transforming power. However, the danger of abuse in this matter does not deny the basic understanding of the Church, which is truly catholic and tries also to work effectively with all others for a better human society.

In my judgment, *Fullness of Faith: The Public Significance of Theology*, by Michael and Kenneth Himes, well illustrates how the Catholic theological tradition addresses and works with all people of goodwill to build a better human society. This book uses the theological concepts of original sin, the Trinity, grace, and the incarnation in developing a public theology for the public Church that is mediated in and through the human and uses the human sources of moral wisdom and knowledge. (Michael Baxter himself has strongly disagreed with the approach of the Himes's book.)[128]

As the century develops, new Catholic moral theologians dealing with recent historical and cultural situations will obviously chart a somewhat new course and approach, but in my judgment the Catholic tradition must be truly catholic, recognizing both the theological and faith dimensions of the discipline but also the reality of mediation and the need for "both-and" approaches.

NOTES

1. McBrien, *Catholicism,* 9–12; Greeley, *Catholic Myth,* 36–64.

2. Aquinas, *Summa theologiae, Ia IIae,* qq. 90–94.

3. Abbott, "Pastoral Constitution on the Church," 233–34n36.

4. For a Catholic analysis of Karl Barth and the differences between Barth and the Catholic theologian Hans Urs von Balthasar on this point, see Steck, *Ethical Thought of von Balthasar,* 58–122.

5. Wawrykow, *God's Grace and Human Action.*

6. John Paul II, *Fides et ratio.*

7. Abbott, "Pastoral Constitution on the Church," 234n36.

8. Donovan, "Alive to the Glory of God," 283–97.

9. Abbott, "Pastoral Constitution on the Church," 210–11n12.

10. Ibid., 226nn21–22.

11. Abbott, "Dogmatic Constitution on the Church," 24–37nn9–17; 78–85nn48–51.

12. Ibid., 85–96nn52–69.

13. Hinze, *Practices of Dialogue in the Roman Catholic Church.*

14. Fuchs, *Natural Law.*

15. Häring, "Conversion."

16. Curran, *New Look at Christian Morality,* 25–71.

17. Conn, *Conversion;* Conn, *Christian Conversion.*

18. Happel and Walter, *Conversion and Discipleship.*

19. O'Keefe, *Becoming Good, Becoming Holy,* 27–43.

20. For an analysis of how three Catholic authors (Gustavo Gutierrez, Bernard Häring, and Rosemary Radford Ruether), among others, have used scripture in moral theology, see Siker, *Scripture and Ethics.*

21. Significant volumes dealing with the role of scripture in moral theology include the following, in chronological order: Curran and McCormick, *Use of Scripture in Moral Theology;* Daly et al., *Christian Biblical Ethics;* Spohn, *What Are They Saying;* Bretzke, *Bibliography on Scripture and Christian Ethics;* Spohn, *Go and Do Likewise.*

22. In addition to Spohn's books listed in the previous note, see Spohn's articles "Jesus and Christian Ethics"; "Morality and the Way of Discipleship"; "Parable and Narrative"; "Use of Scripture in Moral Theology."

23. Ogletree, *Use of the Bible in Christian Ethics,* 15–45.

24. Kelsey, *Use of Scripture in Recent Theology,* 167–78.

25. Spohn, *What Are They Saying,* 5–20.

26. Mouw, *God Who Commands.*

27. Gustafson, "Changing Use of the Bible in Christian Ethics," 141–43.

28. Tambasco, *Bible for Ethics.*

29. Fiorenza, *In Memory of Her;* Fiorenza, *Bread Not Stone.*

30. Spohn, *Go and Do Likewise.*

31. See, for example, Harrington and Keenan, *Jesus and Virtue Ethics.*

32. Siker, *Homosexuality in the Church.*

33. Steck, *Ethical Thought of Hans Urs von Balthasar,* 42–48.

34. Lamb, *Solidarity with Victims,* 11–14.

35. Spohn, *Go and Do Likewise,* 4–26.

36. Steck, *Ethical Thought of Hans Urs von Balthasar,* 62–92.

37. O'Keefe, *Becoming Good, Becoming Holy,* 3–5.

38. E.g., Keating, *Spirituality and Moral Theology;* Billy and Keating, *Conscience and Prayer;* Keating, *Moral Theology.*

39. Keating, *Spirituality and Moral Theology,* 4–7.

40. McDonagh, "Liturgy and Christian Life."

41. E.g., Searle, *Liturgy and Social Justice;* Grosz, *Liturgy and Social Justice;* Empereur and Kiesling, *Liturgy That Does Justice;* Hughes and Francis, *Living No Longer for Ourselves.*

42. Frogomeni and Pawlikowski, *Ecological Challenge.*

43. See Stamps, *To Do Justice.*

44. For the different positions in this debate, see Curran and McCormick, *Distinctiveness of Christian Ethics.* Richard A. McCormick also brought the German debate to the attention of American theologians; see McCormick, *Notes on Moral Theology, 1965–1980,* 632–38.

45. Rigali, "Uniqueness and Distinctiveness." For a festschrift honoring Rigali's contributions, see Salzman, *Method and Catholic Moral Theology.*

46. Rigali, "Dialogue with Richard McCormick" and "Curran's Understanding of Christian Ethics."

47. McCormick, *Notes on Moral Theology, 1965–1980,* 637–38.

48. Curran, "Is There a Distinctively Christian Ethic?"

49. McCormick, *Notes on Moral Theology, 1965–1980,* 633–35.

50. Rigali, "Historical Meaning of *Humanae vitae.*"

51. Rigali, "Theology of the Christian Life."

52. Ramsey, *War and the Christian Conscience,* 66–90.

53. Gustafson, *Christ and the Moral Life,* 98–113.

54. Lehmann, *Ethics in a Christian Context,* 295–302.

55. McCormick and Ramsey, *Doing Evil to Achieve Good.*

56. Curran, *Politics, Medicine, and Christian Ethics.*

57. Fisher and Polish, *Formation of Social Policy;* Polish and Fisher, *Liturgical Foundations;* Pellegrino and Faden, *Jewish and Catholic Bioethics.*

58. Long, *Academic Bonding and Social Concern.*

59. Maguire, *Moral Revolution.*

60. Maguire, *Moral Core of Judaism and Christianity,* 279; for an expanded and revised version, see Maguire, *Moral Creed for All Christians.*

61. Maguire, *Sacred Rights.*

62. Noonan, *Scholastic Analysis of Usury.*

63. Noonan, *Contraception,* 533.

64. Noonan, *Power to Dissolve,* 403.

65. Noonan, *Church That Can and Cannot Change,* 175.

66. Ibid., 120.

67. Noonan, "Development in Moral Doctrine," 669.

68. One recent example of Thomistic historical scholarship in moral theology is Pope, *Ethics of Aquinas.*

69. Dedek, "Moral Absolutes"; "Intrinsically Evil Acts: Historical Study"; "Intrinsically Evil Acts: Emergence"; "Pre-Marital Sex."

70. Curran, *American Catholic Social Ethics;* Curran, *Origins of Moral Theology.*

71. Mackin, *Divorce and Remarriage; Marital Sacrament;* and *What Is Marriage?*

72. Fleming, *Defending Probabilism.*

73. Farley, *Just Love.*

74. Farley, "New Patterns of Relationships." Farley also spoke at the first meeting of Catholic Women in the United States in November 1975 calling for the ordination of women in the Catholic Church.

75. Fiedler, "Dissent within the U.S. Church"; Patrick, *Liberating Conscience,* 118–28.

76. Farley, "Church in the Public Forum."

77. Farley, "Ethics, Ecclesiology, and the Grace of Self-Doubt."

78. Farley, "Feminist Theology and Bioethics."

79. Farley, *Compassionate Respect.*

80. Cahill, *Between the Sexes; Women and Sexuality; Sex, Gender, and Christian Ethics; Family;* and *Theological Bioethics.*

81. Cahill, *Love Your Enemies.*

82. Cahill, *Sex, Gender, and Christian Ethics,* 14–72.

83. Andolsen, Gudorf, and Pellauer, *Women's Consciousness, Women's Conscience.*

84. Andolsen, "*Agape* in Feminist Ethics."

85. Andolsen, "Elements of a Feminist Approach to Bioethics." The volume in which this article appears is a collection of twenty-five articles on Catholic feminist ethics.

86. Andolsen, *Daughters of Jefferson;* Andolsen, *Good Work at the Video Display Terminal.*

87. Andolsen, *New Job Contract.*

88. Gudorf, *Catholic Social Teaching.*

89. Gudorf, *Body, Sex, and Pleasure;* Gudorf, *Victimization.*

90. Stivers, Gudorf, Evans, and Evans, *Christian Ethics;* Wolfe and Gudorf, *Ethics and World Religions.*

91. Patrick, "Women and Religion."

92. Callahan, "Conscience and Gender."

93. Callahan, "Abortion and the Sexual Agenda."

94. Ross, *Extravagant Affections; For the Beauty of the Earth;* "Liturgy and Ethics"; "Bride of Christ."

95. E.g., Hinze, "Bridge Discourse on Wage Justice."

96. Ryan, *Ethics and Economics of Assisted Reproduction.*

97. Traina, *Feminist Ethics and the Natural Law;* DeCrane, *Aquinas, Feminism, and the Common Good.*

98. Jung and Smith, *Heterosexism.*

99. Espin and Diaz, *From the Hearts of Our People.*

100. Conroy, "Profile: Virgilio P. Elizondo."

101. Elizondo, *Galilean Journey.*

102. Elizondo, *Guadalupe;* Elizondo and Matovina, *San Fernando Cathedral.*

103. This information is found on their website, www.achtus.org/.

104. Isasi-Díaz, *En la Lucha;* Isasi-Díaz, *Mujerista Theology.*

105. Isasi-Díaz, "*Burlando al Opresor.*"

106. Rodriguez, *Our Lady of Guadalupe;* Rodriguez, *Stories We Live.*

107. Aquino, *Our Cry for Life;* Aquino, Machado, and Rodriguez, *Reader in Latina Feminist Theology.*

108. Massingale, "African-American Experience."

109. Fahey, "From the Editor's Desk."

110. Phelps, *Black and Catholic;* Davis and Phelps, *Stamped with the Image of God.*

111. Hayes, *Hagar's Daughters;* Hayes, *And Still We Rise;* Hayes and Davis, *Taking Down Our Harps.*

112. Copeland, "Method in Emerging Black Catholic Theology."

113. Mattison, *New Wine, New Wineskins.*

114. Curran, *Catholic Moral Tradition Today;* Gula, *Good Life* and *Call to Holiness;* O'Connell, *Making Disciples.*

115. Rubio, "Beyond the Liberal/Conservative Divide on Contraception."

116. Weaver, "Intimacy with God and Self-Relation in the World."

117. Portier, "In Defense of Mt. St. Mary's"; "Here Come the Evangelical Catholics"; "Foreword," in Mattison, *New Wine, New Wineskins.*

118. Walker, "Introduction," 1.

119. Hauerwas, *With the Grain of the Universe.*

120. Hauerwas, *Character and the Christian Life.*

121. His most systematic presentation is Hauerwas, *Peaceable Kingdom;* see also Hauerwas, *Hauerwas Reader.*

122. Gudorf, "Response to Stanley Hauerwas."

123. Gustafson, "Sectarian Temptation," 86–88.

124. Baxter, "Sign of Peace," especially 33–40.

125. Himes, *Modern Catholic Social Teaching.*

126. Synod of Bishops, *Justitia in mundo,* 289.

127. McCarthy, "Shifting Setting from Subculture to Pluralism" and "Procreation, Development, and Final Destiny."

128. Baxter, "Non-Catholic Character."

FUNDAMENTAL MORAL THEOLOGY

The manuals of moral theology distinguished fundamental moral theology from special moral theology. Fundamental moral theology treated those aspects that were common to all spheres of human life and activity, whereas special moral theology discussed the particular areas of moral endeavor. Most of the manuals developed special moral theology according to the Ten Commandments. Manuals coming out of the Dominican tradition often used the model of the virtues, but in reality the focus was not on virtues but on the acts themselves. The distinction between fundamental and special moral theology is grounded in the *Summa theologiae* of Thomas Aquinas. Despite some problems, the distinction still has relevance today and is often used in contemporary literature. The first section of this chapter looks at the various developments in fundamental moral theology primarily in light of the emphasis on the person. A second section examines how the various authors have synthetically tried to approach fundamental theology, while a third section discusses the understanding of the basic realities involved in fundamental moral theology.

THE RENEWAL OF MORAL THEOLOGY WITH THE EMPHASIS ON THE PERSON

Chapters 1 and 2 pointed out that the manuals of moral theology had as their narrow scope the preparation of confessors to act as judges in the sacrament of penance with regard to the sinfulness and degree of sinfulness of particular actions. These manuals first discussed the morality of human acts in a somewhat practical and superficial way. They then followed with a consideration of law as the objective norm and conscience as the subjective norm of morality. Finally they discussed the meaning of sin. In some manuals, a very few pages were written on virtue.

Vatican II served as the primary but not the only source for the criticism of the approach of the manuals. The Vatican II emphasis on the theological aspect of moral theology strongly supports the emphasis on the person rather than the act. The biblical concepts of discipleship, conversion, and love all emphasize the importance of the person. In addition to Vatican II, the broader Catholic tradition in moral theology as exemplified in the work of Thomas Aquinas was focused not so much on preparing confessors for the sacrament of penance but rather on the person and on a life-centered moral theology. Ethical concerns in the broader Catholic tradition and in contemporary religious and philosophical ethics also support the importance of the person. The good person does good actions; the bad person does bad actions.

Contemporary Catholic moral theologians—despite some differences, especially the difference between conservative and liberal approaches to human acts—are in basic agreement about the importance of the person and the ramifications of that importance for Christian morality. Timothy O'Connell maintains that to achieve a lifestyle of discipleship, a human being needs a clear understanding of personhood itself.[1] Germain Grisez points out that moral theology needs to see how the Christian is a member by adoption of God's family and how Christian love constitutes the person's new nature.[2] Here Grisez recognizes the role of the person as agent, but he also insists on the role of the person as the subject of one's acts, although he does not use that term. Free choices build up human persons and communities. Choice determines the identity of the person.[3] By our actions we make ourselves the type of persons we are. Thus the contemporary Catholic approach, in line with the best of the Catholic tradition, recognizes the important role of the person without, however, denying the need for an independent evaluation of human acts. The person, in a true sense, is more important and more significant morally than the individual act.

One caveat is in order. The individual is most important for moral theology, but the danger exists of a narrow personalism that does not give enough importance to the communitarian, social, ecological, and even global aspects of human existence. Chapter 10 looks at the need to see the human person as related to all these other aspects.

Growth in the Christian Life

Vatican II's insistence on the vocation of all Christians to holiness called for growth and development in the Christian life. The emphasis on scripture and the theological perspective of the discipline of moral theology strongly supports the need for continual growth and development in the Christian moral life. The relationship between spiritual theology and moral theology also contributes to the emphasis on growth and development in Christian moral living. U.S. moral theologians showed the Catholic emphasis on mediation in the growth of the moral life by using philosophical and psychological approaches that studied human development. John W. Crossin recognized the influential psychosocial theory of Erik Erikson and its importance for moral theology. Erikson proposed eight stages of development, from infancy through old age. Responding to these eight different stages is a particular virtue. The virtues attached to these eight different stages are hope, will, purpose, cognition, fidelity, love, care, and wisdom. But Crossin realizes that moral theology needs a critical appropriation of psychological theory in general and of Erikson in particular.[4]

Moral theologians and Catholic educators also dialogued with the very popular structural developmental approaches of Lawrence Kohlberg and James Fowler. Kohlberg's stages of moral development moved from the preconventional level, to the conventional level, to the postconventional level of universal principles of justice. Paul Philibert sees Kohlberg's theory as a helpful but insufficient foundation for understanding Christian moral development and moral education. Philibert criticizes Kohlberg's theory of development for too narrowly emphasizing the aspects of justice and obligation. Conscience development in the best of the Catholic tradition sees conscience as openness to the attractive influence of the good and of value rather than primarily as obligation to obey law. Kohlberg is too Kantian in the philosophical basis of his theory. By emphasizing only justice, Kohlberg does not credit other aspects of Christian moral development such as charity, vocation, character, fidelity, love, and ministerial service to others.[5]

Walter Conn in 1981 published the most systematic Catholic understanding of moral development. Conn relies heavily on Bernard Lonergan's understanding of development in terms of self-transcendence. The psychological theories of Piaget, Erikson, and Kohlberg show that self-transcendence implicitly operates as normative in their theories. Conscious subjectivity has an intrinsic dynamism toward self-transcendence, which, in keeping with the Catholic tradition, is true self-realization. Normative self-transcending subjectivity calls in Lonergan's understanding for a threefold conversion—intellectual conversion, moral conversion, and religious conversion—that involves a total being in love as the efficacious ground of all self-transcendence. In describing religious conversion, Conn stresses the affective aspect of this conversion thus giving primary importance to the transforming power of love.[6]

Virtue

The shift from the primacy of the act to the primacy of the person in the context of a life-centered moral theology focused attention on the virtues and their role in moral life. The broader Catholic tradition outside the manuals had always assigned virtue an important place. According to Thomas Aquinas, virtue is a stable disposition for doing the good. Aquinas recognized the theological virtues and the cardinal moral virtues. The three theological virtues are faith, hope, and charity, which are infused in the believer through grace. The four cardinal virtues are prudence, justice, fortitude, and temperance. These virtues are distinguished by the subjects in which they inhere and which they perfect. Prudence inheres in and perfects the intellect; justice is related to the will; fortitude to the irascible appetites, and temperance to the sensible appetites.[7]

In addition to the Catholic tradition itself, some Protestant ethicists at this time were recognizing the important role of the virtues. The first issue of the *Journal of Religious Ethics* in 1973 published articles debating act-centered Christian ethics and person-centered, or virtue, ethics.[8] Stanley Hauerwas was the most vocal Protestant in employing a person-centered ethic, with his emphasis on character. His 1975 book, a revision of his doctoral dissertation, defends the thesis that Christian ethics is best understood as an ethics of character, since the Christian moral life is fundamentally the orientation of the self.[9] At the same time, many philosophical ethicists became interested in virtue ethics. Alasdair MacIntyre's *After Virtue* (1981) was most influential.

Considering all of these factors, Catholic moral theologians began to pay more attention to the virtues. Jean Porter's *The Recovery of Virtue* (1990) strongly supports the ethical approach of Thomas Aquinas. Writing as a Catholic moral theologian while communicating with many Protestant ethicists, Porter offers a reconstruction of the strictly philosophical aspects of Aquinas's ethical theory in the *Summa theologiae*. She does not consider the properly theological components of the Thomistic approach because she believes that the aspect of Aquinas's moral thought most illuminating for contemporary Christian ethics is his conception of the natural end or good of the human person seen in relationship to his theory of goodness in general.[10]

Romanus Cessario, a Dominican priest, has written extensively on the virtues. His *Moral Virtues and Theological Ethics* (1991) insists on the theological aspect of the virtues by developing the Thomistic understanding that the moral virtues are infused by grace in the believer and not acquired by human effort. In his writings on the virtues, Cessario follows a Thomistic understanding of the theological virtues and the infused cardinal virtues of prudence, justice, fortitude, and temperance. In keeping with the Aristotelian and Thomistic tradition, Cessario understands prudence to be the primary virtue.[11] Although both Porter and Cessario insist on the importance of virtue in the moral life, they differ considerably in their evaluation of particular moral acts. Porter belongs to the liberal or revisionist approach, whereas Cessario belongs to the conservative approach and strongly defends all the particular sexual teachings of the hierarchical magisterium. Cessario bases his moral theology on the magisterium of Pope John Paul II, as found especially in the 1993 encyclical *Veritatis splendor* and the *Catechism of the Catholic Church,* and on the realistic moral theology developed by Thomas Aquinas.[12]

Paul Wadell has also emphasized the virtue approach to moral theology. His *Friendship in the Moral Life* (1989) builds on the Aristotelian and Thomistic emphasis on virtue. The project of the moral life is to become a certain kind of person. Wadell develops his understanding of friendship on the basis of the thought of Aristotle and Thomas Aquinas. The Christian life involves friendship with God and friendship with others in our everyday life.

As mentioned above, Stanley Hauerwas and Alasdair MacIntyre are primary proponents of a virtue ethics, and MacIntyre, like Hauerwas, sees the virtues as formed in a particular community and in that sense as not universal. James Keenan, in his approach to the virtues, well illustrates the Catholic tradition, with its truly catholic character and its insistence on mediation. Keenan recognizes an important role for particular communities and individual uniqueness but still insists that it is possible and necessary to develop cardinal virtues that express what minimally constitutes a virtuous person in all different communities and despite our individual uniqueness.[13] Because of a different anthropological perspective, Keenan parts company with Aquinas in his understanding of the cardinal virtues. Keenan proposes a relational anthropology. We are relational in three ways: generally, specifically, and uniquely. Justice directs our relationships in general; fidelity directs our specific relationships, such as friendships; and self-care directs the unique relationship to one's self. The fourth cardinal virtue, prudence, determines what constitutes the just, faithful, and self-caring life of the person. Keenan, unlike Aquinas, recognizes that conflicts can exist (e.g., between justice and mercy) and sees prudence as integrating the other three virtues into our lives.[14]

William Spohn follows the approach of Thomas Aquinas without explicitly saying so in his recognition that a virtue approach is necessary but not sufficient for a complete moral theology. Moral theology must also consider principles and the consequences of our actions. Strict deontologists give virtue only the instrumental role of providing motivation for what is called for. Strict consequentialists also see virtue simply as instrumental for doing what has the best consequences.

The instrumental role of virtue is insufficient and inadequate for a complete moral theology. Virtue has an independent role in moral theory, but moral theology also needs to consider principles or duties and consequences.[15]

Charles Curran's *The Catholic Moral Tradition Today: A Synthesis* (1999), devotes a chapter to the virtues and their role in the Christian life, thereby illustrating Spohn's understanding. Curran develops virtues on the basis of a relational anthropology that distinguishes the general virtues, which affect all our relationships (e.g., faith, hope, love, creativity, fidelity), from the particular virtues, which affect our different relationships to God (e.g., openness and gratitude), to others, (e.g., justice), to the world (e.g., solidarity with the environment), and to self (e.g., a proper love of self).[16]

Basic Orientation or Option

The emphasis on the actor opens the door to recognizing that some actions are more significant and basic than other actions. Common sense reminds us of this. For example, one's choice of vocation in life guides and directs many other choices that one makes. The person who wants to become a doctor thus will take certain courses in college and probably enroll in a premed program. The biblical teaching also supports the recognition of certain basic acts that influence all other actions. The twofold love command found in the synoptic Gospels—the great commandment on which depends all the law and the prophets—is to love the Lord your God with all your heart, with all your soul, and with all your mind, and to love your neighbor as yourself (Matt. 22:34–40, Mark 12:28–34, and Luke 10:25–28). The basic commitment of discipleship, however it is understood, affects all the other actions of the Christian. Aquinas's teleological approach to moral theology recognizes that the most important choice for all people is the choice of the ultimate end. In light of the ultimate end, one chooses the best means to achieve that end.

One very popular school of post–Vatican II moral theology has understood the basic orientation and fundamental commitment in terms of the fundamental option based on the theology of Karl Rahner. Josef Fuchs has developed the notion of the fundamental option more than any other Catholic moral theologian.[17] Timothy E. O'Connell has explained Fuchs's understanding of the fundamental option to many Americans in his textbook *Principles for a Catholic Morality*, originally published in 1978 and revised in 1990.[18]

This theory rests on two kinds of freedom and two kinds of knowledge related to the different concepts of freedom. The manuals and most ethicists before this time recognized only one type of freedom: the freedom of choice. Thus, for example, one was free to study, to play, or to go to bed. According to the proponents of the fundamental option, this freedom is categorical freedom because it deals with the different categories of acts. There exists, however, a deeper level to the human being where the individual encounters one's self as a subject in the very depths of one's existence. Here the person as subject commits one's self to God, who is also not a categorical object (one of a number of different objects) but is also a subject. At the core of her being, the individual makes this choice of God. The basic yes and commitment to God transcend all our categorical choices and become the fundamental option, but this loving commitment to God on the transcendental level has a significant effect on the categorical choices that we make.

We human beings have two different kinds of knowledge that correspond to these two different aspects of human freedom. On the categorical level, the individual performs this particular act. The act is the object and the person is reflexively conscious of this act precisely because it is differentiated from the person as an object. But on the transcendental level the person determines herself as a subject and consequently cannot have reflexive consciousness of an act, as is possible with categorical acts, with their concrete objects. My awareness of myself as subject differs from the reflex awareness of the object of my categorical choices. The fundamental option, my gracious acceptance of God's love in Jesus through the Spirit, occurs on the transcendental level; consequently, I cannot be reflexively conscious of this as an object of choice. I cannot have absolute certitude that I have even made such an option.

These two actuations of freedom, transcendental and categorical, are not totally discrete acts. The person commits herself to a loving relationship with God in and through her particular categorical acts. The theory thus clearly distinguishes the transcendental level from the categorical level, but it does not hold for two different actions. The act of transcendental freedom occurs in and through the categorical acts.

Not all agree with the concepts of transcendental and categorical freedom and the anthropology that grounds this distinction. The Grisez approach, as represented, for example, by William E. May, maintains that the fundamental option theory is unacceptable because it shifts the locus of self-determination from the free choices we make every day to an alleged act of total self-determination deep within the person that remains incapable of being known in reflexive consciousness.[19] Some revisionists, such as Charles Curran, disagree with the anthropology grounding the two kinds of transcendental and categorical freedom. The person as subject remains too transcendental and becomes separated from concrete social and historical reality. In the fundamental option approach, salvation and grace take place on the transcendental level, but salvation and grace also should take place and influence the categorical level and all the multiple relationships that constitute the person. Curran wants to see the basic orientation of the person in terms of the multiple relationships that constitute the person: relationships to God, neighbor, world, and self. All Catholic moral theologians do not agree with the transcendental-categorical approach, but almost all moral theologians recognize the existence of a basic orientation that tries to influence all our other actions.[20]

Love

Some Catholic moral theologians have developed the fundamental option on the basis of love. Christian thinkers recognize three different types of love: agape, or self-sacrificing love; philia, or friendship love; and eros, or self-fulfilling love. Catholic theologians, on the basis of their own tradition, recognize an important role for proper self-fulfillment or happiness, which is the foundation of the ethics of Thomas Aquinas. They also, in keeping with the Catholic both-and approach, tend to recognize a place for all three kinds of love.

Paul J. Wadell, now of St. Norbert's University, wrote *The Primacy of Love: An Introduction to the Ethics of Thomas Aquinas* (1992) to show that Aquinas's ethic is not rationalistic or simply a matter of natural law. Charity or friendship with God constitutes the core and basis of Aquinas's moral theology. The book, which could readily be used with undergraduates, recognizes the central role of virtue in the ethics of Aquinas, employs a narrative approach, and emphasizes the importance of emotion in the understanding of Aquinas. Jean Porter disagrees with Wadell's reading of Aquinas in a number of areas, including the central claim that for Aquinas *caritas* is a passion. According to Porter, love proper to charity must be distinguished from the properly so-called passion of love.[21]

Three scholarly books have also dealt in more depth with love and its role in the Christian moral life. Edward Collins Vacek, of the Weston School of Theology, insists in *Love, Human, and Divine: The Heart of Christian Ethics* (1994) that love of God is at the heart of Christian life and theology. Vacek brings phenomenology, process theology, and ecumenical perspectives to his understanding of love and its role. Love is an affective, affirming participation in the goodness of a being or a Being. God's covenantal love for us is the affirming love of God, who is Creator, Sustainer, Redeemer, and Sanctifier, but God's love is also a receiving love that receives the beloved into God's self. Thus God is affected by us, our world, and human history. His emphasis on process theology and his understanding of God distinguish Vacek's approach from that of Aquinas and classical theism. Vacek recognizes a place for the three different kinds of human love for God: agape, or love for the sake of the beloved; eros, or love for one's own sake; and philia, or love for the sake of the relationship. For Vacek, philia (*caritas*) or communion is primary, for it is the foundation and goal of the Christian life. The communitarian dimension of the Christian life comes to the fore in philia, whereby we love God not for God's sake or for our sake but for the sake of the covenantal relationships.

Stephen Pope of Boston College calls attention to the need for an ordering of neighbor love. Here he explicitly follows Aquinas on three major points: the fact that grace and charity build on nature, the need for dialogue with the biological knowledge of the day, and the recognition that the given biological inclinations of human beings have an important moral role but cannot be absolutized. Pope faults Catholic personalists, existentialists, feminists, and liberationists for not recognizing the need for an ordering of love that helps to establish moral priorities. While critical of some aspects of neo-Darwinism and sociobiology, Pope appeals to some of these approaches in developing a contemporary analogue to what Aquinas did with Aristotelian biology. He recognizes the dangers of kin and preferential relationships that argue against broader social and communal concerns such as love for the person in need. Love of others can and should, however, build on what is biologically normative as one basis, but not as an absolute basis, for truly personal human flourishing and indicating certain goods that will be included in lives lived well.[22]

Whereas Pope deals explicitly with love of others, Darlene Fozard Weaver of Villanova University, in *Self Love and Christian Ethics* (2002), concentrates on proper love of self but again recognizes the need to see self-love in relationship to the love of God and neighbor. Weaver employs a hermeneutical approach that both criticizes and utilizes Karl Rahner and Paul Tillich. She brings together anthropology and theology as well as morality and religion. Her understanding of love rests on a relational anthropology that sees the self in relationships with God, neighbor, and self. We are all conscious of the dangers of excessive self-love, which uses others, and the defect of self-love in excessive self-denial. Proper self-love consists in a self-determining response to God that is actualized in, but not exhausted by, love of neighbor.

Creative Imagination, Affectivity, and Story

The emphasis on the person, moral development, and dialogue with humanistic psychologists naturally opens the door to understanding the importance of the affective aspect in moral theology. Daniel Maguire, in *The Moral Choice* (1978), was the first Catholic moral theologian to stress the role of creative imagination.[23]

According to Maguire, creative imagination is the supreme faculty of the moral person. Creative imagination in any form is the power to perceive the possible within the actual, and creative action has the ability to bring the possible into the realm of the actual. Moral creativity is an intellectual flowering, but its roots are deep in the affections. There is a tendency to distinguish and even to separate intellect and will, knowledge and desire. In reality, the same person knows and desires. Both types of activity exist in the same conscious vitality. We see Archimedes running from his bath and shouting, "Eureka!" Creative imagination blends the emotional and the intellectual, and the joy of completion is the organically related equal to the desire that animated and sustained the creative process itself.

Maguire develops six conditions for enabling such creative imagination. Enthusiasm is the prerequisite for all success, for creativity has fiery roots. Quietness and passivity, in the sense of contemplation or true leisure rather than the frenetic leisure of so many today, is the second condition. The third condition is work, which is the necessary preparation for the creative imagination. Malleability, as applied to both the individual and the cultural context, is the fourth condition. The fifth condition, *kairos,* refers to the opportunity that is present in a particular time and place and might never come again. Finally, "at-homeness," or absence of alienation, is necessary for the creative imagination to work. As a realist, Maguire recognizes that imagination can go terribly astray. The creative imagination is not the only aspect involved in good moral choosing, but it is a very important one. Subsequent Catholic moral theologians (e.g., Keane and O'Connell) have paid tribute to the pioneering work of Maguire.[24]

Philip S. Keane of Mt. St. Mary's Seminary in Baltimore was the first Catholic moral theologian in the United States to devote a monograph to imagination— *Christian Ethics and Imagination* (1983). Keane was reacting against the tendency of Catholic moral theology and many other types of ethics to rely too heavily on logical and discursive reasoning. But he insists adamantly that there is a place for discursive reasoning and principles in moral theology. Moral theology, however, needs something more—the more that imagination can provide. Imagination involves stories, metaphor, vision, playfulness, prayerful reflection, and a virtuous lifestyle. He begins by pulling together some building blocks for his understanding of imagination from classical authors in various fields (e.g., epistemology, aesthetics) and in dialogue with contemporary authors. He relies heavily on Paul Ricoeur and Hans-Georg Gadamer, but he also considers at some length many of the authors already mentioned in this section—MacIntyre, Hauerwas, Maguire, the virtue theorists, and Kohlberg.

Imagination is important in discerning human values in concrete situations but also in developing the vision of individuals and communities from which our moral judgments come. The imagination both roots us in our tradition and orients us to the future. Keane describes imagination as the basic process by which we bring together the concrete and the universal elements of our human experience. Imagination involves a playful suspension of judgment, leading us toward an appropriate grasp of reality. Moral imagination functions in three main phases. The first phase involves the formation of images, with regard to both principles and actions; the second stage involves associating and reflecting on these images. The third phase, after developing our moral images and playfully reflecting on them, involves making moral judgments. Imaginative moral judgments involve what is fitting and appropriate as to how our actions and principles come together.

Sidney Callahan is trained in psychology, but she writes extensively in moral theology, as exemplified especially in her *In Good Conscience: Reason and Emotion in Moral Decision Making* (1991).[25] The title captures her thesis that emotions have an important role to play in moral decision making. Callahan points out that many philosophical ethicists, with their emphasis on reason, dismiss emotion as something that can get in the way of reason. Some philosophers recognize a role for emotion but insist that emotion must always be tutored by reason. But Callahan, while recognizing that reason has a role in monitoring emotion, maintains that the emotions also must tutor and mentor reason. Emotions tutor reason in negative ways by feelings of mild aversion or even repugnance to some rational arguments that are proposed, such as the use of torture or harvesting neomorts. But emotions also tutor reason in positive ways. Many moral revolutions began because of empathy felt for previously excluded groups: slaves, women, workers, the disabled. Emotions such as love and even anger can inform and guide reason. Anger about what happens to innocent persons can change previous moral thinking.

One expects a humanistic psychologist to recognize the role of emotion in the formation of the moral person and in decision making. In *Virtuous Passions: The Formation of Christian Character* (1993), Simon Harak maintains that Thomas Aquinas recognized the important role of passions and emotions. Aquinas is not just a cognitivist who holds that we should submit our passions to control by reason. Human beings, according to Aquinas, should be drawn to those things that are good for them. Reason cannot get us to our final good and goal, which is union with God; only our passions can do this. Love, not the intellect, is our best approach to God. The whole ensouled, embodied self is integrated in the search for the ultimate possession of God. Giles Milhaven, an important early figure in Catholic revisionism, later devoted a whole book to good anger (1989).[26]

The emphasis on imagination and affectivity in moral theology also involves recognition of the role of stories as proposed by proponents of narrative theology. Stanley Hauerwas was the most significant voice in Christian ethics to call for such a narrative theology. Many Catholic moral theologians recognize the important aspect of narratives and stories but, as Keane has pointed out, they do not see this approach as eliminating the need for the discursive aspect in moral theology. They also continue to insist on the Catholic emphasis on catholicity and some universality. Timothy E. O'Connell, the author of a frequently used textbook in moral theology, confessed that his ministerial students had not really embraced and owned the values that he was teaching them. His book, *Making Disciples,* by utilizing the advances in narrative theology, aims to develop strategies for harnessing the power of imagination for the transmission of values. How do we fulfill the command of Jesus to make disciples? Here again narrative and imagination constitute an important part, though only a part, of moral theology.[27]

SYNTHESES AND TEXTBOOKS

Many teachers of moral theology in the pre–Vatican II period felt uncomfortable with the changes of Vatican II and retired from teaching. A new generation arose to investigate the newer developments and approaches. Obviously the manuals of moral theology could no longer serve as textbooks because of the many important changes that were occurring. In the United States, it took some time before new textbooks came into existence. The cutting edge of Catholic moral theology took place in articles and essays and not in monographs, but all recognized the need for textbooks. In addition to the need for textbooks, a more theoretical force was at work. The Catholic theological tradition has always tried to develop systematic and synthetic approaches that put theology together in a logical and organized way. The *Summa* of Thomas Aquinas, which has been compared with the medieval cathedrals, well illustrates the Catholic penchant for the synthetic and systematic approach.

Once the manuals were discarded in many places in the 1960s, Bernard Häring's three-volume *Law of Christ* often served as a textbook. The English translation of the first volume on fundamental moral theology was published in 1961. It was only in 1978 that Timothy E. O'Connell published the first textbook in moral theology in the United States, which incorporated many of the changes of Vatican II and afterward.[28] O'Connell wrote his doctoral dissertation on Josef Fuchs and depends heavily on Fuchs in his synthesis. Introductory and concluding essays bracket the two major parts of the book. The first part addresses the moral person or Christian anthropology. O'Connell begins the discussion with human action and then the human person; he especially follows Fuchs in recognizing the two levels of freedom: transcendental and categorical. The chapter "Morality: Sin and Virtue" is almost all about sin. After a very significant chapter on conscience, he closes part 1 with a chapter on related dogmatic themes, especially original sin and grace. The earlier chapters on the person are based almost exclusively on human reason and do not have a theological dimension. O'Connell has introductory chapters on biblical morality and Christian morality, but even here he insists that "Christian ethics is human ethics, no more and no less."[29] The second part is about objective morality, which is understood primarily in terms of law and norms, with a heavy emphasis on explaining a revisionist approach to natural law.

O'Connell is a fine pedagogue. One can easily understand why his book was a very popular text and why it was revised in 1990. O'Connell's social location as a seminary professor in Chicago comes through in his focus on teaching seminarians who will be ministers of the sacrament of penance. As a result, the focus of the book is primarily human acts and what is wrong or sinful. The discussion of the book primarily emphasizes the fundamental option involved in mortal sin, with the recognition that mortal sin is a much less frequent occurrence than the manuals claimed.

O'Connell's *Making Disciples: A Handbook of Christian Moral Formation* (1998) takes a more theological approach than his previous work. He is no longer teaching seminarians but is involved at Loyola University in Chicago in the professional education of people ministering in the Church. He now recognizes the importance of the moral formation of the disciples of Jesus and of those ministering in the Church. But this book also illustrates the Catholic emphasis on mediation and "both-and" approaches. He relies heavily on the social sciences and the creative imagination as well as on scripture and theology to ground his understanding of how to invite, celebrate, and live discipleship.

In 1989 Ronald Hamel, now of the Catholic Health Association, and Kenneth Himes, now of Boston College, published *Introduction to Christian Ethics: A Reader,* a nearly six-hundred-page work that serves as a textbook for colleges, seminaries, and universities. The volume includes an ecumenical perspective but concentrates on authors from the progressive school of Catholic moral theology. The themes treated in this book include the background and history of moral theology, the human person, the sources of moral wisdom and knowledge, conscience, and concrete decision making. The Hamel–Himes volume uses the writings of some of the U.S. Catholic authors who are discussed in the post–Vatican II section of the present book. Fuchs, Curran, and McCormick are the only Catholic authors with more than one essay in the Hamel–Himes book.

In 1989 Richard M. Gula published another widely used textbook in fundamental moral theology, *Reason Informed by Faith: Foundations of Catholic Morality.* The book is intended primarily for seminarians and also for graduate students in theology. Gula is a very accomplished pedagogue who writes clearly, succinctly summarizes complex material, uses charts effectively, and keeps the reader's attention through pertinent examples and illustrations. Gula wrote the book to make accessible the work of those who have significantly influenced the recent development of Catholic moral theology. Kenneth R. Himes points out that much of the material will be familiar to those "who have read the work of prominent figures like Charles Curran, Bernard Häring, Louis Janssens, Richard McCormick, or Daniel Maguire."[30] But Gula makes a very important contribution by bringing much of this material into a very readable synthesis. Gula explicitly recognizes the role of mediation and "both-and" approaches for the Catholic tradition and moral theology and for his own work. He also frequently cites and follows James Gustafson, thus engaging in significant ecumenical dialogue.

The short first part of the book deals with the question of the good, which basically is the discussion of the relationship between faith and morality. The longer second section discusses the nature of the human person and conscience, while the third part treats the criteria of the judgment of acts. Gula incorporates into his book three significant developments in Catholic moral theology: a change of focus from the confessional-oriented approach of the manuals to a critical understanding of faith for Christian living; the shift from classicism to historical consciousness; and a more inductive method relating the Gospel and the signs of the times. Like O'Connell, Gula follows the general revisionist perspective with regard to human acts, norms, and dissent from noninfallible teachings. He avoids the two extremes of sectarianism and of a purely philosophical approach. Christian faith affects the person and her character as well as actions and decisions, even though non-Christians may come to the same practical conclusions. In this book Gula mentions aspects that he developed more in later writings—the importance of creative imagination, conscience, and the discernment of the Spirit.[31]

In 1999 Charles Curran published *The Catholic Moral Tradition Today: A Synthesis*. This book is geared to those involved in the graduate study of moral theology but can also be used in theologates and seminaries. The book begins with the importance of the ecclesial context for moral theology. The Catholic Church is universal and inclusive and thus realizes the need for mediation and "both-and" approaches. Bryan Hehir has appreciated Curran's commitment to the Troeltschian argument that Catholicism can and should be a big church and not a sect and how this understanding affects his approach to moral theology and the social mission of the Church.[32] Stance is the logical first step for developing a systematic moral theology. Curran understands the Christian stance as looking at the world and reality in terms of the fivefold Christian mysteries of creation, sin, incarnation, redemption, and resurrection destiny. Thus he accounts for the basic goodness of the created world, which, however, is marred by sin and exists in eschatological tension between the redemption that has already occurred and the fullness of resurrection destiny that will only come at the end of time. *The Catholic Moral Tradition Today,* then, develops the relationality–responsibility model for Christian ethics that sees the person in terms of multiple relationships with God, neighbor, world, and self. The moral person, who is both subject and agent, is understood in light of the theological stance and the relationality-responsibility model. As mentioned earlier, one chapter develops the importance and role of the virtues in light of a relational anthropology. Curran's discussion of moral norms, human acts, and dissent in the Church is based on his earlier writings from a revisionist perspective.

The four syntheses of moral theology discussed above come from the perspective of revisionism in Catholic moral theology. No doubt the great majority of Catholic moral theologians in the United States fit into the revisionist perspective despite many disagreements over specific issues. Other schools of moral theology include the new natural law school of Germain Grisez and his followers. In 1983 Grisez, with the help of others, especially Joseph M. Boyle, published a 971-page fundamental moral theology book, *The Way of the Lord Jesus,* vol. 1, *Christian Moral Principles,* the first of a projected four-volume complete moral theology. Grisez's book is a fundamental moral theology textbook for Catholic seminarians and is original, creative, and very logical and complex. Grisez freely commits himself to following the magisterium of the Church and has a very negative evaluation of much of the Catholic moral theology written after Vatican II.

The first three hundred pages develop his theory, which is described in chapter 5 of this book. Moral theology deals with choices for the good. The basic principle of morality for Grisez is integral human fulfillment understood in the following way: In voluntarily acting for human goods and avoiding what is opposed to them, one ought to choose, and otherwise will, those and only those possibilities whose willing is compatible with a will toward "integral human fulfillment." Eight principles or modes of responsibility spell out this first principle in a formal way. For example, one should not be so moved by one instance of an intelligible good that one chooses to destroy, damage, or impede some other instance of an intelligible good. Grisez then proposes eight basic human goods, discussed in chapter 5 of this volume, that are self-evident; to go against any one of them is a moral evil.

After developing his thought from a philosophical perspective, Grisez discusses sin and the creating and redeeming work of God. Through charity the Christian cooperates in the redemptive work accomplished by God's healing love. Christian morality transforms the first principle of all human morality—that we ought to will only those possibilities that are compatible with the will toward integral human fulfillment—with a more definite principle: To will only what contributes to the integral human fulfillment being realized in the fulfillment of all things in Jesus. The eight modes of Christian response corresponding to the earlier modes of responsibility are the blessings proclaimed in the eight beatitudes. The new Gospel law of love brings the natural law to its perfection and fulfillment, but the new law of love in no way annuls or cancels the natural law with its principles and norms. In fact, faith and love do not conflict with any precepts of the natural law and do not even add new principles to natural law. But faith does generate specific norms proper to Christian life, such as the norm to seek, accept, and faithfully carry out one's personal vocation. Grisez's philosophical and ethical approach is the lens through which he interprets and develops the theological aspects of the discipline. Grisez then, at great length, develops the role of the sacraments—baptism, confirmation, penance, anointing, and the Eucharist—in the Christian moral life. From a practical perspective, Grisez's massive tome is quite intimidating. For that reason, it seems that Grisez and Russell Shaw wrote a 456-page simplified version called *Fulfillment in Christ: A Summary of Christian Moral Principles.* William E. May published an even more concise and quite clear fundamental moral theology based heavily on Grisez's thinking and writing.[33]

Romanus Cessario's *Introduction to Moral Theology* (2001) acknowledges that the authoritative statements of the Roman Catholic Church supply the normative principles for determining what constitutes the basic elements of moral theology. The two primary specific sources for his synthesis are two fundamental documents from the magisterium of Pope John Paul II (the 1993 encyclical *Veritatis splendor* and the *Catechism of the Catholic Church*) and the realist approach to moral theology found in Thomas Aquinas.[34] Cessario understands moral theology as a systematically ordered study of the journey of a human being made in the image and likeness of God back to the Father. He follows the generally accepted approach of Aquinas on virtue, natural law, and the determination of the morality of particular acts based on the object, the end, and the circumstances.

The syntheses mentioned thus far were written primarily for professional moral theologians, graduate students, and ministerial students. There have been some good attempts to provide textbooks for undergraduates and study groups as well. James P. Hanigan's *As I Have Loved You: The Challenge of Christian Ethics* (1986) takes up the usual topics of fundamental moral theology: the person as moral agent, conscience, sin, natural law, and norms. He correctly gives more emphasis to the social and community dimensions of the person, and in keeping with his theological approach he includes a chapter on the counsels of perfection, along with an emphasis on spirituality and liturgy.

Russell Connors and Patrick McCormick have written a text for undergraduates that is pedagogically appealing and user friendly. It also shows great creativity in the way the material is presented.[35] They begin not with theory and principles but with lived experience understood as a "tug" or a call to become a fully human person, to make choices, and to create just community. They develop the importance and role of story, especially in shaping character and the life of the moral person. They respond to the further question of how we know the right thing to do in a particular situation by treating conscience, moral norms, and moral reason developed in a holistic way that also recognizes the role of creative imagination. The book closes with chapters on sin and conversion. Throughout, the authors emphasize the communitarian and social aspects of morality.

James T. Bretzke's *A Morally Complex World: Engaging Contemporary Moral Theology* shows a very knowledgeable moral theologian and another fine pedagogue at work. The book is primarily about decision making in our complex world and not about character and moral development. Bretzke, in keeping with the Catholic tradition, recognizes two theological sources of scripture and tradition and the human sources of reason and experience. He proposes a fascinating double-helix model for the relationship between scripture and ethics and insists that scripture itself is neither self-evident nor self-interpreting nor self-applying. All in all, Bretzke proposes a complex but very clear method of handling issues in our morally complex world.

CONSCIENCE AND SIN

Two of the important topics in the manuals—conscience and sin—underwent a great change in the post–Vatican II period, especially in the writings of the revisionist approach that had been primary in this period. Many of the factors developed in this and preceding chapters contributed to this development.

Conscience

The manuals distinguished conscience as the judgment of the morality of an act from synderesis, the habit of practical reason that knows the first principles of the natural law. In the legal model of the manuals, conscience is the subjective norm of morality, whereas law constitutes the objective norm of morality. Conscience itself involves a rational and deductive reasoning process using the form of a syllogism. The general precept of the natural law (good is to be done) and the more specific principles deduced by moral science from the general principles (e.g., adultery is wrong) constitute the major and minor premises of the syllogism. The decision of conscience is then deduced from the general principle and the more specific principles. For example, evil is to be avoided; adultery is evil; therefore, adultery is to be avoided.

Many contemporary theologians, following Timothy O'Connell, distinguish in an analogous manner three aspects of conscience: conscience as capacity, as process, and as judgment. Conscience on the first level is the unfolding capacity of the human individual for moral goodness; on the second level, conscience is the process we go through in trying to arrive at our decisions; on the third level, conscience is the judgment about what is to be done in a particular situation.[36]

Perhaps the most distinctive characteristic of this contemporary approach to conscience is the personalistic framework in which conscience is cast. There is, however, one caveat. A personalistic framework for conscience should not be understood in a narrow sense that forgets about the social and communal dimension of human and Christian existence. Here one should recall the ultimate dilemma of conscience—I must follow my conscience (in the sense of the judgment of conscience), but my conscience might be wrong. The manuals and the broader Catholic moral tradition recognized that the error of the conscience judgment can be either vincible (my fault) or invincible (not my fault). Why might the conscience decision be wrong? The two general reasons are human finitude and human sinfulness. I see only part of the picture, never the full picture. Sin and bias also affect us in many different ways. Thus we all need to be self-critical and at the same time tap into all the possible resources that can help us in making a decision.

Conscience as capacity is not a static reality. Recall the earlier mention of Walter Conn's emphasis on the growth and development of conscience.[37] The Catholic tradition has consistently recognized a radical drive within each of us to reach out beyond the self to the true and the good that ultimately fulfills the person. The development and growth of conscience as capacity involves deepening our inclination to the good. Conn describes this growth of conscience as the self-transcending subject, going through three different conversions. Notice here how the developmental aspect fits in with the theological aspect of the importance of continuing conversion in the life of the Christian. The virtues also play a very significant role in the growth and development of conscience.

The emphasis on critical imagination, affectivity, and emotion in contemporary Catholic moral theology influences the understanding and role of conscience in all its dimensions. Conscience is not just a discursive process. Sidney Callahan has insisted on the importance of the emotions, affectivity, and intuition in the role of conscience.[38] Callahan recognizes all these sources together with discursive reasoning as involved in the free decision of conscience. But because of human limitation and sinfulness, none of these sources can be absolutized; instead, each must be verified by all of the other factors. Callahan has articulated a broad understanding of conscience as a self-conscious activity of a person who is think-ing, feeling, imagining, and willing action on behalf of moral standards of worth. In this same broad perspective, she calls for a holistic model of moral develop-ment. Moral education can fail by slighting either the need for critical thinking or the need for personal motivations that emerge from empathy, caring, and emo-tional attachments to the vision of the good. With commendable recognition of the complexities involved, Callahan points out the many factors operating in the functioning of conscience: moral freedom and human limits, actively directed thinking and spontaneously free conscience operations, reason and emotion, the individual self, and the constitutive community.

Richard Gula also insists on a holistic understanding of conscience as an ex-pression of the whole self as a thinking, feeling, intuiting, and willing person. Gula refers to practical moral reasoning as discernment, which is at work in all areas except in those actions that are clearly immoral, such as murder. Discernment is a process that, like a four-stranded cable, circles back on itself to intertwine faith, reason, emotion, and intuition. Moral discernment is not a science but an art that can only arrive at moral certitude. The decision of moral discernment rests on an aesthetic judgment of harmony with one's sense of self. The sense of inner harmony and wholeness is the interior sign that we are responding to the grace of God in this moment.[39]

Charles Curran has developed a similar understanding of conscience, insist-ing that the criterion that one has made a good decision is the peace and joy of a good conscience. Curran proposes a number of foundations for this criterion. All recognize that remorse is a sign of an erroneous conscience. Early Christian spirituality proposed criteria for the discernment of spirits. Later spiritual writers, such as Ignatius Loyola and Francis de Sales, insisted on the role of interior peace in decision making. From a more philosophical perspective, the moral subject has a drive for the true and the good. When we achieve the true and the good, peace and joy exist. In any judgments we make, a good criterion is the peace that comes when there are no more pertinent questions to ask. The criterion of peace and joy sees a radical identity between authentic subjectivity and true objectivity. Curran proposes a number of ways to safeguard against abuses that can arise from our limitations and sinfulness.[40]

Sin

Sin, as we have seen, had an important place in the manuals of moral theology, with the primary purpose of training confessors to know what act is a sin and the degree of sinfulness. Sin is an act against the law of God. Mortal sin is an act that turns me away from the love of God and merits eternal damnation. Venial sin is a lesser sin that does not have the dire effects of mortal sin. Three conditions are required for mortal sin—grave matter, full knowledge, and full consent of the will. But the primary criterion in the manuals was the existence of grave matter. In special moral theology the manuals assumed the presence of the other two conditions. Even moral theologians and catechists often spoke of grave sin when they should have spoken only of grave matter. For example, it was generally accepted that it was a mortal sin to miss Mass on Sunday. Thus mortal sin was thought to be a frequent occurrence in the life of Catholics.

Many of the same developments in Catholic moral theology after Vatican II were present in the early changed understanding of mortal sin: the importance of the biblical witness, a greater role given to the theological, and the primary emphasis on the person rather than the act. However, this change with regard to the understanding of mortal sin occurred much more quickly and much earlier than most of the other previously mentioned developments. This quick change was probably due to the important role mortal sin played not only in moral theology but also in Catholic life.

John W. Glazer, in an influential article in *Theological Studies* in 1968 that relied heavily on German theologians such as Karl Rahner and Bruno Schüller, understood mortal sin in light of the fundamental option involving a breaking of one's relationship with God.[41] In three essays written between 1967 and 1969, Curran argued that mortal sin should not be understood in terms of an individual external act.[42] Timothy O'Connell insisted in his 1978 textbook that mortal sin involves a fundamental option and that one cannot even be reflexively conscious of its existence.[43]

Common sense maintains that one does not break deep friendships or relationships many times a day. The biblical and theological notion of conversion talks about a gradual changing process rather than one dramatic act. The concept of sin in Genesis is more than just an act of disobedience. Sin is, of course, the breaking of Adam and Eve's relationship to God, but it is also the breaking of the relationship among people, as illustrated by their children killing another and the breaking of their relationship with the world and even with themselves. Mortal sin involves a breaking of the covenantal relationship with God. Older theologians had pointed out that the move from sin to grace was a process rather than one dramatic act. Some original proponents of the fundamental option saw it as very much in continuity with Aquinas's emphasis on the ultimate end. Mortal sin involves going against God as our ultimate end, not something of less importance.[44]

One of the dramatic changes in Catholic life and practice after Vatican II was the greatly reduced role of confession in the life of Catholics in the pew.[45] With regard to the understanding of sin on the basis of some type of basic orientation, many moral theologians argued for a different format for the sacrament of penance that does not require the confession of all mortal sins according to number and species. Unfortunately, the leadership in the Catholic Church has adamantly refused to change the format of the sacrament of penance. The danger exists that, in neglecting the sacrament of penance, many believers might come to downplay and even forget the reality of human sinfulness. But without the recognition of human sinfulness, continual conversion or growth in the Christian life is not possible. We are all people who have committed sin (what the manuals would call "venial sin") and have been called to change our hearts and grow in our relationships with God, neighbor, world, and self. The changed understanding of sin calls for a changed format for the sacrament of penance. Thus, soon after Vatican II, a newer understanding of mortal sin became widely accepted in Catholic moral theology, and the reasons for the change here prefigured many of the other changes that occurred later in moral theology.

A very significant post–Vatican II development concerned the recognition of social sin. U.S. Catholic moral theologians and the papal magisterium learned the reality of social sin from liberation theologians in Central and South America. Both the papal magisterium and U.S. moral theologians tended at first to emphasize how the personal sins of individuals contribute to the existence of sinful social situations. The consequent call to conversion is not simply a matter of changing one's heart but also of changing those structures that were caused by personal sins. This understanding was in keeping with the more theological approach spawned by Vatican II. Liberation theologians, however, emphasized the sinful structures and institutional violence that have an unconscious effect on how human beings live and act in those structures. Not only do personal sins affect social structures, but social structures influence, often in unconscious and unknown ways, the actions of people who live within those structures.[46]

Principles, Norms, and Casuistry

Post–Vatican II Catholic moral theology has continued to recognize a role for principles and norms in moral theology, even though many no longer adopt a legal model for morality, as had been the practice in the pre–Vatican II manuals. Principles and norms exist primarily to protect and promote moral values and to guide our actions in accord with these values. Post–Vatican II moral theologians continue to recognize, for example, the principle of totality in medical ethics. A part of the human body may be sacrificed for the good of the whole person. The post–Vatican II discussion tended to concentrate on issues of private morality, but principles and norms also come into play in the area of social ethics. We might consider, for example, the importance of human rights and the various types of justice. Principles tend to be more general, for example, the principle of totality wherein norms (e.g., that the direct killing of noncombatants is always wrong) are more specific.

Chapter 5 and to some extent chapter 6 discuss the debate about norms in the post–Vatican II Church, so the present consideration builds on the earlier materials. The manualistic and neoscholastic natural law theorists continue to hold all the norms taught by the hierarchical magisterium based especially on the nature and purpose of the faculty. The new natural law, or the basic goods theory, likewise defends all the norms taught by the hierarchical magisterium and, with the manualistic theory of natural law, also upholds the principle of the double effect. Thus these positions accept the concept of intrinsically evil actions, which are always and everywhere wrong, based on the object of the act apart from the end or the circumstances.

Revisionists challenged some of the norms accepted in pre–Vatican II Catholic moral theology and still taught by the papal magisterium. In general, revisionists defending their approach to norms frequently appeal to the Thomistic understanding that the first principles of the natural law oblige always and everywhere, but that the secondary principles oblige as generally occurs and can admit of some exceptions. The example given by Aquinas is the norm that deposits should be returned. Today we use this same term in referring to bank deposits. The depositor leaves something in possession of another person with the proviso that the other person will return it to the depositor whenever the depositor asks for it. But if the depositor has left you a sword and comes back drunk and threatening to kill people, you should not return the sword to the owner.[47] With regard to the secondary principles of the natural law, complex circumstances and conditions can arise that call for some exceptions to the norm. The Catholic tradition has always recognized that many norms admit of exceptions, such as the norm of promise keeping or of confidentiality. Circumstances might arise in which one is no longer held to keeping the promise or the confidentiality.

Revisionists also point out the existence of different types of norms that would also be generally accepted by others. Russell Connors and Patrick McCormick, basically following the work of Gula and O'Connell, distinguish three types of norms.[48] Formal norms are recognized by all as referring to the persons we are called to be and the virtues that the Christian should have. These norms refer to one's being and not one's doing. Such norms are usually preceded by the verb "be"—for example, be considerate, be loving, be kind. Such norms are very general and admit of no exceptions. Since these norms are formal, they have no material content. What does it mean to be considerate?

Synthetic norms constitute a somewhat more elusive category. These norms are phrased in the language of doing—similar to material norms—and not in the language of being. Synthetic norms are usually phrased negatively—do not lie, do not steal, do not commit murder. These terms (lying, stealing, murder) are synthetic terms that apply to actions that are always wrong. But these are synthetic terms that refer to unjustified false speech, unjustified taking the possession of another, and unjustified killing. Thus these norms do not refer to specific concrete actions as being always wrong. On the other hand, material norms refer to our doing and not our being by pointing out specific concrete actions that are to be done or not done. For example, euthanasia is wrong. Revisionists take different positions on specific absolute material norms.

Richard McCormick, as the premier proportionalist in the United States, developed the theory that one can do premoral evil if there is a proportionate reason. Material values then are not moral values as such but only premoral values. Are our actions involving premoral evil always, everywhere, and in all circumstances wrong? In other words, are they intrinsically evil? McCormick cannot say they are intrinsically evil because one would have to know all the possible combinations of premoral goods and premoral evils involved in every possible concrete act. But in practice McCormick concludes that some material norms are virtually without exception. Examples of such virtually exceptionless or practically exceptionless norms are euthanasia and the direct killing of noncombatants in warfare.[49] Timothy O'Connell, a revisionist, finds some weaknesses in the theory of proportionalism and insists that the direct killing of the innocent is in theory intrinsically evil and not just a virtually exceptionless norm.[50] A more inductive approach, such as the prudential Aristotelian-Thomistic method, could also come to affirm material norms that are always obliging in cases such as human rights and the direct killing of noncombatants.

All agree that principles and norms have a role to play in moral theology, but they are by no means the most important consideration. In reality, very few of the actions that Christians do are taken in light of the existence of concrete material norms.

Casuistry is not a pejorative term in the Catholic understanding unless it is used to describe the whole of moral theology that had no place for the role of the person as moral agent and subject. For many outside the Catholic tradition, casuistry has taken on a pejorative meaning. But in 1988 Albert R. Jonsen, who was trained as a moral theologian, and Stephen Toulmin, a philosopher, published *The Abuse of Casuistry: A History of Moral Reasoning.* Their aim was to show that the casuistic art has a legitimate and even central role to play in practical ethics. Their work together as members of the National Commission for the Protection of Human Subjects of Biomedical and Behavioral Research showed them the importance of the casuistic method, with its comparison of cases with one another and with paradigmatic cases. They understand casuistry as differentiated from the use of principles. Almost a hundred pages of the book deal with high casuistry of the Catholic moral theologians in the period from 1556 to 1656.[51]

In 1995 James F. Keenan and Thomas A. Shannon edited *The Context of Casuistry* in an effort to provide a broader sampling of ethicists, mostly in the Catholic tradition, who used cases to find practical truth in concrete situations. There are different approaches to casuistry and some disagreement over precisely how casuistry functions—for example, what is the role of principles in the use of casuistry? Catholic moral theology will continue to deal with concrete cases and employ some type of casuistry in the process, but casuistry should be only one part of the total reality of moral theology.

In my judgment, casuistry on the objective pole and conscience on the subjective pole exist in some tension with specific material norms. At times the norm guides and directs casuistry and conscience. But casuistry and conscience have modified and clarified norms. Thus, for example, the norm against killing has been sharpened over time. Casuistry and conscience also help to explain why, over time, some specific moral norms taught by the Catholic Church have changed.[52]

This chapter has pointed out the very significant changes that have occurred in fundamental moral theology in the post–Vatican II period. The next three chapters will discuss the developments in marriage and sexual ethics, bioethics, and social ethics.

NOTES

1. O'Connell, *Making Disciples*, 28.

2. Grisez and Shaw, *Fulfillment in Christ*, 279.

3. Ibid., 21–25.

4. Crossin, *What Are They Saying*, 58–81.

5. Philibert, "Conscience." See also Keane, *Christian Ethics and the Imagination*, 155–61.

6. Conn, *Conscience*. See also Conn, *Christian Conversion*.

7. Aquinas, *Summa theologiae, Ia IIae,* qq. 55–70.

8. *Journal of Religious Ethics* 1 (1973): 5–64.

9. Hauerwas, *Character and the Christian Life.*

10. Porter, *Recovery of Virtue,* 32.

11. Cessario, *Moral Virtues and Theological Ethics* and *Virtues or the Examined Life.*

12. Cessario, *Introduction to Moral Theology,* xvi–xvii.

13. Keenan, "Proposing Cardinal Virtues," 714–15.

14. Ibid., 723–28.

15. Spohn, "Return of Virtue Ethics," 64–65.

16. Curran, *Catholic Moral Tradition Today,* 110–36.

17. Fuchs never systematically developed his moral theology. For his most significant essays dealing with fundamental option, see Fuchs, *Human Values and Christian Morality,* 92–111, and *Christian Morality,* 3–133.

18. O'Connell, *Principles for a Catholic Morality,* 57–82 (2d ed., 65–102).

19. May, *Introduction to Moral Theology,* 154–58.

20. Curran, *Catholic Moral Tradition Today,* 96–98.

21. Porter, "Recent Studies in Aquinas's Virtue Ethic," 206–7.

22. Pope, *Evolution of Altruism.* Vacek's and Pope's books were the first two volumes in the Moral Traditions series of Georgetown University Press, edited by James F. Keenan, which now includes more than fifty titles.

23. Maguire, *Moral Choice,* 189–217.

24. Keane, *Christian Ethics and the Imagination,* 15; O'Connell, *Making Disciples,* x.

25. See also Callahan, "Role of Emotion in Ethical Decision Making."

26. Milhaven, *Good Anger.*

27. O'Connell, *Making Disciples,* 105–38.

28. O'Connell, *Principles for a Catholic Morality.*

29. Ibid., 39.

30. Himes, review of Gula's *Reason Informed by Faith,* 293.

31. Gula, *Moral Discernment; Good Life; Call to Holiness.*

32. Hehir, "A Catholic Troeltsch?"

33. May, *Introduction to Moral Theology.*

34. Cessario, *Introduction to Moral Theology,* xi–xvii.

35. Connors and McCormick, *Character, Choice, and Community.*

36. O'Connell, *Principles for a Catholic Morality,* 88–97; Gula, *Reason Informed by Faith,* 130–35; Connors and McCormick, *Character, Choice, and Community,* 122–32.

37. Conn, *Conscience* and *Christian Conversion.*

38. Callahan, *In Good Conscience.*

39. Gula, *Moral Discernment,* 100.

40. Curran, *Catholic Moral Theology Today,* 172–96. Curran first developed this theory of conscience in 1977 in Curran, *Themes in Fundamental Moral Theology,* 191–231.

41. Glazer, "Transition between Grace and Sin."

42. Curran, "Masturbation and Objectively Grave Matter"; "Sexuality and Sin," parts 1 and 2; and "Sacrament of Penance Today."

43. O'Connell, *Principles for a Catholic Morality,* 71–72.

44. E.g., Bretzke, *Morally Complex World,* 191–208; Hanigan, *As I Have Loved You,* 101–18.

45. Gaupin, "More Frequent Communion, Less Frequent Confession."

46. O'Keefe, *What Are They Saying;* Pfeil, "Doctrinal Implications"; Pfeil, "Romero on Social Sin"; Himes, "Social Sin and the Role of the Individual."

47. Aquinas, *Summa theologiae, Ia IIae,* q. 94.

48. Connors and McCormick, *Character, Choice, and Community,* 162–73; Gula, *Reason Informed by Faith,* 283–99; O'Connell, *Principles for a Catholic Morality,* rev. ed., 175–214.

49. For overviews and analyses of McCormick's proportionalism, see Odozor, *Richard A. McCormick and the Renewal of Moral Theology,* 91–118; Walter, "Foundation and Formulation of Norms."

50. O'Connell, *Principles for a Catholic Morality,* rev. ed., 202–14.

51. Jonsen and Toulmin, *Abuse of Casuistry,* 137–227.

52. Curran, *Catholic Moral Tradition Today,* 160–66.

SEXUALITY AND MARRIAGE

The lively debate over *Humanae vitae* in 1968 brought the issue of sexuality to the fore in Catholic life and experience and also in moral theology. From a revisionist perspective, the criticism of the natural law arguments in support of the ban on artificial contraception for spouses logically had to affect other issues of sexuality. Revisionists criticized the approach of *Humanae vitae* and its defenders for failing to appreciate historical consciousness, paying too much attention to the individual act, proposing a morality too narrowly based on the nature and purpose of the faculty, and identifying the human moral act with the physical structure of the act (physicalism). In place of the older natural law criteria for the determination of the morality of sexual acts, the revisionists proposed a more person-centered anthropology, or a relational anthropology, that sees the human person in multiple relationships with God, neighbor, world, and self. Logically, then, the revisionist approach to *Humanae vitae* and contraception applies to other issues of sexuality.

The ensuing debate over sexuality kept alive and even exacerbated the differences between the revisionist approach and the defenders of existing hierarchical teaching with regard to the issues of sexuality and dissent from noninfallible Church teaching.[1] The Vatican took disciplinary action against Anthony Kosnik, Philip Keane, and John McNeill, priests who had questioned existing hierarchical sexual teachings.[2] The strongest Vatican condemnation was the judgment of the Congregation for the Doctrine of the Faith in 1986 that Charles Curran was no longer suitable or eligible to teach Catholic theology because of his dissenting positions. These tensions continued to grow with the 1993 encyclical *Veritatis splendor,* from Pope John Paul II. This encyclical was the first dedicated explicitly to moral theology and was occasioned by what the pope himself called a "genuine crisis" of an "overall and systematic calling into question traditional moral teachings of the Church especially regarding the natural law and the universality and permanent value of its precepts."[3]

The debate over sexuality followed the trajectory that occurred in Catholic moral theology after Vatican II and *Humanae vitae,* as discussed in chapter 4. The leaders of the revisionist approach were young scholars who were just beginning their work as moral theologians. With one or two exceptions, these moral theologians were priests. Lay theologians did not begin writing until the 1980s, after which many women became contributing moral theologians.

The few revisionist moral theologians working in the 1960s and 1970s were so busy dealing with particular issues that they wrote primarily essays rather than monographs. In the area of sexuality, the monographs by Catholic revisionist theologians appeared only in the late 1970s. In the last two decades of the twentieth century and the first years of the twenty-first, many more monographs on sexuality have appeared. This chapter first discusses the particular issues and then the monographs that focus in a more systematic and methodological way on the understanding of human sexuality, marriage, and family.

SPECIFIC SEXUAL ISSUES

The moral theology manuals unanimously taught that in sexual sins there was no parvity of matter—in other words, every sexual sin, even if it is just an internal sin, always involves grave matter. In catechetical and popular parlance, the statement was regularly made that all sins against the sixth commandment are mortal sins.[4]

In a 1966 address to the Catholic Theological Society of America, Charles Curran disagreed with the position that no parvity of matter exists in sexual sin and applied this assertion specifically to masturbation. In light of both Thomas Aquinas's understanding of mortal sin as opposing God as our ultimate end and new fundamental option theories, Curran denied the assertion of no parvity in matters of sexual sin. On the issue of masturbation, current scientific knowledge of the psychological and physical reality of masturbation, theological insights, and the experience of Christians and other people of goodwill argue for a change in the teaching that masturbation always involves grave matter. One of the strong reasons supporting the older position was the fact that in 1612 Claudius Aquaviva, the general of the Society of Jesus, strictly forbade Jesuit theologians to maintain that sexual sins could involve only light matter. From a historical perspective, it is amazing how quickly and easily the newer approach in sexual sins was theologically and pastorally accepted.[5]

Contraception and Artificial Insemination

The basic arguments for and against contraception have not changed substantially since the time of *Humanae vitae*, with one possible exception. Some contemporary defenders of Church teaching on contraception, such as Janet Smith, point to the new arguments proposed by Pope John Paul II, who saw his defense of *Humanae vitae* as trying to incorporate more completely the biblical and personalistic aspects of the encyclical's teaching. Given his theology of the body, the intimate language of the marriage act expresses the total reciprocal self-giving of husband and wife. Contraception, however, contradicts the language of marital love, for it means that husband and wife refuse to give themselves totally to each other.[6] Those Catholics who disagree with *Humanae vitae* reply that the papal teaching still puts too much emphasis on the individual act. The totality of the relationship between husband and wife should express the meaning of this relationship. No one act can ever fully express the total and reciprocal commitment to self-giving of spouses to each other. In addition, marital love includes friendship love and self-fulfilling love, not just self-giving love.

We should remember Pope Pius XII's condemnation of artificial insemination, even with a husband's semen (AIH), and the resultant change in Gerald Kelly's position on this matter. Catholic revisionists who disagree with Church teaching on contraception logically should have no problem with AIH. Although AIH is used in an attempt to have children, whereas contraception is used to avoid having children, the hierarchical consideration of both, in the judgment of revisionists, is based on the same understanding of the need to have the husband's semen deposited into the vagina of the wife. This act analysis, with emphasis on the inviolability of the physical aspect of the act, logically connects AIH and artificial contraception. In 1969 Rodger van Allen explicitly argued in favor of AIH.[7] To my knowledge, no Catholic theologian who accepts artificial contraception opposes AIH. Of course, those who oppose contraception also logically oppose AIH, as is evident in the 1987 "Instruction" from the Congregation for the Doctrine of the Faith.[8] Catholic revisionists differ among themselves on the question of AID—artificial insemination with donor semen.[9]

Sterilization

Logically, a strong connection exists between contraception and sterilization. In accord with the Catholic understanding, contraception is wrong because it goes against the God-given purpose of the sexual act; sterilization is wrong because it goes against the God-given purpose of the sexual faculty or power. Interestingly enough, from the Catholic perspective, the anovulant pill, technically speaking, is a temporary sterilization and not contraception, because it interferes with the sexual faculty and not the sexual act. Logically, the only difference between contraception and sterilization is that most forms of sterilization tend to be permanent. Contraception is thus preferred unless there is a more serious reason permanently avoiding conception.

In his 1977 book on sterilization John P. Boyle points out that in 1973 Charles Curran wrote the first full-length article in this country arguing that direct sterilization is not always wrong.[10] Richard McCormick, in an unpublished paper, also defended the morality of some direct sterilization.[11] John Boyle's book addresses both his assertion of the morality of direct sterilization under certain conditions and the practice of sterilization in Catholic hospitals and health facilities. In the United States at that time the issue of sterilization in Catholic hospitals was becoming quite prominent. Boyle argued that, on the basis of the principle of cooperation, Catholic hospitals in some circumstances (e.g., when the Catholic hospital is the only hospital serving all the people in an area) could allow sterilizations to be done. On the other hand, those who, like William E. May, oppose contraception, also logically oppose direct sterilization.[12]

The issue of sterilization in Catholic hospitals and health care facilities has continued to attract attention. Margaret Farley reported the action of the Vatican Congregation for Religious and Secular Institutes that forced the general administration of the Sisters of Mercy—sponsors at that time of the largest group of nonprofit hospitals in the United States—to rescind a recommendation made in the late 1970s to their hospitals' administrators that tubal ligations be allowed when judged best for the good of the patient. The congregation demanded that the general administration team of the Sisters of Mercy send a new letter prohibiting tubal ligations in their hospitals. The sisters said they would take no public position on sterilization contrary to Church teaching. But the congregation insisted that if an individual sister did not accept this teaching against sterilization, she was to specify the dissent in writing and sign it. Farley describes this episode as an illustration of both power and powerlessness in the Church.[13] Sterilization in Catholic hospitals continues to be discussed, especially in light of mergers of Catholic hospitals with non-Catholic facilities. But the Vatican has been adamant in its prohibition of direct sterilization in Catholic institutions.[14]

These controversies indicate the points at which tension often arises in issues regarding sexuality. Many individual Catholics decide in the forum of conscience that they can dissent from Church teaching on issues such as contraception and sterilization (as well as other issues discussed below), and no public tension results.

Problems arise when issues cannot be solved in the forum of personal conscience but involve the public policy of the Church or of Catholic institutions, as in the cases of sterilization, divorce, remarriage, and the ordination of women.

Homosexuality

A number of factors have contributed to the relatively extensive literature in Catholic moral theology about the morality of homosexual acts. There always have been gay and lesbian Catholics who struggle with the teaching of the Church in this area. The emphasis on a personal and relational approach to sexuality, rather than on the criterion of the nature of the sexual faculty, opened up new possibilities of viewing the morality of homosexual acts. Gay and lesbian movements became vocal during the period after Vatican II; the question could not be ignored. From the viewpoint of moral theology, the issue of homosexual relationships and acts brought into play significant methodological questions. All the sources of moral theology are involved in this issue: scripture, tradition, Church teaching, reason, experience, and the data of the human sciences. Subsequently, many Catholic moral theologians recognized homosexuality as important, not only for its very significant pastoral implications but also because of its importance for the discipline of moral theology itself.

In 1970 John J. McNeill tentatively concluded that responsible homosexual relations could possibly be understood as coming under the principle of choosing the lesser of two evils.[15] In a 1971 article Charles Curran proposed that McNeill's position did not go far enough because such sexual relations in this theory are still regarded as evil. Curran proposed a mediating position, based on his theory of compromise, between the two extreme positions that homosexual acts are always wrong or that they are merely neutral. Curran maintained that homosexual acts in a stable homosexual relationship fall short of the heterosexual ideal but can be justifiable and good for homosexual persons. The article reviewed much of the contemporary literature in Christian ethics and touched on all the sources of knowledge for moral theology that impinge on this question.[16]

In 1976 McNeill published *The Church and the Homosexual* and changed his approach. Scripture condemns perverse homosexual activity by heterosexual persons. The argument that the scriptures were unaware of the reality of the homosexual orientation has been used by many proponents of the goodness of homosexual acts in a committed relationship. An anthropology recognizing radical human freedom argues against the emphasis on human nature in the traditional Catholic condemnation of homosexual acts. Contemporary scientific studies and experience support the goodness of such sexual relationships and acts.

McNeill maintains that the homosexual condition is in accord with the will of God, which is not determined merely by biology. Homosexual acts in a loving and ethically responsible relationship (e.g., a relationship based on mutuality, fidelity, and unselfishness) are morally and spiritually good.

A Challenge to Love (1983), edited by Robert Nugent, contains a number of theological essays that support committed gay and lesbian sexual relationships. Nugent and Jeannine Gramick founded New Ways Ministry to give pastoral support to Catholic gays and lesbians and their families. They are not professional theologians, but they are quite knowledgeable. Together and separately they have published a number of books on gay and lesbian relationships and have addressed the question of morality.[17] *A Challenge to Love* includes a 1980 article by Lisa Cahill, who sees the issue of homosexuality as an illustration of the different sources of moral theology—scripture, tradition, and both descriptive and normative accounts of experience—that inform a controverted and complex issue. Cahill concludes that these sources point unavoidably to a heterosexual norm for human sexuality, which, however, does not exclude exceptional applications in the case of confirmed homosexuals. Thus she adopts a mediating or compromise position in which the heterosexual relation is the ideal but homosexual relations in a committed relationship are morally acceptable.[18]

In the Nugent book Margaret Farley also examines the different sources of knowledge of moral theology and finds no absolute prohibition in these sources of same-sex relations. She then develops the criteria for judging such sexual relationships. In establishing the criteria, love is the problem, not the solution. The question is, what is proper love? Here she appeals to the norms of just love. These criteria or norms include respect for the autonomy and relationality of persons through requirements of mutuality, equality, commitment, and fruitfulness. These criteria should govern same-sex relationships.[19] More than twenty years later, Farley published an extensive monograph on just love.

In the same collection Mary E. Hunt develops a theology of the friendship of women that does not necessarily lead to sexual expression. But there can be a few cherished friendships that are sexual.[20] In a more impressionistic essay, Daniel Maguire argues in favor of same-sex marriage based on the personalist understanding of marriage found in Vatican II.[21]

A Challenge to Love also includes an article by Edward Molloy that develops the thesis of his book on homosexuality, which had recently been published. Molloy tries to prove that the revisionists had not made their case. But most of his book argues against the homosexual way of life as expressed in the social structures and practice of the homosexual subculture.[22] In his 1988 book *Homosexuality*, James Hanigan, using a theological and evangelical approach, defends the thesis that sexuality is vocationally significant and that sexual behavior is morally good only in the vocation of heterosexual marriage.

In the post–Vatican II period John Harvey has written extensively on homosexuality and basically follows the natural law approach of the manuals. Homosexual acts are wrong because such acts cannot fulfill the procreative purpose of the sexual faculty. If procreation can be separated from the sexual act, then any kind of sexual act can be justified. However, Harvey claims that the homosexual orientation is not wrong or evil and that individuals usually have no moral responsibility for their orientation.[23] But in 1986 the Congregation for the Doctrine of the Faith, in a letter to the bishops of the world, stated that the homosexual inclination is not a sin but an objective disorder because it is ordered toward an intrinsically evil act.[24] This statement has occasioned much controversy.[25] The Congregation for the Doctrine of the Faith, however, in accord with the faculty teleology of hierarchical sexual teaching, was compelled to call the inclination disordered. If the inclination or the orientation were good, then some acts coming from that orientation or inclination could be good.

In this early period of the discussion of homosexuality by Catholic moral theologians, John Boswell's 1980 historical study noted the tolerance for same-sex eroticism in the Greco-Roman World in which Christianity arose and maintained that the scriptures did not prove a hostile assessment of homosexuality. His most original historical findings were that early medieval Christians showed no animosity toward same-sex eroticism, and that only in the twelfth and thirteenth centuries did Christian writers take a negative position toward homosexuality.[26] Historians have discussed this book in great depth, and some have praised it lavishly.[27] Catholic theologians have not paid too much attention to it, perhaps because they lack expertise in the historical periods that Boswell discusses.

Since the mid-1980s many more Catholic moral theologians have entered the discussion about homosexual relations, but for the most part the methodological and substantive positions do not depart from the earlier positions. Most of the new voices argue in favor of homosexual relations in a committed relationship, but defenders of the existing hierarchical teaching also continue to write.[28]

Documents and actions by the Congregation for the Doctrine of the Faith strongly defended the existing teaching and sparked discussion. The 1986 "Letter to Bishops on the Pastoral Care of Homosexual Persons" insisted that only in the marital relationship could the use of the sexual faculty be morally good, and pointed out that while the inclination of the homosexual person is not a sin, it is an objective disorder because it is ordered to an intrinsically moral evil.[29] In 1992 the Congregation issued "Observations Regarding Legislative Proposals Concerned with Discrimination toward Homosexual Persons," claiming that homosexuality is not comparable to race, ethnicity, sex, or age with regard to nondiscrimination. Homosexuals, however, have the same rights as all humans, but these rights are not absolute and can be limited, for instance, in placing children for adoption in foster care, the employment of teachers and athletic coaches, and military recruitment. Many Catholic revisionist moral theologians disagreed with aspects of these documents.[30]

In the United States many Catholic bishops have strongly opposed legislation that would legalize same-sex marriage. Observing the way in which many of these arguments are made, Stephen Pope worries that the Church is sending a mixed message about the role and rights of gay people. If the Church is going to argue against same-sex marriage, the bishops should avoid any injustice and antigay bashing. The magisterium, given its reputation for being antigay and not supportive of gay rights, should take proactive steps on behalf of the rights of gay people.[31]

Disciplinary action by the Congregation for the Doctrine of the Faith in the matter of homosexuality also raised significant comment and illustrated the great tension existing in the Catholic Church on these issues. In 1978 the Congregation condemned the teaching in McNeill's book as being opposed to the traditional and actual teaching of the Church. Scandal has been caused by the publication of the book, the *imprimi potest* given by the Jesuit Superior, and McNeill's public promotion of the book and of his ideas. McNeill accepted the order that he not publicly teach the topic of homosexuality.[32] He publicly criticized the 1986 "Letter" and was expelled from the Society of Jesus.[33] Sister Jeannine Gramick and Father Robert Nugent, the directors of New Ways Ministries for Gays and Lesbians, had been under investigation by Church authorities for some time. They never publicly expressed their personal position or disagreed with hierarchical teaching but presented to gay people all that was being said by Church teaching and theologians. In 1999 the CDF permanently prohibited them from any further pastoral work with homosexual persons.[34]

This overview cannot go into detail about all the literature on homosexuality that has been published since the 1980s, but two contemporary authors deserve mention. Mark D. Jordan, who was trained as a philosopher and a medievalist and identifies himself as a gay activist, published *The Invention of Sodomy in Christian Theology* (1997). Jordan understands invention in two senses. In the common sense of discovering something new, the term *sodomy* only came into existence in the twelfth century. In the rhetorical sense of finding the right thing to say or speak, *sodomy* was used for uniting and reifying and for judging and punishing genital acts between persons of the same sex. The confusion and contradictions in the understanding of sodomy cannot be used today for serious theological thinking about sexuality. Jordan concludes that *sodomy* is a term that describes not human behavior but the nervous refusal of theologians to understand how pleasure can survive the preaching of the Gospel. In *The Silence of Sodom: Homosexuality in Modern Catholicism* (2000), Jordan disagrees with the approach taken by most revisionist Catholic moral theologians and most Catholic homosexuals who argue on the basis of homosexual identity. He agrees with Foucault that no such reality as sexual identity exists. Homosexuals have desires, memories, and loves, but not an identity. Revisionist moral theologians in the United States have yet to respond to this argument.

In 1993 Patricia Beattie Jung, from a Catholic perspective, and Ralph F. Smith, from a Lutheran perspective, published *Heterosexism: An Ethical Challenge,* which strongly argues against the homophobia present in their churches. They maintain that the only way to avoid and get rid of this homophobia is to recognize homosexuality as a natural variation and a part of God's original blessing. In 2001 Jung, with Joseph Andrew Coray, edited *Sexual Diversity and Catholicism: Toward the Development of Moral Theology.* Jung points out in the introduction the heterosexual bias in the Catholic tradition that, in general, challenges the present Catholic teaching. The format of the book indicates that moral theologians in the twenty-first century are still dealing with the same facets of the issue that have been present from the earliest writings in the 1970s—the tradition and teaching of the Church, scripture, the social sciences, and human experience.

Divorce and Remarriage

Divorce and remarriage were two other important pastoral issues that revisionist moral theologians began to consider in light of their new methodological approach. Marriage breakdown among Catholics and others was becoming more frequent, but Catholic teaching maintained that a consummated marriage between two baptized persons is indissoluble. At the same time, Catholic scholars were also developing new canonical and pastoral approaches to the question of divorce and remarriage. From the canonical viewpoint, canon lawyers began to annul (not dissolve) more Church marriages on the grounds of a lack of psychological maturity. The couple might have been unable to give the necessary consent because they were unable at the time of the marriage to meet the essential obligations of marriage, especially the indissolubility of marriage. Two types of pastoral or internal forum cases were discussed. In the first case (called the "conflict case"), a valid marriage probably does not exist, but this fact cannot be proved in the external forum of Church law courts. The second case (called the "hardship case") involves a marriage that is presumably valid but has broken down. Much discussion centered on the hardship cases.[35]

The canonical and pastoral approaches lie outside the scope of our consideration, which will deal only with the moral aspect, often phrased in terms of the indissolubility of a consummated sacramental marriage. The question of divorce and remarriage is similar to the homosexuality issue in moral theology because it brings into play how one understands and uses the sources of our moral teaching and theology—scripture, tradition, the teaching of the Church, human reason, and human and Christian experience.

In the first article by an American moral theologian to argue that the Catholic Church should change its teaching on the absolute indissolubility of marriage, Charles Curran touched on all these aspects.[36] Curran reviewed what other scholars were saying about these different sources. Before 1967 U.S. scripture scholars generally understood the New Testament as being in basic agreement with the Catholic Church teaching on the indissolubility of marriage. In 1954 Bruce Vawter wrote an article in this vein, but in 1967 he maintained that the teaching of Jesus on the absolute indissolubility of marriage is a command directed to the conscience of Christians but cannot be made into a divine law binding in all circumstances.[37] Dominic Crossan, at a 1967 symposium of the Canon Law Society of America, came to a similar conclusion with regard to the New Testament.[38] Both authors, and many subsequent writers, see the famous exceptions in Matthew 5:32 and 19:9 (except for *porneia*) as a later redaction and not the words of Jesus. The early Church, as illustrated also by Paul, made some exceptions to the absolute statement of Jesus. Also, they both point to the Sermon on the Mount context, so that Jesus' teaching on divorce belongs to the radical teachings of Jesus that, as a whole, have not been made into absolute norms.

In 1967 Victor Pospishil, a Byzantine Rite Catholic priest and canonist, published *Divorce and Remarriage: Toward a New Catholic Morality,* in which he maintained that the hierarchy has the power of the keys to dissolve truly Christian marriages. There are many inadequacies in his approach, which commentators pointed out later. But his book did bring the question of divorce to the foreground for Catholic moral theologians in the United States immediately after Vatican II. Most of Pospishil's book, including sixty pages of appendices, deals with the historical development of the first ten centuries.

John Noonan, in a careful study presented at the 1967 canon law symposium, deals with the laws of Christian emperors allowing divorce. He concludes that for a substantial period of time many Christians viewed marriage as dissoluble, but this did not prove that the later developments toward indissolubility were wrong.[39] With regard to the historical development of the Catholic tradition, two problems arise. The first problem is in interpreting exactly what the fathers of the Church maintained regarding this point. Most recognize that there were some exceptions (although they differ on how many), but the existence of exceptions raises Noonan's question. Defenders of the existing teaching maintain that there was development in the Church's understanding of the indissolubility of marriage much as there has been development with regard to the position on slavery. Some concessions were made in the past in certain circumstances, but the teaching developed more clearly to recognize the indissolubility of Christian marriage. The other interpretation points out that there were exceptions at that time and that therefore there can be exceptions today.

With regard to Church teaching, U.S. Catholic theologians after Vatican II were aware that the condemnations of divorce in the Council of Trent purposely did not condemn the teaching and practice of the Eastern Orthodox Churches, which through the practice of *oikonomia* allowed second marriages.[40]

What about reason and experience? At the 1967 canon law symposium, Louis and Constance Dupré argued that, at best, reason can prove only a relative indissolubility or stability based on the three values of the relationship of the spouses, the well-being of the children, and the good of society.[41] John Noonan pointed out in a 1969 article that the insistence on a natural law condemnation of divorce arose only in papal documents in the nineteenth and twentieth centuries in order to condemn civil divorce. Noonan notes that the present teaching and practice of the Roman Catholic Church that says that only consummated sacramental marriages are indissoluble means that the great majority of marriages in the world are not indissoluble. Such a position logically denies the natural law argument for indissolubility.[42] In addition to reason, the experience of an ever larger number of broken marriages enters into the discussion, but the question of how to interpret this experience remains.

Curran also saw in the divorce question something analogous to the problem of physicalism in sexual issues. Physicalism identifies the human moral act solely with the physical structure. Something analogous to physicalism exists in the case of indissolubility. The present Catholic teaching maintains that the consent of the spouses produces an indissoluble bond. But this metaphysical bond exists apart from the ongoing relationship of the spouses. The emphasis on the indissoluble bond makes some sense in an approach to marriage that was contractual, substantialist, and static. But in light of Vatican II's understanding of marriage, the contemporary approach to marriage is more covenantal, relational, and developmental. Such a perspective has no room for the consideration of an indissoluble bond.[43] For all these reasons Curran argued that the Catholic Church should change its teaching on the indissolubility of marriage. Lawrence G. Wrenn, a well-respected canonist, proposed in a comparatively brief article in 1973 that the Church move from the indissoluble-invalid approach to a fragile-illicit approach, with the judgment shifting from the tribunal to the parish.[44]

Without doubt, Theodore Mackin's 1984 *Divorce and Remarriage* is the most in-depth and scholarly argument in favor of changing the teaching on the indissolubility of marriage. His 565-page tome is the second of three volumes that Mackin wrote on marriage. His approach is primarily historical. Thus *Divorce and Remarriage* begins with scriptural analysis, the early Church, Jerome and Augustine, the medieval canonists and theologians, and all the other significant historical periods down to Vatican II. He largely provides primary sources and makes little use of secondary sources throughout. For example, the only secondary source mentioned in the chapter on the Pauline tradition is David Daube. With regard to the New Testament evidence, he points out that Jesus did not consider the issue of the inherent indissolubility of marriage, so we cannot say with any certitude that the human will is both powerless and forbidden to dissolve a marriage. Apparently Paul and Matthew, in light of their exceptions, did not think that Jesus taught the inherent indissolubility of marriage.

Only in the twelfth and thirteenth centuries did the canonists develop the concept of an indissoluble juridical bond existing apart from marriage as a human relationship. As a result of this development, Catholic authorities used two dubious strategies to establish the indissolubility of marriage. They wrote into the prescriptive definition of marriage an indissoluble bond and then claimed to find a warrant for this twelfth-century approach in the New Testament itself. Why are consummated sacramental marriages indissoluble, according to the present teaching? Two reasons are given: because marriage is an image of Christ's relationship to the Church and because the imaged sacred reality of Christ's relationship to the Church is indestructible. Therefore the human reality imaging it (the husband-wife relationship) is indissoluble. But there is a problem here. How can a quality in the imaged relationship ontologically cause that same quality in the imaging relationship? Yes, the marriage relationship should strive for indissolubility and for what is found in the relationship of Christ to the Church, but it is not automatically given to the relationship once it is sacramental. The indissoluble bond brought into existence by consent to the marital contract is what Mackin calls the "automatically caused indissolubility of marriage," which exists apart from the marriage relationship itself. The problem here is the substitution of juridical categories for the relational categories upon which Vatican II now insists.

Margaret Farley pointed out that in the 1980s the avalanche of literature in moral theology on marriage breakdown slowed considerably. Most of the interesting ideas were already on the table, and newer canonical and pastoral approaches helped to some degree in solving the issue for some married and divorced Catholics.[45] In addition, even proponents of change recognized that the bigger theological and pastoral problem for the Church is to strengthen and support the commitment to permanent and faithful marriage in light of the many marital breakdowns in our society.[46]

In 1990 Farley herself wrote two essays on divorce and remarriage.[47] She sees the marriage relationship as a moral commitment of a very serious type. Based on her earlier work on commitment, she argues that the very serious commitment of marriage can cease to bind if it becomes impossible to sustain, if the marriage has lost any intrinsic meaning, or if it is in conflict with another very serious obligation.[48] Farley also disagrees with the ontological argument proposed by Pope John Paul II, in which, according to his theology of the body, marriage involves the total gift of one spouse to the other so that they become a new ontological reality. Farley objects that such a position fails to recognize the limitations involved in all free human acts, incorporates a notion of male and female complementarity that has had very negative effects, and fails to recognize that marital love involves not only *agape* but also *philia* and *eros*.

The issue of divorce and remarriage is not going to go away. In 2004 Kenneth R. Himes and James A. Coriden, who wrote a 1996 article on the pastoral care of the divorced and remarried, published in *Theological Studies* a significant article calling for changing the teaching on indissolubility.[49] The article touched the same basics that had been introduced in 1970 to make this argument: the biblical, the historical, the teaching of the Council of Trent, the developments at Vatican II, the problem with the argument based on an indissoluble bond, the marital commitment, and the sacramental signification.

Once again, not all revisionists called for a change in the teaching on the indissolubility of marriage. Richard A. McCormick analyzed the literature in the 1970s and 1980s in his usually succinct way. He rejected the argument for indissolubility based on the indissoluble bond but proposed a moral argument instead. He thought that the problem of divorce and remarriage could be handled on the pastoral level while still upholding the teaching on the indissolubility of marriage.[50] The basic goods approach of Grisez and all those who did not accept dissent strongly continued to maintain the indissolubility of marriage. More important from the ecclesiological perspective is the continued insistence of the hierarchical magisterium on the indissolubility of consummated sacramental marriages.

HIV/AIDS

The last two decades of the twentieth century saw the growing recognition of the AIDS pandemic in the United States and throughout the world. James F. Keenan has summarized well the moral issues involved in general and especially from the perspective of moral theology.[51] In the United States in 1981, 98 percent of AIDS cases came from men having sex with men. But by 1998 that figure had declined to 35 percent. In 1998 approximately one-third of the AIDS cases came from drug-injection equipment and approximately one-third involved women. The three major moral issues involved treatment, education, and prevention.

With regard to treatment, improved drugs have had a very positive effect in prolonging the life of victims of AIDS. Unfortunately, the price of the drugs is a great problem for the poorer areas of the world. In developing new drugs, there is a danger also that victims of AIDS in poorer countries might become guinea pigs.

Most observers recognize the need for a holistic and "both-and" approach to education and prevention of AIDS. Basic behavioral (e.g., permissiveness) and cultural (e.g., the role of women) issues need to be addressed. The most controversial issues in the Catholic context have been the use of condoms and clean-needle exchanges to prevent the transmission of AIDS. The Catholic hierarchies around the world have tended to oppose condoms, with some individual exceptions. In the United States the tension over the use of condoms is evident in the two different documents coming from the United States bishops. The vast majority of Catholic moral theologians have argued that condoms and clean-needle exchanges could be acceptable on the basis of principles found within the Catholic moral theological tradition itself. Theologians have appealed to the Catholic principle of toleration of evil, choosing the lesser of two evils, or material cooperation to justify the use of condoms and clean-needle exchanges to prevent the transmission of AIDS. Of course, the discussion has once again raised questions about the hierarchical teaching on contraception and homosexuality.

TEXTBOOKS AND MONOGRAPHS

Once again, textbooks were needed for Catholic seminaries and colleges. The many controversies about Catholic sexual teaching and ethics occasioned a greater need for textbooks on these subjects, since Catholic colleges and seminaries taught courses on sexual ethics. Two such works appeared in 1977—the first written by a team headed by Anthony Kosnik, and the second by Philip S. Keane.

Early Textbooks

The Kosnik book was the work of a committee established originally by the Catholic Theological Society of America (CTSA) in 1972 to provide helpful and illuminating guidelines amid the reigning confusion about sexual issues. The book discusses most of the particular issues and each discussion ends with pastoral reflections about what should be done in practice. The first three chapters treat the findings of scripture, the tradition of the Church, and the social sciences on sexuality. Their conclusion about the scriptural teaching is in keeping with the basic conclusion of the book: critical scriptural scholarship finds it impossible to approve or reject categorically any particular sexual act outside of its contextual circumstances and intention.[52] The Kosnik team adopted a method, without attempting to prove it, involving four levels of judgment, ranging from the general to the particular. The first level, that of universal principle, calls for sexuality to involve a creative growth toward integration. The authors substitute "creativity" and "integration" for the two traditional ends of sexuality, procreation and love union. The second level spells out, in light of the general principle, seven basic values that must be present in human sexuality: self-liberation, enrichment of the other, honesty, fidelity, service to life, social responsibility, and joy. The third level involves guidelines derived from a conclusion as to whether or not the act serves or destroys these basic values. The authors use the term *guidelines* rather than *norms* because exceptions may occur. The fourth level is the individual conscience decision based on the guidelines.[53] The fifth chapter, which accounts for 60 percent of the book, presents the moral guidelines proposed for marital sexuality, nonmarital sexuality, homosexuality, and other issues. The authors condemn adultery in general but are open to further evidence from the empirical sciences. As for premarital sex, they reject the older absolute prohibition as inadequate because it does not take into account individual circumstances and intention, but they also cannot accept relativism and the failure to see sexuality in light of the values mentioned above. Sexuality in marriage is the ideal, and a serious and growing commitment of the partners is necessary to justify premarital sex. But the people involved must honestly and critically question themselves.

In receiving and not approving the report, the board of the CTSA acted properly. It was not up to the board or the society to agree with it. Obviously, all the members of the society did not agree with all the aspects found in the book. But the book received great public attention precisely because it was a committee report of the CTSA. Dissent from papal moral teachings and the publication of *Human Sexuality* motivated some members of the CTSA and other like-minded Catholic scholars to form the Fellowship of Catholic Scholars, whose members commit themselves to follow the magisterial teachings of the Church.[54] Thus the division among Catholic theologians in general and moral theologians in particular has become so great that a common place for them to meet no longer exists. As we have seen, the Congregation for the Doctrine of the Faith in 1979 published a set of observations condemning positions found in the book that were contradictory to hierarchical Church teaching.[55] Church authorities later took disciplinary actions against Kosnik, the chair of the committee.[56]

Philip Keane's *Sexual Morality: A Catholic Perspective* also tries to deal with all the sexual issues arising in practice, as did the manuals, but his approach is quite different. He briefly treats the theoretical aspects (e.g., sexuality is good but marred by sin) and has a significant chapter on the role of women that argues for equality. The short but very important third chapter, on what has been taught in moral theology recently, emphasizes three aspects: sin in light of the fundamental option, the problem of physicalism in sexual ethics, and the theory of proportionality. Keane proposes his basic criterion: one can commit ontic evil if there is a proportionate reason. Ontic evil describes the evil that is present in the act as distinguished from ultimate moral evil. He recognizes a sliding scale of ontic evil that depends on the particular issue.

Keane applies his basic moral criterion to autosexual acts, homosexual acts, and heterosexual acts. Thus masturbation involves some ontic evil, but there is a sliding scale because of the different realities of masturbation. Therefore, pastoral ministers dealing with this issue must use great discretion and prudence. But masturbation ordinarily is not too significant a problem. Homosexual acts involve significant ontic evil, but they can be morally good. AID (artificial insemination with semen from a donor) contains much ontic evil but it cannot be absolutely ruled out. Keane consistently applies his basic criterion of proportionality to the sexual issues that arise. The Vatican took no public action against Keane, but it pressured the archbishop of Seattle to remove his imprimatur from the book.[57]

In 1987 Vincent J. Genovesi published *In Pursuit of Love*, a textbook on sexuality for college students from a mildly revisionist perspective that explicitly recognizes the possibility of dissent from noninfallible Church teaching. After the opening sections on love as the basis of Christian life, conscience, sin, and the meaning of sexuality, Genovesi treats only the controversial issues of premarital sex, contraception, homosexuality, and masturbation; a chapter on abortion follows. The book basically reviews what revisionist Catholic moral theologians have been saying on these issues. Sometimes the author shies away from giving his own position, perhaps because of the disciplinary actions that have been taken against other Catholic moral theologians writing in this area. The authors he cites most often are McCormick, Häring, Dedek, Kosnik, Keane, and Curran. Thus the focus is on the disputed issues in moral theology, with comparatively little dialogue beyond the Catholic community and no attention to problems of abuse and violence related to sexuality. A second edition in 1996 updated the material and added a short section on the misuse of sexuality, such as rape, pornography, and sexual abuse.

More Scholarly Monographs

Beginning in the 1980s more scholarly monographs on sexuality began to appear that did not have the primary pedagogical or pastoral orientation of the Keane and Kosnik volumes. The work of Lisa Sowle Cahill well illustrates their approach. Cahill is as much interested in methodology as she is in the substantive issue of sexuality. She engages a wide range of authors and perspectives but does not pay much attention to recent writings in Catholic moral theology in the development of her Christian sexual ethics perspective.

In *Between the Sexes: Foundations for a Christian Ethics of Sexuality* (1985), Cahill recognizes four sources of moral theology: scripture, tradition, normative descriptions of the human, and descriptive definitions of the human as found in the human sciences. Scripture is very important, but no single source always trumps the others. Sexual expression is both physical and pleasurable, but it is also an avenue of affective and spiritual relations among people, for good or ill. She agrees with the Christian tradition of evaluating sexual expression by the two criteria of commitment and procreative responsibility, but within a context of equals. Cahill writes here not as a feminist but as a moral theologian who is in dialogue with feminist theology and other approaches.

Cahill concludes that, according to Genesis, difference and cooperation, not supremacy and subordination, are part of God's original creation. Biblical views of male and female together combined with the empirical sciences show that differences ought to be appreciated rather than denigrated, but always within a context of freedom and equality. Separate chapters discuss Thomas Aquinas (strong on reason and natural law) and Martin Luther (strong on scripture). A final chapter applies her criterion of sexual expression, which involves committed partnership, procreation, and equality. Procreative heterosexual marriage is the ideal expression of these values, but sexual expressions can be justified when strict adherence to this norm is inappropriate, difficult, or impossible. Thus Cahill justifies, without any in-depth reasoning, some remarriage after divorce, committed ("preceremonial") premarital sex, and committed homosexual relationships.

In Cahill's *Sex, Gender, and Christian Ethics* (1996), which is also addressed to a broader Christian audience and is not as systematic a study as the earlier book, she writes from within a feminist perspective that emphasizes equality for women in all spheres. However, she opposes some other feminist approaches. Again stressing methodology, she rejects both a postmodernism that does not allow for consensus across cultures and hence cannot be the basis for social criticism, and modernism or liberalism, with its emphasis on autonomy, individualism, and an inability to agree on some substantive values. Her own method builds on the

Aristotelian-Thomistic understanding of human flourishing. Broad areas of agreement about human flourishing can be reached inductively and dialogically through human experience. Cahill again sees sexuality in light of procreation, intimacy, and pleasure, with the same basic applications as in her earlier book. Here she also considers the family and sees the New Testament as calling into question relationships of dominance. The family, with its roles of parenthood and kinship, has an important social function. The Christian family as a kinship group works to overcome every inequality of race, class, and gender, but unfortunately Catholicism has not embraced the range of ecclesial, familial, and social change that women's equality requires.

Christine E. Gudorf is a Roman Catholic moral theologian who writes for a broader Christian audience of general readers. Unlike Cahill's approach, Gudorf's *Body, Sex, and Pleasure* is very critical of the Christian tradition and teaching on sexuality and wants to change it radically. The book challenges the patriarchal, misogynist, and heterosexist attitudes spawned by the Christian tradition. Gudorf gives primacy to the biological and social sciences and to contemporary human experience to criticize scripture and tradition. Scripture contains many nonrevelatory aspects. Procreationism, the assumption that sex is naturally ordered to the creation of life, is the most serious obstacle in developing a just and human sexual ethic today. Gudorf proposes an understanding of sexual pleasure as grace and gift. Sexual pleasure is thus the primary criterion for evaluating sexual activity. More precisely, mutual sexual pleasure is the criterion. Such an approach is not permissive because it calls for a change in all those ways in which sexual activity today is not mutually pleasurable. Gudorf's approach is based on a spirituality of embodiment. This approach differs from others that have proposed multiple values or criteria for governing sexual activity. She also develops the concept of "bodyright"—the right to control one's own body and thereby avoid the dangers of abuse and victimization. In an earlier book Gudorf examined some of the many ways in which Christians and their churches have supported victimization. She frequently points out the violence, injustice, and discrimination against women in sexuality and many other areas.[58]

In 2006 Margaret Farley published her long-awaited *Just Love*, a systematic presentation of Christian sexual ethics proposed for all Christians. The opening chapters trace the historical development in the Western tradition and then different cross-cultural understandings of sexuality today. While recognizing pluralism and diversity with regard to sexuality, she still proposes the meaning of the body, gender, and sexuality as a prelude for developing norms. In developing norms, Farley touches on the four sources of moral wisdom—scripture, tradition, and especially secular disciplines and experience, and also builds on an anthropology recognizing both autonomy and relationality. The just ethic for sexuality involves the following seven norms: no unjust harm, free consent, mutuality, equality, commitment, fruitfulness, and social justice. These norms apply to same-sex as well as to heterosexual relationships. Here again Farley recognizes the legitimate possibility of divorce and remarriage.

In 2002 Mark Jordan, discussed above, published the *Ethics of Sex* for a general Christian audience. His book differs from the other approaches discussed thus far because he writes from a postmodernist perspective and concentrates on Christian rhetoric and speech about sex. He seldom mentions the contemporary human sciences but deals primarily with Christian texts. From earliest Christian times until after the Reformation, Christians did not see sex and marriage primarily in terms of procreation but rather as a way of avoiding the greater sin of nonmarital intercourse for those who were too weak to follow the higher path of virginity. Behind this understanding was the fear of sexual and erotic pleasure. Christian rhetoric saw sex acts in terms of sinful sexual identities, such as the adulterer or the sodomite. The acts became shameful because they reveal the shameful evil identity. The contemporary Christian Church needs to reverse the entire direction of Christian sexual ethics by redeeming erotic pleasure. Bodily and sexual pleasure is good and is basically rooted in creation and redemption. Many have recognized the connection between the mystical and the erotic, but Jordan also sees a connection between prayer and erotic pleasure.

Conservative Approaches

While a pluralism of approaches has emerged among revisionist Catholic moral theologians, defenders of the existing hierarchical Church teachings continue to disseminate their basic approach. The Grisez school is well represented in Grisez's own multivolume contemporary manual of moral theology as well as in other publications. *Catholic Sexual Ethics,* by Ronald Lawler, Joseph Boyle, and William E. May, is a good example of the Grisez approach to sexuality. The authors strongly support the teaching of Pope John Paul II and try to carry out his mandate to develop the biblical foundations, the personalistic appropriateness, and the ethical goods supportive of official Church teaching on sexuality. They oppose what they call the "responsible-relational" approach adopted by many Catholic moral theologians who dissent from Church teachings in many sexual areas. Sex is a good and wonderful gift of God, and intelligently ordered sexual activity can be a humanly perfecting and sanctifying reality. Those actions condemned by the Church harm the basic goods that are at stake in sexual activity. Because these goods are central and important, actions against them are gravely wrong. *Catholic Sexual*

Ethics strongly supports the basic goods methodology and rejects proportionalism. The book includes chapters on biblical teaching, the Catholic tradition, the proper ethical method, and conscience, and discusses the requirements of chastity within and outside the covenant of married love.

In the context of Vatican II's emphasis on a biblical approach, the centrality of the person, and the person's growth in holiness, John Grabowski's *Sex and Virtue* proposes a biblical and virtue-based approach to sexuality that strongly supports the existing teachings of the hierarchical magisterium and opposes any dissent. Grabowski acknowledges that his approach is somewhat similar to Cahill's, but he opposes her proportionalism and defense of some dissenting positions. The Bible sees sex as a covenantal and sacramental reality. Sexual morality is primarily a matter not of rules but of heart and character. The virtue of chastity fosters the capacity for self-giving that is characteristic of covenantal love. Too often today sex is understood in terms of pleasure or individual fulfillment unconnected to any form of covenantal commitment. The primary purpose of sexuality is procreation, which is integrated into the self-donation made possible through chastity. Grabowski strenuously defends the norms proposed in official Catholic teaching.

MARRIAGE AND FAMILY

Writings on marriage in the Catholic tradition involve a number of different disciplines: sacramental, spiritual, systematic, moral, and pastoral theologies, as well as canon law. The following discussion is limited to the aspect of marriage touching on moral theology.

Different Perspectives

One perspective of marriage from a moral theological view is the scholarly perspective, with its intended audience of other scholars and not just students and pastors. Theodore Mackin's trilogy on marriage in the Catholic Church exemplifies this perspective.[59] I referred above to his book on divorce. *What Is Marriage?* traces the historical development of the understanding of marriage from scripture through the new canon law in the early 1980s. Mackin proposes that the Vatican II understanding of marriage as a covenant of love is much better than the older juridical notion of marriage as a contract. In this book, too, he argues that if marriage is a covenant of love, the Church should change its teaching on divorce and remarriage.

The most popular perspective of moral theology to address Christian marriage is the pastoral, or pedagogical, perspective. The pastoral perspective deals with the realities and issues faced by married couples in their lives, while the pedagogical aims at teaching students. Since almost all Catholic colleges taught, and many continue to teach, courses in marriage, many writers approach marriage from this perspective. Until the beginning of the twenty-first century, the pastoral and pedagogical perspectives addressed the moral theology of marriage primarily in terms of the internal life of the Church, especially Vatican II and *Humanae vitae*. The discussion of marriage thus shows the emphasis on these two Church realities as developed in chapter 4. The teachers and professors of these courses matriculated in the context of Vatican II and the discussions of *Humanae vitae*. Vatican II's call for a scriptural approach and emphasis on the person also greatly influenced the approach they took to marriage. In addition, Vatican II specifically understood marriage not as a contract but primarily as the loving covenant between spouses, mirroring the covenant love of Jesus for the Church. The issue of contraception for spouses came up in every class on marriage, as did the issue of divorce and remarriage.

Michael G. Lawler of Creighton University and William P. Roberts of Dayton University both taught marriage courses in Catholic colleges in the last quarter of the twentieth century. They have written extensively on marriage, following this internal Church approach. The first sentence of the foreword to the 1996 Lawler-Roberts coedited volume makes the point very clearly. "Among the paradigm shifts that took place at the Second Vatican Council must be counted the change in the Church's theological understanding of marriage."[60] The purpose of their book is to probe the implications of this change.

Gloria Blanchfield Thomas's contribution to the Lawler-Roberts volume, an article on teaching marriage in a Catholic college, well illustrates the perspective.[61] Thomas, a happily married Catholic and a grandmother, is obviously a good pedagogue and uses lectures, discussions, journaling, and guest speakers to carry out her method of a hermeneutic circle involving experience, scripture, and Church teaching. Her students are apparently predominantly Catholic, although some are alienated from the Church. The students find the teaching on artificial birth control incredible. One-third of their parents are divorced. Premarital sex is an issue for all of them. The women students definitely want equality in marriage and the freedom to pursue careers. They hope that the Church will help them to live out their commitments with consideration of their complex lives. Thus the moral aspects are an important part, but only a part, of the course on marriage. A course on Catholic marriage taught by a committed Catholic to Catholic students in a Catholic college will tend to emphasize an internal Church perspective.

Lawler's 2002 book, *Marriage and the Catholic Church: Disputed Questions*, by definition looks at these issues only from the viewpoint of the Church. Lawler's longest section discusses the bond of marriage and the call for the Church to change its teaching on divorce and remarriage. He ends the book with a proposal concerning cohabitation and marriage in the Catholic community. He proposes bringing back into Catholic practice the ceremony of betrothal as well as marriage. Betrothal could occur between prenuptial cohabiters (not nonnuptial cohabiters), and sexual relations would be approved by the Church as the couple proceeds toward marriage. His earlier book, *Family: American and Christian* (1998), recognized the problems and difficulties of marriage in contemporary American life, but his emphasis is more on the need for the Church to change some of its approaches. However, as we shall see, younger Catholic moral theologians are putting much more emphasis on what the Catholic Church and tradition can and should do to support Catholic marriages in our contemporary society and at the same time contribute to the transformation of society.

The pastoral or pedagogical perspective on marriage is primary in Catholic moral theology, but other perspectives have appeared. James and Kathleen McGinnis are Catholic social activists (James also has a Ph.D. in ethics in the area of nonviolence) who wrote *Parenting for Peace and Justice*, which sold more than sixty thousand copies.[62] Their aim is to show how Catholic parents and families can carry out the call to work for justice, peace, and the transformation of the world.

Rosemary Ruether's *Christianity and the Making of the Modern Family* argues from a broad Christian feminist perspective that the conservative evangelical emphasis today on family values is totally wrong and has no basic support in the Bible or tradition. The concept of family has evolved dramatically in the context of changing sociological, cultural, and economic factors. The New Testament is quite negative about families. The Victorian or "modern" family is the product of a particular social class and a particular historical period. Ruether advocates a pluralism of family forms in which people live together in mutuality with one another and with sustainable communities and environments.

In keeping with her usual style, Lisa Sowle Cahill in *Family: A Christian Social Perspective* (2000), uses biblical, historical, and contemporary Church sources to develop her thesis, with special emphasis on the family as domestic church. The family is a school of intimacy, empathy, and love. As domestic church, the family tries to transform society by bringing these values to bear on the life of all others, especially those suffering from inequality and injustice because of gender, race, or class. Cahill realistically recognizes that at times the larger culture has worked against this vision and ideal of Christian families and has prevented such families from truly carrying out their transformative role. In the process, Cahill also condemns the present American welfare system, which tends to blame the individual persons and does not recognize how social structures create many problems for the poor and disadvantaged. One chapter shows how African American families, even when under duress, offer others the true generosity and help of the domestic church.

Cahill describes her own position as a complex mediation between the evangelical conservative and the mainline feminist. The former extols the existing nuclear family, fails to recognize the transformative role of the family, and even tends to support existing inequalities of gender, race, and class. The mainline feminist approach sees diversity in family forms as true liberation from the patriarchal nuclear family but fails to build better ideals of kin-derived, spousal, and parental relationships and to show how families can better serve the common good. Cahill's mediating position sees the family as created by kinship and marriage as the most basic family form, but it is not the only or exclusively legitimate form. The form has some significant meaning, but the most important criterion is to live out the reality of the domestic church. Cahill also disagrees with the approach of the Religion, Culture, and Family Project, headed by Don Browning at the University of Chicago, with which she had been connected. In her judgment, that approach sees the crisis of families too narrowly in terms of the expressive individualism so rampant in our society that works against marital commitment. Cahill believes that not enough attention is given to the societal aspects and transformative role of the family.

Considerations of marriage and family raise the issue of the role of women in these institutions and in the broader society. Catholic feminist theologians have addressed this issue; in the process they have analyzed and criticized hierarchical Church teaching, including the many writings of Pope John Paul II. Christine Gudorf points out the schizophrenia in papal teaching on the role of women in the public and private realms. Papal social teaching stresses basic equality and a just democratic system, but in the private realm of marriage and family stresses static institutions rooted in divine and natural law, hierarchy, and paternalism.[63]

Cahill traces the development in papal teaching on the family, which has moved away from an earlier emphasis on the husband as the head of the family to a greater emphasis on equality. Pope John Paul II insists on the basic rights and equality of women, with a special concern for the poor; he deplores both violence and discrimination against women. He nowhere calls for the wife to be submissive to the husband within marriage and family. But John Paul II firmly espouses a complementarity model of equality and sees the woman's role primarily as mother. Both the civilization of love and the successful raising of children depend on the father's becoming involved in the motherhood of his wife.[64] Gudorf sees John Paul II as exemplifying the biology-as-destiny school with regard to women but not with regard to men. In addition, John Paul II still endorses the romantic notion of putting women on a pedestal.[65]

Aline Kalbian likewise disagrees with the papal emphasis on complementarity. She points out that, in the papal language, sex and gender are used indiscriminately. As a result, gender is based on biology and no role is given to the cultural formation of gender. Kalbian sees a connection between the moral order, the theological order, and the ecclesiastical order in official Catholic teaching. Perhaps the metaphor of the Church as mother might destabilize some of the understanding of order in these other relationships, which result in a lack of full equality for women.[66] Not all Catholic women agree with Gudorf, Cahill, and Kalbian. Léonie Caldecott warmly embraces John Paul II's "new feminism," with its emphasis on the maternal role of women and the complementarity model.[67]

Behind the papal emphasis on complementarity is the defense of the Catholic Church's teaching and practice of excluding women from ordained ministry. This issue has troubled many women and men in the Church deeply, but it lies beyond the concerns of this book.

TWENTY-FIRST CENTURY APPROACHES

In the twenty-first century moral theologians have begun to write about marriage and family from a different location. They are younger married scholars reflecting on their own experience in light of their Catholic faith. For them, Vatican II and *Humanae vitae* are part of history rather than lived experience. Julie Hanlon Rubio appeals to her own experience, scripture, the marriage liturgy, tradition, the human sciences, and contemporary social sciences. She also quotes frequently from the teaching of John Paul II (with a few gentle disagreements on the mothering role of women and the complementary roles of husband and wife) in her development of a sacramental understanding of the ideal of marriage and family.[68] Obviously there are different types of families, but she wants to hold on to the ideal.

Marriage and family are not based on a romantic love of the partners but are sacramental communities of disciples related to the broader community of the Church, with its call to transform the world around it. The New Testament shows an ambivalence—both a suspicion of marriage (it tends to be idolatrous and keeps people away from discipleship; it also incorporates patriarchal inequality) and a respect for the institution of marriage. The New Testament says little about children in the family; the early Church emphasized the family more. Rubio stresses the dual vocation of parents, with a commitment to the good of the family but also to their work in the world and their efforts to transform the world. Separate chapters discuss mothering, fathering, and welcoming children into the Christian family. She opposes changing the Church teaching on divorce and marriage but supports a pastoral policy that permits the divorced and remarried to share fully in the Eucharist. Rubio does not discuss contraception as an issue or as a problem.

David Matzko McCarthy writes from a similar perspective but gives less emphasis to marriage as a sacrament.[69] He takes a Hauerwasian approach and sees greater opposition between the culture and the Catholic understanding, and maintains there is no role for the family in trying to transform the broader society and world. McCarthy recognizes that his book is not the typical book on marriage and family. He strongly criticizes the understanding of marriage based on romantic love and sexual desire, which results in the closed, isolated, suburban family. Such a model is heavily influenced by the capitalistic market economy and merely contractual social relations. For similar reasons he disagrees with post–Vatican II Catholic personalism, which also narrows the family to an interpersonal place with no room for the politics of neighborhood and the economy of home. As an alternative to the closed, isolated family based on affectionate or interpersonal bonds, he proposes the open public family grounded in the social and economic operations of the neighborhood and households. Neighborhood and community relationships extend the open family outward. Thus the role of the partners in the household is to cultivate the community and neighborhood relationships that make the family truly open and public. McCarthy affirms gender differences, but these differences do not result in different familial or public roles. Marriage, love, and sex must always be seen as part of the venture of a rich social life. In this book McCarthy does not mention his previous support for *Humanae vitae*'s condemnation of artificial contraception.[70]

Like Rubio, Florence Caffrey Bourg appeals to the resources of her Catholic tradition, calls upon her own experience as a spouse and mother of young children, and strongly opposes romantic love as a basis for families in her book on Christian families, *Where Two or Three Are Gathered*. She uses the metaphor of domestic church found in Catholic Church documents since Vatican II and in some other sources to develop her understanding of the Christian family. Bourg sees ordinary family life as a sphere of grace and as an encounter between humans and God. She insists on the equal role of parents in developing the family as the basic cell of society and of the Church in character education, formation of religious identity, and the creation of just social structures. The lives of families as domestic churches constitute the focal point around which she organizes insights about sacramental, virtue, and life ethics theologies. Like her dissertation director,

Lisa Cahill, Bourg sees the purpose and finality of the Christian family as more important than the form that it takes, as the inclusive title of her book suggests.

The consideration of marriage and sexuality in post–Vatican II moral theology exemplifies the tension between those who defend the existing hierarchical teachings and those who advocate change. At the turn of the century, younger Catholic moral theologians have attempted to move beyond these divisions and tensions.

NOTES

1. For an overview of part of this time frame, see Griffin, "American Catholic Sexual Ethics," 468–77.
2. "Congregation for the Doctrine of the Faith on Anthony Kosnik et al."; "Congregation for the Doctrine of the Faith on John McNeill." For the removal of the imprimatur on Keane's book, see Hunthausen, "Hunthausen Withdraws *Imprimatur*."
3. John Paul II, *Veritatis splendor*, 586–87nn4–5.
4. Boyle, *Parvitas Materiae*.
5. Curran, "Masturbation and Objectively Grave Matter." See also Curran, "Sexuality and Sin," parts 1 and 2.
6. Smith, *Humanae vitae, a Generation Later*. Chapter 2 points out that Ford and Kelly had briefly proposed the same argument. See Ford and Kelly, *Contemporary Moral Theology*, 2:289–91.
7. Van Allen, "Artificial Insemination (AIH)."
8. Congregation for the Doctrine of the Faith, "Instruction on Respect for Human Life."
9. Cahill, *Theological Bioethics*, 198–205.
10. Boyle, *Sterilization Controversy*, 24–25; Curran, "Sterilization."
11. McCormick, *Notes on Moral Theology, 1965–1980*, 701n36.
12. May, "Sterilization."
13. Farley, "Power and Powerlessness"; McCormick, *Notes on Moral Theology, 1981–1984*, 187–89.
14. "Bishops Revise Healthcare Directives," *National Catholic Reporter*, June 1, 2001.
15. McNeill, "Christian Male Homosexual."
16. Curran, "Homosexuality and Moral Theology."
17. For Gramick's and Nugent's stories, see Collins, *Modern Inquisition*, 109–63.
18. Cahill, "Moral Methodology."
19. Farley, "Ethic for Same-Sex Relations."
20. Hunt, "Lovingly Lesbian."
21. Maguire, "Morality of Homosexual Marriage."
22. Molloy, "Point/Counterpoint"; Molloy, *Homosexuality and the Christian Way of Life*.
23. Harvey, "Homosexuality." For his most complete work, see Harvey, *Truth about Homosexuality*.
24. Congregation for the Doctrine of the Faith, "Letter to the Bishops," 379.

25. See Nugent, "Sexual Orientation and Vatican Thinking."

26. Boswell, *Christianity, Social Tolerance, and Homosexuality.*

27. See Kuefler, *Boswell Thesis.*

28. Thurston, *Homosexuality and Roman Catholic Ethics.* See also Keenan, "Open Debate."

29. Congregation for the Doctrine of the Faith, "Letter to the Bishops."

30. Keenan, "Open Debate," 129–34.

31. Pope, "Magisterium's Argument against 'Same-Sex Marriage.'"

32. "Congregation for the Doctrine of the Faith on John McNeill."

33. McNeill, *Feet Planted Firmly in Mid-Air.*

34. Collins, *Modern Inquisition,* 161–63.

35. Himes and Coriden, "Notes on Moral Theology."

36. Curran, "Divorce: Doctrine et pratique catholique," published in English as "Divorce: Catholic Theory and Practice."

37. Vawter, "Divorce Clauses in Mt. 5:32 and 19:9"; Vawter, "Biblical Theology of Divorce."

38. Crossan, "Divorce and Remarriage in the New Testament."

39. Noonan, "Novel 22."

40. Fransen, "Divorce on the Ground of Adultery."

41. Dupré and Dupré, "Indissolubility of Marriage and the Common Good."

42. Noonan, "Indissolubility of Marriage and Natural Law."

43. Curran, *Contemporary Problems,* 146–47.

44. Wrenn, "Marriage—Indissoluble or Fragile?"

45. Farley, "Divorce, Remarriage, and Pastoral Practice," 223.

46. Mackin, *Divorce and Remarriage,* 1–2; Curran, "Gospel and Culture."

47. Farley, "Divorce, Remarriage, and Pastoral Practice," and "Divorce and Remarriage."

48. Farley, *Personal Commitments.*

49. Himes and Coriden, "Indissolubility of Marriage." For their earlier article, see note 35.

50. For a study of McCormick's position, see Farley, "Divorce, Remarriage, and Pastoral Practice," 213–23.

51. Fuller and Keenan, "Introduction: At the End of the First Generation of HIV Prevention." The entire volume, *Catholic Ethicists on HIV/AIDS Prevention,* brings together Catholic responses from throughout the world to the AIDS pandemic. See also Cimperman, *When God's People Have HIV/AIDS.*

52. Kosnik et al., *Human Sexuality,* 31.

53. Ibid., 92–98.

54. Hitchcock, "Fellowship of Catholic Scholars," 188–91.

55. "Congregation for the Doctrine of the Faith on Anthony Kosnik et al."; "Congregation for the Doctrine of the Faith on John McNeill." For the removal of the imprimatur on Keane's book, see Hunthausen, "Hunthausen Withdraws *Imprimatur.*"

56. See Griffin, "American Catholic Social Ethics," 474.

57. Keane, *Sexual Morality;* Hunthausen, "Hunthausen Withdraws *Imprimatur.*"

58. Gudorf, *Victimization.*

59. Mackin, *What Is Marriage?* and *The Marital Sacrament.*

60. Lawler and Roberts, *Christian Marriage and Family*, vii.

61. Thomas, "Teaching Marriage in a Catholic College."

62. See also McGinnis and McGinnis, *Parenting for Peace and Justice: Ten Years Later.*

63. Gudorf, "Encountering the Other," 66.

64. Cahill, *Family,* 85–95.

65. Gudorf, "Encountering the Other," 70–85.

66. Kalbian, *Sexing the Church.* See also Traina, "Papal Ideals, Marital Realities."

67. Caldecott, "Sincere Gift."

68. Rubio, *Christian Theology of Marriage and Family.*

69. McCarthy, *Sex and Love in the Home.*

70. McCarthy, "Procreation, Development of Peoples, and Final Destiny."

BIOETHICS

Chapter 2 pointed out the existence of a full-blown area of medical ethics in the pre–Vatican II Roman Catholic tradition. For all practical purposes, Roman Catholics were the only ones interested in medical ethics at that time, for the reasons mentioned in that chapter. Why were other Christian theologians, philosophers, medical and health professionals, and others not interested in medical ethics at this time? For most others there was no conflict between good medicine and good ethics, because the ultimate criterion was the same for both—the good of the patient. Catholic medical ethics called this criterion the "principle of totality." For the good of the person, one could justify sacrificing a part for the good of the whole. As we have seen, many of the problems in Catholic medical ethics concerned the reproductive organs. Here the principle of totality did not apply because the sexual organs had a finality for both the good of the person and the good of the species, its procreative purpose. The procreative purpose, the good of the species, could not be subordinated to or sacrificed for the good of the individual.

What explains the marked and ever growing interest in medical ethics and the emergence of the broader discipline of bioethics since the late 1960s and early 1970s? The answer is simple: tremendous technological advances. The first result of these advances was that they raised questions about the old principle governing medical ethics, that is, the good of the patient. Transplants of organs from one living person to another raised the issue of harming one person (e.g., by taking a kidney) in order to help another. The stunning progress in medicine through drugs, new technologies, and surgeries was fueled by experimentation. All these newer possibilities had to be proved through human experimentation. Experimentation raised another problem with the older criterion, because now an individual was exposed to some harm not for the good of the individual but for the good of knowledge, the good of the species, or the good of another human being. The second result of ongoing development in technology and drugs was the advent of many new technological possibilities for life-saving devices in medicine and of new possibilities of reproductive technologies that began with in-vitro fertilization (IVF) and now involves many other aspects of genetics. These advances raised significant theoretical issues about the relationship between the technological and the human, but they had very significant practical ramifications. Does a dying patient have to use all available life-prolonging technologies and drugs? What is human procreation? Can we enhance human beings through genetics? At present, the ever growing discipline of bioethics involves many different interdisciplinary approaches, including theology, philosophical ethics, medicine, law, and all of the health care professions.

INTRODUCTORY OBSERVATIONS

Catholic bioethicists, like Catholic moral theologians in general, often write as Catholic theologians working from the Catholic tradition for a particularly Catholic audience, but also as Christian theologians writing for a broader Christian audience. Catholic moral theologians in bioethics work from the Catholic tradition and write for a Catholic audience for a number of reasons. The issues themselves are important and also frequently controversial in the Catholic Church. The papal magisterium, especially through the Congregation for the Doctrine of the Faith, has often issued authoritative teachings on these various issues, with a special emphasis on three instructions on abortion, euthanasia, and reproductive technologies.[1] Catholic moral theologians teaching in Catholic colleges and universities teach these courses primarily from the Catholic perspective. Because bioethics is such a popular discipline, many Catholic colleges have undergraduate courses in this area. In addition, Catholic nursing schools and medical schools also teach courses in bioethics from a Catholic perspective.

However, in bioethics there is another institutional reason for Catholic theologians to write for Catholic audiences: the existence of Catholic hospitals and health care facilities. In chapter 2 I mentioned the large number of Catholic hospitals and the *Ethical and Religious Directives* issued by the United States bishops, which governs what is done and not done in those hospitals in accord with Catholic moral teaching. In 2001 the National Conference of Catholic Bishops approved the fourth edition of the *Ethical and Religious Directives for Catholic Health Care Services* as the national code for all Catholic hospitals and health care facilities in the United States.[2] These Catholic hospitals usually also employ a Catholic ethicist who deals with the ethical issues raised in the work of the hospital and works with the hospital ethics committee. Thus a number of factors have influenced the need for Catholic bioethicists writing in the Catholic tradition to address a predominantly Catholic audience. Catholic bioethicists also write from a more general Christian perspective.

Also, many governmental and presidential commissions have come into existence to determine what should be public policy with regard to particular controversial issues. Members of these committees will often include Catholic moral theologians who address the issues from the Roman Catholic perspective. In addition, different medical groups and associations have provided ethical guidelines for their members. Catholics who have worked on these committees are expected to work out of the Catholic tradition but in the context of a pluralistic society.[3]

Different Approaches

Moral theologians writing in bioethics use the same methodologies found in sexual ethics and in the discipline in general. The predominant approach is revisionist, but with the recognition that this model is quite broad and contains a number of different emphases and approaches. Revisionists see in some areas of medical ethics the same problem of physicalism that existed in sexual ethics. The official hierarchical teaching and both natural law approaches continue to insist that the only correct way to bring about procreation is through the physical act of conjugal union whereby the semen of the male is deposited in the vagina of the female. But revisionists often maintain that AIH is acceptable and some also will accept AID, since the physical act of marital intercourse is not the only way for spouses to bring about procreation.[4]

Most but by no means all revisionists oppose euthanasia, and most revisionists reject the blanket moral right of a woman to abortion. All must recognize the issue of physicalism in these two issues.[5] In the abortion debate the primary question is the status of the fetus. Can the individuality of a human being be identical with the physical aspect, and especially with the early physical aspect, of a fertilized ovum? Euthanasia raises a similar issue. The Catholic tradition recognizes that one can remove an extraordinary means to prolong life but one cannot directly intervene to cause the death. The physical act of directly causing death is always wrong. On the other hand, all acknowledge that at times the physical and the human are identical. The accepted medical determination of death employs a physical criterion: the lack of brain waves, circulation, or breathing.

Catholic feminist approaches can be considered a form of revisionism, but such approaches have distinctive features of their own. The feminist perspective is very conscious that too often women have been passive, objectified, and victimized because of male-oriented medicine and bioethics. The female has had to bear the burden of contraception for the most part, even though some forms of contraception, such as some contraceptive pills, have put the woman in danger of possible harm.

The new natural law theorists of the Grisez school also have written extensively in the area of bioethics. Life itself is obviously one of the basic goods that we can never oppose. The neoscholastic natural law model also continues to be employed in discussions of bioethics. Both of these approaches in bioethics, as in all other areas, strongly defend the existing hierarchical teachings. Three journals strongly endorse such approaches. *Health Progress,* the official journal of the Catholic Health Association, contains many articles dealing with all aspects of Catholic health care, including ethical issues. However, the journal publishes only those articles sympathetic to official Catholic teaching but does address controversial issues within the confines of existing hierarchical teaching. The *Linacre Quarterly,* the journal of the Catholic Medical Association begun in the 1930s, considers the philosophy and ethics of medical practice. In the 1970s it published articles from revisionist Catholic moral theologians and had some of these theologians on its editorial board, but since the late 1970s it has not published any article disagreeing with hierarchical Catholic teaching. The *National Catholic Bioethics Quarterly,* the official journal of the National Catholic Bioethics Center, began publishing in 2001 and also does not publish any dissenting articles. Thus these Catholic journals that publish on bioethics strongly support the existing hierarchical teachings and the methodologies in which they are grounded.

Continuities and Agreements

Yes, there are strong differences among Catholic bioethicists, but, as in other areas, there is agreement on the more general aspects of methodology and substance. These different approaches, despite their differences, fit under the general umbrella of the Catholic moral theological tradition. In terms of method, all approaches accept the basic Catholic understanding of mediation and the need for both revelatory and nonrevelatory sources of moral wisdom and knowledge. The acceptance of faith and reason also illustrates their acceptance of the basic Catholic "both-and" rather than the "either-or" approach. Thus they all recognize the need for scripture and tradition, grace and works, faith and reason, Jesus and the Church. Fundamentally, they all agree with the basic grounding of the natural law approach that morality is ultimately what is good and fulfilling for the human person.

All approaches accept the same basic Catholic anthropology: the goodness and dignity of the human person, the social nature of the human person, and the goodness of the body. Human beings are good because they are created in the image of God. The concept of the human being as the image of God goes back to Genesis and has been a central part of the Catholic tradition, as illustrated in the theology of Thomas Aquinas. The ultimate dignity of the human being comes from creation by God. Too often in our society, human dignity and worth are based on what one does, makes, or accomplishes. But in the Christian and Catholic perspective, all people have equal dignity because all alike are creatures of the same God. The basic goodness and equal dignity of all human beings are fundamental anthropological concepts that all Catholic bioethicists accept. Such concepts are central to the development of a Catholic approach to bioethics. But Catholic anthropology also recognizes the existence of sin and its many effects, including sinful social structures.

But the basic goodness and human dignity of the human being is only one part of Catholic anthropology, which also insists on the social nature of the individual. We are not isolated beings existing for our own narrow good. We need all other human beings and relationships in order to fulfill our true humanity. Too often American culture emphasizes only the individual and sees individual happiness and fulfillment in a narrow way apart from the relationship to others. Other people are often only a means to our own happiness. But in the Catholic understanding, others are not means but ends in themselves. We are called to live in all types of relationships with other equal human beings, in marriage, family, friendship, neighborhood, and extending even into the political order. The Catholic belief in the Triune God recognizes that the three persons in one God exist in relationship with one another; this understanding also grounds the relational understanding of humans.

Catholic bioethicists also agree in their recognition of the basic goodness of the human body. Furthermore, they agree that the body has meaning for morality, although they disagree about the specific implications of that moral meaning. The human person is more than just the soul or the spirit. Body and soul form the human person. The Catholic tradition, with its emphasis on hierarchical ordering, recognizes that spiritual values are more important than material values, but in contemporary Catholic bioethics the exact relationship between the bodily and the spiritual or personal aspects is still disputed.

Some continuities between the pre– and post–Vatican II approaches also exist. After Vatican II Catholic moral theologians in biomedical ethics continued to insist on some of the same fundamental principles as those professed before Vatican II, especially the right to life, the principle of stewardship, and the principle of totality. In light of the problems of physicalism, revisionist moral theologians question the principle of double effect and the principle based on the nature, purpose, and ends of sexual organs. Post–Vatican II moral theologians unanimously continue to employ and develop the Catholic position that one does not have to use extraordinary means to preserve life, although they differ in exactly how this is to be understood and applied in some circumstances. In fact, the Catholic tradition on extraordinary means has become almost generally accepted. The early post–Vatican II period also embraced the older casuistic method and emphasis on the solution of particular quandaries. What should the doctor or researcher do? What should the Catholic hospital do? What should government policy be? What should the law be? Some moral theologians have come to question the predominance of this casuistic approach.

LEADING CATHOLIC MORAL THEOLOGIANS IN BIOETHICS

The following section discusses the leading figures in Catholic moral theology and bioethics in light of the four different methodological approaches mentioned earlier: the revisionist, the new natural law theory, the traditional neoscholastic natural law approach, and the feminist perspective. The discussion proceeds historically, addressing the earlier contributors first.

Revisionist Approach

Without doubt, Richard A. McCormick, a leading first-generation revisionist, was the major figure in revisionist Catholic bioethics from Vatican II almost until his death in 2000.[6] McCormick was trained in pre–Vatican II moral theology and wrote his doctoral dissertation in the area of medical ethics. He discussed issues of bioethics in his "Notes on Moral Theology" in *Theological Studies* and in other articles that followed the method of the "Notes" of adroitly analyzing and perceptively criticizing other approaches before developing his own position. His 1980 book of collected essays is subtitled *Dilemmas in Bioethics*.[7] He wrote only one comparatively short monograph, *Health and Medicine in the Catholic Tradition*, which was an extended commentary on a document that he and others had put together called "Ethical Guidelines for Catholic Health Care Institutions." Others recognized McCormick's leading role as a Catholic bioethicist, and he was often asked to serve on governmental commissions and committees of professional medical societies.

McCormick employed his theory of proportionalism with regard to the issues of bioethics. He developed a concern about when and when not to treat patients as he analyzed the many legal cases that came to the fore in the 1970s and early 1980s.[8] Most Catholic moral theologians, except for a few on the far right, view McCormick as a moderate or slightly left-of-center moral theologian. He disagreed with Catholic teaching on contraception, sterilization, and the principle of double effect but strongly opposed euthanasia and abortion except when confronted with another value truly commensurate with life itself.

McCormick proposed six themes to guide his approach to bioethics: life is a basic but not an absolute good, the inclusion of nascent life in this category, love of God and neighbor as the highest and absolute good, the sociality of the human person, the unity of the spheres of life giving and lovemaking (no AID), and permanent heterosexual marriage as normative.[9] In dealing with specific issues, the theological aspect of his approach is primarily implicit, and he often only alludes to the theological.[10] However, later in his career he did explicitly address the phrase he often used: "reason informed by faith." Theology relates to medical ethics in three ways: the protective, the dispositive, and the directional. People without faith or a theological basis can come to the same conclusions as he. McCormick was also willing to use religious language in public, even in pluralistic settings.[11]

Charles Curran, the other leading first-generation revisionist, also made some early contributions to biomedical ethics. As the first U.S. moral theologian to criticize the accepted natural law theory for its physicalism, Curran published an essay in 1968 on absolute norms in medical ethics.[12] In the early 1970s Curran also wrote articles on abortion (arguing for the existence of truly individual human life fourteen days after fertilization), sterilization, experimentation, and genetics. He contributed the article "Roman Catholicism" to the 1978 *Encyclopedia of Bioethics*. By that time, however, he had already decided that he could not give enough time to other areas of moral theology, especially social ethics, if he was to continue in the complex field of bioethics.[13]

John F. Dedek, who was then teaching at Mundelein Seminary in Chicago, wrote two books on medical ethics in the early 1970s.[14] In part 1 of his *Contemporary Medical Ethics* (1975), he discusses surgery, organ transplantation, and human experimentation. In part 2 he treats contraception, homosexuality, and genetic manipulation. The last two parts discuss abortion, euthanasia, and psychosurgery. Dedek does not claim that his research is original but discusses the various positions that have been taken by Catholics and others. He then offers his conclusions as guidance for pastoral ministers. He condemns euthanasia and concludes that the majority of Catholic theologians support the teaching on abortion of the magisterium but that a growing number argue for a few exceptions to the general rule. According to the index, the authors he cites most are McCormick and Curran.

The second generation of revisionist Catholic bioethicists received their degrees after Vatican II and began writing in the late 1970s. David F. Kelly, who taught mostly at Duquesne University, spent his entire academic career in the area of bioethics, beginning with his revised doctoral dissertation, *The Emergence of Roman Catholic Medical Ethics in North America* (1979). The book is a veritable bibliographical gold mine in which he traces, in the style of dissertations, the development of medical ethics. The two principal characteristics of Catholic medical ethics in the twentieth century before Vatican II are its physicalism and ecclesiastical positivism, but many post–Vatican II Catholic bioethicists call into question this physicalism and recognize the legitimacy of theological dissent. A 1991 book focuses on treatment decisions in Catholic hospitals based on Kelly's theoretical understandings and his work in such an institution.[15] His *Contemporary Catholic Health Care Ethics* (2004) has all the virtues of a good textbook. He addresses first the theological basis of health care, and then method, before applying these aspects to particular questions with heavy emphasis on issues of foregoing treatment. He calls his method "intrinsic consequentialism," which he, unlike most Catholic revisionists, describes as a middle position between deontological and utilitarian approaches.

Thomas A. Shannon, professor emeritus at Worchester Polytechnic Institute, has been a prolific contributor to bioethics and social ethics. Paulist Press, a Catholic publisher, in 1976 published his edited anthology on bioethics, which employs a general rather than a Catholic perspective. This book is in its fourth edition.[16] His own *Introduction to Bioethics* is a primer about important bioethical issues, again written from a general rather than a Catholic perspective. But he has also written and edited many volumes from the Catholic perspective as well as frequently contributing to *Theological Studies*.[17] Shannon, using the ethical method of John Duns Scotus and contemporary scientific knowledge, argues for delayed animation in the fetus.[18] James J. Walter, now at Loyola Marymount University, has worked with Shannon on three books, and he has written articles emphasizing especially the theological aspect of Catholic bioethics.[19] In addition, Walter has written a friendly but perceptive analysis and criticism of McCormick's theory of proportionalism.[20] Lisa Sowle Cahill of Boston College certainly fits into this category of second-generation revisionist bioethicists, but she will be discussed under feminist approaches.

James F. Drane, professor emeritus at Edinboro University, has written extensively in bioethics, but not usually from the perspective of a Catholic moral theologian. His significant 1988 book, calling for the role of virtue and character in medical ethics, was copublished by the Catholic Health Association.[21] His *More*

Humane Medicine: A Liberal Catholic Bioethics emphasizes the special relationship of the physician to the patient and the corresponding virtues, while employing a modified natural law approach. His approach is not primarily casuistic, but he does propose some rare and limited exceptions to the Catholic rule against direct and intentional killing.

New Natural Law Theory

Germain Grisez probably would not consider himself a bioethicist, but he has written two massive and erudite books on abortion and euthanasia. No Catholic has treated these issues in greater depth and breadth than Grisez. His seminal 1970 article "Toward a Consistent Natural Law Ethics of Killing" gave direction to his subsequent work in support of a prolife ethic.[22] He opposes abortion, euthanasia, and capital punishment, and has called for the unilateral dismantling of the 1980s U.S. nuclear deterrent because it is based on the moral intention to kill innocent civilians.[23] No one can call him a social conservative. In all these areas Grisez employs his basic goods theory in a consistent and logical way, while at the same time disagreeing with other philosophical and theological approaches.

His 559-page book on abortion (1970) looks at the issue from many different perspectives: biological, sociological, historical, medical, legal, and ethical.[24] He maintains that from the moment of conception the embryo is a truly human individual who must be considered a person. With regard to conflict situations, Grisez actually disagrees somewhat—at least from the philosophical perspective—with the third condition of the principle of double effect. He maintains that the good effect can be achieved by means of the evil effect, provided that a subsequent act is not required to bring about the good effect.

Germain Grisez and Joseph M. Boyle's *Life and Death with Liberty and Justice: A Contribution to the Euthanasia Debate* (1979) takes a much different approach from Grisez's earlier abortion book. This book deals primarily with jurisprudence rather than with morality and ethics. Only in chapters 11 and 12 do the authors develop their basic goods theory, refute other theories, and argue for the immorality of euthanasia and many other forms of killing. Likewise, the book prescinds from any theological aspects. Thus the jurisprudential and legal proposals made in the book do not directly depend upon the moral positions taken. Grisez and Boyle develop a complex understanding of jurisprudence based on liberty and justice. For example, suicide and attempted suicide should not be considered crimes, and the law should avoid interfering with competent adults who freely choose to kill themselves. But they argue against the legalization of voluntary and involuntary euthanasia and assisted suicide based not on the moral precept of the sanctity of life but on the interests of individuals other than those killed—for example, their interest in not standing aloof from an act they abhor.

William E. May has written frequently on bioethical issues and uses the new natural law theory to defend strongly the teachings of the hierarchical magisterium. His 1977 book talks about reproduction, contraception, sterilization, abortion, genetics, and care for the dying.[25] His *Catholic Bioethics and the Gift of Life* (2000) considers the most important bioethical issues raised today. In addition, May has written many articles on bioethics for journals such as the *Linacre Quarterly* and the *National Catholic Bioethics Quarterly*.[26] May also drafted a document signed by other so-called conservative Catholic theologians, including Grisez, that asserts that under ordinary circumstances it is immoral and should not be legally permissible to withhold or withdraw artificial food and hydration from permanently unconscious nonterminal patients.[27]

Neoscholastic and Manualistic Natural Law

Charles J. McFadden and Thomas J. O'Donnell, who wrote textbooks in medical ethics before Vatican II, published new books in the 1970s using the neoscholastic natural law approach.[28] But the most significant book using this approach is *Health Care Ethics: A Theological Analysis*, written by two Dominican priests, Benedict M. Ashley and Kevin D. O'Rourke.[29] Their book basically follows the accepted Thomistic natural law approach and defends the ethical directives proposed by the American bishops for Catholic health care. They call their method "prudential personalism," which is a teleological natural law ethic. O'Rourke has been associated for a long time with the Catholic Health Association. The authors recognize, however, that health care ethics involves much more than a consideration of the disputed moral issues that arise. The book is comprehensive and is not intended as a textbook. The authors, in fact, have written their own textbook based on this more comprehensive volume.[30] The fact that the comprehensive book has gone through five editions and has been repeatedly updated since its publication in 1978 shows the important role it has played in theory and practice in Catholic health care in the United States.

Part 1 is about the dignity of the human being in the community and one's responsibilities and rights with regard to health care. Part 2 considers the responsibilities of the community, the government, and the health care professions in assisting persons in their search for health. Parts 3 and 4 develop the principles for medical ethics and apply them to the many different particular issues. Their theory derives moral principles from the needs of human beings in historically changing communities and thus fits squarely within the accepted Thomistic natural law approach. Their principles correspond with many of the principles developed in the pre–Vatican II understanding of medical ethics. The final part of their book addresses pastoral ministry in health care.

The authors' position on dissent from *Humanae vitae* has hardened since the first edition, which recognized that conscientious individuals can dissent but cannot expect the pastors to approve of their dissenting judgments.[31] The first edition also asks whether the reasons supporting the conclusion of *Humanae vitae* are more probable than the arguments against the position. The authors respond that the authority of the encyclical gives this position a greater weight than theological opinion, but that the value of the arguments remains open to further study and discussion.[32] The fourth edition, by contrast, states that the contrary arguments "are without solid foundation."[33] The first edition sympathetically raises the possibility that artificial contraception within marriage might be only a venial sin.[34] But the fourth edition maintains that contraception is "always objectively a mortal sin."[35]

Edmund D. Pellegrino is not a moral theologian as such but, as a well-known Catholic physician and medical educator, he has written extensively on medicine and health care employing an Aristotelian-Thomistic natural law method. Pellegrino approaches medical ethics in terms of a moral philosophy of the professions, with the emphasis on virtues. The immediate telos or end (an intrinsic Thomistic teleology) of the clinical relationship is the good of the person. Its purpose or end calls for certain character traits in the professional: fidelity, trust, benevolence, truth-telling, intellectual honesty, humility, courage, and suppression of self-interest. The helping professions confront vulnerable, dependent, and anxious human beings who need their skills and help.[36]

The Ethical and Religious Directives for Catholic Health Care Services, officially proposed by the United States bishops (4th edition, 2001) with regard to quandary ethics, obviously strongly supports the existing hierarchical teachings and the natural law methodology on which the directives are based.[37] The moral law is rooted in the whole of human nature. The solutions to the quandaries are the same as those proposed in the pre–Vatican II versions of the *Directives*. These *Directives* condemn contraception, sterilization, artificial insemination, and euthanasia. In keeping with the Catholic tradition, they affirm that a person does not have to use extraordinary or disproportionate means to prolong life. There is a presumption in favor of giving artificial hydration and food as long as such administration is of sufficient benefit to outweigh the burden involved for the patient. However, the *Directives* recognize that health care involves much more than ethical quandaries. The first three parts of the *Directives* consider the social, pastoral, and spiritual responsibilities of Catholic health care and the professional-patient relationship. In light of the biblical mandate to care for the poor, Catholic health care people and institutions have a responsibility to work for adequate health care for the poor, the uninsured, and the underinsured.

This section treats the *Directives* as an illustration of a defense of the existing hierarchical teaching based on a natural law approach. But these *Directives* constitute the official teaching of the Catholic Church and are normative for what is done in Catholic hospitals. Individual Catholics in practice often do dissent from some of these directives, but the Catholic health care institutions must follow them. A particularly urgent problem in the last few years concerns the merger or working together of Catholic institutions with other institutions that do sterilizations and abortions. According to the *Directives,* the Catholic institutions cannot engage in immediate material cooperation with these intrinsically evil actions.

The Catholic Health Association, composed of more than twelve hundred Catholic health care sponsors, facilities, and related organizations, obviously is committed to supporting and acting in accord with the *Directives.* Mention has already been made of their journal, *Health Progress,* which was originally called *Hospital Progress.* But the Catholic Health Association also recognizes that health care ethics involve more than just quandaries. This institution has made a strong commitment to advocate for the poor and to work for a just and adequate health care system in the United States.[38] The National Catholic Bioethics Center, established in 1972, is a very small institution that conducts research, consultations, education, and publishing in support of existing Church teachings in bioethics.[39]

Feminist Approaches

Catholic feminists have also contributed much to the area of bioethics, with their insistence on beginning with the experience of the oppression of women and patriarchy. Margaret Farley bases her call for equality on an anthropology that recognizes the need for both autonomy and relationality.[40] Farley's 2002 published Madeleva Lecture is titled *Compassionate Respect.* Compassion draws us to persons based on their needs. Respect tells us what response to these needs is required and just. Compassionate respect moves beyond the polarities of care and autonomy, care and justice, and persons and principles, by allowing the content of respect or justice to provide the criteria for care.

While they have not written as much as Farley, Barbara Andolsen and Christine Gudorf have also written on bioethics from a feminist perspective. Andolsen points out that the social power to define health and disease has come from a male perspective, thus making normal female biological realities into diseases.

Andolsen insists that care must be governed by the criterion of gender justice.[41] Gudorf maintains that feminist bioethics based on the experience of the alienation of women calls for the well-being and equality of the least powerful and most marginalized members of society. Feminist bioethics insists on an embodied, relational, and social anthropology.[42]

Lisa Sowle Cahill has written more extensively in bioethics than any other Catholic moral theologian since Richard McCormick. In scholarly articles (in the "Notes on Moral Theology" in *Theological Studies,* for example) as well as in popular publications (for example, in *America*), she has covered most of the issues generally discussed in bioethics.[43] In addition to considering the issues involved in the beginning of human life and at the end of human life, she has analyzed and criticized in depth McCormick's method and approach to bioethics.[44]

In the past two decades, her writings have taken a different tack.[45] Bioethics in the Catholic tradition—in keeping with the general approach of bioethics and the specific Western tradition—has dealt primarily with the decisions to be made by an individual person or with policies concerning individual decisions. Cahill wants to expand the horizon of bioethics to include the emphasis on the common good and solidarity in the Christian and Catholic traditions. Health care is a social issue, and she recognizes the attempts made by some Catholic thinkers and institutions, especially the Catholic Health Association, to take seriously the Gospel imperative of a preferential option for the poor in advocating and working toward a just distribution of health care in our society. Today, however, because of globalization, common good and solidarity exist worldwide. Catholic ethics must also be transformative in working to see that health care and bioethics serve the global common good and solidarity. Cahill maintains that Catholics and Christians can and should bring their religious language into the public square as they work with governments and, especially, subsidiary groups and organizations, by advocating, organizing, and networking to have health care and bioethics serve the global common good.

Cahill points out that when bioethics has considered the acts of individuals, it has done so without recognizing the social, cultural, and economic contexts in which decisions are made. We in this country live in a culture that prizes individual choice, scientific progress, technological advance, and a market economy. But do all these realities serve the common good? In discussing reproductive technologies (in vitro fertilization, for example), we must also consider the low success ratio, the disproportionate expense, the priority of other medical needs, and the availability of other solutions, such as adoption.[46]

Cahill's thesis is a good reminder that bioethics must consider more than quandary ethics. The methods discussed in this chapter have all been geared primarily to solving particular cases of what the individual should do. The individual act, however, must always be seen in relationship to the person who places the act and the meaning it has for that person. Catholic bioethics has begun to consider, but must give more importance to, the meaning of pain, suffering, frailty, aging, and death in light of the Catholic tradition truly to give meaning to people as they make their particular decisions. In addition, the social aspects of common good and solidarity raise questions about how health care is delivered in our country and in the world and what we can do to transform the present systems. Quandary issues will always remain, but they are not the only issues. In many ways, they are not even the most important issues in bioethics. Emphasis on these broader issues will also enable the different approaches within the Catholic tradition to find common ground and areas of agreement.

ETHICAL QUANDARIES

This section looks at the ethical quandaries in bioethics in three different areas: the beginning of life, the end of life, and the enhancement of life.

Beginning of Life

The primary ethical quandary involving the beginning of life is abortion. The moral analysis of abortion logically entails two questions: What is the value of the fetus? And how do you solve conflict situations?

Papal and hierarchical teaching is clear on both issues. In a somewhat solemn manner, Pope John Paul II, in his 1995 encyclical *Evangelium vitae*—in accord with the unchanged and unchangeable tradition of the Church—declared "that direct abortion, that is, abortion intended as an end or as a means, always constitutes a grave moral disorder."[47] In November 1974 the Congregation for the Doctrine of the Faith issued a longer, more detailed analysis of abortion in its "Declaration on Procured Abortion."[48]

Some revisionists, such as John T. Noonan Jr., strongly support the position that from the time of fertilization the fetus has all the protections of a human being.[49] But other revisionists have proposed differing positions. In 1973, on the basis of André Helleger's research on fetal development, Charles Curran contended that in the first fourteen days a truly individual human being does not exist.[50] Richard McCormick was somewhat open to this position in his "Notes on Moral Theology" in 1973 and continued throughout the years to defend and develop this assertion.[51] The following arguments have been made in support of this position:

the high percentage of miscarried fertilized ova during this fourteen-day period, the fluid individuality of the pre-embryo, the possibility of twinning and recombination occurring before the fourteenth day, and the insufficiency of the genetic code of the fertilized ovum to govern its development apart from maternal genetic influences. But McCormick still gives great value to the pre-embryo. In principle, one cannot exclude nontherapeutic experiments on the early embryo, but he concludes that there is a strong prima facie obligation to treat the pre-embryo as a person.[52] But supporters of the existence of a human person from the time of fertilization have tried to refute the arguments proposed by McCormick and others.[53]

As early as 1967 Joseph Donceel, a Jesuit philosopher at Fordham University, defended the Thomistic theory of delayed animation because the soul can only be received into matter capable of receiving it. Donceel admits that he is not certain about when the soul is infused, but this cannot be before the formation of human organs such as the nervous system and the brain.[54] In the 1990s Thomas A. Shannon, building on the philosophical approach of John Duns Scotus and St. Bonaventure in the Franciscan tradition and in light of contemporary biology, argued for a later animation, or coming of personhood. Shannon maintains that there is no person before individuality occurs, at about two weeks. But individuation is a necessary but not a sufficient criterion for true personhood. He maintains that true personhood in the full moral sense cannot occur without an integrated neural system that takes place at about twenty-one weeks after conception. Shannon admits, however, that even before personhood, the fetus has some value, but he does not clearly state the nature of that value.[55] Mark Johnson of Marquette University strongly disagreed with Shannon's arguments in an extended exchange in *Theological Studies*.[56]

In light of the differing theological opinions about when personhood occurs, Carol Tauer argued on the basis of traditional Catholic moral theological teaching on probablism that Catholics can accept as probable the opinion that the early human embryo is not a person.[57] Daniel Maguire maintained a similar position.[58]

Proponents of the new natural law theory strongly support the existence of personhood from conception. Germain Grisez developed a two-step argument. The first step is based on the fact that a new individual comes into existence at conception. Second, this individual is a person who will develop on the basis of the already existing individualized fertilized ovum.[59] Grisez in 1990 refuted some of the newer arguments proposing delayed animation.[60]

William E. May argued that the very early fetus is an individual human being with the potential to develop already built in and not depending on any other outside force. Thus it is a human person. One of the significant questions is how one evaluates that potentiality. May insists that the potentiality is already built in and that nothing else is required for future development.[61] May also tried later to refute the newer arguments proposed against personhood from the moment of conception.[62]

Ashley and O'Rourke, the best-known contemporary representatives of natural law teaching in defense of existing Church teaching, defend human personhood from the time of conception. They correctly point out that official Catholic teaching recognizes the existence of theoretical doubt about when personhood occurs, but in practice the human being is to be treated as a person from the moment of conception. They claim that the Aristotelian and Thomistic positions of delayed animation were based on the inaccurate biology of the time, which knew nothing about the fertilized ovum. They refute the arguments in favor of delayed animation based on individuality and the large number of miscarriages.[63]

Catholic feminists have also addressed the question of the status of the fetus and when personhood begins. But something should be said about the historical and cultural context in which Catholic feminists were writing. Many observers, but especially Catholic feminists, have pointed out that the U.S. bishops have made public policy on the legal issue of abortion paramount and central to the detriment of many other aspects of Catholic teaching on economic justice, peace, and the equal rights of women.[64] Defenders of the bishops could point out that the late Cardinal Bernardin developed the consistent ethic of life to embrace all the life issues.[65] But, in practice, abortion has been the central issue and the only issue over which individual bishops have taken disciplinary action against Catholic legislators who support *Roe v. Wade.*

One significant event occurred in October 1984, when ninety-six Catholics signed a statement that appeared as an advertisement in the *New York Times* maintaining that there is a diversity of opinion among Catholics on the morality of abortion and that Catholics should not oppose the legal freedom of religion of women who want abortions. Among the signers were several Catholic moral theologians, including Margaret Farley, Mary Hunt, Daniel Maguire, Giles Milhaven, and Thomas Shannon. As mentioned in chapter 6, the Vatican reacted only against the twenty-four religious women who signed the statement, insisting that they publicly retract. Twenty-two of these women found ways in the next two years to settle the matter without making a public retraction.[66]

Margaret Farley has drawn attention to the impasse today in public debate between strong anti-abortionists and strong pro-abortionists. One position about which both sides are possibly in bad faith is on the nature of the fetus. The pro-abortion position often maintains that the fetus is simply tissue in the pregnant woman. On the other hand, the anti-abortion position acknowledges no ambiguity or uncertainty about the nature of the fetus and argues for an absolute prohibition of abortion.[67]

Sidney Callahan strongly defends prolife feminism. She argues for a more inclusive understanding of justice, rather than the narrow right of the autonomy of a woman to control her body. Unique individual embryonic life brings with it membership in the species or collective human family and is the basis for human solidarity, equality, and natural human rights.[68]

Lisa Cahill holds that the developing fetus has developing moral worth. We will probably never find that magic moment when true personhood begins. She fears that those who propose such a moment do so in order to erode the respect due to early developing human life. From the very beginning the embryo is a living member of the human species, even if it does not have all the safeguards of personhood. All our decisions about the status of the fetus take place in the context of uncertainty, but Cahill fears that American individualism, the market economy, and the scientific imperative will erode the human value of the fetus. In terms of public policy, all should work for better social and economic conditions for women so that they will not be faced with the dilemma of aborting.[69]

The vast majority of Catholic moral theologians hold to a very early origin of human personhood or at least give great value to the early embryo and fetus. One of the primary reasons for this position comes from the Catholic insistence that the equal dignity of all human beings comes from their creation by God. Human dignity is not based on what one does, makes, or accomplishes.

The status of the fetus is one important issue in the question of abortion. The other important question is how to solve conflict situations in which the fetus is involved. For those in the Catholic tradition who hold that the fetus has the rights of a true human person from the moment of conception, or at least from the fourteenth day—and this involves the great majority of Catholic moral theologians—the conflict involves the life of the fetus as a human person. According to official Catholic teaching and the principle of double effect, direct abortion is always wrong, but indirect abortion can be permitted for a proportionate reason. A direct abortion is an act that by the intention of the agent or the nature of the act aims at killing the fetus either as a means or as an end. As pointed out above, removing a cancerous uterus or pathological fallopian tube that contains a fetus are indirect abortions. But one cannot directly kill the fetus in order to save the mother's life. Revisionists justify an abortion in order to save the life of the mother or for a value commensurate with life itself. The issue of abortion does not directly arise with the pre-embryo except in the case of an abortifacient pill because the woman does not know she is pregnant. Lisa Cahill and Thomas Shannon do not maintain that the early embryo, even after fourteen days, is truly a person. Their writings suggest that Cahill gives much more value to the early fetus than does Shannon.[70] Daniel Maguire has also defended the moral and legal acceptance of abortion.[71]

Embryonic stem cell research also involves the issue of the worth or value of the early embryo because in the process of this research the early embryo is destroyed. The hierarchical magisterium and all who hold that the fetus must be treated as a human person from fertilization strongly oppose stem cell research precisely because the early embryo is destroyed. Those who hold that personhood begins only after the fourteenth day are open to such research depending on the value they give to the pre-embryo as compared with the possible good coming from scientific research. Thomas Shannon, for example, supports such stem cell research.[72] Lisa Cahill is concerned that individualistic liberalism, scientific imperative, and private economic gain that support such stem cell research erode the respect due to pre-embryonic human life. Cahill points out the optimism of the scientists, which may well be exaggerated. Theological bioethics should use narrative and prophetic approaches to raise questions about an uncritical acceptance of stem cell research as a scientific and research imperative.[73] Paul Lauritzen does not hold that the early embryo is a human person, but he uses the analogy with just war criterion of last resort to oppose stem cell research because there are other possible ways to get similar benefits.[74] In one symposium, two Catholic theologians condemned stem cell research as the taking of human life. Four other theologians did not give the pre-embryo such status, but they discouraged such research because of respect for fetal life and social justice issues.[75]

Assisted reproductive technology (ART), often in the form of in-vitro fertilization and embryo transfer, is frequently used today. Official Catholic teaching, as we have seen, opposes even AIH. As in the case of artificial contraception, it separates the procreative and unitive aspects of the sexual act. Logically, anyone (e.g., Ashley and O'Rourke) who sees contraception as morally wrong also views AIH as morally wrong.[76] Richard McCormick accepts AIH (not AID) and defended the simple or standard IVF where the pre-embryo from the husband's gametes is implanted in the uterus of the wife. He recognizes problems involving the moral status of the pre-embryo, especially related to spare embryos and what to do with them, but he maintains that prenascent life at this stage does not deserve the same protection as life after fourteen days.[77] Other Catholic moralists, such as Paul Lauritzen and Jean Porter, are not totally opposed to the use of donor semen or ova.[78] Feminists such as Margaret Farley raise questions about the effect of such procedures on women and their roles in society.[79] Maura Ryan, on the basis of her moral theology and her own experience, puts the issue of ART in a broader social justice and common good perspective. She concludes that in principle IVF should be eligible for funding (e.g., by insurance companies) as a medical treatment, but there must also be limits on IVF in light of other medical needs.[80] Lisa Cahill does not oppose all ART, but she wants the low success rate, the disproportionate expense, the priority of other medical needs, and the availability of other solutions (e.g., adoption) to be part of the public dialogue.[81]

Death and Dying

The traditional Catholic approach worked out in the pre–Vatican II era was that euthanasia is wrong, but one does not have to do everything possible to keep physical life in existence. David Kelly rightly claims that this position became the generally accepted American consensus in the latter part of the twentieth century despite some arguments in favor of euthanasia.[82] Papal documents and instructions from the Congregation for the Doctrine of the Faith and the *Ethical and Religious Directives for Catholic Health Care Services* all recognize and spell out this basic Catholic approach.[83] The vast majority of Catholic moral theologians accept this twofold approach, but there are some disputes about particular issues.

Responding to many legal cases throughout the 1970s and 1980s, Richard A. McCormick developed his own position on when to treat and when not to treat the critically ill. Physical or biological life is a relative rather than an absolute value. McCormick, like most Catholic commentators, cites the 1957 address of Pope Pius XII that the use of extraordinary or disproportionate means "would be too burdensome . . . and would render the attainment of the higher, more important goods, too difficult. Life, death, and all temporal activities are in fact subordinated to spiritual ends." When the struggle for mere survival would be all-encompassing and would exclude room for the significant relationships of human persons is the criterion McCormick uses for the decision to suspend treatment. But he strongly opposes not treating mildly retarded newborns, as in the case of Down syndrome babies. For infants and incompetent adults, the criterion for not treating should be the best interests of the person, including some considerations of the later quality of life and the length that life would be prolonged. The analysis involved here is a question of burdens and benefits. The analysis obviously recognizes and gives importance to the quality of life, but the quality of life is understood not in terms of social utility to others but in terms of the continued physical existence of the person involved. McCormick commented on many of the legal cases surrounding these issues in the 1970s and 1980s.[84] John J. Paris, now of Boston College, often discussed these issues, sometimes in collaboration with McCormick.[85]

One disputed area in the late twentieth and early twenty-first centuries concerned the withholding or withdrawal of artificial nutrition and hydration from patients in a persistent vegetative state. The issue raises the question of how one evaluates burdens and benefits. On the whole, the revisionist moral theologians generally accept the possibility of withholding or withdrawing such hydration and nutrition because there is no obligation to continue using ineffective means that will not offer any reasonable hope of success. Proponents of such a position see a parallel with the withholding or withdrawal of a respirator. Since the water and food are supplied by a medical intervention, as in the case of the respirator, withholding or withdrawing them is not the same as not giving the patient food and drink.[86] But as Ashley and O'Rourke point out, many who "base their views squarely on magisterial teachings," like themselves, also hold that artificial hydration and nutrition can be withheld or withdrawn in such cases. This is not the same as not providing ordinary food and water to the patient. Ashley and O'Rourke cite Directive 58 of the *Ethical and Religious Directives*: "There should be a presumption in favor of providing nutrition and hydration to all patients, including patients who require medically assisted nutrition and hydration, as long as this is of sufficient benefit to outweigh the burdens involved to the patient." But Ashley and O'Rourke also point out that individual theologians and groups of bishops have insisted on the obligation not to withdraw or withhold artificial hydration and nutrition for patients in a persistent vegetative state because they have a right to food and water.[87]

Two contexts—the Terry Schiavo case in Florida and the 2004 allocution of Pope John Paul II—fueled this debate. John Paul II maintained that tubes are not a medical act and that their use always represents a natural means of preserving life, which is a part of normal care.[88] Discussion has taken place about the exact meaning of the Pope's allocution and the strength of its authoritative nature. But the vast majority of Catholic moral theologians continue to allow for withholding or withdrawing artificial hydration and nutrition when it is burdensome to the patient and does not offer hope of success. In addition, the Ethical and Religious Directive 58 has not been changed in any way.[89]

The second prong of the Catholic teaching—the condemnation of euthanasia or mercy killing—is upheld by the vast majority of Catholic moral theologians in the United States today. Pope John Paul II's 1995 encyclical *Evangelium vitae* strongly condemned euthanasia as a grave violation of the law of God, a teaching that is based upon natural law and the written word of God.[90] The hierarchical teaching and all those who accept the principle of double effect condemn all euthanasia as direct killing of an innocent human being. Those who follow the new natural law theory likewise condemn direct euthanasia.

Revisionists on the whole oppose euthanasia, but a proportionalist approach does not accept the position that the direct killing of the innocent is always wrong.

Direct in this sense, as we have seen, is based not only on intention but also on the physical structure of the act itself. Proportionalists hold that such nonmoral evil could be done if there is a proportionate reason. McCormick maintains that the prohibition of euthanasia is at least a virtual exceptionless norm in light of the possibly and probably short-term and long-term effects of accepting euthanasia.[91] David Kelly likewise disagrees with the concept of direct and indirect killing and at one time favored euthanasia, but now he opposes almost all euthanasia. Kelly concludes that euthanasia is almost always morally wrong, given the possibility of proper pain management, and should not be legalized.[92]

Lisa Cahill, like Margaret Farley and others, also does not see an absolute difference between direct killing and not using extraordinary means, but Cahill still upholds the general Christian consensus that direct killing does not respect human dignity. Furthermore, instituting general practices of killing in such cases is detrimental to the common good. Cahill goes on to show the narrowness and ineffectiveness of a quandary ethics approach. The best response to the call for euthanasia and assisted suicide involves creating a social ethos that accepts dependency and decline as part of the human condition and uses the best medical knowledge to ameliorate pain while drawing on spiritual traditions to offer patients and caregivers hope in transcendent meaning beyond their present condition. Theological bioethics as participatory transformation should work to achieve this approach.[93]

Daniel Maguire has used the proportionalist approach to justify active euthanasia. Taking a life is wrong unless there is a proportionate reason to do so. Judgments often do vary about what is a proportionate reason, but he maintains that there are proportionate reasons to justify active euthanasia. For Maguire, active euthanasia is now an open moral question. Yes, abuses might follow, but abuse does not take away the use.[94] Dick Westley, while upholding the Catholic ideal, accepts the moral legitimacy of some active euthanasia.[95] But the vast majority of Catholic moral theologians disagree with these positions.

Human Enhancement

Experimentation has been one of the principal reasons for the growth and progress of pharmacology and biomedical technology. New drugs and procedures have to be tested before they can be safely employed. Bioethicists in general have written much on experimentation, but Catholic bioethicists have seldom addressed the issue. It is safe to say that Catholic bioethicists would generally accept the understanding proposed in Directive 31 of the *Ethical and Religious Directives:* "No one should be the subject of medical or genetic experimentation, even if it is therapeutic, unless the person or surrogate first has given free and informed consent. In instances of nontherapeutic experimentation, the surrogate can give this consent only if the experiment entails no significant risk to the person's well being. Moreover, the greater the person's incompetency and vulnerability, the greater the reasons must be to perform any medical experimentation, especially nontherapeutic."[96] The guideline is rightly quite general, and there can be different ways of interpreting and applying it. One area debated by a few Catholic moral theologians concerns parents giving consent for their children to be involved in nontherapeutic experimentation with minimal risks involved. Of course, official Catholic teaching rejects any nontherapeutic experimentation on the embryo.[97]

In the pre–Vatican II period Catholic moral theologians worked out the basic principles governing organ transplants. Gerald Kelly, we recall, on the basis of charity, justified organ transplants between two living human beings if the donor's functional integrity is maintained. Thus one could donate one of two kidneys.[98] Again, bioethicists in general have written much on organ transplants, but Catholic bioethicists have not dealt extensively with this subject. Four questions arise in terms of transplanting organs from recently deceased people. First, how should such organs be fairly distributed, since there is always more need than there are organs available? Second, if the voluntary giving of organs does not provide a sufficient number of them, should we allow people to sell their organs? Third, who pays for organ transplants? The present system in the United States is somewhat mixed, but there is no doubt that those who can pay for these expensive procedures are much better off than those who cannot. This certainly raises issues of justice and equality. Fourth, what are the legitimate means of trying to obtain more organs? On this score, Philip Boyle and Kevin O'Rourke, on the basis of the common good, propose a presumption in favor of organ donation by all people who have just died. Those who disagree could object to such procedures, and their organs would not be taken.[99]

The completion of the mapping of the human genome in 2003 raised the issue of human enhancement through genetic engineering. But some Catholic moral theologians in the early 1970s had already addressed the issue of genetics. Charles Curran's anthropology, recognizing both the creativity and freedom of the person, together with the creatureliness and sinfulness, calls for a genetic approach that opposes both an unqualified yes and an intransigent no to genetic possibilities. The scientific and the technological are important, but they are only one aspect of the human. At times the human and the moral must say no to the technological.[100] Richard McCormick, in commenting on Curran's article on this subject, and many others have adopted a similar "both-and" anthropology and approach to genetics in general.[101]

Contemporary Catholic bioethicists such as James Walter and David Kelly adopt a similar anthropological understanding in approaching issues of genetics.[102] Most of the possibilities in genetic enhancement lie in the future, but some possibilities already exist. There are currently four possible approaches—somatic cell therapy, germ line therapy, somatic cell enhancement, and germ line enhancement—but the distinction between therapy and enhancement is not always absolute. The theological-ethical criterion governing any therapeutic approach is the ultimate good of the person. Enhancement raises many ethical questions.[103] Again, bioethicists should discuss genetics in light of the need for a more equitable distribution of health care and in light of the dangers of an approach that emphasizes individual freedom, access to genetic medicine based on ability to pay, and a science that is interested only in technological progress.[104]

Cloning is intimately connected with the issue of stem cell research. The president's Council on Bioethics (2002) distinguished reproductive cloning, which it opposed, and therapeutic cloning involving the use of the clone for research purposes and for stem cell research. On the issue of therapeutic cloning, seven members favored regulation approving and governing such cloning, while ten members affirmed a four-year moratorium.[105] The moral issues and differences are similar to the related case of stem cell research. Those who hold to a moral human person from the moment of conception oppose all cloning. Defenders of therapeutic cloning, such as James Drane, claim that a human person is not present before the fourteenth day.[106] Some Catholic theologians who hold that the early embryo is not a person discourage stem cell research because of their respect for developing fetal life and for reasons of social justice.[107]

M. Cathleen Kaveny, a lawyer and theologian at Notre Dame, has written on the jurisprudential aspects of three emerging issues connected with genetics: cloning, discrimination on the basis of genetic information, and patenting of genetic material. The Catholic approach to these issues should challenge the individualistic, voluntaristic approach most common in this country by insisting on a legal policy based on the virtue of solidarity.[108]

BROADER APPROACHES TO BIOETHICS

In addition to discussing the morality of particular acts, Catholic bioethicists have considered somewhat the person who acts and the virtues of that actor. Also, the social aspects of health care and especially its just distribution have come to the fore. In aspects of justice, the context is now global rather than national or regional.

The Person and Virtues

Edmund Pellegrino and David Thomasma, in a number of books and articles, have criticized the emphasis on quandary ethics, with its problem-solving skills, because such an approach ignores that acts are done by the members of the health care team. Thus character and virtues remain most important for medical ethics and practice. Following a neoscholastic approach, they recognize both natural and supernatural virtues. They also see the need for principles, but the virtues in general and the Christian virtues in particular modify the principles. Thus, for example, for the Christian, justice is transformed into charitable justice and what is owed to another is governed by Christian love.[109]

James Drane, as we have seen, has emphasized the role of virtues and character in medical ethics. Writing from a broadly human perspective, he shows how the virtues of benevolence, truthfulness, respect, friendliness, justice, and religion should affect the role and function of the physician.[110] James F. Keenan has brought to genetic medicine his understanding of the four cardinal virtues based on a relational anthropology: justice, fidelity, self-care, and prudence, which determine what is the just, faithful, and self-caring way of life.[111]

Catholic bioethicists have paid less attention to the patient, the virtues of the patient, and the meaning of all these medical interventions for the person undergoing them. Most Catholic books dealing with bioethics have only a comparatively short discussion of suffering.[112] In keeping with their focus on Catholic health care facilities, Ashley and O'Rourke have an important section on pastoral care, which is obviously a very significant reality for the patient.[113] However, Ashley and O'Rourke focus primarily on the givers of pastoral care rather than on those who receive it.

Catholic bioethics needs to say more about the spirituality and meaning for the person involved in all medical interventions. To its credit, Catholic sacramental theory and practice recognize the important role of the sacrament of the sick, but this sacramental reality needs to be developed and seen as permeating all aspects of the sick person's relationship to life in general and medical care in particular. Many medical interventions raise the issue of suffering and its place in the Christian life. Christian approaches recognize the complexity and even the paradox of suffering. We should do everything we can to overcome suffering, but in the last analysis, suffering will be a part of every human life. Christians see such suffering in light of the redemptive suffering of Jesus. Most health care and its expenses go to the elderly. Here the individual patient must deal with the reality of frailty, aging, dependency, and death itself. The meaning that older patients seek in the midst of many medical surgeries, drugs, and interventions is the most important reality from the perspective of the patient involved.

Medical Care, Justice, and the Common Good

Catholic moral theologians have also addressed the just distribution of health care in the United States. Papal and hierarchical teachings have insisted on the right to health care. In the encyclical *Pacem in terris* (1963), Pope John XXIII recognized that every human being has a right to the means suitable for the proper development of life: food, clothing, shelter, rest, medical care, and necessary social services.[114] In a 1981 pastoral letter the U.S. Catholic bishops maintained that the basic right to adequate health care follows from the sanctity of life and the dignity of the person. The federal government should guarantee a basic level of health care for all, with special attention to the needs of the poor.[115]

In 1979 Charles Curran argued for a right to adequate health care for all. This right is based on the Catholic understanding of the role of the state, the common good, distributive justice, and the recognition that the goods of creation exist to serve the needs of all.[116] But Curran did not get into the structural issues of how all this should be accomplished. In a 1993 book written before President Clinton's proposal for health care reform, Philip S. Keane insisted on a communitarian perspective, the common good, and distributive justice as grounding the right to a reasonable level of health care for all. This approach is best carried out through a national single-payer insurance system to be administered by the states, with the delivery of health care remaining largely in private hands and with a strong emphasis on preventive care.[117] Catholic moral theologians generally agree on the person's right to adequate medical care.

The *Ethical and Religious Directives,* in its recent edition, shows an important development from the original format, which dealt only with actions that could not or usually could not be performed in a Catholic health care facility. In the recent edition, the first of six parts deals with the social responsibility of Catholic health care. Catholic health care is grounded in the promotion of human dignity and is committed to the biblical mandate of caring for the poor, working for the common good, and exercising responsible stewardship of health care resources.[118] A mutual relationship exists between the Catholic Health Association (CHA) and the *Ethical and Religious Directives,* and both have moved in recent decades to a greater concern about the social dimensions of health care. The CHA advocates for health care reform in accord with the demands of social justice through legislation. The CHA also works with other hospitals, nonprofit groups, and state and federal governments to improve the way in which the ill, the old, and the dying participate in their communities.[119] Much more needs to be done to put flesh and blood into this Catholic approach, which calls for a more just health care system based on the right of all to a reasonable or adequate level of health care.

The social justice aspects of health care distribution today have a global dimension. The Catholic Church is a universal church, and its members and theologians should have a global perspective. The AIDS pandemic has helped to make Catholic moral theologians in the United States more aware of the global dimensions of the common good and of justice with regard to health care. AIDS is primarily a justice issue, not a sexual issue, that involves poverty, racism, patriarchy, and exploitive economic systems. Catholic theologians in the United States have become conscious of the global dimension of AIDS, with special concern about the problem in Africa. The sinful social structures that support AIDS must be changed. Lower-cost treatments need to be provided for the victims in addition to changing the structures that serve to spread the disease. Catholic, other religious, interfaith, nonprofit, and also governmental organizations are working to improve the situation. U.S. Catholic moral theologians James Keenan, Lisa Cahill, and Margaret Farley have made Catholic moral theologians in the United States aware of the global reality of AIDS.[120]

This chapter has developed the different methodological approaches to bioethics in post–Vatican II moral theology: revisionism, new natural law theory, scholastic natural law, and feminism. However, these different approaches all share the basic characteristics of the Catholic moral theological tradition. Catholic moral theologians also discussed in detail the disputed issues and quandaries that arose during this period. As time went on, more attention was paid to the person, virtues, and the meaning of illness, suffering, and death for the Christian, as well as the social aspects of medical care in light of the common good. The social and justice dimensions are not just one part of bioethics. They should also form the context and background within which one addresses all issues involved in bioethics.

NOTES

1. For a collection of magisterial teachings on medical ethics and bioethics, see O'Rourke and Boyle, *Medical Ethics*.
2. See www.nccbuscc.org/bishops/directives.shtml.
3. For Richard A. McCormick's understanding of his role in such situations, see McCormick, *Critical Calling*, 191–208.

4. Vacek, "Vatican Instruction on Reproductive Technology."

5. Abortion and euthanasia are considered in some depth below.

6. For an overview of McCormick's work, see Odozor, *Richard A. McCormick and the Renewal of Moral Theology*. For McCormick's work in bioethics, see Cahill, "On Richard McCormick."

7. McCormick, *How Brave a New World?*

8. Clark, *To Treat or Not to Treat*. For a broader discussion of the same issue, see Sparks, *To Treat or Not to Treat*. Richard Sparks made a significant contribution by publishing many monographs in moral theology when he was an editor at Paulist Press.

9. McCormick, *Health and Medicine*, 51–58.

10. Himes, "Contribution of Theology."

11. McCormick, *Corrective Vision*, 100–109.

12. Curran, "Absolute Norms and Medical Ethics."

13. For Curran's own description of his work in medical ethics, see Curran, *Loyal Dissent*.

14. Dedek, *Human Life* and *Contemporary Medical Ethics*.

15. Kelly, *Critical Care Ethics*.

16. Shannon, *Bioethics*.

17. E.g., Shannon, *Made in Whose Image?*; Shannon and Cahill, *Religion and Artificial Reproduction*; Jung and Shannon, *Abortion and Catholics*.

18. Shannon and Wolter, "Reflections on the Moral Status of the Pre-Embryo," 603–26.

19. Walter and Shannon, *Quality of Life*; Shannon and Walter, *New Genetic Medicine*; Walter and Shannon, *Contemporary Issues in Bioethics*. See Walter's essays in Shannon and Walter, *New Genetic Medicine*.

20. Walter, "Foundation and Formulation of Norms."

21. Drane, *Becoming a Good Doctor*.

22. Grisez, "Toward a Consistent Natural Law Ethics of Killing."

23. Grisez, Finnis, and Boyle, *Nuclear Deterrence, Morality, and Realism*.

24. Grisez, *Abortion*.

25. May, *Human Existence, Medicine, and Ethics*.

26. For May's complete bibliography, see May's homepage www.christendom-awake.org/pages/may/may.html.

27. May, "Feeding and Hydrating."

28. McFadden, *Dignity of Life*; O'Donnell, *Medicine and Christian Morality*.

29. Ashley and O'Rourke, *Health Care Ethics* (4th ed., 1997); Ashley, deBlois, and O'Rourke, *Ethics* (5th ed., 2006).

30. Ashley and O'Rourke, *Ethics of Health Care* (3d ed., 2002).

31. Ashley and O'Rourke, *Health Care Ethics* (1st ed., 1978), 75.

32. Ibid., 275.

33. Ashley and O'Rourke, *Health Care Ethics* (4th ed., 1997), 277.

34. Ashley and O'Rourke, *Health Care Ethics* (1st ed., 1978), 302.

35. Ashley and O'Rourke, *Health Care Ethics* (4th ed., 1997), 309.

36. For Pellegrino's own summary of his many writings, see Pellegrino, "From Medical Ethics."

37. See www.nccbuscc.org/bishops/directives.shtml.

38. See the Catholic Health Association website (www.chausa.org/), which describes their many involvements in health care.

39. See the National Catholic Bioethics Center website, www.ncbcenter.org/.

40. Farley, "Feminist Theology and Bioethics," 163–85.

41. Andolsen, "Elements of a Feminist Approach to Bioethics."

42. Gudorf, "Feminist Critique of Biomedical Principleism."

43. E.g., Cahill, "'Seamless Garment'"; "Sanctity of Life"; "Bioethical Decisions to End Life"; "Embryo and the Fetus"; and "Bioethics."

44. Cahill, "On Richard McCormick."

45. Cahill, *Theological Bioethics*; Cahill, *Bioethics and the Common Good.*

46. Cahill, *Theological Bioethics*, 210.

47. John Paul II, *Evangelium vitae*, 729n61.

48. Sacred Congregation for the Doctrine of the Faith, "Declaration on Procured Abortion."

49. Noonan, "Almost Absolute Value in History," and *Private Choice.*

50. Curran, "Abortion."

51. McCormick, *Notes on Moral Theology, 1965–1980*, 499, 515–16.

52. McCormick, *Corrective Vision*, 176–88.

53. For a summary of some of these refutations, see Cahill, "Notes on Moral Theology, 1992."

54. Donceel, "Abortion," and "Immediate Animation and Delayed Hominization."

55. Shannon and Wolter, "Reflections on the Moral Status of the Pre-Embryo"; Shannon, "Human Embryonic Stem Cell Therapy."

56. Johnson, "Reflections on Some Recent Catholic Claims." For the last exchange, see Johnson and Shannon, "*Quaestio Disputata.*"

57. Tauer, "Tradition of Probabilism."

58. Maguire, "Abortion." See also Burtchaell and Maguire, "Catholic Legacy and Abortion."

59. Grisez, *Abortion*, 273–87.

60. Grisez, "When Do People Begin?"

61. May, *Human Existence, Medicine, and Ethics*, 93–105.

62. May, "Moral Status of the Embryo."

63. Ashley and O'Rourke, *Health Care Ethics*, 4th ed., 222–40.

64. Gudorf, "To Make a Seamless Garment"; Farley, "Church in the Public Forum"; Cahill, *Theological Bioethics*, 183–89. See also Byrnes and Segers, *Catholic Church and the Politics of Abortion.*

65. Bernardin et al., *Consistent Ethic of Life.*

66. Patrick, *Liberating Conscience*, 118–28.

67. Farley, "Liberation, Abortion, and Responsibility," 635.

68. Callahan, "Abortion and the Sexual Agenda."

69. Cahill, *Theological Bioethics*, 170–79.

70. Shannon and Wolter, "Reflections on the Moral Status of the Pre-Embryo"; Shannon, "Human Embryonic Stem Cell Therapy"; Cahill, *Theological Bioethics*, 170–79.

71. Maguire, *Sacred Rights*. Maguire is president of the Religious Consultation on Population, Reproductive Health, and Ethics.

72. Shannon, *New Genetic Medicine,* 140–60, and personal correspondence, November 2006.

73. Cahill, *Theological Bioethics,* 229–35.

74. Lauritzen, "Neither Person nor Property."

75. Snow, *Stem Cell Research.*

76. Ashley and O'Rourke, *Health Care Ethics,* 4th ed., 240–48.

77. McCormick, *Critical Calling,* 329–52.

78. Lauritzen, *Pursuing Parenthood,* 89–97; Porter, "Human Need and Natural Law," 105.

79. Farley, "Feminist Theology and Bioethics."

80. Ryan, *Ethics and Economics of Assisted Reproduction.* For Lauritzen's theological ethical reflection on his own experience, see Lauritzen, *Pursuing Parenthood.*

81. Cahill, *Theological Bioethics,* 193–210.

82. Kelly, *Contemporary Catholic Health Care Ethics,* 127.

83. For references to all these documents and others, see Ashley and O'Rourke, *Health Care Ethics,* 4th ed., 411–32.

84. See McCormick's seminal article, "To Save or Let Die." For analysis and commentaries on McCormick's developing position in this area, see McCartney, "Issues in Death and Dying"; Clark, *To Treat or Not to Treat;* Cahill, "McCormick's 'To Save or Let Die.'"

85. E.g., McCormick and Paris, "Saving Defective Infants" and "Living Will Legislation Reconsidered." For further discussion of the abundant literature on this subject, see, in addition to the general treatments of Catholic health care today, Christie, *Last Rites,* and Kelly, *Medical Care at the End of Life.* Kelly's book updates what he wrote on this subject in his *Contemporary Health Care Ethics.*

86. E.g., Kelly, *Contemporary Catholic Health Care Ethics,* 188–91.

87. Ashley and O'Rourke, *Health Care Ethics,* 4th ed., 426–28. See also O'Rourke, "Catholic Tradition on Forgoing Life Support," 549.

88. John Paul II, "Care for Patients in a Permanent Vegetative State."

89. Shannon and Walter, "Assisted Nutrition and Hydration and the Catholic Tradition"; Paris, Keenan, and Himes, "*Quaestio Disputata*"; Shannon and Walter, "Reply to Professors Paris, Keenan, and Himes."

90. John Paul II, *Evangelium vitae,* 732n65.

91. McCormick, "New Medicine and Morality," 318–20.

92. Kelly, *Contemporary Catholic Health Care Ethics,* 199–205.

93. Cahill, *Theological Bioethics,* 112–30.

94. Maguire, *Death by Choice,* 2d ed., 60–61.

95. Westley, *When It's Right to Die.* See also May and Westley, *Catholic Perspectives.*

96. See www.nccbuscc.org/bishops/directives.shtml.

97. Ashley and O'Rourke, *Health Care Ethics,* 4th ed., 350–51.

98. Kelly, *Medico-Moral Problems,* 245–57.

99. Ashley and O'Rourke, *Health Care Ethics,* 4th ed., 331–39; Boyle and O'Rourke, "Presumed Consent for Organ Donation."

100. Curran, "Theology and Genetics."

101. McCormick, *Notes on Moral Theology, 1965–1980,* 278–90, 401–22.

102. Shannon and Walter, *New Genetic Medicine,* 7–17, 31–40; Kelly, *Contemporary Catholic Health Care Ethics,* 260–69.

103. Kelly, *Contemporary Catholic Health Care Ethics,* 260–69.

104. Cahill, *Theological Bioethics,* 235–51.

105. Kass, *Human Cloning and Human Dignity,* xxxix–lx.

106. Drane, *More Humane Medicine,* 317–25.

107. See notes 72–74.

108. Kaveny, "Jurisprudence and Genetics."

109. Pellegrino and Thomasma, *Virtues in Medical Practice* and *Christian Virtues in Medical Practice.*

110. Drane, *Becoming a Good Doctor.*

111. Keenan, "What Does Virtue Ethics Bring to Genetics?"

112. E.g., Kelly, *Contemporary Catholic Health Care Ethics,* 42–44, 220–25.

113. Ashley and O'Rourke, *Health Care Ethics,* 4th ed., 433–62.

114. John XXIII, *Pacem in terris,* 132n11.

115. U.S. Bishops, "Pastoral Letter on Health and Health Care," 264–67.

116. Curran, *Transition and Tradition in Moral Theology,* 139–70.

117. Keane, *Health Care Reform.*

118. See www.nccbuscc.org/bishops/directives.shtml.

119. For the various involvements of the Catholic Health Association, see Cahill, *Theological Bioethics,* 82–86, 148–54.

120. Keenan, *Catholic Ethicists on HIV/AIDS Prevention;* Cahill, *Theological Bioethics,* 156–68; Farley, "Partnership in Hope."

SOCIAL ETHICS

This chapter begins by situating Catholic social ethics in the United States in the post–Vatican II period in relationship to the pre–Vatican II period and in relationship to other aspects and areas of moral theology. The second section addresses the different methodological approaches, and the third section considers the primary issues discussed.

INTRODUCTORY ASPECTS

Strong continuities exist between the pre– and post–Vatican II approaches to social ethics. The anthropological underpinnings of Catholic social ethics continue to insist on both the dignity and the social nature of the individual person. Catholic social ethics continues to oppose the two extremes of individualism and collectivism. In light of this anthropology, Catholic social ethics sees the political order or the state as natural, necessary, and good. We are by nature social and political and are called to form political government in order to achieve the common good. In keeping with the middle position between individualism and collectivism, the common good ultimately redounds to the good of the individual. The principle of subsidiarity guides the role and function of the state. The state should assist individuals and all intermediate groups, such as families, neighborhoods, voluntary societies and institutions such as schools, the press, and churches to do all they can on their own for the common good, but the state should intervene directly to do what the individual and the lesser mediating institutions cannot do on their own.

In accord with this basic anthropology, there are three types of justice: Commutative justice governs one-on-one relationships; legal or social justice grounds the individual's obligations and contributions to the whole of the society or the state; distributive justice governs how society and the state distribute their burdens and their goods, with a heavy emphasis on need in the latter case. Post–Vatican II Catholic social ethics has developed the understanding of human rights, stressing both political and civil rights, such as basic freedoms in society, but also recognizing social and economic rights, such as the right to food, clothing, shelter, education, and adequate health care. Also, contemporary Catholic social ethics insists even more on the social aspect of all property because the goods of creation exist to serve the needs of all. In somewhat new and different ways, contemporary Catholic social ethics has developed the basic biblical mandate to have concern for the poor and the needy.

As pointed out in chapter 3, official Catholic social teaching and social ethics gradually gave more importance to the freedom of the individual and the importance of democratic political structures. The post–Vatican II era continued developing that trajectory in terms of freedom and democracy. The Catholic tradition has been associated with just war theory, and this association has continued in general after Vatican II. Thus there are significant continuities between the pre– and post–Vatican II approaches to social ethics.

What about discontinuities? One source of discontinuity comes from the many new realities that appeared in the social order in this period. Significant developments have occurred in all areas. Think, for example, of the end of colonialism, the developing world, the East-West confrontation, the women's movement, nuclear weapons, the ecological movement, globalization, and the AIDS pandemic, to mention just a few.

Two other methodological discontinuities relate to two developments in post–Vatican II Catholic moral theology in general. First, biblical and theological emphasis is increased. The basic methodological approach to social ethics was no longer solely on the basis of natural law. Biblical and theological concepts became increasingly central. For example, in light of the biblical approach, post–Vatican II Catholic social ethics developed the preferential option for the poor. The second methodological discontinuity concerned the philosophical aspect of natural law. Historical consciousness came to the fore. The particular, the contingent, the historical, and the individual focuses were emphasized. Catholic social ethics still recognizes a significant role for the universal, but not as much as in the pre–Vatican II period. This difference also affected the methodological approach, placing more emphasis upon the inductive aspect.

Post–Vatican II Catholic social ethics in the United States differs from all the other areas of moral theology already considered. In this area there is no great difference between the revisionist and the conservative or traditionalist approaches, as exist in all other areas. Why is there no difference in Catholic social ethics? As already mentioned, there are many significant continuities between pre–Vatican II and post–Vatican II social ethics, so that there is no large group of theologians disagreeing with positions that were strongly held in the pre–Vatican II Church and continue to be strongly held in the post–Vatican II Church. The specific problems that created the differences in the other areas do not exist in the area of social ethics. The primary area of contention in all other aspects of moral theology is what revisionists call the "problem of physicalism"—the moral aspect of the act becomes identified with the physical structure of the act. This problem, however, does not exist in the area of social ethics. Behind the problem of physicalism is the teleological criterion based on the nature of the faculty and its purposes. But Catholic social ethics, since it deals with persons and society, never mentions the finality of the faculty, especially the sexual faculty. Almost by definition, the problem of physicalism does not exist in the area of social ethics.

The second reason for strong disagreements in all other areas was the issue of dissent over noninfallible papal teaching. This dissent, as mentioned in the previous chapters, exists primarily in areas where the problem of physicalism is involved. But, again, in social ethics there is no group of Catholic theologians explicitly dissenting from the existing papal teaching.

In this context, revisionist Catholic theologians pointed out the methodological differences between papal social teaching and papal sexual teaching in the post–Vatican II era. Significant methodological shifts have occurred in papal social teaching since Leo XIII's encyclical *Rerum novarum* (1891). The first shift from classicism to historical consciousness also emphasized a more inductive methodological approach. The second shift involved moving away from an emphasis on human nature, order, some inequality, and obedience to controlling authorities to the primacy of the human person, with the concomitant need for freedom, equality, and participation in the life of society. The third shift involved a move from a predominantly legal ethical model to a relationality-responsibility ethical model. These three shifts developed over time, and most of the development came at the time of Vatican II and afterward. These shifts did not occur in papal and hierarchical sexual teaching. The emphasis remained on classicism, with a deductive approach; on human nature and faculties, with their God-given purpose; and on a legal ethical model. If the methodological shifts in papal social teaching were used in papal sexual teaching, these teachings would logically have to go through some change and development.[1]

Papal social teaching has obviously played an important role in Catholic social ethics in the United States. The important documents include the Pastoral Constitution on the Church in the Modern World and the Declaration on Religious Freedom of Vatican II. Pope Paul VI issued the encyclical *Populorum progressio* (1967), the apostolic letter *Octogesima adveniens* (1971), and the apostolic exhortation *Evangelii nuntiandi* (1975). The 1971 International Synod of Bishops issued *Justitia in mundo*. Pope John Paul II wrote three encyclicals dealing with social issues—*Laborem exercens* (1981), *Sollicitudo rei socialis* (1987), and *Centesimus annus* (1991).[2] Catholic moral theologians often made commentaries on these individual documents and also on the whole corpus of the papal teaching.[3]

In the 1980s the U.S. bishops issued two pastoral letters on the issues of peace, war, and especially nuclear deterrence and the U.S. economy.[4] Both of these documents were critical of aspects of U.S. policy. Perhaps the most innovative aspect of these documents was the way in which they were written. In both cases a committee of bishops held hearings involving a good number of experts from all fields, including theology, and then published their early drafts in order to have feedback and discussion. As a result, these documents were truly owned by the bishops themselves and by many in the Church. In the process of writing and discussing these documents, Catholic social ethicists were heavily involved. The U.S. bishops deserve great credit for focusing the attention of the Church and of Catholic theologians on these significant social issues in the 1980s.

DIFFERENT APPROACHES AND SIGNIFICANT AUTHORS

Three generic approaches exist in U.S. Catholic social ethics in the post–Vatican II period, which are based on the relationship between the Christian Catholic understanding and the U.S. cultural and political ethos. The majority position is somewhat critical of the U.S. ethos and structures and is also called, at least by those who disagree with it, the "liberal or progressive position." The neoconservative approach is much more supportive of the existing U.S. moral, cultural, and political ethos and disagrees with the first approach, which it finds too critical of the U.S. scene. Most radical is the third approach, which in general sees great incompatibility between the Catholic vision and the U.S. ethos, even to the point of arguing against working with others as a public Church to change U.S. ethos and structures for the better. Such an approach has significant continuity with the pre–Vatican II radical approach of the Catholic Worker movement.

Progressive Approach

The somewhat critical or progressive approach sees itself as working in the tradition of "Catholic social teaching," the name given to papal and hierarchical teaching, and opposes the individualistic anthropology behind problematic aspects of the U.S. ethos and structures. It is quite supportive of many of the social stances taken by the U.S. bishops in the latter part of the twentieth century. The U.S. bishops in the 1970s and 1980s advocated public policy issues using different means, such as pastoral letters, resolutions, congressional testimony, and legislative activity. As pointed out in the previous chapter, abortion was a significant issue for the U.S. Catholic bishops throughout this period, but they also were significantly vocal on three other issues: nuclear war and deterrence, the economy, and U.S. foreign policy, especially in Central America. The 1983 pastoral letter on peace, in light of just war criteria, placed very radical restrictions on the use of nuclear weapons and a restrictive and conditional acceptance only of counterforce and not countercity nuclear deterrence. The 1986 pastoral letter on the economy—on the basis of the common good, distributive justice, and the obligations of the state—strongly criticized the domestic and international dimensions of Reaganomics. On the basis of social justice, human rights, and noninterference, the bishops were quite critical of U.S. support for conservative political regimes in Central America.[5]

Catholic progressive or liberal social ethicists in general supported such initiatives and even encouraged such initiatives by the U.S. bishops, and also staked out other socially progressive positions in relation to existing U.S. policies. But the great majority of such progressive Catholic social ethicists also disagreed with the physicalism of post–Vatican II hierarchical sexual teaching, thus indicating again the two different methodologies involved in the two genres of sexual and social hierarchical teaching.

In social ethics, as in the other areas already described, it took some time for post–Vatican II Catholic theologians to establish themselves. J. Bryan Hehir has provided an early and continuing contribution to Catholic social ethics, although he has never written a monograph. Hehir worked for the U.S. bishops' conference from 1973 to 1992 and had a significant role in formulating and articulating the bishops' proposals on domestic and international policy issues. He was the chief staff person for the bishops' pastoral letter on peace in 1983, often testified before congressional committees on international political issues, such as the need for human rights against some conservative governments in South America, and worked closely with Cardinal Joseph Bernardin in developing the concept of a consistent ethic of life. His work with the bishops' conference made him the target of attacks by some conservatives in the Catholic Church who thought his positions were much too progressive. In his numerous essays and articles he addressed, especially, international policy issues, with a heavy emphasis on peace and war. Hehir also wrote frequently and incisively on how the Catholic Church as a public Church should work with all others for more just domestic and international policies. Hehir saw himself as following in the tradition of John Courtney Murray.

He later became a professor and dean of Harvard Divinity School and also taught in the Kennedy School of Government at Harvard. He developed specific policy positions in light of his Catholic ethical understandings and his public reading of the concrete situation.[6]

David Hollenbach's 1979 *Claims in Conflict*, based on his dissertation, strives, as the subtitle says, to retrieve and renew the Catholic human rights tradition, which is a more adequate approach than either Marxism or individualistic liberalism. Hollenbach moves away from the pre–Vatican II neoscholastic approach in developing eight areas of human rights (e.g., religious, bodily, political, economic, etc.), each with its personal, social, and instrumental rights. This inclusive set of rights is ultimately based on human dignity. The Catholic tradition has been reluctant to recognize conflicts, but Hollenbach develops three strategic moral priorities: the needs of the poor, the freedom of the dominated, and the participation of marginalized people.

Hollenbach, now at Boston College, served as the chief staff person for the 1986 bishops' pastoral letter on the economy and continued to develop his understanding of human rights and their ramifications for domestic and international issues.[7] He also addressed the role of religion in general and the Catholic Church in particular in working for a just society in the midst of our existing pluralisms.[8] Hollenbach's 2002 book tries to make the Catholic concept of the common good and its ramifications better understood and accepted by many who are unaware of such an approach. He develops a pluralistic, analogical understanding of the common good and a sense of community in the midst of great pluralism. He then illustrates his approach in dealing with the poverty and hopelessness of our inner cities and the ambiguities of globalization that are detrimental to human equality.[9]

Charles E. Curran's *American Catholic Social Ethics* (1982) analyzed and criticized the methodological approaches of five U.S. Catholic social ethicists in the twentieth century—John A. Ryan, William J. Engelen, Paul Hanly Furfey, John Courtney Murray, and James W. Douglass—to the relationship between being Catholic and being American. Curran points out that at times the Catholic Church has rightly criticized the shortcomings of the U.S. ethos, especially its individualism, but at other times the Church has learned from the United States, especially in areas such as freedom and democracy. He applies to social ethics his basic stance of the fivefold mysteries of creation, sin, incarnation, redemption, and resurrection destiny. He wrote essays on social ethics in the subsequent years; some of the earlier ones were collected in *Directions in Catholic Social Ethics* (1985). His *Catholic Social Teaching, 1891–Present: A Historical, Theological, and Ethical Analysis* (2002) analyzes and criticizes the historical development of the official papal and hierarchical Catholic social teaching. The methodological chapters consider the theological, ethical, and ecclesial approaches, while the substantive chapters discuss anthropology and the social and political orders. Curran points out the historical developments and changes that have occurred within papal social teaching, especially in light of Vatican II. His *The Moral Theology of Pope John Paul II* (2005), while generally positive about the papal social teaching—although having some problems with its unwillingness to deal with conflict—points out once again the significant methodological differences in papal sexual and social teaching.

Two Jesuits who were trained in other disciplines have also contributed to Catholic social ethics and Catholic social teaching. With a doctorate in sociology, John Coleman, now at Loyola Marymount University, has been publishing articles for over thirty years. His 1982 book *An American Strategic Theology* brought together some earlier articles. His work joins his sociological concern for the impact of religion on society with a post–Vatican II Catholic emphasis on the Church's social mission. Coleman edited an important book on the hundredth anniversary of *Rerum novarum,* bringing together the most significant contributors to a progressive Catholic social ethics in the United States.[10] He likewise coedited many volumes for the *Concilium* series.

John Langan of the Woodstock Institute and Georgetown University received his Ph.D. in philosophy, but he has edited a number of volumes often resulting from the work of task forces and groups dealing with human rights, nuclear deterrence, and national security.[11] His own writings have dealt with the issues mentioned above as well as with business ethics and even aspects of bioethics.

In addition to his many writings on bioethics, Thomas A. Shannon has published in the area of social ethics, beginning with his revised doctoral dissertation, *Render unto God: A Theology of Selective Obedience.* Shannon has written on social ethics and war and peace, including two volumes with Thomas Massaro of the Weston Jesuit Theologate.[12] Massaro's revised dissertation dealt with a Catholic analysis of welfare reform.[13]

Michael J. Himes and Kenneth R. Himes's *Fullness of Faith: The Public Significance of Theology* (1993) is a work of public theology that interprets the meaning of basic Christian symbols and concepts such as creation, sin, the Trinity, grace, creation, incarnation, and the communion of saints for transforming society in a more just manner. Kenneth Himes, now of Boston College, has also written articles on many aspects of Catholic social teaching, especially on military intervention.[14] In 2005, after three years of meetings and discussions, he published the edited volume *Modern Catholic Social Teaching: Commentaries and Interpretations.* This large reference volume has extensive commentaries on the papal and conciliar documents comprising Catholic social teaching, as well as essays on the fundamentals of Catholic social teaching and its reception and future in the United

States. All the contributors take a progressive and liberal approach to Catholic social ethics.

Marvin L. Krier Mich, in *Catholic Social Teaching and Movements* (1998), takes the unique perspective of telling the story of Catholic social teaching "from above," discussing the documents of the hierarchical magisterium, but also "from below," considering the movements and activists in the United States who both express and shape the teaching. Mary Elsbernd and Reimund Bieringer's book on justice responds to seven dilemmas of justice faced by middle-class Christians today. It develops an understanding of justice that calls for involvement and active participation of all, especially the poor and marginalized in society.[15] Elsbernd has also written a significant essay showing how the social encyclicals of Pope John Paul II moved away from the methodological approach found in Pope Paul VI's *Octogesima adveniens.*[16]

Daniel Finn and Albino Barrera, two Catholic theologians with degrees in economics, have tried to develop an economic ethic and also the economic background and ramifications of Catholic social teaching. Finn has written books on economic ethics and just trading as well as articles about Catholic social teaching.[17] Lately he has focused on markets, arguing that self-interest can be a legitimate moral motive in economic matters, provided that the consequences of the action do not harm or result in an injustice to others. Four elements are involved in what he calls the "moral ecology of markets": markets limited by law, communal provision of goods and services, the morality of individuals and groups, and mediating institutions of civil society.[18]

Albino Barrera brings his knowledge of economics to the body of Catholic social teaching. For example, he adapts the Catholic insistence on universal access to material goods to the social and economic conditions of the new information age. He proposes a participatory egalitarianism in the new knowledge economy.[19] His 2005 book shows how Christians can and should work for progressive social and economic policies to bring about a just sharing of material goods.[20]

Catholic Neoconservatives

The Catholic neoconservative movement coalesced in the early 1980s and has been identified especially with Michael Novak, Richard John Neuhaus, and George Weigel. Neoconservatives believe that the current crisis in the Church is not a crisis of authority, as the liberals hold, but rather a crisis of faith.[21] The neoconservative position opposes both the liberals and the restorationists, who do not want to accept Vatican II. Neoconservatives accept Vatican II but oppose the liberal interpretation of the council that dominated the chief intellectual and organizational networks of U.S. Catholicism. Neoconservatives disagree with the public policy positions often taken by the bishops, their advisors, and liberal Catholic intellectuals. The liberals were too insouciant about the threat of communism, too unconcerned about persecution of the Church behind the Iron Curtain, too nervous about the prolife position on abortion, too statist on social welfare policy, and too vulnerable to the siren songs of *Tercer Mundismo* that swept through liberal Protestantism.

Catholic neoconservatives initiated a dialogue with conservative evangelical Protestants. They employed a theological method that challenged the dominant ways of thinking in the academy and strongly opposed the various claims—racial, class, and gender—of political correctness. Neoconservatives called for a social, cultural, and political transformation of American society with a religiously grounded public philosophy capable of informing and disciplining the moral argument that is the lifeblood of democracy.

Catholic neoconservatives believe that Catholic liberals have been too critical of U.S. foreign policy and capitalism. They disagree with the positions taken by the U.S. bishops, especially in their pastoral letters on peace and the economy, but they strongly support the teachings of John Paul II. In fact, the neoconservatives claim that John Paul II corrected the liberal excesses of progressive U.S. Church officials and intellectuals. The neoconservatives strongly support papal teaching and, generally speaking, do not allow dissent of any kind; liberals often dissent on issues of sexual morality.

Michael Novak's *The Spirit of Democratic Capitalism* (1982) sounded the clarion call for Catholic neoconservatives. Novak, from the American Enterprise Institute, sees a close connection between the political, the economic, and the cultural orders and insists that all these orders should be relatively free. The ethos of democratic capitalism includes a special evolution of pluralism, respect for contingency and unintended consequences, a sense of sin, and a new and distinctive conception of community, the individual, and the family. From a pragmatic perspective, democratic capitalism alone can create wealth and thus help to overcome poverty, while from a theological perspective it is in keeping with the basic doctrines of the Trinity, the incarnation, competition, original sin, the separation of the realms, and charity. It is an empirical fact that socialism failed primarily because it failed to unleash human creativity and gave too much power to the state.

In the *Spirit of Democratic Capitalism*, Novak devotes two chapters to liberation theology, concluding with the worry that this path to liberation is ill defined against state tyranny, is vulnerable to a new union of church and state coming from the left, and is likely to lead to economic decadence.[22] In subsequent years Novak has continued his dialogue with liberation theology. In this dialogue and in

257

his other writings he has claimed to be following in the footsteps of Isaac Hecker, the founder of the Paulist Fathers, and John Courtney Murray, who proposed a theology based on the *novus ordo seclorum* found in the United States. Capitalism emphasizes economic activism, commerce, invention, discovery, entrepreneurship, enterprise, investment, and creation of wealth. Capitalism in the United States is not perfect, but democratic capitalism is the best economic system both in terms of its foundation in Christian theology and in its practical effect of creating wealth and overcoming poverty. Novak agrees with liberationists on the option for the poor, but he argues that liberation theology does not truly liberate, while democratic capitalism is the system most compatible with democracy and most likely to help the poor.[23]

Novak is a prolific author who has written on many subjects, but between 1978 and 1999 he wrote eight books on Catholic social thought, all of them in homage to Pope John Paul II.[24] Novak and other neoconservatives were most laudatory about John Paul II's encyclical *Centesimus annus*. John Paul II accepts and confirms the U.S. vision of a free economy within a moral culture energized by a democratic polity. Thus John Paul II has brought economic liberty and democracy into Catholic social teaching, just as Vatican II brought in religious liberty.[25] Todd David Whitmore of Notre Dame has claimed that Novak actually disagrees with John Paul II in the areas of economic rights, the gap between the rich and the poor, restrictions on the accumulation of private property, and regarding capitalism as the only acceptable economic system.[26]

In 1987 George Weigel published *Tranquillitas Ordinis: The Present Failure and Future Promise of American Catholic Thought on War and Peace*. The phrase "tranquility of order," which Weigel understands as the order created by a just political community and as mediated through law, comes from St. Augustine. The tranquility of order and peace is brought about by the instruments of politics, including, if necessary, the use of armed force. But Weigel claims that the Catholic heritage, starting with Augustine, developed by Aquinas, and expressed in this country by John Courtney Murray, has been abandoned in light of many factors, especially the controversies over the Vietnam War and the interpretation given by many to Vatican II's call for "an entirely new attitude" toward peace and war.

The 1983 U.S. bishops' pastoral letter was a decisive moment in the abandonment of the heritage. The principal deficiency of the pastoral letter is to ignore the political context in which the debate about nuclear weapons and deterrence should take place. The letter is too negative on U.S. structures and policies and fails to appreciate the huge threat of totalitarianism and communism, and does not adequately emphasize the first condition of going to a just war—the need for a just cause. The pastoral letter mistakenly claims that just war theory and pacifism are interrelated approaches to the analysis of warfare, and thus wrongly maintains that there is a presumption against a resort to armed force.[27]

Progressive and liberal Catholic social ethicists pointed out the polemical nature of Weigel's book and strongly disagreed with the contention that Bryan Hehir and the U.S. bishops as a whole had abandoned the Catholic tradition.[28] Novak and Weigel claim to be the true disciples of John Courtney Murray, and they emphasize Murray's defense of the American political system, freedom, and democracy, and his opposition to communism. But Catholic progressives such as Hehir and Hollenbach see themselves as continuing to build on the legacy of Murray in light of post–Vatican II theological developments and the changing historical realities of the times. In fact, a cottage industry has developed involving studies of Murray and how to interpret him today.[29] The Catholic progressives disagree among themselves on whether Murray used only a natural law approach or also some theological concepts in addressing the general American society and what is the proper way for Catholic theological ethicists today to address the general American public.[30]

Weigel's 1989 *Catholicism and the Renewal of American Democracy* espoused many of the same neoconservative positions—a strong defense of U.S. political structures and policies, a sharp attack against Catholic liberals for denigrating the U.S. experiment and policies, a claiming of the mantle of John Courtney Murray, and the Catholic liberals' unwillingness to accept the vision and thought of Pope John Paul II. Weigel has continued to publish often in developing his Catholic neoconservative approach and has also written a very favorable biography of Pope John Paul II.[31]

Richard John Neuhaus, a Lutheran pastor and a leading opponent of the Vietnam War, became a Christian neoconservative in the 1980s. His 1984 book, *The Naked Public Square: Religion and Democracy in America,* addressed the role of religion as a support for democracy from a neoconservative perspective. He opposes the religious right, but he is even more opposed to the secularizing tendencies in the United States and the inability of liberal Protestant churches to do anything about it. The public square is "naked" because Americans have removed religious values from debates about public policy. Neuhaus wants a role for religion in addressing the values and beliefs that are the basis for the U.S. political system and its policies. He fears that the naked public square will only facilitate the growth of state totalitarianism at the expense of mediating institutions.

In 1987 Neuhaus wrote *The Catholic Moment,* which develops the thesis that the Roman Catholic Church can and should be the leading Church in the world in proclaiming the Gospel; now is the moment for the U.S. Roman Catholic Church to assume its rightful role in the culture-forming task of constructing a religiously informed philosophy for the U.S. experiment in ordered liberty. In this book Neuhaus aligns himself with Catholic neoconservatives and develops similar positions—high praise for John Paul II and Cardinal Ratzinger, criticism of the approaches often taken by the U.S. bishops and especially by the liberal elite Catholic intellectuals, sharp opposition to liberation theology, insistence on the need for mediating institutions in society, and a great fear of the state becoming too powerful. But he retains his Lutheran understanding of seeing the relationship between Christ (or grace) and culture in terms of paradox, whereas most Catholic theologians after Vatican II, including the neoconservatives, adopt either explicitly or implicitly an understanding of Christ, or grace, as the transformer of culture.

In 1990 Neuhaus became a Roman Catholic and joined Novak and Weigel in forming a triumvirate. He also started publishing *First Things*, a very significant journal addressing religion and public life from the neoconservative perspective. This journal has a wider audience than the journal started by Michael Novak in 1982, *Catholicism in Crisis*, which in 1986 changed its name simply to *Crisis*.

The progressive or liberal approach and the neoconservative approach, despite their differences, share a basic outlook in many ways. They both claim to accept Catholic social teaching, call for a religious voice in U.S. public life, and believe in a public Church that tries to influence the existing political and social order. As mentioned, the eschatology or the Church and culture relationship of both approaches is often that of Christ transforming culture. Culture is seen in light of the goodness of creation and incarnation, and redemption by Christ, but also as affected by sin and always falling short of the fullness of the reign of God.

Radical or Countercultural Approach

The radical approach logically employs a Christ-against-culture model that sees the Church primarily as countercultural. The world and its institutions tend to be identified much more with sin than in the other two approaches. There is some debate over whether this general approach should be called sectarian, but as authors of an anthology on radical Catholicism note, the Church is definitely called to be an alternative community in the midst of culture and powers that operate on assumptions and procedures not grounded in the ethics of the Gospel. The Church is called to be countercultural.[32]

The post–Vatican II Catholic radicals in many ways continue the radicalism of the Catholic Worker and the approach enunciated by the early Paul Hanly Furfey, as mentioned in chapter 3. The work of Michael J. Baxter of Notre Dame has already been mentioned in chapter 5. Baxter develops his radical Catholic social ethics on the basis of the radical ethical teaching of Jesus, the experience of the Catholic

Worker movement, and the theology of Stanley Hauerwas. The public Church approach of both liberals and neoconservatives is an ideology that ultimately dilutes the Christian message. Communities should be resisting societies and not spend most of their time propping up the existing political and economic structures.[33]

Michael Budde, a political scientist, and Robert Brimlow, a philosopher, are both Catholic, but at times they write from a broader Christian perspective. They call for a countercultural Church, based on the radical ethic of the Sermon on the Mount, that will not be a chaplain to nations and corporations. The chapter "John Locke in Ecclesial Drag? The Problem with *Centesimus Annus*" criticizes John Paul II for accepting and justifying capitalism, thus making the Gospel subject to the dominant powers and structures.[34] Academic defenders of the radical approach are comparatively few, but adherents of the more radical Catholic Worker type of Catholicism continue to be a significant presence in the life of the Catholic Church.

Other Approaches

David Schindler, in opposition to liberation theology as well as to the political liberalism of both the progressive and neoconservative U.S. approaches, developed a theological approach based on the *communio* ecclesiology of Hans Urs von Balthasar. Theologians must embrace the world without becoming identified with it and must die to the world without separating themselves from the world. The political liberalism advocated by Murray and the neoconservatives is basically a dualistic approach based on the distinction between nature and grace that prevents the Church from really transforming the natural order. All that exists, including the natural, is a gift from God and must be ordered by grace to the service of God and others. Schindler stays on the level of theory and does not get into practical aspects of political and economic ethics.[35]

Catholic feminist scholars have also published in the area of social ethics. Christine Gudorf's doctoral dissertation analyzed Catholic social teaching from a liberationist perspective.[36] In addition to the previously mentioned book on victimization, she has also written on population and environmental ethics.[37] As noted earlier, Lisa Sowle Cahill has written a monograph on peace and war and has continued to write on just peacemaking and on global ethics.[38] Christine Firer Hinze, now at Fordham University, published her revised doctoral dissertation on power and has written on Catholic social ethics from a feminist perspective.[39]

Mary E. Hobgood, of the College of Holy Cross, has written two monographs that propose a radical feminist liberationist approach to economic ethics. Her 1991 book analyzes and criticizes papal and hierarchical economic teachings. She maintains that three different and even conflicting approaches are used as these documents analyze the problems in the economic sector: the organic, the orthodox, and the radical. However, the papal teaching proposes solutions to the problem only on the basis of the first two approaches and not on the basis of the radical model, which would call for a moving away from the traditional Catholic support of private property. For a variety of institutional reasons, the hierarchical documents fear to carry out all the logical consequences of their own more radical analysis. Hobgood's 2000 monograph, *Dismantling Privilege*, does not deal much with the Catholic tradition. A just society in the United States requires that we recognize and do away with the unearned privileges of race, class, and gender that are so prevalent in the U.S. structures and institutions and to reconstruct these structures and institutions on the basis of the politics of solidarity.[40]

THE ISSUES

This section considers some of the more significant issues in social ethics: peace and war, capitalism, racism, law and morality, ecology, and globalization.

Peace and War

Catholic moral theologians in the post–Vatican II period spent more time addressing the issues of peace, war, and deterrence than any other topic. A number of factors explain this emphasis. The Pastoral Constitution on the Church in the Modern World addressed the issue in some depth and pointed out the horrors of war, especially modern weapons of destruction. While calling for an evaluation of war with an entirely new attitude and the recognition of pacifism and conscientious objection as legitimate options for individuals, the document basically follows the just war theory, with heavy emphasis on the *ius in bello* criterion of condemning any act of indiscriminate killing—countercity warfare. Events in the world, especially the Vietnam War and the strong reaction to it in the United States among some Catholics, brought this issue to the fore. In addition, the cold war raised very important issues especially with regard to deterrence strategy, and this debate gradually moved out of the narrow corridors of policymakers to a broader public forum. In 1983 the pastoral letter of the U.S. bishops, *The Challenge of Peace*, brought this issue to the attention of the Church and a broader secular society in a very open way through a public drafting process that involved discussions and debate.[41]

The radical position in this area has taken the form of pacifism and has been identified not so much with moral theologians as with activists and movements that have often been called the "Catholic peace movement" or the "Catholic left."[42] This movement definitely finds some continuity with the Catholic Worker movement and received its greatest publicity in the civil disobedience of the Berrigan brothers in trying to stop the Vietnam War. Even at the Vatican Council, three people associated with the group called Pax, Eileen Egan of the Catholic Worker movement, James W. Douglass, and Gordon Zahn, lobbied the bishops at Vatican II to accept the pacifist position.[43] Since then the Catholic peace movement has grown considerably at the grassroots level. *The Challenge of Peace* recognized that there exist in the Church two traditions—just war and pacifism—as individual choices but not as something required of individuals or states.

Five significant persons articulated the pacifist position at this time—Thomas Merton, Gordon Zahn, James W. Douglass, and Daniel and Philip Berrigan. They based their pacifism on the Gospels and the teachings of Jesus. Thomas Merton, the Trappist monk, recognized that a just war was theoretically possible but argued that the Christian is called to be a peacemaker. On a pragmatic level, the danger of war escalating to dangerous proportions makes it imperative to find solutions other than war.[44] Gordon Zahn was a conscientious objector during World War II and then studied sociology under Paul Hanly Furfey at Catholic University. Zahn insisted that the early Church was pacifist and that pacifism should be the position of the Church today. He also vigorously maintained that just war theory is no longer operable in the context of modern war.[45] James W. Douglass based his pacifism theologically on an eschatological understanding that we are living in the end times and on a Christology of the nonviolent Cross. From an ethical perspective, we need a radical transformation to make peace and justice real in our world.[46] Daniel Berrigan, a Jesuit priest and poet, used the strategy of civil disobedience to eliminate weapons of war. Influenced by both Thomas Merton and the Catholic Worker movement, Berrigan's pacifism is based on scripture and the liturgy.[47]

Among these figures there were some disagreements based ultimately on two different types of pacifism. Gordon Zahn, with strong ties to the Catholic Worker movement, and Paul Hanly Furfey defended Christian witness pacifism—we are called to bear witness to the pacifist Jesus no matter what happens and even if we are not successful in the short run. The Berrigans, in their acts of civil disobedience, used pacifism as an effective way of trying to bring about social change. Zahn expressed some disagreements about certain tactics used by the Berrigans but insisted that his differences with them were much fewer than his differences with those who accepted the possibility of just war.[48]

Lisa Sowle Cahill's 1994 *Love Your Enemies: Discipleship, Pacifism, and Just War Theories* looked at pacifism and just war in light of the discipleship of Jesus, with emphasis on the Sermon on the Mount and Jesus' command to love one's enemies. In keeping with the method used in her other books, she treats the matter historically—from the early Church, Augustine, Aquinas, Luther, Calvin, and down to and through the twentieth century. Her book is more analytical than normative and remains very much on the level of academic theory, but she definitely accepts the pacifist approach.

Just War Theory and Differences between Liberals and Neoconservatives

The majority of Catholic moral theologians work from a just war theory. One must emphasize that this theory tries to limit as much as possible the going to war and also to limit the way in which any war is waged. The call to peace and nonviolence is a Gospel imperative and a moral challenge, especially in our global society. There is general agreement that the following conditions must be met to justify going to war (*ius ad bellum*): just cause, last resort, declaration by competent authority, probability of success, and proportionality. The two conditions for waging war (*ius in bello*) are the principle of proportionality and the principle of discrimination that forbids direct killing of noncombatants. An eschatology that recognizes that we live in an imperfect and even sinful world and that the fullness of the reign of God will never be realized here serves as the theological basis justifying the possibility and the need for violence and war. In this imperfect world the use of force to defend and protect the innocent might be necessary. The differences between the more liberal Catholic approaches and the neoconservative and other conservative approaches arise in understandings of the finer points of the just war theory and in how it should be applied.

The discussion in the 1970s and 1980s centered on the cold war, nuclear weapons, and especially nuclear deterrence. Here the U.S. bishops' pastoral letter *The Challenge of Peace* made significant contributions and set the parameters for the discussion by Catholic moral theologians and even for many non-Catholics. With regard to just war theory, the pastoral letter recognized that pacifism is a legitimate tradition and position for individuals today. Furthermore, pacifism and just war theory share some common ground. The letter understood just war theory to involve a presumption against the use of force that can, however, be overcome in accord with just war principles. But such a presumption against the use of force made any resort to force more restrictive. As Bryan Hehir reported, most of the progressive and liberal Catholic moral theologians accepted such an understanding.[49]

Both Michael Novak and George Weigel have strongly disagreed with the presumption against using force. They advocate a return to the Augustinian tradition that the just war theory does not begin with the presumption against force but with a presumption of the obligation of public authority to justice and charity in light of our sinful world, in which injustice and violence against the innocent will always be present.[50]

The pastoral letter takes three positions on the use of nuclear weapons: no use of nuclear weapons against civilian population targets; no first use of nuclear weapons; and, while highly skeptical of the possibility of limiting any nuclear war, the bishops do not absolutely reject the use of retaliatory counterforce nuclear weapons as distinguished from counterpopulation or countercity weapons. The letter gives a strictly conditional moral acceptance to a limited counterforce nuclear deterrent that can never be the basis for a true peace. The bishops' theory of deterrence depends upon their theory of the use of nuclear weapons because they hold the position that one cannot threaten to do what it is morally wrong to do. If they were to condemn all use, they logically would have to call for unilateral nuclear disarmament. In the course of writing the pastoral letter, the bishops obviously never wanted to require unilateral nuclear disarmament. Mutual nuclear disarmament is one of the principles that must guide the approach to deterrence. More specifically, the bishops accept a limited counterforce deterrent that is not destabilizing, does not possess hard-target kill capability, and is limited to preventing nuclear war and not to fighting a limited nuclear war. Sufficiency to deter a nuclear war, and not superiority in the arms race, is another limiting criterion of moral deterrence.

The progressive wing of Catholic moral theology was in general agreement with the positions of the bishops but with some differences in theory and application.[51] The pacifists obviously did not think that the pastoral letter went far enough. The strongest opposition came from the Catholic neoconservative camp. In reaction to the first draft of the pastoral letter, Michael Novak wrote his own version of what a pastoral letter on this issue should be, and a number of other Catholic conservatives signed the document. The bishops' draft, according to Novak, was too idealistic and did not recognize the realities of the current world, especially the communist threat, with the corresponding need at times to use and to threaten to use nuclear weapons.[52] We should remember that George Weigel, in *Tranquillitas Ordinis,* made a similar criticism of the pastoral letter.[53]

The 1990s and the present century have seen the issue of military intervention in other countries come to the fore. Intervention can be proposed for a number of reasons: for humanitarian reasons, to defend against state-sponsored terrorism, and to stop the proliferation of weapons of mass destruction. Humanitarian intervention is easy to justify in light of just war criteria. Many point out, for example, our failure to intervene in Rwanda. Bryan Hehir holds that there is a "marginal possibility" for military intervention where there is very clear evidence of the existence of weapons of mass destruction and the intention to use them. But the danger exists that this marginal possibility will make easier the resort to war.[54] In all questions of intervention, Hehir, Kenneth Himes, and John Langan agree that the intervention should be multilateral and not taken by only one country.[55]

Kenneth Himes, with many others, distinguishes between a preemptive strike and a preventive war. As a legitimate form of self-defense, a preemptive strike is justified when the threat is clear, substantial, and imminent. But a preventive war is based on some eventual or possible outcome that a state views as undesirable. It is launched in response to a future and uncertain threat. Many opposed the second Iraq War precisely because it was a war of prevention that was not necessary.[56]

Both George Weigel and Michael Novak have strongly supported the U.S. invasion of Iraq in 2003. This war was just, they argue, because of the legitimate aim of defending the tranquility of order violated by the aggression of Saddam Hussein.[57] William Cavanaugh, from his Hauerwasian perspective, disagrees with Weigel and Novak's understanding of just war theory as a task of statecraft and also their application of it to defend the war in Iraq. Cavanaugh points out that the Novak and Weigel position is not in accord with the teaching of Pope John Paul II.[58] Michael Schuck of Loyola University in Chicago has proposed that an *ius post bellum* be added to just war theory to deal with what occurs after the war is over.[59] Kenneth Himes understands such a condition as requiring the establishment of a public order that satisfies basic human rights.[60] In my judgment, such a condition reminds us of the inherent limitation in any use of force. Force can and at times should be used to stop an injustice, but it can never bring about true justice and peace. In conclusion, one notes that both Pope John Paul II and the liberal U.S. moral theologians have significantly limited and restricted the conditions that would justify the resort to war in the post–Vatican II period.[61]

CAPITALISM

It is impossible to consider all the aspects involved in the economic order. This section concentrates on the discussion about capitalism and the U.S. economic system that took place especially in preparation for and in response to the 1986 pastoral letter of the U.S. bishops, *Economic Justice for All*, and the 1991 encyclical of John Paul II, *Centesimus annus*.

Economic Justice for All went through earlier drafts that were publicly discussed not only by Catholics and other Christians but even by secular thinkers in the United States. The bishops based their proposals on the biblical and theological themes of human beings created in the image of God, the covenant, the reign of God, discipleship, and its relationship to riches and poverty. The ethical grounding of the bishops' letter includes the dignity of the human person, human rights, love and solidarity, participation, the three forms of justice (but especially distributive justice), and an option for the poor. A just economic order requires the participation of all and guarantees economic rights to a minimally decent level of food, clothing, shelter, health care, and basic education. A creative and participatory economic system assures these rights through employment, but for those unable to work or to find work, society has an obligation to provide for basic economic needs, just as it has a duty to guarantee the fundamental freedoms in the political sphere. The bishops also find the disparity of income and wealth in the United States unacceptable. Just as the founders of the country met the challenge of their day by embracing political and civil rights, the time has come for a similar experiment in securing economic rights for all. The letter deals with the four specific areas of employment, poverty, food and agriculture, and the U.S. economy and developing nations. The final chapter calls for a new American experiment of partnership for the public good that recognizes the need for economic planning that includes a role for government together with all economic actors.[62]

Catholic commentators, including Michael Novak, recognize that the pastoral letter follows the liberal progressive Catholic approach to social ethics predominant in the United States at that time. However, Novak strongly disagrees with the pastoral letter. In fact, he was the primary author of *A Lay Letter* on the economy published even before the first draft of the U.S. bishops' letter.[63] The *Letter* recognized the need for the Catholic approach to the economy to avoid the two opposite dangers of collectivism and individualism; it insisted on the three basic Catholic principles of the dignity of the person, the social nature of the person, and the obligation to assign social decisions to the proper level of authority. *A Lay Letter* is much less critical of the U.S. economy than the bishops are, and above all does not recognize any role for economic rights. Novak strongly opposed the concept of economic rights found in the bishops' pastoral letter. In 1978 he maintained that economic rights were incomprehensible because they failed to identify who had the duty to supply the right.[64] In 1985 and 1987 he insisted that economic rights are not truly rights but goods that are indispensable to a full human life.[65] David Hollenbach challenged Novak on the issue of human rights.[66] In response Novak moved, in the words of Darrel Trimiew, from skepticism to reluctant support of economic rights.[67] In 1987 Novak concluded that operationally he comes out in the same place as Hollenbach.[68]

Novak found both good and bad news in John Paul II's *Sollicitudo rei socialis* (1987). The good news is the pope's insistence on a democratic polity, an economy that embraces private initiative, and a moral culture marked by freedom, autonomy, and self-determination. The bad news is the pope's insistence on condemning the systems of both the East and the West and even on seeing "moral equivalence" between them.[69]

But Novak was ecstatic about John Paul II's 1991 encyclical *Centesimus annus*—"a great encyclical, the greatest in a hundred years." "It is the single best statement in our lifetime by the Catholic Church . . . of the moral vision of the political economy such as that of the United States," he wrote.[70] Novak's *The Catholic Ethic and the Spirit of Capitalism* (1993) saw the pope as embracing an economic system that recognizes the fundamental and positive role of business, the market, private property, and the resulting responsibility for the means of production as well as for human activity in the economic sector. We are all capitalists now, even the pope.

Progressives such as Hollenbach, Curran, and Whitmore saw in *Centesimus annus* a more complex judgment of capitalism and also a criticism of aspects of the U.S. system.[71] Yes, John Paul II harshly criticizes the social assistance state, or the welfare state, and supports the market, profit, creativity, and initiative. But he insists that the economic sector be circumscribed within a strong juridical framework looking to the common good. The free market alone cannot fully satisfy human needs. In fact, John Paul II insists that it is unacceptable to say that the defeat of so-called real socialism leaves capitalism as the only model of economic organization.[72]

Our focus here is capitalism and the U.S. economy, especially in light of reactions to significant documents of the hierarchical magisterium, which obviously is only a part of the total picture. It is safe to say, however, that three basic positions exist in the Catholic Church in the United States. The progressive or liberal position is critical of the existing U.S. system and calls for significant changes, without, however, abandoning the present system. The radical or countercultural approach, by definition, tends to separate itself from the existing economic system. The conservative approach is more favorably disposed to and supportive of the U.S. economy. However, neoconservatives like Michael Novak are not guilty of individualism since they take seriously the common good, justice, and the option for the poor.

Racism

The record of Catholic moral theology in the United States in the post–Vatican II period on racism is abysmal. Bryan Massingale, a young African American moral theologian, pointed out in the "Notes on Moral Theology" in *Theological Studies* that in the post–Vatican II period there was no sustained attention to racial injustice. The blame here does not rest only with the authors of these "Notes," because they were reporting and analyzing what was found in the literature. The

Proceedings of the Catholic Theological Society of America in the post–Vatican II period had only one article or even seminar that focused on racism. In 1974 Joseph Nearon, the first African American member of the Catholic Theological Society of America, accused Catholic theology of being racist, but he did this not to condemn but to awaken. However, the silence in later *Proceedings* is deafening. Nearon's call was not heard.[73] Charles Curran has acknowledged that there is no concentrated discussion of racism in his many writings on social ethics.[74]

The only exception to this dismal picture is Daniel Maguire's *A New American Justice: Ending the White Male Monopolies* (1980).[75] Maguire here made the case that preferential affirmative option for blacks is primary and paradigmatic, while still recognizing that Native Americans, women, and Hispanics are also disempowered, but not in the same way as blacks.

In the area of racism the U.S. Catholic bishops were more aware of the problem than Catholic moral theologians. In 1979 the U.S. bishops issued a pastoral letter on racism—*Brothers and Sisters to Us*. The document, like most of the bishops' documents, did not go through the lengthy and public drafting process and had little or no effect on either the Church or the broader society. Groups of bishops and individual bishops have also issued letters on racism. Bryan Massingale criticizes most of these documents as seeing the problem only in personal terms and not in institutional or structural terms, as being naïve in relying on moral suasion to solve the problem, and failing to recognize the complicity of white Catholics in the ideology of white supremacy. Massingale calls for white Catholic theologians to see the issue not in terms of racism but in terms of white privilege.[76]

Some in the white Catholic theological community have been open to the call to examine white privilege. Jon Nilson's presidential address to the 2003 convention of the Catholic Theological Society of America was titled "Confessions of a White Racist Catholic Theologian." In 2004 Laurie Cassidy and Alex Mikulich formed a group at the Catholic Theological Society meeting for ongoing reflection on why dialogue on racism and white privilege is a moral imperative for white Roman Catholic theologians in the United States.[77] White Catholic theologians and the white Catholic Church in the United States must also recognize and support the growing Hispanic and Latino/a transformation of the U.S. Church.

Church, Morality, Public Policy, and Law

In light of Vatican II's call for overcoming the split between faith and daily life, the 1971 Synod of Bishops declared, "Action on behalf of justice and participation in the transformation of the world fully appear to us as a constitutive dimension of the preaching of the Gospel, or in other words, of the Church's mission for the redemption of the human race and its liberation from a very oppressive situation."[78] Since the social mission of the Church is a constitutive dimension, the Church cannot exist without it. Thus the social mission must be a part of the life of the individual Catholic Christian, the parish community, and the local, national, and universal Church. The Church works for justice and the transformation of the world at all of these levels. From an ecclesiological perspective, some problems arise when the leaders of the Church, the bishops, speak for the whole Church in proposing what should be public policy or law in a particular area.

The U.S. bishops dealt with this issue in their pastoral letters in the 1980s on peace and the economy. In the pastoral letter on peace the bishops recognized different levels of their teaching: universally binding moral principles, official Church teaching, and the application of principles to particular issues. These applications involve a prudential judgment made on the basis of specific circumstances that can be interpreted differently by people of goodwill and with the same basic faith commitment. Those who share the same basic principles and the same faith can and do disagree on complex social issues.[79] With regard to the economic pastoral, the bishops distinguished between prudential judgments and their enunciation of principles. There can be different Catholic approaches on specific policy recommendations.[80]

With this approach the bishops are avoiding two extremes. The one extreme says that the Gospels and the Church have nothing to say with regard to the specific areas of peace and the economy. The other extreme maintains that Christians and churches can know readily, quickly, and with great certitude what should be done in these complex issues. The approach of the bishops well illustrates the Catholic notion of mediation. The Gospel is mediated in and through the human. But, as the human becomes more complex and more specific, one cannot expect to find certitude and agreement even among those who profess the same faith. Such a theological approach is in agreement with the practical experience of disagreements among Catholics on many specific and complex public policy issues. The ultimate ecclesiological question involved here is the legitimate unity and diversity within the Church.

Without doubt abortion has been the most controversial public policy issue in the U.S. Catholic Church. In the 1973 *Roe v. Wade* decision the Supreme Court ruled that a woman is free to abort with no restrictions concerning the fetus until the third trimester. The U.S. bishops strongly opposed the Supreme Court decision and have been working ever since to find a way to overturn it. There can be no doubt that the U.S. bishops put more effort and money into the abortion issue than any other question of public policy.[81]

Before every presidential election, beginning in 1976, the U.S. bishops have issued a document about the election and Catholic voters. The bishops declare they do not want the formation of a Catholic voting block and do not support or oppose any individual candidate. They urge voters to elect candidates on the basis of a full range of issues and on the character of the individual politician. For example, in 1996 the document mentions twenty different issues in alphabetical order, beginning with abortion.[82] In the 1980s Cardinal Joseph Bernardin of Chicago developed his understanding of a consistent ethic of life to bring all the life issues together.[83]

In addition to the primacy of the abortion issue with the bishops as a whole, individual bishops have taken different levels of disciplinary actions against Catholic legislators who have not voted pro-life. These disciplinary actions have ranged from not allowing such Catholic politicians to speak in Catholic facilities to telling them they should not present themselves for communion.[84]

Catholic moral theologians and lawyers have taken stands on abortion laws and on the theory of the proper relationship of law and morality. Those in favor of a legal proscription of abortion, such as Germain Grisez and John Noonan, insist that the primary purpose of law is to protect the right to life of all as a part of the common good, especially those who are weak and vulnerable. No one is weaker and more vulnerable than the fetus.[85]

Others propose a different approach. In 1968 Robert F. Drinan, a Jesuit priest, then dean of the Boston College Law School and future congressman, maintained that there was no such thing as the Catholic position on the jurisprudence of abortion law. Writing before *Roe v. Wade,* he opted for the total decriminalization of abortion and the establishment of civil regulations governing it. If some abortions are made legal and others illegal, the state gives the impression of sanctioning abortion. The state should be morally neutral on the practice of abortion and not sanction some abortions.[86]

Writing after *Roe v. Wade,* Charles E. Curran pointed out two different Catholic theories of the relationship between law and morality.[87] The older approach, based on Thomas Aquinas, sees civil law in light of natural law, but there is not an exact correspondence between the two. Civil law deals only with what affects the common good. Also, since the majority of human beings are imperfect and sinful, civil law should suppress the more grievous evils from which the majority can abstain, and especially those that are harmful to others. In this context, Aquinas approves of Augustine's toleration and civic regulation of prostitution.

The newer approach accepts the role of law as found in the Declaration on Religious Freedom of Vatican II and in the writings of John Courtney Murray.

Freedom in society should be respected as far as possible and curtailed only when and insofar as necessary. Law should intervene on the basis of the criterion of public order, which is a narrower concept than common good. Public order involves an order of peace, justice, and public morality. But in a pluralistic society law also has prudential, pragmatic, and feasibility aspects. In light of this theory, one could argue in favor of a law against abortion based on the public need for justice, especially to protect the right to life of the most poor and vulnerable. But in light of the pragmatic and feasibility considerations, seen from the perspective of the first criterion of as much freedom as possible and as little restraint as necessary, one holding the hierarchical Church teaching on human life of the fetus could still argue against overturning *Roe v. Wade*, as Curran has done. Curran has pointed out that the Roman magisterium continues to use the older Thomistic approach and has not accepted the public order approach of the Declaration on Religious Freedom.[88] Mary Ann Glendon's theory wants to hold on to both a pedagogical aspect of law promoting the social good and its pragmatic and feasible aspects. On this basis she criticized American approaches to the philosophy of law for not giving enough importance to the positive pedagogical function of law.[89]

In chapter 6 I pointed out that Catholic feminists—Lisa Cahill, Margaret Farley, and Christine Gudorf, among others—have criticized the U.S. bishops for the primacy and centrality with which they have addressed the issue of abortion law. These three do not hold that a truly human person is present from conception, and this obviously affects their approach. But one could criticize the primacy given to abortion and the disciplinary actions taken against some Catholic legislators in light of the theoretical doubt in the Catholic tradition about when truly individual human life begins, and in light of the theory of law based on what is found in the Declaration on Religious Freedom, which recognizes the importance of freedom and some feasible, prudential, and pragmatic aspects of law. The hierarchical magisterium can and should use means other than law to support its prolife position. On the other hand, supporters of the action of the bishops insist on the fundamental importance of protecting innocent human life.

The hierarchical magisterium has strongly opposed the legalization of same-sex marriages. This position builds on the immorality of homosexual acts and the special good of marriage as a social institution, while accepting the human dignity of all, including gays, and opposing unjust discrimination.[90] The new natural law theorists, especially John Finnis, have written extensively on this issue and insist that granting legal status to same-sex marriages threatens the well-being, stability, and integrity of the family, which the state must strongly support and uphold.[91] Stephen J. Pope of Boston College, appealing to John Courtney Murray, is not convinced by the arguments proposed by the magisterium and also urges the hierarchical magisterium, in defending the importance of the social institution of marriage, not to question the worth and dignity of gay and lesbian people.[92] Paul Griffiths, a self-described orthodox Catholic, argues that the Catholic Church and its teaching would be better off if same-sex marriages were legalized. Griffiths argues that there is much greater opposition between the U.S. ethos and the Catholic understanding than the hierarchical magisterium recognizes.[93]

Ecology

Environmental ethics is a very significant issue in our world, but ecology has become a major concern only in the past few decades. The Catholic discussion of ecology shows the complexity of the issue and the many perspectives from which scholars can and should address it. At the same time, the ecological discussion in Roman Catholicism in the United States illustrates the porous and somewhat artificial boundaries of what constitutes the discipline of moral theology.

An anthology titled *Embracing Earth: Catholic Approaches to Ecology* (1994), edited by Albert J. La Chance and John E. Carroll, includes contributions from eighteen Catholic authors, none of them professional moral theologians. This anthology illustrates the different perspectives that one can and should bring to the consideration of ecology: spirituality, mysticism, creation theology, cosmology, scripture, sacramental theology, and feminism. This book begins with a two-page comment by Thomas Berry, written in 1982, maintaining that the future of the Catholic Church in the United States will depend on its capacity to accept responsibility for the fate of the earth. Berry, a Passionist priest and scholar of Indian religions, has written extensively on ecology for four decades from a somewhat radical perspective influenced by the thought of Teilhard de Chardin.[94] A 1987 book developed his thought in dialogue with some Catholic critics.[95]

Feminism has been an important ally to ecology. Ecofeminism sees an intimate connection between patriarchal domination of women and the domination of the earth. Rosemary Radford Ruether, the acknowledged mother of feminism in Catholic circles in the United States, has written extensively in this area. Ruether would never consider herself a moral theologian, but she has often touched on subjects dealing with the area of moral theology. She was one of the first Catholics to call for a change in the teaching on artificial contraception in the early 1960s.[96] Her voluminous writings have addressed the role of women in society and in the Church. Her contribution to sexual ethics is discussed in chapter 8. Her last work in ecofeminism, *Integrating Ecofeminism: Globalization and World Religions* (2005), stresses the connection between the oppression of women, ecological harm, and global corporate exploitation, and how the world religions can help to overcome these harms and injustices.

Elizabeth Johnson, the leading Catholic feminist theologian in the United States today, has also addressed ecology. Her 1993 Madaleva Lecture sees hierarchical dualism as the source of ecological degradation, and she develops three neglected sources of wisdom as building blocks for an alternative vision: women's wisdom, human connectedness to the earth, and the Creator Spirit.[97]

Catholic moral theologians and social ethicists arrived on the scene of ecology a little late, and often analyzed the ecological issue in light of Catholic social teaching. Charles M. Murphy's *At Home on Earth: Foundations for a Catholic Ethic of the Environment* (1989), a popular book aimed at a more general audience, calls for a sacramental consciousness that appreciates God's presence within nature and love for nature. He praises, perhaps too uncritically, the role of papal teaching in proposing a Catholic ethic of the environment.[98]

Daniel J. Cowdin has written significant articles on the environment. He has traced John Paul II's move somewhat away from an anthropocentric approach that does not give enough importance to the intrinsic value of the earth.[99] Cowdin maintains, on theological and ethical grounds, that the earth has intrinsic value apart from its relationship to human beings, but he also sees a special place for humans within creation. Cowdin criticizes the narrowness of some contemporary Catholic moral theology, with its turn to the subject, which often contrasts the human person and nonhuman nature. He calls for a turn to the objective and the natural without, however, losing the gains for the person made by the turn to the subject. Cowdin recognizes his as a middle position that also will not please radical environmentalists because it recognizes conflict among human, social, and ecological values.[100] Cowdin's article appeared in an anthology that included perspectives from scripture, systematic theology, and sacramental theology.[101]

In 1996 the United States Catholic Conference published *And God Saw That It Was Good: Catholic Theology and the Environment.* This book includes papal and hierarchical documents on the ecology from different bishops' conferences around the world as well as contributions from two Catholic moral theologians. Christine Firer Hinze agrees with Cowdin's basic perspective. Bodily and personal ecology, social and economic ecology, and cosmological ecology are interactive and mutually influencing.[102] Drew Christiansen sees Catholic social teaching as open to a planetary common good, which calls for sustainable development and thereby differs from the more radical approaches of Deep Ecology.[103] Once again, the influence of the Catholic "both-and" is apparent. Maura A. Ryan and Todd David Whitmore edited a 1997 volume about the ethics of global stewardship in general and the particular problems of population, environment, and development. It also expands the discussion to include children, national security, U.S. immigration policy, and environmental racism.[104]

Dawn M. Nothwehr, a Franciscan religious woman who taught at the Chicago Theological Union, creatively brought together articles from the Franciscan tradition dealing with theology of the environment. Nineteenth- and twentieth-century Catholic theology made the Thomistic tradition central and practically neglected all other traditions. Here, Nothwehr brings together twenty contributors representing the Franciscan tradition from the perspective of scripture, the approaches of St. Francis and St. Clare, the medieval approaches of St. Bonaventure and John Duns Scotus, and contemporary Franciscan praxis.[105]

Globalization

In the past few decades we have become conscious of the global reality of many issues, from climate to economics. The previously discussed issues of human rights and ecology have a global dimension to them. Human interdependence on a global scale reminds us, at a bare minimum, of the need to search for a global ethic to avoid the problems of injustice, terrorism, and poverty. A significant impetus calling for the world religions to come together in terms of a global ethic came from the World Parliament of Religions in 1993 and the work of the German Catholic theologian Hans Küng. Religion in the past and even today has been a source of division and even violence in our world. Küng maintains that today the religions of the world can and must agree on certain core fundamental values, and must put them into practice to bring about greater peace, justice, and unity in the world in which we live.[106]

The history of the Catholic tradition strongly suggests that it is open to the concept of a global ethic. The Catholic Church sees itself as a universal community open to all people and all cultures living in all parts of the world. The neo-scholastic understanding of natural law insists on the existence of universal and immutable principles that are true for all human beings. Catholic moral theologians who basically accept a similar understanding of natural law, or of basic goods that are common to all human beings, are most open to the possibility and need for a global ethic.

In the post–Vatican II period, liberal or progressive Catholic moral theologians have become extremely conscious of pluralism, diversity, historical consciousness, and the influence of social location on all human moral knowing. Generally speaking, however, even the progressive or liberal Catholic moral theologians today still hold to some possibility of a global ethic. William O'Neill and Jean Porter do not recognize in theory or in principle the existence of a common morality based on the truly human, but they nonetheless insist on the possibility of some practical consensus across cultural boundaries. O'Neill, for example, recognizes that human rights cannot be derived from a rational common morality, but he claims that we can still find some agreement on human rights through rhetorical persuasion by providing reasons that others in different cultures might find acceptable.[107] In a similar way, Jean Porter denies a common understanding of the truly human but argues that different cultures can overcome moral disagreements on an ad hoc and pragmatic basis. The success in coming to such agreements shows that significant communalities exist in human existence, even across cultures, making moral consensus on a practical level a real possibility.[108]

Lisa Cahill wants to go further and defend in principle some generalized knowledge about human goods and relationships based on an Aristotelian-Thomistic understanding of moral rationality, with a heavy emphasis on prudence linked to narrative or traditions and practices historically reappropriated.[109] Cahill's position of a chastened universalism seems to be in agreement with many of the other progressive Catholic moral theologians discussed here.

Most Catholic moral theologians recognize that the level of agreement is in the area of the general and not the specific. Thomas Aquinas himself acknowledged a great difference between the primary principles of natural law, which are universal and always obliging, and the secondary principles, which can admit of exceptions in particular cases.[110] The greater the specificity, the greater the complexity and the possibility of differences.

This chapter on social ethics underscores the danger of a narrow personalism that fails to give enough importance to the social, political, economic, ecological, and global aspects of human existence. Catholic moral theology in the immediate post–Vatican II and post–Humanae vitae era rightly emphasized the person. The renewal of moral theology challenged the act-centered approach of the manuals and called for the role of the person as subject and agent. The biblical influence strengthened the emphasis on the person who is called to conversion, change of heart, and love of God and neighbor. In reaction to the anthropology used in Humanae vitae, revisionist theologians made the person and the person's relationships, rather than the purpose of the faculty, the basic moral criterion.

But the person must always be seen in multiple relationships with God and with different kinds of neighbors, ranging from those to whom one is committed, to strangers and those in need, to the world in which we live, to the self. A narrow personalism fails to give enough importance to the many aspects of human existence that have been described in this chapter. The danger exists of forgetting these broader dimensions and relationships in considering issues that, on the surface, seem to be only personal. In reality, there is very little that is only personal.

Our personal actions are always embedded in a broader framework and have political, economic, and ecological aspects. The Catholic "both-and" and inclusive
approaches avoid the dangers of a narrow personalism.

This chapter also illustrates the tremendous growth in post–Vatican II moral
theology. By definition, social ethics deals with all the issues facing society. Globalization now reminds us that every issue has broad dimensions. New issues such as
ecology, the role of women, worldwide poverty, economic development, and wars
of intervention have come to the fore. In addition, the number of Catholic moral
theologians writing in areas of social ethics in the past fifty years has increased
dramatically.

NOTES

1. Curran, *Tensions in Moral Theology*, 119–37.
2. All these documents can be found in O'Brien and Shannon, *Catholic Social Thought*.
3. Himes, *Modern Catholic Social Teaching*.
4. U.S. Catholic Bishops, "Challenge of Peace," and "Economic Justice for All."
5. Hehir, "Catholic Church and Political Order."
6. Gould, "Father J. Bryan Hehir."
7. Hollenbach, *Justice, Peace, and Human Rights*.
8. Hollenbach, *Global Face of Public Faith*.
9. Hollenbach, *Common Good and Christian Ethics*.
10. Coleman, *One Hundred Years of Catholic Social Thought*.
11. E.g., Hennelly and Langan, *Human Rights in the Americas*; O'Brien and Langan, *Nuclear Dilemma and Just War Tradition*.
12. Massaro and Shannon, *American Catholic Social Teaching*; Massaro and Shannon, *Catholic Perspectives on Peace and War*.
13. Massaro, *Catholic Social Teaching and U.S. Welfare Reform*.
14. Himes, "Morality of Humanitarian Intervention," and "Intervention, Just War, and U.S. National Security."
15. Elsbernd and Bieringer, *When Love Is Not Enough*.
16. Elsbernd, "Whatever Happened to *Octogesima Adveniens*?"
17. Pemberton and Finn, *Toward a Christian Economic Ethic*; Finn, *Just Trading*.
18. Finn, "John Paul II and the Moral Ecology of Markets"; Finn, *Moral Ecology of Markets*.
19. Barrera, *Modern Catholic Social Documents*.
20. Barrera, *God and the Evil of Scarcity*.
21. The following description of Catholic neoconservatives is taken from Weigel, "Neoconservative Difference."
22. Novak, *Spirit of Democratic Capitalism*, 287–314.
23. Novak, *Liberation Theology and the Liberal Society*, and *Will It Liberate?*

24. See www.nd.edu/~cstprog/19990427.htm.

25. Novak, "Tested by Our Own Ideals."

26. Whitmore, "John Paul II, Michael Novak, and the Differences."

27. Weigel, *Tranquillitas ordinis*, 280–85. See also Weigel, "Moral Clarity in a Time of War."

28. E.g., Hollenbach, "War and Peace in American Catholic Thought."

29. For two edited books dealing with the Murray legacy from somewhat different perspectives, see Hunt and Grasso, *John Courtney Murray and the American Civil Conversation;* and Hooper and Whitmore, *John Courtney Murray and the Growth of Tradition.*

30. Whitmore, "Growing End."

31. Weigel, *Witness to Hope.*

32. Budde and Brimlow, *Church as Counterculture.*

33. For a lengthy summary of Baxter's position, see Heyer, *Prophetic and Public.* In this book Heyer tries to bring together the progressive and radical approaches.

34. Budde and Brimlow, *Christianity Incorporated,* 109–28.

35. Schindler, *Heart of the World.*

36. Gudorf, *Catholic Social Teaching on Liberation Themes.*

37. Gudorf, "Resymbolizing Life."

38. Cahill, "Just Peacemaking" and "Toward Global Ethics."

39. Hinze, *Comprehending Power in Christian Social Ethics* and "U.S. Catholic Social Thought, Gender, and Economic Livelihood."

40. Hobgood, *Catholic Social Teaching and Economic Theory* and *Dismantling Privilege.*

41. U.S. Catholic Bishops, "Challenge of Peace."

42. For the best history of the Catholic peace movement, see McNeal, *Harder than War.*

43. Ibid., 98–99.

44. Ibid., 105–30.

45. Au, *Cross, the Flag, and the Bomb,* 107–16.

46. See Curran, *American Catholic Social Ethics,* 243–82.

47. McNeal, *Harder than War,* 173–210.

48. Zahn, "The Berrigans: Radical Activism Personified."

49. Hehir, "Catholic Teaching on War and Peace."

50. Novak, "Argument That the War against Iraq Is Just"; Weigel, "Just War Case for the War."

51. Hehir, "Catholic Teaching on War and Peace." See also Hollenbach, *Nuclear Ethics,* and Langan, "Pastoral on War and Peace."

52. Novak, "Moral Clarity in the Nuclear Age" and *Moral Clarity in the Nuclear Age.*

53. Weigel, *Tranquillitas ordinis,* 257–85.

54. For a summary statement of Hehir's position drawn from a number of different sources, see Himes, "Intervention, Just War, and U.S. National Security," 149–50.

55. Ibid., and Langan, "To Intervene or Not to Intervene."

56. Himes, "Intervention, Just War, and U.S. National Security," 147–48.

57. Hehir, "Catholic Teaching on War and Peace." See also Hollenbach, *Nuclear Ethics,* and Langan, "Pastoral on War and Peace."

58. Cavanaugh, "At Odds with the Pope."

59. Schuck, "When the Shooting Stops."

60. Himes, "Intervention, Just War, and U.S. National Security," 154–56.

61. Curran, *Moral Theology of Pope John Paul II*, 234–38.

62. U.S. Catholic Bishops, "Economic Justice for All," 492–571.

63. Lay Commission on Catholic Social Teaching, *Toward the Future*; Novak, *Freedom with Justice*.

64. Novak, "Human Rights and Whited Sepulchres."

65. Novak, "Economic Rights," 13, and "Rights and Wrongs of 'Economic Rights.'"

66. Hollenbach, "Growing End of an Argument."

67. Trimiew, "Economic Rights Debate," 90–95.

68. Novak, "Rights and Wrongs of 'Economic Rights,'" 49.

69. Novak, "Development of Nations."

70. Novak, "Pope, Liberty, Capitalism."

71. Hollenbach, "Christian Social Ethics after the Cold War"; Curran, *Catholic Social Teaching 1891–Present*, 206–9; Whitmore, "John Paul II, Michael Novak, and the Differences."

72. John Paul II, *Centesimus annus*, 461–72nn30–43.

73. Massingale, "African-American Experience," 81–86.

74. Curran, "White Privilege."

75. Reissued as Maguire, *Case for Affirmative Action*.

76. Massingale, "James Cone and Recent Catholic Episcopal Teaching on Racism."

77. Cassidy, "White Privilege and Racism." See also Cassidy and Mikulich, *Interrupting White Privilege*.

78. Synod of Bishops, *Justitia in mundo*, 289.

79. U.S. Catholic Bishops, "Challenge of Peace," 494–95nn9–14.

80. U.S. Catholic Bishops, "Economic Justice for All," 576n20.

81. Byrnes and Segers, *Catholic Church and the Politics of Abortion*.

82. Administrative Board of U.S. Catholic Conference, *Political Responsibility*. For the most recent document, see U.S. Catholic Bishops, "Faithful Citizenship."

83. Bernardin, *Consistent Ethic of Life*.

84. For a defense of this position, see Donoghue, "Manifest Lack of Proper Disposition for Communion." For an opposite approach, see D'Antonio, "Church Pays Cost of Abortion Absolutism," 7.

85. Grisez, *Abortion*, 347–466; Noonan, *Private Choice*.

86. Drinan, "Morality of Abortion Laws," and "Jurisprudential Options on Abortion."

87. Curran, *Ongoing Revision in Moral Theology*, 107–43.

88. Curran, *Moral Theology of Pope John Paul II*, 230–34.

89. Glendon, *Abortion and Divorce in Western Law*.

90. Congregation for the Doctrine of the Faith, "Considerations Regarding Proposals," and "Observations Regarding Legislative Proposals."

91. Finnis, "Law, Morality, and 'Sexual Orientation.'"

92. Pope, "Magisterium's Argument against 'Same-Sex Marriage.'"

93. Griffiths, "Legalized Same-Sex Marriage."

94. Berry, *Teilhard in the Ecological Age*.

95. Lonergan and Richards, *Thomas Berry and the New Cosmology*.

96. Ruether, "Birth Control and the Ideals of Marital Sexuality."

97. Johnson, *Women, Earth, and Creator Spirit*.

98. For a good overview, see Hart, *What Are They Saying*.

99. Cowdin, "John Paul II and Environmental Concerns."

100. Cowdin, "Toward an Environmental Ethics."

101. Irwin and Pellegrino, *Preserving the Creation*.

102. Hinze, "Catholic Social Teaching and Theological Ethics."

103. Christiansen, "Ecology and the Common Good."

104. Ryan and Whitmore, *Challenge of Global Stewardship*.

105. Nothwehr, *Franciscan Theology of the Environment*.

106. Küng and Kuschel, *Global Ethic*; Küng, *Global Responsibility*. For my reaction to the declaration, see Curran, "Global Ethic."

107. O'Neill, "Babel's Children," 164.

108. Porter, "Search for a Global Ethic."

109. Cahill, "Toward Global Ethics," 331–44.

110. Aquinas, *Summa theologiae*, Ia IIae, q. 94, a. 4.

CONCLUSIONS: LOOKING BACKWARD AND FORWARD

Francis Kenrick, Aloysius Sabetti, and other U.S. Catholic moral theologians in the late nineteenth century could never have anticipated the future developments of moral theology. Likewise, twentieth-century moral theologians writing before Vatican II could never have predicted the course that moral theology would take in the later twentieth and early twenty-first centuries.

What explains the dramatic changes that have occurred? Earlier chapters have pointed out the three publics as the most significant factors affecting the development of moral theology: the Church, the academy, and society at large.

Developments in the Church have had the greatest effect on the discipline of moral theology. The manuals of moral theology in place before Vatican II had the primary purpose of training future confessors for their role, especially as judges in the sacrament of penance, which was then popularly called "confession." The faithful had to confess their sins according to number and species. Moral theology courses in the seminary trained future priests to know the sinfulness and the degree of sinfulness of particular actions.

Many pastoral and moral theologians have called for a change in the celebration of penance so that it does not necessarily call for the confession of sins according to number and species. A greater appreciation of the person, and the recognition of both sin and conversion in relational terms, means that one can never judge the state of the person merely on the basis of knowing the objective good or evil of the actions of that person. Above all, the sacrament of penance should celebrate the joyful forgiveness of God's mercy through the community of the Church and the penitent's recognition of the need for continual conversion to grow in the fundamental relationships with God, neighbor, world, and self. Unfortunately, the hierarchical magisterium has adamantly refused to make any significant changes in the format of the sacrament of penance. In reality, the Catholic faithful, by their actions and practice, have shown that confession as it exists today no longer plays a very significant a role in their lives. Thus the primary reason for the focus of the manuals of moral theology has lost much of its importance.

No theologian in the early twentieth century could have foreseen the work of Vatican II. This council changed moral theology in three important ways: through the basic purpose and scope of the discipline, its method, and its ecumenical dimension. Vatican II recognized the universal call of all Christians to holiness and thus saw moral theology as considering the whole of the Christian life. The focus could no longer be on the minimal aspects of what acts are sinful and the degree of sinfulness. The manuals, with their narrow focus, had neglected the role of the person, the fundamental change of heart of the person, and the virtues that modify the Christian as subject and agent.

Second, Vatican II called for a change in the methodology of moral theology. The council insisted that moral theology give more importance to the role of faith and grace in the moral life and the scriptural and theological bases for understanding Christian morality. The narrow concerns of the manuals had put all the emphasis on determining the morality of particular acts in light of natural law theory and the teachings of the hierarchical magisterium. Moral theology after Vatican II gave much greater emphasis to the theological dimensions of the discipline while still recognizing an important role for human reason and experience.

Finally, Vatican II called for an ecumenical dialogue with all other Christians and also for interfaith dialogue. The ecumenical dialogue has had an enormous impact on Catholic moral theology. Francis Kenrick, the author of the first textbook in moral theology in the United States, engaged in ecumenical dialogue, especially with Episcopalians, to show the broader areas of agreement between Catholics and others. But his successors seldom followed his example. Catholic theology in general and moral theology in particular, especially after the condemnations of Americanism and modernism in the early twentieth century, existed in their own Catholic ghetto. By definition, Catholic moral theology today is ecumenical. No one can study moral theology without its ecumenical dimension. In fact, the ecumenical aspect blurs the boundaries and parameters of Catholic moral theology. Catholic moral theologians today address not only a Catholic audience but often a broader, ecumenical audience.

Humanae vitae (1968) raised the issue of the role of authoritative hierarchical teaching in moral matters and the possibility of dissent from the noninfallible hierarchical magisterium. Previously it was generally accepted that authoritative papal teaching was the ultimate answer settling all disputed issues. The changed understanding of ecclesiology at Vatican II, together with the debates about moral theology in general and artificial contraception in particular, made some Catholic theologians more aware of the possibility and legitimacy of dissent from some noninfallible teachings. The discussion about dissent has spread to other issues besides contraception and has become a central issue in both moral theology and the life of the Catholic Church.

The second influence in the development of moral theology is the academy. The shift in the primary home of moral theology from the seminary to the college and university accentuated the academic nature of moral theology and contributed to the growing scholarly depth of the discipline after Vatican II. The proliferation of Ph.D.-granting programs in the United States greatly enhanced the research component of the discipline. Those teaching in such institutions were expected to contribute to the development of knowledge in this area. The Ph.D. students learned the importance of research and writing through their doctoral dissertation. These newly minted Ph.D.s then began teaching in Catholic colleges, where publishing and research formed part of their academic work. As a result, publications in moral theology have increased to the extent that more monographs are published in one year than were published in the early decades of the twentieth century. As a result of this academic depth, no one can any longer claim to be an expert in all aspects of moral theology. Moral theologians must specialize in one particular area within the general category of moral theology.

As a result of this shift, the number of moral theologians has multiplied. The United States, with its more than 220 Catholic colleges, has more moral theologians than any other country and even more than any other continent in the world. Not only has the number of moral theologians increased but also their diversity. In the pre–Vatican II period, moral theologians, for all practical purposes, were celibate male priests. Today moral theologians more closely resemble the faithful in the community of the baptized—women and men; married and single; lay, clerical, and religious.

The college and university home of moral theology calls for academic freedom in research and publishing. Academic freedom, together with the related issue of dissent from noninfallible Church teaching, has become a much-disputed issue in the life of the Church and the Catholic academy. Before the 1960s no one associated academic freedom with the work of professors of moral theology. But today in the United States, most Catholic moral theologians defend the need for academic freedom in developing their discipline in the academy.

Dialogue within the academy has brought moral theology into contact with the principal thought currents of the contemporary scholarly world. The shift from classicism to historical consciousness in post–Vatican II moral theology owes much to this broader academic dialogue. Postmodernism has raised many questions for moral theology. Feminist theories have also played a significant part in new approaches to moral theology.

The third, or public, factor influencing moral theology is the broader human society itself. The growth of bioethics, for example, owes much to the scientific and technological breakthroughs that have occurred in contemporary times. As shown in the chapter on social ethics, the growing global dimension of all social issues as well as many new issues continues to arise in our fast-changing world.

Dialogue with the broader society also brings moral theology into contact with newer and different theoretical understandings and approaches.

These three publics, or factors, influencing moral theology explain why no one could have predicted how moral theology has developed in the United States since its beginnings in the latter part of the nineteenth century. Looking backward also helps us to look forward. As a result of all that we have learned from the past developments in moral theology and the factors influencing these changes, predicting how moral theology will develop in the future is impossible for anyone. One can only surmise that there will be as many changes in the next hundred years as there have been in the past hundred years, and probably more. The discontinuities that have surfaced in the past will arise again in the future.

But there will also be significant continuities, which exist primarily in the areas of method and general concepts. The fundamental bases and approaches of Catholic moral theology are not going to change. Chapter 6 discussed three approaches of Catholic method that Vatican II affirmed in continuity with the broader Catholic theological tradition: mediation, catholicity, with its "both-and" approach, and Catholic theology as part of a living tradition.

Mediation recognizes the divine as coming to us in and through the human. The incarnation well illustrates mediation. God comes to us in and through the human nature of Jesus. The Catholic understanding of Church and sacraments shows mediation at work. In moral theology, mediation recognizes the basic goodness of the human, despite human sinfulness, and the important role for human sources of moral wisdom and knowledge. Moral theology's emphasis on natural law well exemplifies the effects of mediation in moral theology. Yes, Catholic theologians will continue to discuss the meaning of human reason and human nature, but Catholic moral theology in the future will also continue to recognize the importance of the human and human reason.

The Catholic Church and tradition are catholic—inclusive and striving to embrace all. Thus the characteristic approach of Catholic moral theology is "both-and" rather than "either-or." The Catholic Church is not a sect that withdraws from the world; rather, it lives in the world and tries to transform it. Catholic moral theology in the future will continue to insist on "both-and" approaches— scripture and tradition, grace and nature, faith and reason, Jesus and the Church.

Mediation and catholicity help to explain why the Catholic tradition is a living tradition. Yes, the Church must always be faithful to the word and work of Jesus, but one must understand, appropriate, and live out the word and work of Jesus in light of the changing circumstances of time and place. Through the gift of the life-giving Spirit and with broad and inclusive dialogue with all possible sources of knowledge, the Church strives to understand what humans and human communities are called to be and to do in our world.

The fundamental bases of Catholic moral theology will remain in substantial continuity with the tradition. Take, for example, anthropology. Moral theology will continue to defend the equal dignity of all human beings. Too often our contemporary society attributes dignity to people on the basis of what they do, make, or accomplish. But the Catholic theological position bases human dignity on the fact that we all were created in the image and likeness of God and called to share in God's friendship. The equal dignity of all, regardless of gender, race, ethnicity, health, or economic status, serves as the basis for protecting and promoting the sanctity of all human beings. The history described in these pages shows the fundamental nature of this anthropology.

In addition to insistence on the equal dignity of all human beings, the Catholic approach to anthropology will accentuate the social nature of human beings. We are not isolated individuals but are called by God to live in relationships with others and to form communities, beginning with the family and extending to the neighborhood and ultimately to political and civil society on the local, state, and federal levels. The Catholic tradition recognizes the need for worldwide cooperation in striving to achieve the common good of all. At times, different terms have been used to express this reality. Thomas Aquinas spoke of the human person as being social and political by nature. Pope John Paul II introduced the virtue of solidarity. In light of this social and communitarian emphasis, the Catholic tradition has now and will in the future oppose individualistic approaches that fail to see the human being called to live with all others and to work for the common good of society.

Because of the discontinuities coming from changed understandings in the Church, the academy, and the broader society, predicting how Catholic moral theology will develop in specific ways in the future is impossible. But the discipline in the future, as in the past, will continue to employ the methods and fundamental bases that make the Catholic theological tradition a living tradition.

BIBLIOGRAPHY

Abbott, Walter J., "Constitution on the Sacred Liturgy." In *Documents of Vatican II*, ed. Walter J. Abbott, 136–78. New York: Guild, 1966.

———. "Decree on Ecumenism." In *Documents of Vatican II*, ed. Walter J. Abbott, 341–66. New York: Guild, 1966.

———. "Decree on Priestly Formation." In *Documents of Vatican II*, ed. Walter J. Abbott, 437–57. New York: Guild, 1966.

———. *Documents of Vatican II*. New York: Guild, 1966.

———. "Dogmatic Constitution on the Church." In *Documents of Vatican II*, ed. Walter J. Abbott, 14–96. New York: Guild, 1966.

———. "Pastoral Constitution on the Church in the Modern World." In *Documents of Vatican II*, ed. Walter J. Abbott, 199–308. New York: Guild, 1966.

Administrative Board of the U.S. Catholic Conference. *Political Responsibility*. Washington, DC: U.S. Catholic Conference, 1996.

Allsopp, Michael E., and John J. O'Keefe. *Vertiatis splendor: American Responses*. Kansas City, MO: Sheed & Ward, 1995.

Andolsen, Barbara Hilkert. "*Agape* in Feminist Ethics." *Journal of Religious Ethics* 9 (1981): 69–83.

———. *Daughters of Jefferson, Daughters of Bootblacks: Racism in American Feminism*. Macon, GA: Mercer University Press, 1986.

———. "Elements of a Feminist Approach to Bioethics." In *Feminist Ethics and the Catholic Moral Tradition*, ed. Charles E. Curran, Margaret A. Farley, and Richard A. McCormick, 350–63. New York: Paulist Press, 1996.

———. *Good Work at the Video Display Terminal: A Feminist Ethical Analysis of Changes in Clerical Work*. Knoxville: University of Tennessee Press, 1989.

———. *The New Job Contract: Economic Justice in an Age of Insecurity*. Cleveland: Pilgrim, 1998.

Andolsen, Barbara Hilkert, Christine E. Gudorf, and Mary E. Pellauer, eds. *Women's Consciousness, Women's Conscience: A Reader in Feminist Ethics*. Minneapolis: Winston, 1985.

Angelini, Guiseppe, and Ambrogio Valsecchi. *Disegno storico della teologia morale*. Bologna: Dehoniane, 1972.

Antoninus, Saint. *Summa theologica, pars tertia*. Verona: Typographia Seminarii, 1740.

Appleby, Scott. *Church and Age Unite: The Modernist Impulse in American Catholicism*. Notre Dame: University of Notre Dame Press, 1992.

Aquinas, Thomas. *Summa theologiae*. 4 vols. Rome: Marietti, 1952.

Aquino, Maria Pilar. *Our Cry for Life: Feminist Theology from Latin America*. Maryknoll, NY: Orbis Books, 1993.

Aquino, Maria Pilar, Daisy L. Machado, and Jeanette Rodriguez, eds. *A Reader in Latina Feminist Theology: Religion and Justice*. Austin: University of Texas Press, 2002.

Ashley, Benedict M. *Living the Truth in Love: A Biblical Introduction to Moral Theology.* New York: Alba House, 1996.

Ashley, Benedict M., Jean K. DeBlois, and Kevin D. O'Rourke. *Health Care Ethics: A Catholic Theological Analysis.* 5th ed. Washington, DC: Georgetown University Press, 2006.

Ashley, Benedict M., and Kevin D. O'Rourke. *Ethics of Health Care: An Introductory Textbook.* 3d ed. Washington, DC: Georgetown University Press, 2002.

———. *Health Care Ethics: A Theological Analysis.* St. Louis, MO: Catholic Health Association, 1978.

———. *Health Care Ethics: A Theological Analysis.* 4th ed. Washington, DC: Georgetown University Press, 1997.

Au, William A. *The Cross, the Flag, and the Bomb: American Catholics Debate War and Peace, 1960–83.* Westport, CT: Greenwood, 1985.

Aubert, Roger, et al. *The Church in the Age of Liberalism: History of the Church.* Vol. 8. New York: Crossroad, 1981.

Barrera, Albino. *God and the Evil of Scarcity.* Notre Dame: University of Notre Dame Press, 2005.

———. *Modern Catholic Social Documents and the Political Economy.* Washington, DC: Georgetown University Press, 2001.

Bassett, William W., ed. *The Bond of Marriage.* Notre Dame: University of Notre Dame Press, 1968.

Baxter, Michael J. "The Non-Catholic Character of the 'Public Church.'" *Modern Theology* 11 (1995): 243–58.

———. "The Sign of Peace: The Mission of the Church to the Nations." *Proceedings of the Catholic Theological Society of America* 59 (2004): 19–41.

Beckley, Harlan. *Passion for Justice: Retrieving the Legacies of Walter Rauschenbusch, John A. Ryan, and Reinhold Niebuhr.* Louisville, KY: Westminster/John Knox, 1992.

———. "Theology and Prudence in John Ryan's Economic Ethics." In *Religion and Public Life: The Legacy of Monsignor John A. Ryan,* ed. Robert G. Kennedy et al., 35–60. Lanham, MD: University Press of America, 2001.

Bernardin, Joseph Cardinal. *Consistent Ethic of Life.* Edited by Thomas G. Fuechtmann. Kansas City, MO: Sheed & Ward, 1988.

Berry, Thomas Mary. *Teilhard in the Ecological Age.* Chambersburg, PA: Anima, 1982.

Bihlmeyer, Karl, and Hermann Tüchle. *Church History.* Vol. 1, *Christian Antiquity.* Westminster, MD: Newman, 1958.

Billy, Dennis J., and James F. Keating. *Conscience and Prayer: The Spirit of Catholic Moral Theology.* Collegeville, MN: Liturgical Press, 2001.

"Bishops Revise Healthcare Directives." *National Catholic Reporter,* June 1, 2001, 11.

Boere, John C. "A Survey of the Content and Organization of the Curriculum of the Theological Departments of Major Seminaries in the United States of America." Master's thesis, Catholic University of America, 1963.

Boswell, John. *Christianity, Social Tolerance, and Homosexuality: Gay People in Western Europe from the Beginning of the Christian Era to the Fourteenth Century.* Chicago: University of Chicago Press, 1980.

Bouquillon, Thomas. "Condemnation des doctrines Rosminiennes." *Le Messager des Fidèles de Maredsous* 5 (1888): 199–207.

———. "Dix années de pontificat." *Le Messager des Fidèles de Maredsous* 5 (1888): 4–9.

———. "Les droits de l'Eglise." *Le Messager des Fidèles de Maredsous* 5 (1888): 533–46.

———. *Education: To Whom Does It Belong?* Baltimore: John Murphy, 1891.

———. *Institutiones theologiae moralis fundamentalis.* Bruges: Beyaert-Defoort, 1873.

———. *Institutiones theologiae moralis specialis: De virtute religionis.* Bruges: Beyaert-Storie, 1880.

———. "Léon XIII et la Bavière." *Le Messager des Fidèles de Maredsous* 5 (1888): 74–87.

———, ed. *Leonis Papae XIII allocutiones, epistolae, constitutiones aliaque acta praecipua.* 2 vols. Bruges: Desclée De Brouwer, 1887.

———. "Le libéralisme d'après l'Encyclique *Libertas.*" *Le Messager des Fidèles de Maredsous* 5 (1888): 361–70.

———. "La liberté chrétienne d'après l'Encyclique *Libertas.*" *Le Messager des Fidèles de Maredsous* 5 (1888): 399–404.

———. "Moral Theology at the End of the Nineteenth Century." *Catholic University Bulletin* 5 (1899): 244–68.

———. *Theologia moralis fundamentalis.* 2d ed. Bruges: Beyaert-Storie, 1890.

———. *Theologia moralis fundamentalis.* 3d ed. Bruges: Car. Beyaert, 1903.

Bourg, Florence Caffrey. *Where Two or Three Are Gathered: Christian Families as Domestic Churches.* Notre Dame: University of Notre Dame Press, 2004.

Bouscaren, T. Lincoln. *Ethics of Ectopic Operations.* 2d ed. Milwaukee: Bruce, 1944.

Boyle, John P. "The American Experience in Moral Theology." *Proceedings of the Catholic Theological Society of America* 41 (1986): 23–46.

———. *Church Teaching Authority: Historical and Theological Studies.* Notre Dame: University of Notre Dame Press, 1995.

———. *The Sterilization Controversy: A New Crisis for the Catholic Hospital?* New York: Paulist Press, 1977.

Boyle, Patrick J. *Parvitas Materiae in Sexto in Contemporary Catholic Thought.* Lanham, MD: University Press of America, 1987.

Boyle, Philip, and Kevin D. O'Rourke. "Presumed Consent for Organ Donation." *America* 155 (November 22, 1986): 326–37.

Bretzke, James T. *Bibliography on Scripture and Christian Ethics.* Lewiston, NY: Edwin Mellen, 1997.

———. *A Morally Complex World: Engaging Contemporary Moral Theology.* Collegeville, MN: Liturgical Press, 2004.

Briggs, Kenneth A. *Holy Siege: The Year That Shook Catholic America.* San Francisco: HarperSanFrancisco, 1992.

Broderick, Francis L. "But Constitutions Can Be Changed . . ." *Catholic Historical Review* 49 (1963): 393.

———. "The Encyclicals and Social Action: Is John A. Ryan Typical?" *Catholic Historical Review* 55 (1969): 3.

———. *Right Reverend New Dealer: John A. Ryan.* New York: Macmillan, 1963.

Brokhage, Joseph D. *Francis Patrick Kenrick's Opinion on Slavery.* Washington, DC: Catholic University of America Press, 1955.

Budde, Michael L., and Robert M. Brimlow. *Christianity Incorporated: How Big Business Is Buying the Church.* Grand Rapids: Brazos, 2002.

———. *The Church as Counterculture.* Albany: State University of New York Press, 2000.

Burtchaell, James Tunstead, and Daniel Charles Maguire. "The Catholic Legacy and Abortion: A Debate." *Commonweal* 114 (November 20, 1987): 657–63.

Butler, Christopher. "Authority and the Christian Conscience." In *The Magisterium and Morality.* Readings in Moral Theology No. 3, ed. Charles E. Curran and Richard A. McCormick, 171–87. New York: Paulist Press, 1982.

Byrnes, Timothy A., and Mary C. Segers. *The Catholic Church and the Politics of Abortion: A View from the States.* Boulder: Westview, 1992.

Cahill, Lisa Sowle. *Between the Sexes: Foundations for a Christian Ethics of Sexuality.* Minneapolis: Fortress, 1985.

———. "Bioethical Decisions to End Life." *Theological Studies* 52 (1991): 107–27.

———. "Bioethics." *Theological Studies* 67 (2006): 120–42.

———. *Bioethics and the Common Good.* 2004 Père Marquette Lecture in Theology. Milwaukee: Marquette University Press, 2004.

———. "The Embryo and the Fetus: New Moral Contexts." *Theological Studies* 54 (1993): 124–42.

———. *Family: A Christian Social Perspective.* Minneapolis: Fortress, 2000.

———. "Just Peacemaking: Theory, Practice and Prospects." *Journal of the Society of Christian Ethics* 23, no. 1 (2003): 195–212.

———. *Love Your Enemies: Discipleship, Pacifism, and Just War Theory.* Minneapolis: Fortress, 1994.

———. "Moral Methodology: A Case Study." In *A Challenge to Love: Gay and Lesbian Catholics in the Church,* ed. Robert Nugent, 78–92. New York: Crossroad, 1983.

———. "Notes on Moral Theology, 1992: The Embryo and the Fetus; New Moral Contexts." *Theological Studies* 54 (1993): 132–36.

———. "On Richard McCormick: Reason and Faith in Post–Vatican II Catholic Ethics." In *Theological Voices and Medical Ethics,* ed. Allen Verhey and Stephen E. Lammers, 78–105. Grand Rapids: William B. Eerdmans, 1993.

———. "Richard A. McCormick, S.J.'s 'To Save or Let Die': The Dilemma of Modern Medicine." In *The Story of Bioethics: From Seminal Works to Contemporary Explorations,* ed. Jennifer K. Walter and Eran P. Klein, 131–48. Washington, DC: Georgetown University Press, 2003.

———. "Sanctity of Life, Quality of Life, and Social Justice." *Theological Studies* 48 (1987): 105–23.

———. "'The Seamless Garment': Life in Its Beginnings." *Theological Studies* 46 (1985): 64–80.

———. *Sex, Gender, and Christian Ethics.* Cambridge: Cambridge University Press, 1996.

———. "Sexual Ethics." In *A Call to Fidelity: On the Moral Theology of Charles E. Curran,* ed. James J. Walter, Timothy E. O'Connell, and Thomas A. Shannon, 113–33. Washington, DC: Georgetown University Press, 2002.

————. *Theological Bioethics: Participation, Justice, and Change.* Washington, DC: George-town University Press, 2005.

————. "Toward Global Ethics." *Theological Studies* 63 (2002): 324–44.

————. *Women and Sexuality.* 1992 Madaleva Lecture in Spirituality. New York: Paulist Press, 1992.

Caldecott, Léonie. "Sincere Gift: The Pope's 'New Feminism.'" In *John Paul II and Moral Theology.* Readings in Moral Theology No. 10, ed. Charles E. Curran and Richard A. McCormick, 216–34. New York: Paulist Press, 1998.

Callahan, Sidney. "Abortion and the Sexual Agenda: A Case for Pro-Life Feminism." In *Feminist Ethics and the Catholic Moral Tradition,* ed. Charles E. Curran, Margaret A. Farley, and Richard A. McCormick, 422–39. New York: Paulist Press, 1996.

————. "Conscience and Gender." In *Conscience.* Readings in Moral Theology No. 14, ed. Charles E. Curran, 113–29. New York: Paulist Press, 2004.

————. *In Good Conscience: Reason and Emotion in Moral Decision-Making.* San Francisco: Harper, 1991.

————. "The Role of Emotion in Ethical Decision Making." *Catholic International* 12 (May 2001): 143–48.

Campana, J. H. "Gury, Jean Pierre." In *New Catholic Encyclopedia,* 6:866–67. New York: McGraw-Hill, 1967.

Capellmann, Carl. *Medicina Pastoralis.* 7th ed. Aquisgrani, Germany: R. Barth, 1879.

Capone, Domenico. "Per la norma morale: Ragione, coscienza, legge." In *Historia: Memoria futurae; Mélanges Louis Vereecke,* ed. Réal Tremblay and Dennis J. Billy, 199–225. Rome: Editiones Academiae Alphonsianae, 1991.

Carey, Patrick W. "College Theology in Historical Perspective." In *American Catholic Traditions: Resources for Renewal,* ed. Sandra Yocum Mize and William L. Portier, 242–71. Maryknoll, NY: Orbis Books, 1997.

————. "Introduction." In *American Catholic Religious Thought: The Shaping of a Theological and Social Tradition,* 2d ed., ed. Patrick W. Carey, 60–71. Milwaukee: Marquette University Press, 2004.

Carlen, Claudia, ed. *The Papal Encyclicals, 1903–39.* Wilmington, NC: McGrath, 1981.

Cassidy, Laurie M. "White Privilege and Racism." *Proceedings of the Catholic Theological Society of America* 59 (2004): 151–52.

Cassidy, Laurie M., and Alex Mikulich, eds. *Interrupting White Privilege: Catholic Theologians Break the Silence.* Maryknoll, NY: Orbis Books, 2007.

Catholic Hospital Association. "Ethical and Religious Directives for Catholic Hospitals." In *Medical Ethics,* Edwin F. Healy, 393–401. Chicago: Loyola University Press, 1956.

Catholic University of America, School of Religious Studies. *A Century of Religious Studies: Faculty and Dissertations.* Washington, DC: Catholic University of America, 1989.

Cavanaugh, William. "At Odds with the Pope." *Commonweal* 130 (May 23, 2003): 11–13.

Cessario, Romanus. *Introduction to Moral Theology.* Washington, DC: Catholic University of America Press, 2001.

————. *The Moral Virtues and Theological Ethics.* Notre Dame: University of Notre Dame Press, 1991.

————. *The Virtues or the Examined Life.* New York: Continuum, 2002.

Christiansen, Drew. "Ecology and the Common Good: Catholic Social Teaching and Environmental Responsibility." In *"And God Saw That It Was Good": Catholic Theology and the Environment,* ed. Drew Christiansen and Walter Grazer, 183–95. Washington, DC: United States Catholic Conference, 1996.

Christiansen, Drew, and Walter Grazer, eds. *"And God Saw That It Was Good": Catholic Theology and the Environment.* Washington, DC: United States Catholic Conference, 1996.

Christie, Dolores L. *Adequately Considered: An American Perspective on Louis Janssens' Personalist Morals.* Louvain: Peeters, 1990.

———. *Last Rites: A Catholic Perspective on End-of-Life Decisions.* Lanham, MD: Rowman & Littlefield, 2003.

Cimperman, Maria. *When God's People Have HIV/AIDS: An Approach to Ethics.* Maryknoll, NY: Orbis Books, 2005.

Clark, Peter A. *To Treat or Not to Treat: The Ethical Methodology of Richard A. McCormick, S.J., as Applied to the Treatment Decisions for Handicapped Newborns.* Omaha, NE: Creighton University Press, 2003.

Coffey, J. "Callan, Charles Jerome." In *New Catholic Encyclopedia,* 2:1077–78. New York: McGraw-Hill, 1967.

———. "McHugh, John Ambrose." In *New Catholic Encyclopedia,* 9:34. New York: McGraw-Hill, 1967.

Coleman, John A. *An American Strategic Theology.* New York: Paulist Press, 1982.

———, ed. *One Hundred Years of Catholic Social Thought: Celebration and Challenge.* Maryknoll, NY: Orbis Books, 1991.

Collins, Paul. *The Modern Inquisition: Seven Prominent Catholics and Their Struggles with the Vatican.* Woodstock, NY: Overlook, 2002.

Congar, Yves. "A Brief History of the Forms of the Magisterium and Its Relations with Scholars." In *The Magisterium and Morality.* Readings in Moral Theology No. 3, ed. Charles E. Curran and Richard A. McCormick, 314–31. New York: Paulist Press, 1982.

Congregation for the Doctrine of the Faith. "Considerations Regarding Proposals to Give Legal Recognition to Unions between Homosexual Persons." *Origins* 33 (2003): 177–82.

———. "Instruction on the Ecclesial Vocation of the Theologian (*Donum veritatis*)." *Origins* 20 (1990): 117–26.

———. "Instruction on Respect for Human Life in Its Origin and on the Dignity of Procreation (*Donum vitae*)." *Origins* 16 (1987): 697–711.

———. "Letter to the Bishops of the Catholic Church on the Pastoral Care of Homosexual Persons." *Origins* 16 (1986): 377–82.

———. "Observations Regarding Legislative Proposals Concerned with Discrimination toward Homosexual Persons." *Origins* 22 (1992): 173–77.

"Congregation for the Doctrine of the Faith on Anthony Kosnik et al., *Human Sexuality,* July 13, 1979." In *Dialogue about Catholic Sexual Teaching.* Readings in Moral Theology No. 8, ed. Charles E. Curran and Richard A. McCormick, 485–90. New York: Paulist Press, 1993.

"Congregation for the Doctrine of the Faith on John McNeill, *The Church and the Homosexual*, Summer 1978." In *Dialogue about Catholic Sexual Teaching. Readings in Moral Theology* No. 8, ed. Charles E. Curran and Richard A. McCormick, 491–97. New York: Paulist Press, 1993.

Conn, Walter E. *Christian Conversion: A Developmental Interpretation of Autonomy and Surrender.* New York: Paulist Press, 1986.

———. *Conscience: Development and Self-Transcendence.* Birmingham, AL.: Religious Education Press, 1981.

———, ed. *Conversion: Perspectives on Personal and Social Transformation.* Staten Island: Alba House, 1978.

Connell, Francis J. *Morals in Politics and Professions: A Guide for Catholics in Public Life.* Westminster, MD: Newman, 1946.

———. *Outlines of Moral Theology.* 2d ed. Milwaukee: Bruce, 1958.

———. "Prizefighting and Boxing." *American Ecclesiastical Review* 122 (1950): 58–59.

———. "The Theological School in America." In *Essays on Catholic Education in the United States,* ed. Roy J. Deferrari, 219–33. Washington, DC: Catholic University of America Press, 1942.

Connery, John. *Abortion: The Development of the Roman Catholic Perspective.* Chicago: Loyola University Press, 1977.

Connors, Russell B., Jr., and Patrick T. McCormick. *Character, Choice, and Community: The Three Faces of Christian Ethics.* New York: Paulist Press, 1998.

Conroy, Ed. "Profile: Virgilio P. Elizondo." *National Catholic Reporter,* October 8, 2004, 19.

Copeland, M. Shawn. "Method in Emerging Black Catholic Theology." In *Taking Down Our Harps: Black Catholics in the United States,* ed. Diana L. Hayes and Cyprian Davis, 120–44. Maryknoll, NY: Orbis Books, 1998.

Coppens, Charles. *Moral Principles and Medical Practice: The Basis of Medical Jurisprudence.* New York: Benziger Brothers, 1897.

Coriden, James A. "The Canonical Doctrine of Reception." *Jurist* 50 (1990): 58–82.

Cowdin, Daniel M. "John Paul II and Environmental Concerns: Problems and Possibilities." *Living Light* 28 (1991): 44–52.

———. "Toward an Environmental Ethics." In *Preserving the Creation: Environmental Theology and Ethics,* ed. Kevin W. Irwin and Edmund D. Pellegrino, 112–47. Washington, DC: Georgetown University Press, 1994.

Crews, Clyde E. *An American Holy Land: A History of the Archdiocese of Louisville.* Wilmington, DE: Glazier, 1987.

Cronin, Daniel A. *The Moral Law in Regard to the Ordinary and Extraordinary Means of Conserving Life.* Rome: Pontificia Università Gregoriana, 1958.

Cronin, John F. "Forty Years Later: Reflections and Reminiscences." *American Ecclesiastical Review* 164 (1971): 310–18.

———. *Social Principles and Economic Life.* Milwaukee: Bruce, 1959.

Cross, Robert D. *The Emergence of Liberal Catholicism in America.* Cambridge: Harvard University Press, 1958.

Crossan, Dominic. "Divorce and Remarriage in the New Testament." In *The Bond of Marriage,* ed. William W. Bassett, 1–33. Notre Dame: University of Notre Dame Press, 1968.

Crossin, John W. *What Are They Saying about Virtue?* New York: Paulist Press, 1985.

Curran, Charles E. "Abortion: Law and Morality in Contemporary Catholic Theology." *Jurist* 33 (1973): 162–83.

———. "Absolute Norms and Medical Ethics." In *Absolutes in Moral Theology?* ed. Charles E. Curran, 108–53. Washington, DC: Corpus, 1968.

———. "Absolute Norms in Moral Theology." In *Norm and Context in Christian Ethics,* ed. Gene H. Outka and Paul Ramsey, 39–74. New York: Charles Scribner's Sons, 1968.

———, ed. *Absolutes in Moral Theology?* Washington, DC: Corpus, 1968.

———. *American Catholic Social Ethics: Twentieth-Century Approaches.* Notre Dame: University of Notre Dame Press, 1982.

———. *Catholic Higher Education, Theology, and Academic Freedom.* Notre Dame: University of Notre Dame Press, 1990.

———. *The Catholic Moral Tradition Today: A Synthesis.* Washington, DC: Georgetown University Press, 1999.

———. *Catholic Social Teaching 1891–Present: A Historical, Theological, and Ethical Analysis.* Washington, DC: Georgetown University Press, 2002.

———, ed. *Change in Official Catholic Moral Teachings.* Readings in Moral Theology No. 13. New York: Paulist Press, 2003.

———. *Contemporary Problems in Moral Theology.* Notre Dame: Fides, 1970.

———, ed. *Contraception: Authority and Dissent.* New York: Herder and Herder, 1969.

———. *Directions in Catholic Social Ethics.* Notre Dame: University of Notre Dame Press, 1985.

———. "Divorce: Catholic Theory and Practice." *American Ecclesiastical Review* 168 (1974): 3–34, 75–97.

———. "Divorce: Doctrine et pratique catholique aux États Unis." *Recherches de Science Religieuse* 61 (1973): 575–624.

———. *Faithful Dissent.* Kansas City, MO: Sheed & Ward, 1986.

———. "The Global Ethic." *Ecumenist* 37 (spring 2000): 6–10.

———. "The Gospel and Culture: Christian Marriage and Divorce Today." *Social Thought* 2 (winter 1976): 9–28.

———. "Homosexuality and Moral Theology: Methodological and Substantive Considerations." *Thomist* 35 (1971): 447–81.

———. "Is There a Distinctively Christian Ethic?" In *Metropolis: Christian Presence and Responsibility,* ed. Philip D. Morris, 92–120. Notre Dame: Fides, 1970.

———. *Loyal Dissent: Memoir of a Catholic Theologian.* Washington, DC: Georgetown University Press, 2006.

———. "Masturbation and Objectively Grave Matter: An Exploratory Discussion." *Proceedings of the Catholic Theological Society of America* 21 (1966): 95–109.

———, ed. *Moral Theology: Challenges for the Future; Essays in Honor of Richard A. McCormick.* New York: Paulist Press, 1990.

———. *The Moral Theology of Pope John Paul II.* Washington, DC: Georgetown University Press, 2005.

———. "Natural Law and Contemporary Moral Theology." In *Contraception: Authority and Dissent,* ed. Charles E. Curran, 151–75. New York: Herder and Herder, 1969.

———. *A New Look at Christian Morality: Christian Morality Today II.* Notre Dame: Fides, 1968.

———. *Ongoing Revision in Moral Theology.* Notre Dame: Fides, 1975.

———. *The Origins of Moral Theology in the United States.* Washington, DC: Georgetown University Press, 1997.

———. *Politics, Medicine, and Christian Ethics: A Dialogue with Paul Ramsey.* Philadelphia: Fortress, 1973.

———. "The Problem of Conscience and the Twentieth-Century Christian." In *Ecumenical Dialogue at Harvard: The Roman Catholic-Protestant Colloquium,* ed. Samuel H. Miller and G. Ernest Wright, 262–73. Cambridge: Belknap Press of Harvard University Press, 1964.

———. "Relevance: Contemporary Moral Concerns." In *Jesus Christ Reforms His Church: Twenty-Six North American Liturgical Week,* 3–13. Washington, DC: Liturgical Conference, 1966.

———. "Roman Catholicism." In *Encyclopedia of Bioethics,* rev. ed., ed. Warren T. Reich, 4:2321–31. New York: Simon & Schuster/Macmillan, 1995.

———. "The Sacrament of Penance Today." *Worship* 43 (1969): 510–31, 590–619.

———. "Sexuality and Sin: A Current Appraisal." Part 1. *Homiletic and Pastoral Review* 68 (September 1968): 1005–14.

———. "Sexuality and Sin: A Current Appraisal." Part 2. *Homiletic and Pastoral Review* 69 (October 1968): 27–34.

———. "Sterilization: Roman Catholic Theory and Practice." *Linacre Quarterly* 40 (1973): 97–108.

———. *Tensions in Moral Theology.* Notre Dame: University of Notre Dame Press, 1988.

———. *Themes in Fundamental Moral Theology.* Notre Dame: University of Notre Dame Press, 1977.

———. "Theology and Genetics: A Multifaceted Dialogue." *Journal of Ecumenical Studies* 7 (1970): 61–89.

———. *Transition and Tradition in Moral Theology.* Notre Dame: University of Notre Dame Press, 1979.

———. "White Privilege." *Horizons* 32 (2005): 361–63.

Curran, Charles E., Margaret A. Farley, and Richard A. McCormick, eds. *Feminist Ethics and the Catholic Moral Tradition.* Readings in Moral Theology No. 9. New York: Paulist Press, 1996.

Curran, Charles E., et al., *Dissent In and For the Church: Theologians and Humanae vitae.* New York: Sheed & Ward, 1969.

Curran, Charles E., and Richard A. McCormick, eds. *Dialogue about Catholic Sexual Teaching.* Readings in Moral Theology No. 8. New York: Paulist Press, 1993.

———. *Dissent in the Church.* Readings in Moral Theology No. 6. New York: Paulist Press, 1988.

———. *The Distinctiveness of Christian Ethics.* Readings in Moral Theology No. 2. New York: Paulist Press, 1980.

———. *The Magisterium and Morality.* Readings in Moral Theology No. 3. New York: Paulist Press, 1982.

————. *The Use of Scripture in Moral Theology*. Readings in Moral Theology No. 4. New York: Paulist Press, 1984.

Daly, Robert J., et al. *Christian Biblical Ethics: From Christian Revelation to Contemporary Christian Praxis; Method and Content*. New York: Paulist Press, 1984.

D'Antonio, William V. "Church Pays Cost of Abortion Absolutism." *National Catholic Reporter*, July 2, 2004, 7.

Davis, Cyprian. *The History of Black Catholics in the United States*. New York: Crossroad, 1990.

Davis, Cyprian, and Jaime T. Phelps, eds. *Stamped with the Image of God: African-Americans as God's Image in Black*. Maryknoll, NY: Orbis Books, 2003.

Davis, Henry. *Moral and Pastoral Theology*. 4 vols. 6th ed. London: Sheed & Ward, 1949.

DeCrane, Susanne M. *Aquinas, Feminism, and the Common Good*. Washington, DC: Georgetown University Press, 2004.

Dedek, John F. *Contemporary Medical Ethics*. New York: Sheed & Ward, 1975.

————. *Human Life: Some Moral Issues*. New York: Sheed & Ward, 1972.

————. "Intrinsically Evil Acts: The Emergence of a Doctrine." *Recherches de Théologie ancienne et médiévale* 50 (1983): 191–226.

————. "Intrinsically Evil Acts: An Historical Study of the Mind of St. Thomas." *Thomist* 43 (1979): 385–413.

————. "Moral Absolutes in the Predecessors of St. Thomas." *Theological Studies* 38 (1977): 654–80.

————. "Pre-Marital Sex: The Theological Argument from Peter Lombard to Durand." *Theological Studies* 41 (1980): 643–67.

Dietrich, Wendell. "*Gaudium et Spes* and Häring's Personalism." In *Oecumenica: An Annual Symposium of Ecumenical Research* (1968): 274–83.

Dolan, Jay P. *The American Catholic Experience: A History from Colonial Times to the Present*. Notre Dame: University of Notre Dame Press, 1992.

Donceel, Joseph F. "Abortion: Mediate or Immediate Animation." *Continuum* 5 (1967): 167–71.

————. "Immediate Animation and Delayed Hominization." *Theological Studies* 31 (1970): 76–105.

Donoghue, John F. "A Manifest Lack of Proper Disposition for Communion." *Origins* 34 (2004): 188–89.

Donovan, John Timothy "Crusader in the Cold War: A Biography of Fr. John F. Cronin, S.S. (1908–1994)." Ph.D. diss., Marquette University, 2000.

Donovan, Mary Ann. "Alive to the Glory of God: A Key Insight in St. Irenaeus." *Theological Studies* 49 (1988): 283–97.

Dooley, Patrick J. *Woodstock and Its Makers*. Woodstock, MD: College Press, 1927.

Dorszynski, Julius A. *Catholic Teaching about the Morality of Falsehood*. Washington, DC: Catholic University of America Press, 1949.

Drane, James F. *Becoming a Good Doctor: The Place of Virtue and Character in Medical Ethics*. Kansas City, MO: Sheed & Ward, 1988.

————. *More Humane Medicine: A Liberal Catholic Bioethics*. Edinboro, PA: University of Edinboro Press, 2003.

Drinan, Robert F. "The Jurisprudential Options on Abortion." *Theological Studies* 31 (1970): 149–69.

———. "The Morality of Abortion Laws." *Catholic Lawyer* 14 (1968): 191–98.

Dulles, Avery. "Criteria of Catholic Theology." *Communio* 20 (1995): 303–15.

———. "Doctrinal Authority for a Pilgrim Church." In *The Magisterium and Morality. Readings in Moral Theology* No. 3, ed. Charles E. Curran and Richard A. McCormick, 264–65. New York: Paulist Press, 1982.

———. "The Two Magisteria: An Interim Reflection." *Proceedings of the Catholic Theological Society of America* 35 (1980): 155–69.

Dupré, Louis, and Constance Dupré. "The Indissolubility of Marriage and the Common Good." In *The Bond of Marriage*, ed. William W. Bassett, 181–99. Notre Dame: University of Notre Dame Press, 1968.

Elizondo, Virgilio P. *The Future Is Mestizo: Life Where Cultures Meet*. Oak Park, IL: Meyer-Stone, 1988.

———. *Galilean Journey: The Mexican American Promise*. Rev. ed. Maryknoll, NY: Orbis Books, 2000.

———. *Guadalupe: Mother of the New Creation*. Maryknoll, NY: Orbis Books, 1997.

Elizondo, Virgilio P., and Timothy Matovina. *San Fernando Cathedral: Soul of the City*. Maryknoll, NY: Orbis Books, 1998.

Ellis, John Tracy. "American Catholics and the Intellectual Life." *Thought* 30 (1955–56): 351–88.

———. "The Formation of the American Priest: An Historical Perspective." In *The Catholic Priest in the United States: Historical Investigations*, ed. John Tracy Ellis, 3–110. Collegeville, MN: St. John's University Press, 1971.

Elsbernd, Mary. "Whatever Happened to *Octogesima Adveniens?*" *Theological Studies* 56 (1995): 39–60.

Elsbernd, Mary, and Reimund Bieringer. *When Love Is Not Enough: A Theo-Ethic of Justice*. Collegeville, MN: Liturgical Press, 2002.

Empereur, James L., and Christopher G. Kiesling. *The Liturgy That Does Justice*. Collegeville, MN: Liturgical Press, 1990.

Espin, Orlando O., and Miguel H. Diaz, eds. *From the Hearts of Our People: Latino/a Explorations in Catholic Systematic Theology*. Maryknoll, NY: Orbis Books, 1999.

Fahey, Michael A. "From the Editor's Desk." *Theological Studies* 61 (2000): 603.

Farley, Margaret A. "The Church in the Public Forum: Scandal or Prophetic Witness?" *Proceedings of the Catholic Theological Society of America* 55 (2000): 87–101.

———. *Compassionate Respect: A Feminist Approach to Medical Ethics and Other Questions*. 2002 Madaleva Lecture in Spirituality. New York: Paulist Press, 2002.

———. "Divorce and Remarriage: A Moral Perspective." In *Divorce and Remarriage: Religious and Psychological Perspectives*, ed. William P. Roberts, 107–27. Kansas City, MO: Sheed & Ward, 1990.

———. "Divorce, Remarriage, and Pastoral Practice." In *Moral Theology: Challenges for the Future; Essays in Honor of Richard A. McCormick*, ed. Charles E. Curran, 213–39. New York: Paulist Press, 1990.

———. "An Ethic for Same-Sex Relations." In *A Challenge to Love: Gay and Lesbian Catholics in the Church*, ed. Robert Nugent, 93–106. New York: Crossroad, 1983.

———. "Ethics, Ecclesiology, and the Grace of Self-Doubt." In *A Call to Fidelity: On the Moral Theology of Charles E. Curran,* ed. James J. Walter, Timothy E. O'Connell, and Thomas A. Shannon, 55–75. Washington, DC: Georgetown University Press, 2002.

———. "Feminist Theology and Bioethics." In *On Moral Medicine: Theological Perspectives in Medical Ethics,* 2d ed., ed. Stephen E. Lammers and Allen Verhey, 98–101. Grand Rapids: William B. Eerdmans, 1998.

———. "Feminist Theology and Bioethics." In *Theology and Bioethics: Exploring the Foundations and Frontiers,* ed. Earl Shelp, 163–86. Dordrecht, Holland: D. Reidel, 1985.

———. *Just Love: A Framework for Christian Sexual Ethics.* New York: Continuum, 2006.

———. "Liberation, Abortion, and Responsibility." In *On Moral Medicine: Theological Perspectives in Medical Ethics,* 2d ed., ed. Stephen E. Lammers and Allen Verhey, 633–38. Grand Rapids: William B. Eerdmans, 1998.

———. "New Patterns of Relationships: Beginnings of a Moral Revolution." *Theological Studies* 36 (1975): 627–46.

———. "Partnership in Hope: Gender, Faith, and Responses to HIV/AIDS in Africa." *Journal of Feminist Studies in Religion* 20 (2004): 33–48.

———. *Personal Commitments: Beginning, Keeping, Changing.* San Francisco: Harper & Row, 1986.

———. "Power and Powerlessness: A Case in Point." *Proceedings of the Catholic Theological Society of America* 37 (1982): 116–19.

"Father Aloysius Sabetti: A Fellow Professor's Reminiscences." *Woodstock Letters* 29 (1900): 228.

Fiedler, Maureen. "Dissent within the U.S. Church: The Case of the Vatican '24.'" In *Church Polity and American Politics: Issues in Contemporary American Catholicism,* ed. Mary C. Segers, 303–12. New York: Garland, 1990.

Finn, Daniel Rush. "John Paul II and the Moral Ecology of Markets." *Theological Studies* 59 (1998): 662–79.

———. *Just Trading: On the Ethics and Economics of International Trade.* Nashville, TN: Abingdon, 1996.

———. *The Moral Ecology of Markets: Assessing Claims about Markets and Justice.* Cambridge: Cambridge University Press, 2006.

Finney, Patrick A. *Moral Problems in Hospital Practice: A Pastoral Handbook.* St. Louis, MO: B. Herder, 1922.

———. *Moral Problems in Hospital Practice: A Practical Handbook.* Rev. ed. Edited by Patrick O'Brien. St. Louis, MO: B. Herder, 1956.

Finnis, John. *Fundamentals of Ethics.* Washington, DC: Georgetown University Press, 1983.

———. "Law, Morality, and 'Sexual Orientation.'" *Notre Dame Law Review* 69, no. 5 (1994): 1049–76.

———. *Moral Absolutes, Tradition, Revision, and Truth.* Washington, DC: Catholic University of America Press, 1991.

———. *Natural Law and Natural Rights.* Clarendon Law Series. Oxford: Clarendon Press, 1980.

Finucane, Daniel J. *Sensus Fidelium: The Use of a Concept in the Post–Vatican II Era.* San Francisco: International Scholars, 1996.

Fiorenza, Elizabeth Schüssler. *Bread Not Stone: The Challenge of Feminist Biblical Interpretation*. Boston: Beacon Press, 1984.

————. *In Memory of Her: A Feminist Reconstruction of Christian Origins*. New York: Crossroad, 1983.

Fisher, Eugene J., and Daniel F. Polish, eds. *The Formation of Social Policy in the Catholic and Jewish Traditions*. Notre Dame: University of Notre Dame Press, 1980.

Fleming, Julia. *Defending Probabilism: The Moral Theology of Juan Caramuel*. Washington, DC: Georgetown University Press, 2006.

Focus: Virtue and Obligation in Religious Ethics. *Journal of Religious Ethics* 1 (Fall 1973): 5–64.

Fogarty, Gerald P. *American Catholic Biblical Scholarship: A History from the Early Republic to Vatican II*. San Francisco: Harper & Row, 1989.

Ford, John C. *Man Takes a Drink: Facts and Principles about Alcohol*. New York: P. J. Kennedy, 1955.

————. "The Morality of Obliteration Bombing." *Theological Studies* 5 (1944): 261–309.

Ford, John C. and Gerald Kelly. *Contemporary Moral Theology*. Vol. 1, *Questions in Fundamental Moral Theology*. Westminster, MD: Newman, 1958.

————. *Contemporary Moral Theology*. Vol. 2, *Marriage Questions*. Westminster, MD: Newman, 1963.

Ford, John T. "John Paul II Asks for Forgiveness." *Ecumenical Trends* 27 (December 1998): 173–75.

Franklin, R. W., and Robert L. Spaeth. *Virgil Michel: American Catholic*. Collegeville, MN: Liturgical Press, 1988.

Fransen, Piet. "Divorce on the Ground of Adultery—the Council of Trent (1563)." In *The Future of Marriage as Institution*, ed. Franz Böckle, 89–100. New York: Herder and Herder, 1970.

Frogomeni, Richard N., and John T. Pawlikowski, eds. *The Ecological Challenge: Ethical, Liturgical, and Spiritual Responses*. Collegeville, MN: Liturgical Press, 1994.

Fuchs, Josef. *Christian Ethics in a Secular Arena*. Washington, DC: Georgetown University Press, 1984.

————. *Christian Morality: The Word Becomes Flesh*. Washington, DC: Georgetown University Press, 1987.

————. *Human Values and Christian Morality*. Dublin: Gill & Macmillan, 1970.

————. *Moral Demands and Personal Obligations*. Washington, DC: Georgetown University Press, 1993.

————. *Natural Law: A Theological Investigation*. New York: Sheed & Ward, 1965.

————. *Personal Responsibility and Christian Morality*. Washington, DC: Georgetown University Press, 1983.

Fuller, John D., and James F. Keenan. "Introduction: At the End of the First Generation of HIV Prevention." In *Catholic Ethicists on HIV/AIDS Prevention*, ed. James F. Keenan, 22–38. New York: Continuum, 2000.

Furfey, Paul Hanly. *Fire on the Earth*. New York: Macmillan, 1936.

————. *The Respectable Murderers*. New York: Herder and Herder, 1968.

Gaillardetz, Richard. "The Ordinary Universal Magisterium: Unresolved Questions." *Theological Studies* 63 (2002): 447–71.

————. *Teaching with Authority: A Theology of the Magisterium in the Church.* Collegeville, MN: Liturgical Press, 1997.

Gallagher, John A. *Time Past, Time Future: A Historical Study of Catholic Moral Theology.* New York: Paulist Press, 1990.

Gallagher, Raphael. "The Fate of the Moral Manual since St. Alphonsus." In *History and Conscience: Studies in Honor of Father Sean O'Riordan CSSR,* ed. Raphael Gallagher and Brendan McConvery, 212–39. Dublin: Gill & MacMillan, 1989.

Gardella, Peter. *Innocent Ecstasy: How Christianity Gave America an Ethic about Sexual Pleasure.* New York: Oxford University Press, 1985.

Gaupin, Linda. "More Frequent Communion, Less Frequent Confession." *Living Light* 20 (1984): 254–60.

Genovesi, Vincent J. *In Pursuit of Love: Catholic Morality and Human Sexuality.* 2d ed. Collegeville, MN: Liturgical Press, 1996.

George, Robert P., ed. *Natural Law and Moral Inquiry: Ethics, Metaphysics, and Politics in the Work of Germain Grisez.* Washington, DC: Georgetown University Press, 1998.

Glazer, John W. "Transition between Grace and Sin." *Theological Studies* 29 (1968): 260–74.

Glazier, Michael, and Thomas J. Shelley. *The Encyclopedia of American Catholic History.* Collegeville, MN: Liturgical Press, 1997.

Gleason, Philip. *The Conservative Reformers: German American Catholics and the Social Order.* Notre Dame: University of Notre Dame Press, 1968.

Glendon, Mary Ann. *Abortion and Divorce in Western Law: American Failures, European Challenges.* Cambridge, MA: Harvard University Press, 1987.

Goodwine, John A. "A Problem of Periodic Continence." *American Ecclesiastical Review* 137 (1957): 164–65.

Gould, William J. "Father J. Bryan Hehir: Priest, Policy Analyst, and Theologian of Dialogue." In *Religious Leaders and Faith-Based Politics: Ten Profiles,* ed. Jo Renee Formicola and Hubert Morken, 197–223. Lanham, MD: Rowman & Littlefield, 2001.

Grabowski, John S. *Sex and Virtue: An Introduction to Sexual Ethics.* Washington, DC: Catholic University of America Press, 2003.

Graham, Mark E. *Josef Fuchs on Natural Law.* Washington, DC: Georgetown University Press, 2002.

Greeley, Andrew M. *The Catholic Myth: The Behavior and Beliefs of American Catholics.* New York: Charles Scribner's Sons, 1990.

————. *From Backwater to Mainstream: A Profile of Catholic Higher Education.* Carnegie Commission Studies. New York: McGraw-Hill, 1969.

Greeley, Andrew M., William C. McCready, and Kathleen McCourt. *Catholic Schools in a Declining Church.* Kansas City, MO: Sheed & Ward, 1976.

Griese, Orville N. *The Morality of Periodic Continence.* Washington, DC: Catholic University of American Press, 1942.

Griffin, Leslie. "American Catholic Sexual Ethics, 1789–1989." In *Dialogue about Catholic Sexual Teaching.* Readings in Moral Theology No. 8, ed. Charles E. Curran and Richard A. McCormick, 453–84. New York: Paulist Press, 1993.

Griffiths, Paul J. "Legalized Same-Sex Marriage: Why Law and Morality Can Part." *Commonweal* 130, no. 18 (October 24, 2003): 10–14.

Grisez, Germain. *Abortion: The Myths, the Realities, and the Arguments.* New York: Corpus, 1970.

———. "How to Deal with Theological Dissent." In *Dissent in the Church.* Readings in Moral Theology No. 6, ed. Charles E. Curran and John A. McCormick, 442–72. New York: Paulist Press, 1988.

———. "Infallibility and Specific Moral Norms: A Review Discussion." *Thomist* 49 (1985): 248–87.

———. "*Quaestio Disputata:* The Ordinary Magisterium's Infallibility; A Reply to Some New Arguments." *Theological Studies* 55 (1994): 720–32, 737–38.

———. "Toward a Consistent Natural Law Ethics of Killing." *American Journal of Jurisprudence* 15 (1970): 64–96.

———. *The Way of the Lord Jesus.* Vol. 1, *Christian Moral Principles.* Chicago: Franciscan Herald, 1983.

———. *The Way of the Lord Jesus.* Vol. 2, *Living a Christian Life.* Quincy, IL: Franciscan, 1993.

———. *The Way of the Lord Jesus.* Vol. 3, *Difficult Moral Questions.* Quincy, IL: Franciscan, 1997.

———. "When Do People Begin?" *Proceedings of the American Philosophical Association* 63 (1990): 37.

Grisez, Germain, and Joseph M. Boyle Jr. *Life and Death with Liberty and Justice: A Contribution to the Euthanasia Debate.* Notre Dame: University of Notre Dame Press, 1979.

Grisez, Germain, Joseph M. Boyle Jr., and John Finnis. "Practical Principles, Moral Truth, and Ultimate Ends." *American Journal of Jurisprudence* 32 (1987): 99–151.

Grisez, Germain, John M. Finnis, and Joseph M. Boyle Jr. *Nuclear Deterrence, Morality, and Realism.* Oxford: Oxford University Press, 1987.

Grisez, Germain, and Russell Shaw. *Fulfillment in Christ: A Summary of Christian Moral Principles.* Notre Dame: University of Notre Dame Press, 1991.

———. *Personal Vocation: God Calls Everyone by Name.* Huntington, IN: Our Sunday Visitor, 2003.

Grosz, Edward M., ed. *Liturgy and Social Justice: Celebrating Rites—Proclaiming Rights.* Collegeville, MN: Liturgical Press, 1989.

Gudorf, Christine E. *Body, Sex, and Pleasure: Reconstructing Christian Sexual Ethics.* Cleveland: Pilgrim, 1994.

———. *Catholic Social Teaching on Liberation Themes.* Lanham, MD: University Press of America, 1980.

———. "Encountering the Other: The Modern Papacy on Women." In *Feminist Ethics and the Catholic Moral Tradition.* Readings in Moral Theology No. 9, ed. Charles E. Curran, Margaret A. Farley, and Richard A. McCormick, 66–89. New York: Paulist Press, 1996.

———. "A Feminist Critique of Biomedical Principleism." In *A Matter of Principles? Ferment in U.S. Bioethics,* ed. Edwin R. DuBose, Ronald P. Hamel, and Lawrence J. O'Connell, 164–81. Valley Forge, PA: Trinity Press International, 1994.

———. "A Response to Stanley Hauerwas." *Proceedings of the Catholic Theological Society of America* 61 (2006): 77–80.

———. "Resymbolizing Life: Religion on Population and Environment." *Horizons* 28 (2001): 183–210.

———. "To Make a Seamless Garment, Use a Single Piece of Cloth." *Cross Currents* 34 (1984): 473–91.

———. *Victimization: Examining Christian Complicity.* Philadelphia: Trinity Press International, 1992.

Guerber, Jean. *Le ralliement du clergé français à la morale liguorienne.* Rome: Gregorian University Press.

Gula, Richard M. *The Call to Holiness: Embracing a Fully Christian Life.* New York: Paulist Press, 2003.

———. *The Good Life: Where Morality and Spirituality Converge.* New York: Paulist Press, 1999.

———. *Moral Discernment.* New York: Paulist Press, 1997.

———. *Reason Informed by Faith: Foundations of Catholic Morality.* New York: Paulist Press, 1989.

Gustafson, James M. "The Changing Use of the Bible in Christian Ethics." In *The Use of Scripture in Moral Theology.* Readings in Moral Theology No. 4, ed. Charles E. Curran and Richard A. McCormick, 133–50. New York: Paulist Press, 1984.

———. *Christ and the Moral Life.* New York: Harper & Row, 1968.

———. *Protestant and Roman Catholic Ethics: Prospects for Rapprochement.* Chicago: University of Chicago Press, 1978.

———. "The Sectarian Temptation: Reflections on Theology, the Church, and the University." *Proceedings of the Catholic Theological Society of America* 40 (1985): 83–94.

Hallett, Garth L. *Greater Good: The Case for Proportionalism.* Washington, DC: Georgetown University Press, 1996.

Hamel Ronald P., and Kenneth R. Himes, eds. *Introduction to Christian Ethics: A Reader.* New York: Paulist Press, 1989.

Hanigan, James P. *As I Have Loved You: The Challenge of Christian Ethics.* New York: Paulist Press, 1986.

———. *Homosexuality: The Test Case for Catholic Sexual Ethics.* New York: Paulist Press, 1988.

Happel, Stephen, and James J. Walter. *Conversion and Discipleship: A Christian Foundation for Ethics and Doctrine.* Philadelphia: Fortress, 1986.

Harak, Simon. *Virtuous Passions: The Formation of Christian Character.* Notre Dame: University of Notre Dame Press, 1993.

Häring, Bernard. "La conversion." In *Pastorale du peché,* ed. Philippe Delhaye, 65–145. Tournai, Belgium: Desclée & Cie, 1961.

———. *Free and Faithful in Christ: Moral Theology for Clergy and Laity.* 3 vols. New York: Seabury, 1978–81.

———. *The Law of Christ: Moral Theology for Priests and Laity.* 3 vols. Westminster, MD: Newman, 1961–66.

———. *My Witness for the Church.* Translated by Leonard Swidler. New York: Paulist Press, 1992.

Harrington, Daniel J., and James F. Keenan. *Jesus and Virtue Ethics: Building Bridges between New Testament Studies and Moral Theology.* Lanham, MD: Sheed & Ward, 2002.

Hart, John. *What Are They Saying about Environmental Theology?* New York: Paulist Press, 2004.

Harvey, John F. "Homosexuality." In *New Catholic Encyclopedia,* 7:116–19. New York: McGraw-Hill, 1967.

———. *The Truth about Homosexuality.* San Francisco: Ignatius, 1996.

Hauerwas, Stanley. *Character and the Christian Life: A Study in Theological Ethics.* San Antonio, TX: Trinity University Press, 1975.

———. *The Hauerwas Reader.* Edited by John Berkman and Michael Cartwright. Durham, NC: Duke University Press, 2001.

———. *The Peaceable Kingdom: A Primer in Christian Ethics.* Notre Dame: University of Notre Dame Press, 1983.

———. *With the Grain of the Universe: The Church's Witness and Natural Theology, Being the Gifford Lectures Delivered at the University of St. Andrew's in 2001.* Grand Rapids: Brazos, 2001.

Hauerwas, Stanley, and Samuel Wells, eds. *The Blackwell Companion to Christian Ethics.* Malden, MA: Blackwell, 2004.

Hayes, Diana L. *Hagar's Daughters: Womanist Ways of Being in the World.* 1995 Madaleva Lecture in Spirituality. New York: Paulist Press, 1995.

———. *And Still We Rise: An Introduction to Black Liberation Theology.* New York: Paulist Press, 1996.

Hayes, Diana L., and Cyprian Davis, eds. *Taking Down Our Harps: Black Catholics in the United States.* Maryknoll, NY: Orbis Books, 1998.

Healy, Edwin F. *Medical Ethics.* Chicago: Loyola University Press, 1956.

Heck, Theodore. *The Curriculum of the Major Seminary in Relation to Contemporary Conditions.* Washington, DC: Catholic University of America Press, 1935.

Hehir, J. Bryan. "The Catholic Church and the Political Order." In *The Church's Public Role: Retrospect and Prospect,* ed. Dieter T. Hessel, 176–97. Grand Rapids: William B. Eerdmans, 1993.

———. "Catholic Teaching on War and Peace: The Decade 1979–1989." In *Moral Theology: Challenges for the Future; Essays in Honor of Richard A. McCormick,* ed. Charles E. Curran, 369–76. New York: Paulist Press, 1990.

———. "A Catholic Troeltsch? Curran on the Social Ministry of the Church." In *A Call to Fidelity: On the Moral Theology of Charles E. Curran,* ed. James J. Walter, Timothy E. O'Connell, and Thomas A. Shannon, 191–207. Washington, DC: Georgetown University Press, 2002.

Hennelly, Alfred, and John Langan, eds. *Human Rights in the Americas: The Struggle for Consensus.* Washington, DC: Georgetown University Press, 1982.

Heuser, Herman J. "Note." *American Ecclesiastical Review* 1 (1889): 70.

Heyer, Kristen E. *Prophetic and Public: The Social Witness of U.S. Catholicism.* Washington, DC: Georgetown University Press, 2006.

Hill, Brennan R. "Bernard Häring and the Second Vatican Council." *Horizons* 33 (2006): 78–100.

Hillquit, Morris, and John A. Ryan. *Socialism: Promise or Menace?* New York: Macmillan, 1914.

Himes, Kenneth R. "The Contribution of Theology to Catholic Moral Theology." In *Moral Theology: Challenges for the Future; Essays in Honor of Richard A. McCormick,* ed. Charles E. Curran, 48–73. New York: Paulist Press, 1990.

———."Eucharist and Justice: Assessing the Legacy of Virgil Michel." *Worship* 62 (1988): 201–24.

———. "Intervention, Just War, and U.S. National Security." *Theological Studies* 65 (2004): 141–57.

———, ed. *Modern Catholic Social Teaching: Commentaries and Interpretations.* Washington, DC: Georgetown University Press, 2004.

———. "The Morality of Humanitarian Intervention." *Theological Studies* 55 (1994): 82–105.

———. Review of *Reason Informed by Faith: Foundations of Catholic Morality,* by Richard M. Gula. *Journal of Religion* 71 (1991): 293–94.

———. "Social Sin and the Role of the Individual." *Annual of the Society of Christian Ethics* (1986): 183–218.

Himes, Kenneth R., and James A. Coriden. "The Indissolubility of Marriage: Reasons to Reconsider." *Theological Studies* 65 (2004): 453–99.

———. "Notes on Moral Theology: Pastoral Care of the Divorced and Remarried." *Theological Studies* 57 (1996): 97–123.

Himes, Michael J., and Kenneth R. Himes. *Fullness of Faith: The Public Significance of Theology.* New York: Paulist Press, 1993.

Hinze, Bradford E. *Practices of Dialogue in the Roman Catholic Church: Aims and Obstacles, Lessons and Laments.* New York: Continuum, 2006.

Hinze, Christine Firer. "Bridge Discourse on Wage Justice: Roman Catholic and Feminist Perspectives on the Family Living Wage." In *Feminist Ethics and the Catholic Moral Tradition.* Readings in Moral Theology No. 9, ed. Charles E. Curran, Margaret A. Farley, and Richard A. McCormick, 511–40. New York: Paulist Press, 1996.

———. "Catholic Social Teaching and Theological Ethics." In *"And God Saw That It Was Good": Catholic Theology and the Environment,* ed. Drew Christiansen and Walter Grazer, 165–82. Washington, DC: United States Catholic Conference, 1996.

———. *Comprehending Power in Christian Social Ethics.* Atlanta: Scholars Press, 1995.

———. "U.S. Catholic Social Thought, Gender, and Economic Livelihood." *Theological Studies* 66 (2005): 568–91.

Hitchcock, James. "The Fellowship of Catholic Scholars: Bowing Out of the New Class." In *Being Right: Conservative Catholics in America,* ed. Mary Jo Weaver and R. Scott Appleby, 186–210. Bloomington: University of Indiana Press, 1995.

Hittinger, Russell. *First Grace: Rediscovering Natural Law in a Post-Christian World.* Wilmington, DE: ISI Books, 2003.

———. "Natural Law as 'Law': Reflections on the Occasion of *Veritatis splendor.*" *American Journal of Jurisprudence* 39 (1994): 1–32.

———. "The Pope and the Theorists: The Oneness of Truth." *Crisis* 11 (December 1993): 31–36.

Hobgood, Mary E. *Catholic Social Teaching and Economic Theory: Paradigms in Conflict.* Philadelphia: Temple University Press, 1991.

———. *Dismantling Privilege: An Ethic of Accountability.* Cleveland: Pilgrim, 2002.

Hogan, John B. "Christian Faith and Modern Science." *American Catholic Quarterly Review* 22 (1897): 382–99.

———. *Clerical Studies.* Boston: Marlier, Callanan, 1898.

Hogan, Linda. *Confronting the Truth: Conscience and the Catholic Tradition.* New York: Paulist Press, 2000.

Hollenbach, David. "Christian Social Ethics after the Cold War." *Theological Studies* 53 (1992): 75–95.

———. *Claims in Conflict: Retrieving and Renewing the Catholic Human Rights Tradition.* New York: Paulist Press, 1979.

———. *The Common Good and Christian Ethics.* Cambridge: Cambridge University Press, 2002.

———. "Freedom and Truth: Religious Liberty as Immunity and Empowerment." In *John Courtney Murray and the Growth of Tradition,* ed. Leon J. Hooper and Todd David Whitmore, 129–48. Kansas City, MO: Sheed & Ward, 1996.

———. *The Global Face of Public Faith: Politics, Human Rights, and Christian Ethics.* Washington, DC: Georgetown University Press, 2003.

———. "The Growing End of an Argument." *America* 153 (November 30, 1985): 363–66.

———. *Justice, Peace, and Human Rights: American Catholic Social Ethics in a Pluralistic World.* New York: Crossroad, 1988.

———. *Nuclear Ethics: A Christian Moral Argument.* New York: Paulist Press, 1983.

———. "War and Peace in American Catholic Thought: A Heritage Abandoned." *Theological Studies* 48 (1987): 711–26.

Hooper, J. Leon, ed. *John Courtney Murray, Religious Liberty: Catholic Struggles with Pluralism.* Louisville, KY: Westminster/John Knox, 1993.

———. "The Theological Sources of John Courtney Murray's Ethics." In *John Courtney Murray and the Growth of Tradition,* ed. Leon J. Hooper and Todd David Whitmore, 106–25. Kansas City, MO: Sheed & Ward, 1996.

Hooper, J. Leon, and Todd David Whitmore, eds. *John Courtney Murray and the Growth of Tradition.* Kansas City, MO: Sheed & Ward, 1996.

Hoose, Bernard. *Proportionalism: The American Debate and Its European Roots.* Washington, DC: Georgetown University Press, 1987.

Hughes, Kathleen, and Mark R. Francis, eds. *Living No Longer for Ourselves: Liturgy and Justice in the Nineties.* Collegeville, MN: Liturgical Press, 1991.

Hunt, Mary E. "Lovingly Lesbian: Toward a Feminist Theology of Friendship." In *A Challenge to Love: Gay and Lesbian Catholics in the Church,* ed. Robert Nugent, 135–55. New York: Crossroad, 1983.

Hunt, Robert P., and Kenneth L. Grasso, eds. *John Courtney Murray and the American Civil Conversation.* Grand Rapids: William B. Eerdmans, 1992.

Hunthausen, Raymond G. "Archbishop Hunthausen Withdraws *Imprimatur.*" *Origins* 14 (1984): 15–16.

Husslein, Joseph C. *The Christian Social Manifesto: An Interpretive Study of the Encyclicals Rerum Novarum and Quadragesimo Anno of Pope Leo XIII and Pope Pius XI.* Milwaukee: Bruce, 1931.

Irwin, Kevin W., and Edmund D. Pellegrino, eds. *Preserving the Creation: Environmental Theology and Ethics.* Washington, DC: Georgetown University Press, 1994.

Isasi-Díaz, Ada Maria. *"Burlando al Opresor:* Mocking/Tricking the Oppressor; Dreams and Hopes of Hispanas/Latinas and *Mujeristas."* *Theological Studies* 65 (2004): 340–63.

———. *En la Lucha—In the Struggle: A Hispanic Women's Liberation Theology.* Minneapolis: Fortress, 2004.

———. *Mujerista Theology: A Theology for the Twenty-First Century.* Maryknoll, NY: Orbis Books, 1996.

Joblin, Joseph. "Le Saint-Siege face à la guerre: Continuité et renouvellement de son action pour la paix a l'époque contemporaine." *Gregorianum* 80 (1999): 333–52.

John XXIII. *Pacem in Terris.* In *Catholic Social Thought: The Documentary Heritage,* ed. David J. O'Brien and Thomas A. Shannon, 131–62. Maryknoll, NY: Orbis Books, 1992.

John Paul II. "Ad tuendam fidem." *Origins* 28 (1998): 116–19.

———. "Care for Patients in a Permanent Vegetative State." *Origins* 33 (2004): 737–40.

———. *Centesimus annus.* In *The Encyclicals of Pope John Paul II,* ed. J. Michael Miller, 511–61. Huntington, IN: Our Sunday Visitor, 2001.

———. *Dominum et vivificantem.* In *The Encyclicals of Pope John Paul II,* ed. J. Michael Miller, 243–302. Huntington, IN: Our Sunday Visitor, 2001.

———. *Evangelium vitae.* In *The Encyclicals of Pope John Paul II,* ed. J. Michael Miller, 681–762. Huntington, IN: Our Sunday Visitor, 2001.

———. *Fides et ratio.* In *The Encyclicals of Pope John Paul II,* ed. J. Michael Miller, 850–913. Huntington, IN: Our Sunday Visitor, 2001.

———. "Incarnationis mysterium." *Origins* 28 (1998): 450–51.

———. "Jubilee Characteristic: The Purification of Memory." *Origins* 29 (2000): 649–50.

———. *Laborem exercens.* In *The Encyclicals of Pope John Paul II,* ed. J. Michael Miller, 153–93. Huntington, IN: Our Sunday Visitor, 2001.

———. *Redemptor hominis.* In *The Encyclicals of Pope John Paul II,* ed. J. Michael Miller, 48–89. Huntington, IN: Our Sunday Visitor, 2001.

———. *The Role of the Christian Family in the Modern World* (*Familiaris Consortio*). Boston: St. Paul, 1981.

———. *Sollicitudo rei socialis.* In *The Encyclicals of Pope John Paul II,* ed. J. Michael Miller, 379–420. Huntington, IN: Our Sunday Visitor, 2001.

———. "Tertio millennio adveniente." *Origins* 24 (1994): 401–16.

———. *The Theology of the Body: Human Love in the Divine Plan.* Boston: Pauline, 1997.

———. *Ut unum sint.* In *The Encyclicals of Pope John Paul II,* ed. J. Michael Miller, 782–831. Huntington, IN: Our Sunday Visitor, 2001.

———. *Veritatis splendor.* In *The Encyclicals of Pope John Paul II,* ed. J. Michael Miller, 583–661. Huntington, IN: Our Sunday Visitor, 2001.

Johnson, Elizabeth A. *Women, Earth, and Creator Spirit.* 1993 Madeleva Lecture in Spirituality. New York: Paulist Press, 1993.

Johnson, Mark. "Reflections on Some Recent Catholic Claims for Delayed Hominization." *Theological Studies* 56 (1995): 743–63.

Johnson, Mark, and Thomas A. Shannon. *"Quaestio Disputata:* Delayed Hominization." *Theological Studies* 58 (1997): 708–17.

Jonsen, Albert R., and Stephen Toulmin. *The Abuse of Casuistry: A History of Moral Reasoning.* Berkeley and Los Angeles: University of California Press, 1988.

Jordan, Mark D. *The Ethics of Sex.* Malden, MA: Blackwell, 2002.

———. *The Invention of Sodomy in Christian Theology.* Chicago: University of Chicago Press, 1997.

———. *The Silence of Sodom: Homosexuality in Modern Catholicism.* Chicago: University of Chicago Press, 2000.

Jung, Patricia Beattie, and Joseph Andrew Coray, eds. *Sexual Diversity and Catholicism: Toward the Development of Moral Theology.* Collegeville, MN: Liturgical Press, 2001.

Jung, Patricia Beattie, and Thomas A. Shannon, eds. *Abortion and Catholics: The American Debate.* New York: Crossroad, 1988.

Jung, Patricia Beattie, and Ralph F. Smith. *Heterosexism: An Ethical Challenge.* Albany: State University of New York Press, 1993.

Kaczor, Christopher. *Proportionalism and the Natural Law Tradition.* Washington, DC: Catholic University of America Press, 2002.

Kaiser, Robert Blair. *The Politics of Sex and Religion: A Case History in the Development of Doctrine, 1962–1984.* Kansas City, MO: Leaven, 1985.

Kalbian, Aline H. "The Catholic Church's Public Confession: Theological and Ethical Implications." *Annual of the Society of Christian Ethics* 21 (2001): 175–89.

———. *Sexing the Church: Gender, Power, and Ethics in Contemporary Catholicism.* Bloomington: Indiana University Press, 2005.

———. "Where Have All the Proportionalists Gone?" *Journal of Religious Ethics* 30 (2002): 3–22.

Kass, Leon R. *Human Cloning and Human Dignity: The Report of the President's Council on Bioethics.* New York: Public Affairs, 2002.

Kauffman, Christopher. *Tradition and Transformation in Catholic Culture: The Priests of St. Sulpice in the United States from 1791 to the Present.* New York: Macmillan, 1988.

Kaveny, M. Cathleen. "Jurisprudence and Genetics." *Theological Studies* 60 (1999): 135–47.

Keane, Philip S. *Christian Ethics and the Imagination.* New York: Paulist Press, 1984.

———. *Health Care Reform: A Catholic View.* New York: Paulist Press, 1993.

———. *Sexual Morality: A Catholic Perspective.* New York: Paulist Press, 1977.

Keating, James F., ed. *Moral Theology: New Directions and Fundamental Issues; Festschrift for James P. Hanigan.* New York: Paulist Press, 2004.

———, ed. *Spirituality and Moral Theology: Essays from a Pastoral Perspective.* New York: Paulist Press, 2000.

Keenan, James F., ed. *Catholic Ethicists on HIV/AIDS Prevention.* New York: Continuum, 2000.

———. *Goodness and Rightness in Thomas Aquinas's Summa theologiae.* Washington, DC: Georgetown University Press, 1992.

———. "The Moral Agent: Actions and Normative Decision Making." In *A Call to Fidelity: On the Moral Theology of Charles E. Curran,* ed. James J. Walter, Timothy E. O'Connell, and Thomas A. Shannon, 37–53. Washington, DC: Georgetown University Press, 2002.

———. "The Open Debate: Moral Theology and the Lives of Gay and Lesbian Catholics." *Theological Studies* 64 (2003): 127–50.

————. "Proposing Cardinal Virtues." *Theological Studies* 56 (1995): 709–29.

————. "What Does Virtue Ethics Bring to Genetics?" In *Genetics, Theology, and Ethics: An Interdisciplinary Conversation,* ed. Lisa Sowle Cahill, 97–113. New York: Crossroad, 2005.

Keenan, James F., and Thomas A. Shannon, eds. *The Context of Casuistry.* Washington, DC: Georgetown University Press, 1995.

Kelly, David F. *Contemporary Catholic Health Care Ethics.* Washington, DC: Georgetown University Press, 2004.

————. *Critical Care Ethics: Treatment Decisions in American Hospitals.* Kansas City, MO: Sheed & Ward, 1991.

————. *The Emergence of Roman Catholic Medical Ethics in North America: An Historical-Methodological-Biographical Study.* New York: Edwin Mellen, 1979.

————. *Medical Care at the End of Life: A Catholic Perspective.* Washington, DC: Georgetown University Press, 2006.

Kelly, Gerald A. "Current Theology: Notes on Moral Theology." *Theological Studies* 8 (1947): 106–10.

————. *The Good Confessor.* New York: Sentinel, 1951.

————. *Medico-Moral Problems.* St. Louis, MO: Catholic Hospital Association, 1958.

————. *Modern Youth and Chastity.* St. Louis, MO: Queen's Work, 1941.

————. "The Morality of Artificial Insemination." *American Ecclesiastical Review* 101 (1939): 109–18.

Kelly, Kevin. "Serving the Truth." In *Dissent in the Church.* Readings in Moral Theology No. 6, ed. Charles E. Curran and John A. McCormick, 478–83. New York: Paulist Press, 1988.

Kelsey, David. *The Use of Scripture in Recent Theology.* Philadelphia: Fortress, 1975.

Kennedy, Robert G., et al., eds. *Religion and Public Life: The Legacy of Monsignor John A. Ryan.* Lanham, MD: University Press of America, 2001.

Kenny, John P. *Principles of Medical Ethics.* Westminster, MD: Newman, 1952.

————. *Principles of Medical Ethics.* 2d ed. Westminster, MD: Newman, 1962.

Kenrick, Francis Patrick. *Theologia moralis.* 3 vols. Philadelphia: Eugene Cummiskey, 1841–43.

Komonchak, Joseph A. "The Church in Crisis: Pope Benedict's Theological Vision." *Commonweal* 132, no. 11 (June 3, 2005): 11–14.

————. "Ordinary Papal Magisterium and Religious Assent." In *Contraception: Authority and Dissent,* ed. Charles E. Curran, 102–14. New York: Herder and Herder, 1969.

Konings, Anthony. *Theologiae moralis Sancti Alphonsi Compendium.* Cincinnati: Benziger, 1888.

Kosnik, Anthony, William Carroll, Agnes Cunningham, Ronald Modras, and James Schulte. *Human Sexuality: New Directions in American Catholic Thought.* New York: Paulist Press, 1977.

Kuefler, Matthew, ed. *The Boswell Thesis: Essays on Christianity, Social Tolerance, and Homosexuality.* Chicago: University of Chicago Press, 2006.

Küng, Hans. *Global Responsibility: In Search of a New World Ethic.* New York: Crossroad, 1991.

Küng, Hans, and Karl Josef Kuschel, eds. *Global Ethic: The Declaration of the Parliament of the World's Religions*. New York: Continuum, 1993

Küng, Hans, and Leonard Swidler, eds. *The Church in Anguish: Has the Vatican Betrayed Vatican II?* San Francisco: Harper & Row, 1987.

La Chance, Albert J., and John E. Carroll, eds. *Embracing Earth: Catholic Approaches to Ecology*. Maryknoll, NY: Orbis Books, 1994.

Lamb, Matthew. *Solidarity with Victims: Toward a Theology of Social Transformation*. New York: Crossroad, 1982.

Lammers, Stephen E., and Allen Verhey. *On Moral Medicine: Theological Perspectives in Medical Ethics*. 2d ed. Grand Rapids: William B. Eerdmans, 1998.

Langan, John. "Direct and Indirect—Some Recent Exchanges between Paul Ramsey and Richard A. McCormick." *Religious Studies Review* 5 (1979): 95–101.

———. "Pastoral on War and Peace: Reactions and New Directions." *Theological Studies* 46 (1985): 80–101.

———. "To Intervene or Not to Intervene." *Christian Century* 113 (January 24, 1996): 81–85.

Langlois, John. "Callan, Charles Jerome (1877–1962)." In *The Encyclopedia of American Catholic History*, ed. Michael Glazier and Thomas J. Shelley, 194. Collegeville, MN: Liturgical Press, 1997.

———. "McHugh, John Ambrose (1880–1950)." In *The Encyclopedia of American Catholic History*, ed. Michael Glazier and Thomas J. Shelley, 887. Collegeville, MN: Liturgical Press, 1997.

Laubacher, J. A. "Tanquery, Adophe Alfred." In *New Catholic Encyclopedia*, 13:934. New York: McGraw-Hill, 1967.

Lauritzen, Paul. "Neither Person nor Property: Embryo Research and the Status of the Early Embryo." *America* 184 (March 26, 2001): 20–23.

———. *Pursuing Parenthood: Ethical Issues in Assisted Reproduction*. Bloomington: University of Indiana Press, 1993.

Lawler, Michael G. *Family: American and Christian*. Chicago: Loyola University Press, 1998.

———. *Marriage and the Catholic Church: Disputed Questions*. Collegeville, MN: Liturgical Press, 2002.

Lawler, Michael G., and William P. Roberts, eds. *Christian Marriage and Family: Contemporary, Theological, and Pastoral Perspectives*. Collegeville, MN: Liturgical Press, 1996.

Lawler, Ronald, Joseph Boyle, and William E. May. *Catholic Sexual Ethics: A Summary, Explanation, and Defense*. Huntington, IN: Our Sunday Visitor, 1985.

Lay Commission on Catholic Social Teaching and the U.S. Economy. *Toward the Future: Catholic Social Teaching and the U.S. Economy; A Lay Letter*. New York: American Catholic Committee, 1994.

Lécrivain, Ph. "Saint Alphonse aux risques du rigorisme et du liguorisme." *Studia Moralia* 25 (1987): 376–93.

Lehmann, Paul. *Ethics in a Christian Context*. New York: Harper & Row, 1963.

Leo XIII. *Longinqua oceani*. In *The Papal Encyclicals, 1879–1903*, ed. Claudia Carlen, 363–70. Wilmington, NC: McGrath, 1981.

Levada, William. "Dissent and the Catholic Religion Teacher." In *Dissent in the Church.* Readings in Moral Theology No. 6, ed. Charles E. Curran and John A. McCormick, 133–51. New York: Paulist Press, 1988.

———. "Infallible Church Magisterium and the Natural Moral Law." S.T.D. diss., Pontifical Gregorian University, 1970.

Ligorio, Alphonsus de. *Dissertatio scholastico-moralis pro usu moderato opinionis probabilis.* Neapoli, 1749.

———. *Theologia moralis.* 9th ed. Edited by Leonardus Gaudé. 4 vols. Rome: Typographia Vaticana, 1905.

Lonergan, Anne, and Caroline Richards, eds. *Thomas Berry and the New Cosmology.* Mystic, CT: Twenty-Third Publications, 1987.

Lonergan, Bernard. "The Transition from a Classicist World-View to Historical Mindedness." In *Law for Liberty: The Role of Law in the Church Today,* ed. James E. Biechler, 126–33. Baltimore: Helicon, 1967.

Long, Edward LeRoy, Jr. *Academic Bonding and Social Concern: The Society of Christian Ethics, 1959–1983.* Washington, DC: Georgetown University Press, 1985.

Love, Thomas T. *John Courtney Murray: Contemporary Church-State Theory.* Garden City, NY: Doubleday, 1965.

MacIntyre, Alasdair. *After Virtue: A Study in Moral Theory.* Notre Dame: University of Notre Dame Press, 1981.

Mackin, Theodore. *Divorce and Remarriage.* New York: Paulist Press, 1984.

———. *The Marital Sacrament.* New York: Paulist Press, 1989.

———. *What Is Marriage? Marriage in the Catholic Church.* New York: Paulist Press, 1982.

Maguire, Daniel C. "Abortion: A Question of Catholic Honesty." *Christian Century* 100 (1983): 803–7.

———. *A Case for Affirmative Action.* Dubuque, IA: Shepherd, 1992.

———. *Death by Choice.* Garden City, NY: Doubleday, 1974.

———. *Death by Choice.* 2d ed. Garden City, NY: Image, 1984.

———. "Moral Absolutes and the Magisterium." In *Absolutes in Moral Theology?* ed. Charles E. Curran, 57–107. Washington, DC: Corpus, 1968.

———. *The Moral Choice.* Garden City, NY: Doubleday, 1978.

———. *The Moral Core of Judaism and Christianity: Reclaiming the Revolution.* Minneapolis: Fortress, 1993.

———. *A Moral Creed for All Christians.* Minneapolis: Fortress, 2005.

———. "The Morality of Homosexual Marriage." In *A Challenge to Love: Gay and Lesbian Catholics in the Church,* ed. Robert Nugent, 118–34. New York: Crossroad, 1983.

———. *The Moral Revolution: A Christian Humanist Vision.* New York: Harper & Row, 1986.

———. *A New American Justice: Ending the White Male Monopoly.* Garden City, NY: Doubleday, 1980.

———, ed. *Sacred Rights: The Case for Contraception and Abortion in World Religions.* New York: Oxford University Press, 2003.

Mahoney, John. *The Making of Moral Theology: A Study of the Roman Catholic Tradition.* Oxford: Oxford University Press, 1987.

Mahony, Roger. "The Magisterium and Theological Dissent." In *Dissent in the Church. Readings in Moral Theology No. 6*, ed. Charles E. Curran and John A. McCormick, 164–75. New York: Paulist Press, 1988.

Massaro, Thomas J. *Catholic Social Teaching and United States Welfare Reform.* Collegeville, MN: Liturgical Press, 1998.

Massaro, Thomas J., and Thomas A. Shannon, eds. *American Catholic Social Teaching.* Collegeville, MN: Liturgical Press, 2002.

———. *Catholic Perspectives on Peace and War.* Lanham, MD: Rowman & Littlefield, 2003.

Massingale, Bryan. "The African-American Experience and U.S. Roman Catholic Ethics: 'Strangers and Aliens No Longer?'" In *Black and Catholic: The Challenge and Gift of Black Folks*, ed. Jaime T. Phelps, 79–101. Milwaukee: Marquette University Press, 1997.

———. "James Cone and Recent Catholic Episcopal Teaching on Racism." *Theological Studies* 61 (2000): 700–730.

Mattison, William C., III. "The Changing Face of Natural Law: The Necessity of Belief for Natural Law Norm Specification." *Journal of the Society of Christian Ethics* 27, no. 1 (2007): 251–77.

———, ed. *New Wine, New Wineskins: A Next Generation Reflects on Key Issues in Catholic Moral Theology.* Lanham, MD: Sheed & Ward, 2005.

May, William E. *Catholic Bioethics and the Gift of Life.* Huntington, IN: Our Sunday Visitor, 2000.

———. "Catholic Moral Teachings and the Limits of Dissent." In *Vatican Authority and American Catholic Dissent: The Curran Case and Its Consequences*, ed. William W. May, 87–102. New York: Crossroad, 1987.

———, coordinator of drafting committee. "Feeding and Hydrating the Permanently Unconscious and Other Vulnerable Persons." *Issues in Law and Medicine* 3 (winter 1987): 203–17.

———. *Human Existence, Medicine, and Ethics: Reflections on Human Life.* Chicago: Franciscan Herald, 1977.

———. *An Introduction to Moral Theology.* Huntington, IN: Our Sunday Visitor, 1991.

———. "The Moral Status of the Embryo." *Linacre Quarterly* 59 (1992): 76–83.

———. "Sterilization: Catholic Teaching and Practice." *Homiletic and Pastoral Review* 77 (August–September 1977): 9–22.

May, William E., and Richard Westley. *Catholic Perspectives: The Right to Die.* Chicago: Thomas More, 1980.

McAvoy, Thomas E. *Americanist Heresy in Roman Catholicism.* Notre Dame: University of Notre Dame Press, 1963.

McBrien, Richard P. *Catholicism.* Rev. ed. San Francisco: HarperCollins, 1994.

McCarraher, Eugene B. "The Church Irrelevant: Paul Hanly Furfey and the Fortunes of American Catholic Radicalism." *Religion in American Culture* 7, no. 2 (summer 1997): 163–94.

McCarthy, David Matzko. "Procreation, the Development of Peoples, and the Final Destiny of Humanity." *Communio* 26 (1999): 698–721.

———. *Sex and Love in the Home: A Theology of the Household.* London: SCM, 2001.

———. "Shifting Setting from Subculture to Pluralism: Catholic Moral Theology in an Evangelical Key." *Communio* 31 (2004): 85–110.

McCartney, James J. "Issues in Death and Dying (Including Newborns)." In *Moral Theology: Challenges for the Future; Essays in Honor of Richard A. McCormick,* ed. Charles E. Curran, 264–84. New York: Paulist Press, 1990.

McCool, Gerald A. *Catholic Theology in the Nineteenth Century: The Quest for a Unitary Method.* New York: Seabury, 1977.

McCormick, Richard A. "A Commentary on the Commentaries." In *Doing Evil to Achieve Good: Moral Choice in Conflict Situations,* ed. Richard A. McCormick and Paul Ramsey, 193–267. Chicago: Loyola University Press, 1978.

———. *Corrective Vision: Explorations in Moral Theology.* Kansas City, MO: Sheed & Ward, 1994.

———. *The Critical Calling: Reflections on Moral Dilemmas since Vatican II.* Washington, DC: Georgetown University Press, 1989.

———. *Health and Medicine in the Catholic Tradition.* New York: Crossroad, 1984.

———. *How Brave a New World? Dilemmas in Bioethics.* Garden City, NY: Doubleday, 1981.

———. "The New Medicine and Morality." *Theology Digest* 21 (1973): 308–21.

———. *Notes on Moral Theology, 1965–1980.* Washington, DC: University Press of America, 1981.

———. *Notes on Moral Theology, 1981–1984.* Washington, DC: University Press of America, 1984.

———. "The Search for Truth in the Catholic Context." In *Dissent in the Church.* Readings in Moral Theology No. 6, ed. Charles E. Curran and John A. McCormick, 421–34. New York: Paulist Press, 1988.

———. "To Save or Let Die." *Journal of the American Medical Association* 229 (1974): 172–76.

McCormick, Richard A., and John J. Paris. "Living Will Legislation Reconsidered." *America* 145 (August 29–September 5, 1981): 86–89.

———. "Saving Defective Infants: Options for Life or Death." *America* 148 (April 23, 1981): 313–17.

McCormick, Richard A., and Paul Ramsey, eds. *Doing Evil to Achieve Good: Moral Choice in Conflict Situations,* Chicago: Loyola University Press, 1978.

McDonagh, Enda. "Liturgy and Christian Life." In *New Dictionary of Sacramental Worship,* ed. Peter E. Fink, 742–53. Collegeville, MN: Liturgical Press, 1990.

McDonough, Peter. *Men Astutely Trained: A History of the Jesuits in the American Century.* New York: Free Press, 1992.

McDonough, William. "'New Terrain' and a 'Stumbling Stone' in Redemptorist Contributions to *Gaudium et Spes*: On Relating and Juxtaposing Truth's Formulations and Its Experience." *Studia Moralia* 35 (1997): 9–48.

McFadden, Charles J. *The Dignity of Life: Moral Values in a Changing Society.* Huntington, IN: Our Sunday Visitor, 1976.

———. *Medical Ethics.* 2d ed. Philadelphia: F. A. Davis, 1949.

———. *Medical Ethics.* 4th ed. Philadelphia: F. A. Davis, 1956.

———. *Medical Ethics for Nurses.* Philadelphia: F. A. Davis, 1946.

McGinnis, James, and Kathleen McGinnis. *Parenting for Peace and Justice.* Maryknoll, NY: Orbis Books, 1981.

———. *Parenting for Peace and Justice: Ten Years Later.* Maryknoll, NY: Orbis Books, 1990.

McGreevy, John T. *Catholicism and American Freedom: A History.* New York: W. W. Norton, 2003.

McHugh, John A., and Charles J. Callan, *Moral Theology: A Complete Course Based on St. Thomas Aquinas and the Best Modern Authorities.* 2 vols. New York: Joseph F. Wagner, 1929.

———. *Moral Theology: A Complete Course Based on St. Thomas Aquinas and the Best Modern Authorities.* 2nd ed. Edited by Edward P. Farrell. 2 vols. New York: Joseph F. Wagner, 1960.

McInerny, Ralph. *Ethica Thomistica: The Moral Philosophy of Thomas Aquinas.* Rev. ed. Washington, DC: Catholic University of America Press, 1997.

McKeever, Paul E. "Seventy-Five Years of Moral Theology in America." *American Ecclesiastical Review* 152 (1965): 19–20.

McKeown, Elizabeth. "After the Fall: Roman Catholic Modernism at the American Academy of Religion." *U.S. Catholic Historian* 20 (summer 2002): 111–31.

McNeal, Patricia. *Harder than War: Catholic Peacemaking in Twentieth-Century America.* New Brunswick, NJ: Rutgers University Press, 1992.

McNeill, John J. "The Christian Male Homosexual." *Homiletic and Pastoral Review* 70 (1970): 667–77, 747–58, 828–36.

———. *The Church and the Homosexual.* Kansas City, MO: Sheed & Ward, 1976.

———. *Feet Planted Firmly in Mid-Air: My Spiritual Journey.* Louisville, KY: Westminster/John Knox, 1998.

Menius, Margaret Kelly. "John Cuthbert Ford, S.J.: His Contribution to Twentieth-Century Catholic Moral Theology on the Issue of Contraception." Ph.D. diss., St. Louis University, 1998.

Messori, Vittorio. "Colloquio con il cardinale Josef Ratzinger, ecco perché la fede é in crisi." *Jesus* (November 1984): 67–81.

Mich, Marvin L. Krier. *Catholic Social Teaching and Movements.* Mystic, CT: Twenty-Third, 1998.

Michel, Virgil. *Christian Social Reconstruction.* Milwaukee: Bruce, 1937.

———. *The Social Question: Essays on Capitalism and Christianity.* Edited by Robert L. Spaeth. Collegeville, MN: St. John's University Press, 1987.

Milhaven, John Giles. *Good Anger.* Kansas City, MO: Sheed & Ward, 1989.

———. *Toward a New Catholic Morality.* Garden City, NY: Doubleday, 1970.

Miller, J. Michael, ed. *The Encyclicals of Pope John Paul II.* Huntington, IN: Our Sunday Visitor, 2001.

Mize, Sandra Yocum. *Joining the Revolution in Theology: The College Theology Society.* New York: Rowman & Littlefield, 2007.

———. "On Writing a History of the College Theology Society." *Horizons* 31 (2004): 94–104.

Molloy, Edward A. *Homosexuality and the Christian Way of Life.* Lanham, MD: University Press of America, 1981.

————. "Point/Counterpoint." In *A Challenge to Love: Gay and Lesbian Catholics in the Church,* ed. Robert Nugent, 107–17. New York: Crossroad, 1983.

Moran, Terrence J. "Connell, Francis (1888–1967)." In *The Encyclopedia of American Catholic History,* ed. Michael Glazier and Thomas J. Shelley, 371–72. Collegeville, MN: Liturgical Press, 1997.

Mouw, Richard J. *The God Who Commands: A Study in Divine Command Ethics.* Notre Dame: University of Notre Dame Press, 1990.

Murphy, Charles M. *At Home on Earth: Foundations for a Catholic Ethic of the Environment.* New York: Crossroad, 1989.

Murray, John Courtney. "The Church and Totalitarian Democracy." *Theological Studies* 13 (1952): 525–63.

————. "Contemporary Orientation of Catholic Thought on Church and State in the Light of History." *Theological Studies* 10 (1949): 177–234.

————. "Dr. Morrison and the First Amendment." *America* 78 (1948): 683–86.

————. "Intercreedal Co-operation: Its Theory and Its Organization." *Theological Studies* 4 (1943): 257–68.

————. "Leo XIII: Separation of Church and State." *Theological Studies* 14 (1953): 145–214.

————. "Leo XIII: Two Concepts of Government." *Theological Studies* 14 (1953): 551–67.

————. "Leo XIII: Two Concepts of Government II: Government and the Order of Culture." *Theological Studies* 15 (1954): 1–33.

————. "Leo XIII and Pius XII: Government and the Order of Religion." In *John Courtney Murray, Religious Liberty: Catholic Struggles with Pluralism,* ed. Leon J. Hooper, 49–125. Louisville, KY: Westminster/John Knox, 1993.

————. "Leo XIII on Church and State: The General Structure of the Controversy." *Theological Studies* 14 (1953): 1–30.

————. "Letter to the Editor." *Theological Studies* 4 (1943): 472–74.

————. *The Problem of Religious Freedom.* Westminster, MD: Newman, 1965.

————. "The Problem of State Religion." *Theological Studies* 12 (1951): 155–78.

————. "Vers une intelligence du développement de la doctrine de l'Église sur la liberté religieuse." In *Vatican II: La liberté religieuse, declaration 'Dignitatis humanae personae,'* ed. J. Hamer and Y. Congar, 111–47. Paris: Éditions du Cerf, 1967.

————. *We Hold These Truths: Catholic Reflections on the American Proposition.* New York: Sheed & Ward, 1960.

National Conference of Catholic Bishops. *Brothers and Sisters to Us: U.S. Bishops' Pastoral Letter on Racism in Our Day.* Washington, DC: United States Catholic Conference, 1979.

Neuhaus, Richard John. *The Catholic Moment: The Paradox of the Church in the Postmodern World.* San Francisco: Harper & Row, 1987.

————. *The Naked Public Square: Religion and Democracy in America.* Grand Rapids: William B. Eerdmans, 1984.

Newman, John Henry. *On Consulting the Faithful in Matters of Doctrine.* Edited by John Coulson. London: Collins Liturgical Press, 1986.

Nilson, Jon. "Confessions of a White Racist Catholic Theologian." *Proceedings of the Catholic Theological Society of America* 58 (2003): 64–82.

Nolan, Hugh J. *The Most Reverend Francis Patrick Kenrick, Third Bishop of Philadelphia.* Washington, DC: Catholic University of America Press, 1948.

Noldin, H. *Summa theologiae moralis: Complementum de Castitate.* 36th ed. Edited by Godefridus Heinzel. Innsbruck: Rauch, 1958.

Noonan, John T., Jr. "An Almost Absolute Value in History." In *The Morality of Abortion: Legal and Historical Perspectives,* ed. John T. Noonan Jr., 1–59. Cambridge, MA: Harvard University Press, 1970.

———. "The Amendment of Papal Teaching by Theologians." In *Contraception: Authority and Dissent,* ed. Charles E. Curran, 41–75. New York: Herder and Herder, 1969.

———. *A Church That Can and Cannot Change: The Development of Catholic Moral Teaching.* Notre Dame: University of Notre Dame Press, 2005.

———. *Contraception: A History of Its Treatment by the Catholic Theologians and Canonists.* Cambridge, MA: Belknap Press of Harvard University Press, 1965.

———. "Development in Moral Doctrine." *Theological Studies* 54 (1993): 662–77.

———. "Indissolubility of Marriage and Natural Law." *American Journal of Jurisprudence* 14 (1969): 79–88.

———. "Novel 22." In *The Bond of Marriage,* ed. William W. Bassett, 41–90. Notre Dame: University of Notre Dame Press, 1968.

———. *Power to Dissolve: Lawyers and Marriages in the Courts of the Roman Curia.* Cambridge, MA: Belknap Press of Harvard University Press, 1972.

———. *A Private Choice: Abortion in America in the Seventies.* New York: Free Press, 1979.

———. *The Scholastic Analysis of Usury.* Cambridge, MA: Harvard University Press, 1957.

Nothwehr, Dawn M. ed. *Franciscan Theology of the Environment: An Introductory Reader.* Quincy, IL: Franciscan, 2002.

Novak, Michael. "An Argument That the War against Iraq Is Just." *Origins* 32 (2003): 593–98.

———. *The Catholic Ethic and the Spirit of Capitalism.* New York: Free Press, 1993.

———. "The Development of Nations." In *Aspiring to Freedom: Commentaries on John Paul II's Encyclical, the Social Concerns of the Church,* ed. Kenneth A. Myers, 67–109. Grand Rapids: William B. Eerdmans, 1988.

———. "Dissent in the Church." In *Dissent in the Church.* Readings in Moral Theology No. 6, ed. Charles E. Curran and John A. McCormick, 112–26. New York: Paulist Press, 1988.

———. "Economic Rights: The Servile State." *Catholicism in Crisis* 3 (October 1985): 8–15.

———. *Freedom with Justice, Catholic Social Thought, and Liberal Institutions.* San Francisco: Harper & Row, 1984.

———. "Human Rights and Whited Sepulchres." In *Human Rights and U.S. Human Rights Policy,* ed. Howard J. Wiarda, 74–80. Washington, DC: American Enterprise Institute, 1982.

———, ed. *Liberation Theology and the Liberal Society.* Washington, DC: American Enterprise Institute, 1987.

———. *Moral Clarity in the Nuclear Age.* Nashville, TN: T. Nelson, 1983.

———. "Moral Clarity in the Nuclear Age: A Letter from Catholic Clergy and Laity." *Catholicism in Crisis* 1 (March 1983): 3–23.

———. "The Pope, Liberty, Capitalism." *National Review* 43, no. 4 (1991) (special supplement): 11–12.

———. "The Rights and Wrongs of 'Economic Rights': A Debate Continued." *This World* (spring 1987): 43–52.

———. *The Spirit of Democratic Capitalism.* New York: Simon & Schuster, 1982.

———. "Tested by Our Own Ideals." In *John Paul II and Moral Theology.* Readings in Moral Theology No. 10, ed. Charles E. Curran and Richard A. McCormick, 331–33. New York: Paulist Press, 1998.

———. *Will It Liberate? Questions about Liberation Theology.* New York: Paulist Press, 1986.

Nuesse, C. Joseph. *The Catholic University of America: A Centennial History.* Washington, DC: Catholic University of America Press, 1990.

———. "Thomas Joseph Bouquillon (1840–1902): Moral Theologian and Precursor of the Social Sciences in the Catholic University of America." *Catholic Historical Review* 72 (1986): 601–19.

Nugent, Robert, ed. *A Challenge to Love: Gay and Lesbian Catholics in the Church.* New York: Crossroad, 1983.

———. "Sexual Orientation and Vatican Thinking." In *The Vatican and Homosexuality,* ed. Jeannine Gramick and Pat Furey, 48–58. New York: Crossroad, 1988.

O'Brien, David J., and Thomas A. Shannon, eds. *Catholic Social Thought: The Documentary Heritage.* Maryknoll, NY: Orbis Books, 1992.

O'Brien, William V., and John Langan, eds. *The Nuclear Dilemma and the Just War Tradition.* Lexington, MA: Lexington Books, 1986.

O'Connell, Timothy E. "Changing Roman Catholic Moral Theology: A Study in Josef Fuchs." Ph.D. diss., Fordham University, 1974.

———. *Making Disciples: A Handbook of Christian Moral Formation.* New York: Crossroad, 1998.

———. *Principles for a Catholic Morality.* Rev. ed. San Francisco: Harper & Row, 1990.

O'Dea, Thomas F. *American Catholic Dilemma: An Inquiry into the Intellectual Life.* New York: Sheed & Ward, 1958.

O'Donnell, Thomas J. *Medicine and Christian Morality.* New York: Alba House, 1976.

———. *Morals in Medicine.* Westminster, MD: Newman, 1956.

———. *Morals in Medicine.* 2d ed. Westminster, MD: Newman, 1959.

Odozor, Paulinus Ikechukwu. *Richard A. McCormick and the Renewal of Moral Theology.* Notre Dame: University of Notre Dame Press, 1995.

Ogletree, Thomas. *The Use of the Bible in Christian Ethics.* Philadelphia: Fortress, 1983.

O'Keefe, Mark. *Becoming Good, Becoming Holy: On the Relationship of Christian Ethics and Spirituality.* New York: Paulist Press, 1995.

———. *What Are They Saying about Social Sin?* New York: Paulist Press, 1990.

O'Neill, William R. "Babel's Children: Reconstructing the Common Good." *Annual of the Society of Christian Ethics* 18 (1998): 161–76.

O'Rourke, Kevin D. "The Catholic Tradition on Forgoing Life Support." *National Catholic Bioethics Quarterly* 5 (2005): 537–53.

O'Rourke, Kevin D., and Philip Boyle, eds. *Medical Ethics: Sources of Catholic Teaching.* St. Louis, MO: Catholic Health Association of the United States, 1989.

Örsy, Ladislas. *The Church Learning and Teaching: Magisterium, Assent, Dissent, Academic Freedom.* Collegeville, MN: Liturgical Press, 1991.

Outka, Gene H., and Paul Ramsey, eds. *Norm and Context in Christian Ethics.* New York: Charles Scribner's Sons, 1968.

Paris, John J., James F. Keenan, and Kenneth R. Himes. "*Quaestio Disputata*: Did John Paul II's Allocution on Life-Sustaining Treatments Revise Tradition? A Response to Thomas A. Shannon and James J. Walter." *Theological Studies* 67 (2006): 163–68.

Patrick, Anne. *Liberating Conscience: Feminist Explorations in Catholic Moral Theology.* New York: Continuum, 1996.

———. "Women and Religion: A Survey of Significant Literature, 1965–1974." *Theological Studies* 36 (1975): 737–65.

Paul VI. "Address to the Second General Conference of Latin American Bishops, Medellín, Columbia, August 24, 1968." *Acta Apostolicae Sedis* 60 (1968): 639–49.

———. *Humanae vitae.* In *The Papal Encyclicals, 1958–1981,* ed. Claudia Carlen, 223–36. Wilmington, NC: McGrath, 1981.

Pellegrino, Edmund D. "From Medical Ethics to a Moral Philosophy of the Professions." In *The Story of Bioethics: From Seminal Works to Contemporary Explorations,* ed. Jennifer K. Walter and Eran P. Klein, 3–15. Washington, DC: Georgetown University Press, 2003.

Pellegrino, Edmund D., and Alan I. Faden, eds. *Jewish and Catholic Bioethics: An Ecumenical Dialogue.* Washington, DC: Georgetown University Press, 1999.

Pellegrino, Edmund D., and David C. Thomasma. *Christian Virtues in Medical Practice.* Washington, DC: Georgetown University Press, 1996.

———. *The Virtues in Medical Practice.* New York: Oxford University Press, 1993.

Pelotte, Donald E. *John Courtney Murray: Theologian in Conflict.* New York: Paulist Press, 1976.

Pemberton, Prentiss L., and Daniel Rush Finn. *Toward a Christian Economic Ethic: Stewardship and Social Power.* Minneapolis: Winston, 1986.

Pfeil, Margaret. "Doctrinal Implications of Magisterial Use of the Language of Social Sin." *Louvain Studies* 27 (2002): 132–52.

———. "Romero on Social Sin." *Living Light* 37, no. 4 (summer 2001): 65–71.

Phelps, Jaime T., ed. *Black and Catholic: The Challenge and Gift of Black Folks.* Milwaukee: Marquette University Press, 1997.

Philibert, Paul J. "Conscience: Developmental Perspectives from Rogers and Kohlberg." *Horizons* 6 (1979): 1–25.

Pilarczyk, Daniel. "Dissent in the Church." In *Dissent in the Church.* Readings in Moral Theology No. 6, ed. Charles E. Curran and John A. McCormick, 152–63. New York: Paulist Press, 1988.

Pius XI. *Casti connubii.* In *The Papal Encyclicals, 1903–39,* ed. Claudia Carlen, 391–414. Wilmington, NC: McGrath, 1981.

———. *Quadragesimo anno.* In *The Papal Encyclicals, 1903–39,* ed. Claudia Carlen, 415–43. Wilmington, NC: McGrath, 1981.

Pius XII. *Humani generis*. In *The Papal Encyclicals, 1939–1958*, ed. Claudia Carlen, 178. Wilmington, NC: McGrath, 1981.

———. "To the Italian Catholic Union of Midwives." In Pope Pius XII, *Moral Questions Affecting Married Life*, 3–23. Washington, DC: National Catholic Welfare Conference, 1951.

———. "Morality and Eugenics." *The Pope Speaks* 6 (1960): 392–400.

———. "The Prolongation of Life [November 24, 1957]." In *Medical Ethics: Sources of Catholic Teaching*, ed. Kevin D. O'Rourke and Philip Boyle, 207–8. St. Louis, MO: Catholic Health Association of the United States, 1989.

Polish, Daniel F., and Eugene J. Fisher, eds. *Liturgical Foundations of Social Policy in Catholic and Jewish Traditions*. Notre Dame: University of Notre Dame Press, 1983.

Pope, Stephen J., ed. *The Ethics of Aquinas*. Washington, DC: Georgetown University Press, 2002.

———. *The Evolution of Altruism and the Ordering of Love*. Washington, DC: Georgetown University Press, 1994.

———. "The Magisterium's Argument against 'Same-Sex Marriage': An Ethical Analysis and Critique." *Theological Studies* 65 (2004): 530–65.

Porter, Jean. "Human Need and Natural Law." In *Infertility: A Crossroad of Faith, Medicine, and Technology*, ed. Kevin William Wildes, 93–106. Boston: Kluwer Academic, 1997.

———. "In the Wake of a Doctrine: A Reassessment of the Doctrine of Natural Law as Developed in *We Hold These Truths*." In *John Courtney Murray and the Growth of Tradition*, ed. Leon J. Hooper and Todd David Whitmore, 24–40. Kansas City, MO: Sheed & Ward, 1996.

———. "The Moral Act in *Veritatis splendor* and Aquinas's *Summa theologiae*." In *Vertiatis Spendor: American Responses*, ed. Michael E. Allsopp and John J. O'Keefe, 278–95. Kansas City, MO: Sheed & Ward, 1995.

———. *Moral Action and Christian Ethics*. New York: Cambridge University Press, 1995.

———. *Natural and Divine Law: Reclaiming the Tradition for Christian Ethics*. Grand Rapids: William B. Eerdmans, 1999.

———. *Nature as Reason: A Thomistic Theology of Natural Law*. Grand Rapids: William B. Eerdmans, 2005.

———. "Recent Studies in Aquinas's Virtue Ethic: A Review Essay." *Journal of Religious Ethics* 266 (1998): 191–215.

———. *The Recovery of Virtue: The Relevance of Aquinas for Christian Ethics*. Louisville, KY: Westminster/John Knox, 1990.

———. "The Search for a Global Ethic." *Theological Studies* 62 (2001): 105–21.

Portier, William L. "In Defense of Mt. St. Mary's: They Are Evangelical, Not Conservative." *Commonweal* 127 (February 11, 2000): 31–33.

———. "Foreword." In *New Wine, New Wineskins: A Next Generation Reflects on Key Issues in Catholic Moral Theology*, ed. William C. Mattison III, ix–xii. Lanham, MD: Sheed & Ward, 2005.

———. "Here Come the Evangelical Catholics." *Communio* 31 (2004): 35–66.

Pospishil, Victor J. *Divorce and Remarriage: Toward a New Catholic Teaching*. New York: Herder and Herder, 1967.

Pottmeyer, Hermann J. "Reception and Submission." *Jurist* 51 (1991): 262–92.

Rahner, Karl. "The Dispute Concerning the Teaching Office of the Church." In *The Magisterium and Morality.* Readings in Moral Theology No. 3, ed. Charles E. Curran and Richard A. McCormick, 113–28. New York: Paulist Press, 1982.

Ramsey, Paul. *War and the Christian Conscience: How Shall Modern War Be Conducted Justly?* Durham, NC: Duke University Press, 1961.

Ratzinger, Josef, and Tarcisio Bertone. "Commentary on Profession of Faith's Concluding Paragraph." *Origins* 28 (1998): 116–19.

Regan, Richard J. *Conflict and Consensus: Religious Freedom and the Second Vatican Council.* New York: Macmillan, 1967.

Reher, Margaret Mary. "Pope Leo XIII and Americanism." *Theological Studies* 34 (1973): 679–89.

Reilly, Daniel F. *The School Controversy, 1891–93.* Washington, DC: Catholic University of America Press, 1943.

Rigali, Norbert J. "Charles Curran's Understanding of Christian Ethics." *Chicago Studies* 22 (1983): 123–32.

———. "Dialogue with Richard McCormick." *Chicago Studies* 16 (1977): 299–308.

———. "The Historical Meaning of *Humanae vitae*." *Chicago Studies* 15 (1976): 127–38.

———. "On the Theology of the Christian Life." In *Moral Theology: New Directions and Fundamental Issues; Festschrift for James P. Hanigan,* ed. James F. Keating, 3–23. New York: Paulist Press, 2004.

———. "The Uniqueness and Distinctiveness of Christian Morality and Ethics." In *Moral Theology: Challenges for the Future; Essays in Honor of Richard A. McCormick,* ed. Charles E. Curran, 74–93. New York: Paulist Press, 1990.

Riley, Lawrence J. "Moral Aspects of Periodic Continence." *Homiletic and Pastoral Review* 57 (1957): 824.

Rodgers, Rosemary. *A History of the College Theology Society, 1954–2004.* Villanova, PA: College Theology Society/Horizons, 1983.

Rodriguez, Jeanette. *Our Lady of Guadalupe: Faith and Empowerment among Mexican-American Women.* Austin: University of Texas Press, 1994.

———. *Stories We Live: Hispanic Women's Spirituality—Cuentos que vivimos.* 1996 Madaleva Lecture in Spirituality. New York: Paulist Press, 1996.

Ross, Susan A. "The Bride of Christ and the Body Politic: Body and Gender in Pre–Vatican II Marriage Theology." *Journal of Religion* 71 (1991): 345–61.

———. *Extravagant Affections: A Feminist Sacramental Theology.* New York: Continuum, 1998.

———. *For the Beauty of the Earth: Women, Sacramentality, and Justice.* 2006 Madaleva Lecture in Spirituality. New York: Paulist Press, 2002.

———. "Liturgy and Ethics: Feminist Perspectives." In *Annual of the Society of Christian Ethics* 20 (2000): 263–74.

Rubio, Julie Hanlon. "Beyond the Liberal/Conservative Divide on Contraception." *Horizons* 32 (2005): 70–94.

———. *A Christian Theology of Marriage and Family.* New York: Paulist Press, 2003.

Ruether, Rosemary Radford. "Birth Control and the Ideals of Marital Sexuality." In *Contraception and Holiness: The Catholic Predicament,* ed. Thomas D. Roberts, 72–91. New York: Herder and Herder, 1964.

———. *Christianity and the Making of the Modern Family.* Boston: Beacon Press, 2000.

———. *Integrating Ecofeminism, Globalization, and World Religions.* Lanham, MD: Rowman & Littlefield, 2005.

Rush, Ormond. "*Sensus fidei:* Faith 'Making Sense' of Revelation." *Theological Studies* 62 (2001): 231–61.

Ryan, E. G. "Bouquillon Controversy." In *New Catholic Encyclopedia,* 2:731–32. New York: McGraw-Hill, 1967.

Ryan, John A. *A Better Economic Order.* New York: Harper and Brothers, 1935.

———. "Comment by Dr. Ryan." *American Ecclesiastical Review* 81 (1929): 70–72.

———. *Declining Liberty and Other Papers.* New York: Macmillan, 1927.

———. *Distributive Justice: The Right and Wrong of Our Present Distribution of Wealth.* New York: Macmillan, 1916.

———. "Family Limitation." *American Ecclesiastical Review* 54 (1916): 684–96.

———. "The Immorality of Contraception." *American Ecclesiastical Review* 79 (1928): 408–11.

———. *A Living Wage: Its Ethical and Economic Aspects.* New York: Macmillan, 1906.

———. "The Method of Teleology in Ethics." *New York Review* 2 (July–August 1906): 409–29.

———. *Moral Aspects of Sterilization.* Washington, DC: National Catholic Welfare Conference, 1930.

———. *The Norm of Morality Defined and Applied to Particular Actions.* Washington, DC: National Catholic Welfare Conference, 1952.

———. "The Place of the Negro in American Society." *Catholic Mind* 41 (July 1943): 13–22.

———. "Private Ownership and Socialism." *Catholic World* 94 (January 1912): 497–504.

———. *Seven Troubled Years, 1930–36: A Collection of Papers on the Depression and on the Problems of Recovery and Reform.* Ann Arbor: Edwards Brothers, 1937.

———. *Social Doctrine in Action: A Personal History.* New York: Harper and Brothers, 1941.

Ryan, John A., and Francis J. Boland, eds. *Catholic Principles of Politics.* New York: Macmillan, 1940.

Ryan, John A., and Moorhouse F. Millar, eds. *The State and the Church.* New York: Macmillan, 1922.

Ryan, Maura A. *Ethics and Economics of Assisted Reproduction: The Cost of Longing.* Washington, DC: Georgetown University Press, 2001.

Ryan, Maura A., and Todd David Whitmore, eds. *The Challenge of Global Stewardship: Roman Catholic Responses.* Notre Dame: University of Notre Dame Press, 1997.

Sabetti, Aloysius. "Animadversiones in controversia de ectopicis conceptibus." *American Ecclesiastical Review* 11 (1894): 129–34.

———. "The Catholic Church and Obstetrical Science." *American Ecclesiastical Review* 13 (1895): 129–30.

———. "Commentary on the Decree *Quemadmodum*." *American Ecclesiastical Review* 6 (1892): 166.

———. *Compendium theologiae moralis*. 7th ed. New York: Pustet, 1892.

———. *Compendium theologiae moralis*. 34th ed. Edited by Daniel Creeden. New York: Pustet, 1939.

Sacred Congregation for the Doctrine of the Faith. "Declaration on Procured Abortion [November 18, 1974]." In *Medical Ethics: Sources of Catholic Teaching*, ed. Kevin D. O'Rourke and Philip Boyle, 37–39. St. Louis, MO: Catholic Health Association of the United States, 1989.

Salaverri, Joachim. *Sacrae theologiae summa*. Vol. 1, *Theologia fundamentalis*. 3d ed. Madrid: Biblioteca de Autores Cristianos, 1955.

Salzman, Todd A., ed. *Method and Catholic Moral Theology: The Ongoing Reconstruction.* Omaha: Creighton University Press, 1999.

———. *What Are They Saying about Catholic Ethical Method?* New York: Paulist Press, 2003.

Sampers, A. "Konings, Anthony." In *New Catholic Encyclopedia*, 8:249. New York: McGraw-Hill, 1967.

Schindler, David L. *Heart of the World, Center of the Church: Communio Ecclesiology, Liberalism, and Liberation*. Grand Rapids: William B. Eerdmans, 1996.

Schuck, Michael. "When the Shooting Stops: Missing Elements in Just War Theory." *Christian Century* 101 (October 26, 1994): 982–84.

Searle, Mark, ed. *Liturgy and Social Justice*. Collegeville, MN: Liturgical Press, 1980.

Selling, Joseph A., ed. *Personalist Morals: Essays in Honor of Professor Louis Janssens*. Leuven, Belgium: Leuven University Press, 1988.

———. "The Reaction to *Humanae vitae*: A Study in Special and Fundamental Theology." S.T.D. diss., Catholic University of Louvain, 1977.

Shannon, Thomas A., ed. *Bioethics: Basic Writings on the Key Questions That Surround the Major, Modern Biological Possibilities and Problems*. 4th ed. New York: Paulist Press, 1993.

———. "Human Embryonic Stem Cell Therapy." *Theological Studies* 62 (2001): 811–24.

———. *Introduction to Bioethics*. 2d ed. New York: Paulist Press, 1987.

———. *Made in Whose Image? Genetic Engineering and Christian Ethics*. Amherst, NY: Humanity, 2000.

———. *Render unto God: A Theology of Selective Obedience*. New York: Paulist Press, 1974.

Shannon, Thomas A., and Lisa Sowle Cahill. *Religion and Artificial Reproduction: An Inquiry into the Vatican "Instruction on Regard for Human Life in Its Origin and on the Dignity of Human Reproduction."* New York: Crossroad, 1988.

Shannon Thomas A., and James J. Walter. "Assisted Nutrition and Hydration and the Catholic Tradition." *Theological Studies* 66 (2005): 651–62.

———. *The New Genetic Medicine: Theological and Ethical Reflections*. Lanham, MD: Rowman & Littlefield, 2003.

———. "Reply to Professors Paris, Keenan, and Himes." *Theological Studies* 67 (2006): 169–74.

Shannon, Thomas A., and Allan B. Wolter. "Reflections on the Moral Status of the Pre-Embryo." *Theological Studies* 51 (1990): 603–26.

Shannon, William H. *The Lively Debate: Response to Humanae vitae.* New York: Sheed & Ward, 1970.

Shaw, Russell. "The Making of a Moral Theologian." *Catholic World Report* (March 1996). Available at www.ewtn.com/library/homelibr/grisez.txt.

Siker, Jeffrey S., ed. *Homosexuality in the Church: Both Sides of the Debate.* Louisville, KY: Westminster/JohnKnox, 1994.

———. *Scripture and Ethics: Twentieth-Century Portraits.* New York: Oxford University Press, 1997.

Slater, Thomas. *A Manual of Moral Theology for English-Speaking Countries.* 3d ed. New York: Benziger, 1908.

Sloyan, Gerard S. "Present at the Sidelines of the Creation." *Horizons* 31 (2004): 88–93.

Smith, Janet E. *Humanae vitae, a Generation Later.* Washington, DC: Catholic University of America Press, 1991.

Smith, John Talbot. *Our Seminaries: An Essay on Clerical Training.* New York: William H. Young, 1896.

Smith, William B. "Selected Methodological Questions in the Fundamental Moral Theology of Francis J. Connell, C. SS. R." S.T.D. diss., Catholic University of America, 1971.

Snow, Nancy E., ed. *Stem Cell Research: New Frontiers in Science and Ethics.* Notre Dame: University of Notre Dame Press, 2003.

Sparks, Richard C. *To Treat or Not to Treat: Bioethics and the Handicapped Newborn.* New York: Paulist Press, 1988.

Spohn, William C. *Go and Do Likewise: Jesus and Ethics.* New York: Continuum, 1999.

———. "Jesus and Christian Ethics." *Theological Studies* 56 (1995): 92–107.

———. "Morality and the Way of Discipleship: The Use of Scripture in *Veritatis splendor.*" In *Vertiatis splendor: American Responses,* ed. Michael E. Allsopp and John J. O'Keefe, 83–105. Kansas City, MO: Sheed & Ward, 1995.

———. "Parable and Narrative in Christian Ethics." *Theological Studies* 51 (1990): 100–114.

———. "The Return of Virtue Ethics." *Theological Studies* 53 (1992): 64–65.

———. "Use of Scripture in Moral Theology." *Theological Studies* 47 (1986): 88–102.

———. *What Are They Saying about Scripture and Ethics?* Rev. ed. New York: Paulist Press, 1995.

Stamps, Mary E., ed. *To Do Justice and Right upon the Earth: Papers from the Virgil Michel Symposium on Liturgy and Social Justice.* Collegeville, MN: Liturgical Press, 1993.

Steck, Christopher. *The Ethical Thought of Hans Urs von Balthasar.* New York: Crossroad, 2001.

Stivers, Robert L., Christine E. Gudorf, Alice Frazer Evans, and Robert A. Evans, eds. *Christian Ethics: A Case Method Approach.* 3d ed. Maryknoll, NY: Orbis Books, 2005.

Sullivan, Francis A. *The Magisterium: Teaching Authority in the Catholic Church.* New York: Paulist Press, 1983.

———. "The Papal Apology." *America* 182, no. 12 (April 8, 2000): 17–22.

———. "Reply to Germain Grisez." *Theological Studies* 55 (1994): 732–37.

———. "The 'Secondary Object' of Infallibility." *Theological Studies* 54 (1993): 536–50.

Swidler, Arlene. "Catholics and the E.R.A." *Commonweal* 103 (1976): 585–89.

Synod of Bishops. *Justitia in mundo* [1971]. In *Catholic Social Thought: The Documentary Heritage,* ed. David J. O'Brien and Thomas A. Shannon, 288–300. Maryknoll, NY: Orbis Books, 1992.

Tambasco, Anthony J. *The Bible for Ethics: Juan Luis Segundo and First-World Ethics.* Washington, DC: Catholic University Press of America, 1981.

Tauer, Carol. "The Tradition of Probabilism and the Moral Status of the Early Embryo." *Theological Studies* 45 (1984): 3–13.

Tentler, Leslie Woodcock. *Catholics and Contraception: An American History.* Ithaca, NY: Cornell University Press, 2004.

Thomas, Gloria Blanchfield. "Teaching Marriage in a Catholic College." In *Christian Marriage and Family: Contemporary, Theological, and Pastoral Perspectives,* ed. Michael G. Lawler and William P. Roberts, 176–91. Collegeville, MN: Liturgical Press, 1996.

Thomas, Samuel J. "A 'Final Disposition . . . One Way or Another': The Real End of the First Curran Affair." *Catholic Historical Review* 91 (2005): 714–42.

Thurston, Thomas. *Homosexuality and Roman Catholic Ethics.* San Francisco: International Scholars Publications, 1996.

Traina, Cristina L. H. *Feminist Ethics and the Natural Law: The End of the Anathemas.* Washington, DC: Georgetown University Press, 1999.

———. "Papal Ideals, Marital Realities: One View from the Ground." In *Sexual Diversity and Catholicism: Toward the Development of Moral Theology,* ed. Patricia Beattie Jung and Joseph Andrew Coray, 269–88. Collegeville, MN: Liturgical Press, 2001.

Trimiew, Darryl M. "The Economic Rights Debate: The End of One Argument, the Beginning of Another." *Annual of the Society of Christian Ethics* (1991): 85–108.

U.S. Catholic Bishops. "Challenge of Peace: God's Promise and Our Response." In *Catholic Social Thought: The Documentary Heritage,* ed. David J. O'Brien and Thomas A. Shannon, 492–571. Maryknoll, NY: Orbis Books, 1992.

———. "Economic Justice for All." In *Catholic Social Thought: The Documentary Heritage,* ed. David J. O'Brien and Thomas A. Shannon, 572–680. Maryknoll, NY: Orbis Books, 1992.

———. "*Ex Corde Ecclesiae:* An Application to the United States." *Origins* 26 (1996): 381–84.

———. "Faithful Citizenship: A Catholic Call to Political Responsibility." *Origins* 33 (2003): 321–30.

———. *Human Life in Our Day.* Washington, DC: U.S. Catholic Conference, 1968.

———. "Pastoral Letter on Health and Health Care." In *Medical Ethics: Sources of Catholic Teaching,* ed. Kevin D. O'Rourke and Philip Boyle, 264–67. St. Louis, MO: Catholic Health Association of the United States, 1989.

Vacek, Edward Collins. *Love Human and Divine: The Heart of Christian Ethics.* Washington, DC: Georgetown University Press, 1994.

———. "Vatican Instruction on Reproductive Technology." *Theological Studies* 49 (1988): 110–31.

Van Allen, Rodger. "Artificial Insemination (AIH): A Contemporary Re-Analysis." *Homiletic and Pastoral Review* 70 (1969–70): 363–72.

Vawter, Bruce. "The Biblical Theology of Divorce." *Proceedings of the Catholic Theological Society of America* 22 (1967): 223–43.

———. "The Divorce Clauses in Mt. 5:32 and 19:9." *Catholic Biblical Quarterly* 16 (1954): 155–67.

Vereecke, Louis. "Le concile de Trent et l'enseignement de la théologie morale." In Louis Vereecke, *De Guillaume d'Ockham à Saint Alphonse de Liguori: Études d'histoire de la théologie morale moderne 1300–1789,* 495–508. Rome: Collegium S. Alfonsi de Urbe, 1986.

———. "La conscience selon Saint Alphonse de Liguori." In Louis Vereecke, *De Guillaume d'Ockham à Saint Alphonse de Liguori: Études d'histoire de la théologie morale moderne 1300–1789,* 555–60. Rome: Collegium S. Alfonsi de Urbe, 1986.

———. *De Guillaume d'Ockham à Saint Alphonse de Liguori: Études d'histoire de la théologie morale moderne 1300–1789.* Rome: Collegium S. Alfonsi de Urbe, 1986.

———. "History of Moral Theology (700 to Vatican Council I)." *New Catholic Encyclopedia* 9:1119–22. New York: McGraw-Hill, 1967.

———. "Storia della teologia morale." In *Nuovo dizionario di teologia morale,* ed. Francesco Compagnoni, Giannino Piana, and Salvatore Privitera, 1314–38. Milan: Paoline, 1990.

Vidal, Marciano. *La morale di Sant' Alfonso: Dal rigorismo alla benignità.* Rome: Editiones Academiae Alphonsianae, 1992.

Wadell, Paul J. *Friendship and the Moral Life.* Notre Dame: University of Notre Dame Press, 1989.

———. *The Primary of Love: An Introduction to the Ethics of Thomas Aquinas.* New York: Paulist Press, 1992.

Walker, Adrian J. "Introduction." *Communio* 31 (2004): 1–3.

Walter, James J. "The Foundation and Formulation of Norms." In *Moral Theology: Challenges for the Future; Essays in Honor of Richard A. McCormick,* ed. Charles E. Curran, 125–54. New York: Paulist Press, 1990.

Walter, James J., Timothy E. O'Connell, and Thomas A. Shannon. *A Call to Fidelity: On the Moral Theology of Charles E. Curran.* Washington, DC: Georgetown University Press, 2002.

Walter, James J., and Thomas A. Shannon. *Contemporary Issues in Bioethics: A Catholic Perspective.* Lanham, MD: Rowman & Littlefield, 2005.

———. *The Quality of Life: The New Medical Dilemma.* New York: Paulist Press, 1990.

Walter, Jennifer K., and Eran P. Klein, eds. *The Story of Bioethics: From Seminal Works to Contemporary Explorations.* Washington, DC: Georgetown University Press, 2003.

Wawrykow, Joseph B. *God's Grace and Human Action: "Merit" in the Theology of Thomas Aquinas.* Notre Dame: University of Notre Dame Press, 1995.

Weaver, Darlene Fozard. "Intimacy with God and Self-Relation in the World: The Fundamental Option and Categorical Activity." In *New Wine, New Wineskins: A Next Generation Reflects on Key Issues in Catholic Moral Theology,* ed. William C. Mattison III, 160. Lanham, MD: Sheed & Ward, 2005.

———. *Self Love and Christian Ethics.* New York: Cambridge University Press, 2002.

Weaver, Mary Jo, and R. Scott Appleby, eds. *Being Right: Conservative Catholics in America.* Bloomington: University of Indiana Press, 1995.

Weigel, George. *Catholicism and the Renewal of American Democracy.* New York: Paulist Press, 1989.

———. "The Just War Case for the War." *America* 188 (March 31, 2003): 7–10.

———. "Moral Clarity in a Time of War." *First Things* 128 (January 2003): 20–27.

———. "The Neoconservative Difference, a Proposal for the Renewal of Church and Society." In *Being Right: Conservative Catholics in America,* ed. Mary Jo Weaver and R. Scott Appleby, 138–62. Bloomington: University of Indiana Press, 1995.

———. *Tranquillitas ordinis: The Present Failure and Future Promise of American Catholic Thought on War and Peace.* New York: Oxford University Press, 1987.

———. *Witness to Hope: The Biography of Pope John Paul II.* New York: Cliff Street Books, 1999.

Weiss, Otto. "Alphonso de Liguori und die Deutsche Moraltheologie im 19 Jahrhundert." *Studia Moralia* 25 (1987): 123–61.

Werner, Stephen A. *Prophet of the Christian Social Manifesto: Joseph Husslein, S.J., His Life, Work, and Social Thought.* Milwaukee: Marquette University Press, 2001.

Westley, Dick. *When It's Right to Die: Conflicting Voices, Difficult Choices.* Mystic, CT: Twenty-Third, 1995.

White, Joseph M. *The Diocesan Seminary in the United States: A History from the 1780s to the Present.* Notre Dame: University of Notre Dame Press, 1989.

———. "Theological Studies at the Catholic University of America: Organization and Leadership before Vatican Council II." *U.S. Catholic Historian* 7 (1988): 453–66.

Whitmore, Todd David. "The Growing End: John Courtney Murray and the Shape of Murray Studies." In *John Courtney Murray and the Growth of Tradition,* ed. Leon J. Hooper and Todd David Whitmore, v–xxvii. Kansas City, MO: Sheed & Ward, 1996.

———. "John Paul II, Michael Novak, and the Differences between Them." *Annual of the Society of Christian Ethics* 21 (2001): 215–32.

———. "The Reception of Catholic Approaches to Peace and War in the United States." In *Modern Catholic Social Teaching: Commentaries and Interpretations,* ed. Kenneth R. Himes, 493–521. Washington, DC: Georgetown University Press, 2004.

Wilkins, John, ed. *Understanding Veritatis splendor.* London: SPCK, 1994.

Wister, Robert J. "The Curran (Charles) Controversy." In *The Encyclopedia of American Catholic History,* ed. Michael Glazier and Thomas J. Shelley, 400–402. Collegeville, MN: Liturgical Press, 1997.

———. "Theology in America." In *The Encyclopedia of American Catholic History,* ed. Michael Glazier and Thomas J. Shelley, 1381–84. Collegeville, MN: Liturgical Press, 1997.

Wojtyla, Karol. *Person and Community: Selected Essays.* Translated by Theresa Sandok. New York: Peter Lang, 1993.

Wolfe, Regina Wentzel, and Christine E. Gudorf, eds. *Ethics and World Religions: Cross-Cultural Case Studies.* Maryknoll, NY: Orbis Books, 1999.

Woods, Walter J. *Walking with Faith: New Perspectives on the Sources and Shaping of Catholic Moral Life.* Collegeville, MN: Liturgical Press, 1998.

Wrenn, Lawrence G. "Marriage—Indissoluble or Fragile?" In *Divorce and Remarriage in the Catholic Church,* ed. Lawrence G. Wrenn, 134–49. New York: Paulist Press, 1973.

Zahn, Gordon C. "The Berrigans: Radical Activism Personified." In *The Berrigans,* ed. William VanEtten Casey and Philip Nobile, 97–112. New York: Avon, 1971.

ABOUT THE AUTHOR

Charles E. Curran, a Roman Catholic priest of the Diocese of Rochester, New York, is Elizabeth Scurlock University Professor of Human Values at Southern Methodist University. He was the first recipient of the John Courtney Murray Award for Theology and has served as president of the Catholic Theological Society of America, the Society of Christian Ethics, and the American Theological Society. In 2003, Curran received the Presidential Award of the College Theology Society for a lifetime of scholarly achievements in moral theology, and in 2005, Call to Action presented him with its leadership award. He is the author of *Loyal Dissent: Memoir of a Catholic Theologian, The Moral Theology of Pope John Paul II,* and *Catholic Social Teaching, 1891–Present,* all published by Georgetown University Press.

INDEX

abortifacient pill, 235
abortion, 232–36
  beginning of life issues, 57, 232–36
  conflict issues involving, 235–36
  craniotomy, 21, 58
  dissent on, 152, 234
  double effect, principle of, 58
  ectopic pregnancies. *See* ectopic pregnancy
  ensoulment of fetus, 57, 232–36
  Grisez and new natural law theory on, 227
  legal access to, 234, 271
  in medical ethics before Vatican II, 54,
    57–59
  morning-after pill, 235
  in nineteenth century, 8, 21
  as public policy issue, 152, 234, 270–72
  Religious Consultation on Population,
    Reproductive Health, and Ethics, 148
  revisionist moral theology on, 221, 232–33
  Roe v. Wade, 270, 271, 272
  Sabetti on, 21
  to save life of mother, 58–59
  therapeutic, 57–59
  unjust aggressor argument regarding, 21, 58
  in U.S. bishops' political agenda, 152, 234,
    270–71, 272
absolute consequentialism, 107–8
absolute moral norms, 106, 107, 150, 185–87
academy, 1–2
  Church teaching, theologians' role in,
    115–16, 122
  demands for academic freedom, 92
  development of moral theology influenced
    by, 282–83
  John Paul II on duties and loyalties of, 89–91
  lay and women theologians, 93
  mandatum, 90
  professionalization of Catholic theological
    teaching, 92–93
  after Vatican II. *See under* twentieth century
    moral theology after Vatican II
  before Vatican II, 39–43

Academy of Catholic Hispanic Theologians of
  the United States (ACHTUS), 155–56
ACLU (American Civil Liberties Union), 69
adultery, 205
Aeterni patris, 10
affectivity and emotion, 175
affirmative action, Maguire on, 148
agape, 172
aggiornamento, 84
AID (artificial insemination with donor
  semen), 52, 59, 193, 206, 225, 236
AIDS/HIV, 203–4, 244
AIH (artificial insemination with husband's
  semen), 52, 59, 193, 221, 236
Alan of Lille, 1
alcoholism, 40
Alexander VII (pope), 4
Alexander VIII (pope), 4
Alphonsian approach to moral theology. *See*
  Liguori, Alphonsus
American Civil Liberties Union (ACLU), 69
American culture
  Catholic neoconservative position on, 256–60
  dissent from hierarchical magisterium
    identified with, 91
  Kenrick's emphasis on love and pleasure
    in sexuality and marriage influenced
    by, 14–15
  Murray on contiguity between Catholicism
    and, 72, 77–79
  natural law and, 78, 79
  papal condemnation of Americanism and
    modernism, 35–37, 41
  social ethics as critical of, 252
analogical imagination, 131–32
Andolsen, Barbara Hilkert, 153, 230–31
animation of fetus, delayed, 57, 232–36
anovulant pills, use of, 48, 194
anthropology, Catholic, 222–23, 249, 285
Antoninus of Florence, 2, 50
apocalyptic aspects of scripture, 139
Aquaviva, Claudius, 192

329

social ethics (continued)
  continuity with Catholic tradition, 259
  globalization, 275–76
  war and peace, 265, 266
  public policy issues, 269–73
  racism, 71–72, 99, 148, 154–57, 268–69
  radical or countercultural approach to,
    260–61, 262–63, 268
  in revisionist moral theology, 250–52
  sin, social, recognition of, 185
  teleological approach to, 63, 65–66
  unique methodological approach of, 63–64
  U.S. cultural and political ethos, criticism
    of, 252
  before Vatican II, 63–82
    *Central Blatt and Social Justice
      Review,* 70
    Cronin, John F., 71–72
    economics, need for harmony with, 66
    Furfey, Paul Hanley, 70, 71
    Hussleim, Joseph, 70
    Michel, Virgil, 70
    Murray, John Courtney, 72–79
    natural law and. *See under* natural law
    papal teachings on, 67–68, 71, 75
    pre- and post-Vatican II continuities,
      249–52
    Ryan, John A., 64–69, 70, 71–72
    unique methodological approach of,
      63–64
    WWII and peace movements, 70–71, 78
Social Gospel School, 75, 78
social injustices of members of Church, John
  Paul II's apologies for, 88
social or legal justice, 239
Social Principles and Economic Life
  (Cronin), 72
socialism, 69, 70
society as a whole, changes in moral theology
  wrought by, 98–99, 283–84
Society of Catholic College Teachers of Sacred
  Doctrine, 92
Society of Christian Ethics, 147
Society of Jesus. *See* Jesuits
sociobiology, 173
sodomy, 198–99
Sollicitudo rei socialis, 87, 252, 267–68
somatic cell therapy/enhancement, 242

Spalding, John Lancaster, 22
special moral theology, 24, 27, 38, 165, 184
Spellman, Francis, 73
spiritual theology and moral theology, 141–43
Spohn, William, 137–38, 141, 169–70
St. Mary's in Notre Dame, 92
state
  church and. *See* church and state
  law of state and morality. *See* public policy
  Ryan on role of, 68–69
Steck, Christopher, 141
stem cell research, 236, 241
sterilization, 48, 55, 59, 106, 193–95
stewardship over own bodies and persons,
  54, 56
Stoeckle, Bernard, 144
story or narrative theology, 175–76
structural developmental approach, 167
Suarez, Francisco, 25, 26, 27
suicide, 56–57, 227–28, 239. *See also* euthanasia
Sullivan, Francis, 114, 124
Sullivan, William L., 37
Sulpicians, 11–12, 22
suspicion, hermeneutic of, 151
Syllabus of Errors, 8
syllogism in decisions of conscience, 181
synthetic norms, 187
systematic and synthetic approach in Catholic
  theological tradition, 176

Tambasco, Anthony, 138
Tanquerey, Adolphe, 22
Tauer, Carol, 233
Taylor, Jeremy, 16
teaching office of the Church
  bishops, role of, 26, 49, 116, 122–24
  Bouquillon on, 26
  duality of, 116
  feminist response to, 152
  infallible teachings. *See* infallible teachings
  ordinary universal magisterium, 122–24
  papal. *See* papacy and papal authority
  theologians, role of, 115–16, 122
  Vatican II on, 112, 113–14, 117
Teilhard de Chardin, Pierre, 273
teleological approach, 63, 65–66, 107, 170
temperance, 168
Testem benevolentiae, 36